TO FEED

AND BE FED

To Feed and Be Fed

THE COSMOLOGICAL BASES OF AUTHORITY AND IDENTITY IN THE ANDES

Susan Elizabeth Ramírez

STANFORD UNIVERSITY PRESS
STANFORD, CALIFORNIA 2005

Stanford University Press
Stanford, California

Printed in the United States of America on
acid-free, archival-quality paper

LIBRARY OF CONGRESS CATALOGING-IN-PUBLICATION DATA

Ramírez, Susan E., date–
To feed and be fed : the cosmological bases of authority and identity in the Andes / Susan Elizabeth Ramírez.
p. cm.
Includes bibliographical references and index.
ISBN 0-8047-4921-3 (cloth : alk.papar)—ISBN 0-8047-4922-1 (pbk : alk. paper)
1. Inca cosmology. 2. Incas—Kings and rulers. 3. Incas—Politics and government. 4. Indians of South America—First contact with Europeans—Andes Region. 5. Peru—History—Conquest, 1522-1548. I. Title.

F3429.3.C74R36 2005
985'00498323—dc22 2005000235

Original Printing 2005

Last figure below indicates year of this printing:
14 13 12 11 10 09 08 07 06 05

Typeset by G&S Book Services in 10/12.5 and Sabon

To you, so that you may remember.
If not for you, for whom?

Table of Contents

Figures and Tables

Figures

Table

Acknowledgments

This book could not have been written without the generous support of many people and institutions. I first thank the personnel of the many archives that I frequented to find the local and imperial-level sources that provided the data for this reimagining of the Andean peoples and their institutions in the sixteenth and seventeenth centuries. Their help in locating and copying materials proved priceless. Next, I thank the funding institutions, such as the Institute for Advanced Studies in Princeton; the School for American Research in Santa Fe, New Mexico; the American Philosophical Society; the Fulbright Commission; and the authorities of De Paul University for time off and the opportunity to spend months thinking culturally unthinkable thoughts without worrying about the next lecture or whether a given student earned a B+ or an A−. The administration at Texas Christian University, my most recent academic home, and especially Dean Mary Volcansek, Associate Provost Larry Adams, and Provost R. Nowell Donovan, also gave most valuable and timely assistance in speeding the book into production. Finally, I thank the many colleagues, friends, and family members who shared thoughts, bibliographies, and even unpublished papers, and/or who paid my bills or otherwise took care of my apartment and mail so that I could escape the routine and take advantage of the opportunities to think myself into the encounter-and-contact era. Without the conjunction of these many types of support, I might only now be finishing Chapter 3.

TO FEED
AND BE FED

1 *A Personal Odyssey*

> [It has been] argued that "native" histories are mentally enigmatic to the Western observer because they respond to a cultural logic that is impenetrable to Western modes of thought.
>
> — Neil L. Whitehead

The exploration of "the other" has been a fascination and a challenge to scholars and other curious beings for centuries. This is certainly true of Western observers on the subject of the Incas and other Andean peoples since first contact. The result of both casual and intimate association has been a corpus of firsthand descriptions, what I call the classical chronicles, that inform us that the Incas had built a huge empire. At its largest the empire extended over territory that is now defined as southern Colombia; highland and coastal Ecuador and Peru; highland Bolivia; northwestern Argentina; and about half of Chile. Travel and communication throughout this landmass was facilitated by an intricate system of linked roads that went north and south in the mountains and along the coast, tied together by east-west trails through the river valleys. Messengers (*chasquis*) ran relay style along these highways, carrying messages and fresh fish, stopping at way stations to pass on their responsibility to another, who sprinted on to the next stop, and so forth. The Inca rulers had urban complexes built, we are told, at various spots throughout the empire: at Cuzco, considered the capital of their jurisdiction; at Huánuco Viejo; Incahuasi; Tomebamba; and elsewhere, places that the native chronicler Felipe Guamán Poma de Ayala identified as many Cuzcos. But most of the population of this multiethnic empire were peasants, who cultivated the land to produce maize, potatoes, maca, and other vegetables and fruit, and shepherded large numbers of llamas and alpacas. They also, as tribute, lent their labor to build the roads, bridges, storehouses, ceremonial centers, and irrigation canals and agricultural terraces that directly benefited themselves or others like them. Smaller numbers served as fishermen and skilled artisans and specialists. This was an organized, rationalized realm with a bureaucracy. Officials had jurisdiction over units of population, categorized according to a decimal system, beginning with units of forty thousand households and extending down to as few as five.[1]

These early eyewitness descriptions include less information about native religion, initially, because the Spanish, confident that the Christian god had given them victory against the Moors on the Iberian peninsula and opened the Americas to them to continue to spread their faith, dismissed the Andeans as pagans and infidels whose gods were fictitious, impotent inventions and, therefore, of little importance. But short or fragmentary references to ritual, polytheism, ancestor worship, and the attendant human and other animal and plant sacrifices, even in the earliest documents, provide sound evidence that the Andean people were profoundly spiritual beings.

Given that these chroniclers rarely recorded the native voice in the first decades after the invasion and first encounters, the Spanish depictions and view became predominant. They established what amounted to a near monopoly on the selection, summation, and transmittal of information. So their view, in large part, became the basis for our views. Scholars have read, analyzed, and synthesized these mostly Spanish accounts to write myriad interpretations of various aspects of Andean civilization. William Prescott used them in the nineteenth century to produce a sweeping, aggressive history of the Incas. In the twentieth century, Heinrich Cunow used the same sources to describe this civilization, in whole or in part, as a socialist paradise where the needs of all were met in a communal setting. Karl Wittfogel thought the Andean people were a good example of an oriental despotism. More recently, several authors described the Andean realm in Marxist terms.[2]

During the last several decades, other approaches to the study of the Incas have dominated scholarly endeavors. Basing his writings on a detailed analysis and mostly literal interpretation of his sources, the archaeologist John Rowe developed what has been labeled a historicist approach in some classic articles that are often cited and are only now being, in part, revised. The anthropologist John V. Murra's political economy approach, which emphasized verticality, reciprocity, and redistribution, added new insights to sometimes ambiguous, contradictory, and hard-to-understand economic data. Finally, R. Tom Zuidema's structural interpretations, beginning with the shrine system (*ceque*) near the purported Inca capital, have drawn attention to rituals and belief systems. The publication and use of more localized notarial and administrative and judicial records—pioneered by Waldemar Espinoza Soriano, María Rostworowski, John V. Murra, Franklin Pease, and Noble David Cook—moved studies down to a more personal level, resulting in a sometimes daily and more intimate glimpse of an active population. Such work showed the often large gap between imperial generalization and local, practical, semiautonomous reality.[3]

But the secular focus continued to predominate, with a few recent exceptions, such as the notable essays on Andean religion of Luis Millones; subsequent publications by historians, anthropologists, and archaeologists such as Guillermo Cock Carrasco, Mary Doyle, Lorenzo Huertas, Liliana Regalado de Hurtado, Arthur Demarest, and Geoffrey Conrad; and more recently, by Peter Gose and Kenneth Mills. Many of these, to a lesser or greater extent, relied on the records of idolatry that are most abundant for the seventeenth century. It was after 1600 that the viceregal ecclesiastical establishment became aware that the native conversion to Catholicism was superficial and that elements of local cults, most dedicated to the ancestors, had survived hidden from the eyes of or with the tacit consent of Spanish authorities. Alarmed at this chilling realization, clerical judges traveled to distant settlements to survey these survivals and look underneath the thin veneer of Christianity in an effort to "know thine enemy." These tours of extirpation became one of the first systematic efforts to eliminate Andean religions. The investigators who used these local documents deepened our understanding of Andean belief systems that had eluded or been neglected by earlier generations.[4]

In this process of writing and rewriting Andean history, scholars began to recognize that each manuscript has a perspective and conscious or unconscious objectives. Even native sources, such as those written by the Spanish-schooled Guamán Poma de Ayala and the Inca Garcilaso de la Vega, must be read with caution and questioned, for peculiar to each are its own filters, biases, and goals. Gary Urton's work on Pacaritanbo (also Pacariqtambo or Pacarictambo) provides a good, accessible example at a more localized level of how to decode, appraise, and evaluate a document to better ascertain the reliability of the information it contains. Karen Powers's ingenious work on indigenous wills also comes to mind. These scholars comprehended that words cannot be taken literally, uncritically, and out of context. Meanings change over time; the same words had other connotations in other temporal and geographic settings. For instance, the field moved from thinking that the *encomienda* had a territorial dimension to its rightful definition of the labor obligations of a given social group; and that "tribute" in the pre-Hispanic Andes was not assessed as quantities of goods as it was under the Nahuatl-speaking Mexicas, but instead that it was measured in terms of labor service. Likewise, a structure identified as a "fortress" by sixteenth-century Spanish observers was not necessarily strictly defensive, but instead a temple and sacred precinct within sometimes labyrinthine protective walls. In other words, the world portrayed by the Spanish and Hispanicized native writers in early colonial times is not necessarily and in all aspects what their words lead us to imagine it was today.[5]

Yet, for all the advances, many still cling to an image of an empire ruled by a king who himself had a clear order in a dynastic sequence; where primogeniture was indicated and normative, if not always the followed preference in choosing an heir; where the empire was demarcated and its far-flung corners were well connected through a series of admirably engineered roads and bridges; where an elaborate and ubiquitous bureaucracy controlled every "province"; where every person and every tribute-produced carrying cloth and tunic were counted and accounted for; and where centralization was omnipresent and inescapable. In sum, this is what we think we know about the Incas.[6]

I write "think we know" because the records contain other problematic words, inexplicable phrases, contradictions, inconsistencies, and unexpected silences and gaps that lead me to think that we still have much to learn about native society as it existed at the time of or shortly after contact with the Europeans. For example, in the few instances where the native voice is recorded, I found phrases or statements that were intriguingly incomprehensible and obtuse at first. I happened upon two such statements researching my last book. Both pointed in the same direction. They taught me to slow down, to ponder, to imagine, to empathize, and to question the sources, my own assumptions, and the meanings of words, whose conventional, present definitions did not fit the context and circumstances in which they were used. They sent me into the archives to read and reconsider the records of idolatry. These detailed reports of religious persecution by sometimes overzealous extirpators charged first with uncovering the secret religious practices of the provincial natives, and second, with converting the practitioners, contained information on the cosmology or belief system of peasants and the organization and practice of ancestor worship, including accounts of divination and other esoteric and occult rituals. The continuities in thought and deed, between the state theater that I read about in the chronicles and the ceremonies that were still practiced among the distant rural peoples in the late sixteenth and early and mid-seventeenth centuries, helped me comprehend the words and phrases that, at first, had been beyond my understanding. In other instances, I did not find the documentation to support what I assumed to have occurred. These frustrations and appraisals pried open my own window to the past and helped me see through the filters of the Spanish and Hispanicized native writers and (more important) my own. Opening was slow and gradual; the vision was fuzzy at first. The outlines became progressively less blurry as multiple documents were found; as the various possible definitions of words were considered; and as words were compared to behavior to better envision context. I finally realized that we, in part, were the distortionists.[7]

It is a theoretical near impossibility to totally penetrate the mind of another, especially of a person or people brought up in a different tradition. The question is how to understand the other's worldview from the outside and, then, how to translate that belief system and culture into terms that can be understood by a Western audience of one's peers. How to bridge the gap between our own and native concepts is also a challenge of modern ethnographic work. The same decentering task faces the ethnographic historian.

But the task of historical anthropology is even harder than that of ethnography because scholars must rely on the reports of Europeans (or the Europeanized) who were not consciously attempting to be anthropologists but were nonetheless often trying to explain to their colleagues and superiors the native situation for their own purposes. Moreover, we cannot go back and rephrase and decenter questions to comprehend better original meanings and intent, to penetrate the sometimes hastily stated colloquialisms or idioms that are replete with assumptions about basic local lore. Therefore, investigators must excavate mentally through various layers of meanings. They must unpack the historical records that usually contain the words of Lima or provincial urban lawyers, court-appointed translators (*lenguas*), or officials (such as the protector of Indians), who reframe what native informants said that they thought, saw, heard, or experienced. This usually implies the translation of native words from the original languages, such as Quechua, Aymara, Mochic (or Yunga), or any of the others that were spoken in the Andes, into Spanish. We scholars, then, translate them again sometimes into English, Portuguese, German, French, Japanese, Polish, and other languages. Translations are never totally equivalent. Because the sense of words changes over time, the Spanish words used by the classic chroniclers and the translators of the sixteenth and seventeenth centuries must be kept in historical context to understand their referents. Translating meaning between two cultures also involves conveying one conceptualization into terms and categories that are often foreign to the original.

Imprecision also hinders understanding. As will be shown in Chapter 2, the Spanish often used words like *province* without ever establishing a generic and universally accepted definition or telling us to what they precisely referred. They used a word like *tierra,* literally understood as "land," when they specifically referred to people or persons.[8] Complicating things, too, were the terms native Andeans used to refer to phenomena outside their everyday experience. Like the Nahuatl speakers of central Mexico, who called Hernando Cortés's boats "towers" or "houses," and horses "deer," and who also equated the Spanish to gods because their use of muskets and cannons made them think that the Spanish controlled thunder and lightning, the Andeans fit occurrences into their own cultural context as best they could. Edmundo Guillén Guillén amassed the early testimonials of Andeans showing that they called the Spanish *viracochas* after an all-powerful creator god.[9] Indigenous informants elsewhere talked about planted fields (*chacras*). The Spanish translated the word sometimes as "lands," sometimes as "properties," not comprehending that the natives distinguished between planted land and unplanted land, and that unplanted land was not a chacra. This gave rise to debates over private property that, in the Andes, was not entirely equivalent to the Western institution before the Spanish incursion. The problem becomes one of how, if one can somehow understand them, a native mind-set and culture can be described accurately so that a Westerner can comprehend them without distortion and loss of the essence of that understanding. The challenge is to make sense of the other's world without deforming it or depicting it as a pale reflection of one's own culture.[10]

Having worked in the northern provinces of Peru for most of my professional life, dealing with regional aspects of the local political economy and social structure—and, of late, particularly the native chiefs (*curacas, caciques*) and their people—I was immediately struck with the bravura and obviously exaggerated stories of the Incas portrayed in some of the chronicles, when I had the opportunity to revisit them in recent years. The vision transmitted in many of the early Spanish or Hispanicized native accounts was, it soon became clear, often a largely Europeanized, sanitized, and simplified one. Research into the authors' lives, travels, professions, the other experiences, and the motivations behind their writings by me and others taught me to be wary of their class biases and skeptical (sometimes in the extreme) of their blanket statements. Many early reports I found to be Cuzco- and Inca-centric, just like later histories of the colonial and republican eras tended to be Lima- and elite-centered. Moreover, as research into a chief and his people, or chieftainships (*curacazgos, cacicazgos*), brought me inevitably into the study of the relationship between local polities and the imperial state, I realized just how the Spanish cultural predilections and my own had prevented us from "seeing," just how much our upbringing and learning determined how we reconstructed the past, and just how many scholars tended to disregard native voices, even when we encountered them.[11]

A major breakthrough in my thinking occurred soon after the Quincentenary, the five-hundredth anniversary of Columbus's "discovery" of the so-called New World, when a statement in a 1990 article by Franklin Pease made me recall a footnote in a book by Raul Porras Barrenechea. Both authors, the acknowledged experts for their time on the Incas and Peruvian history in general, stated and then dismissed as obviously wrong the incontrovertible fact that in the earliest accounts and reports from the "front(ier)" between Pizarro's moving expeditionary force and the natives of the west coast and highlands of South America, the individual rulers were called "the Cuzco." That statement, so casually and confidently disregarded, got stuck somewhere in my subconscious. I pondered that enigma throughout the next few years, until one day, when I was about to write the second chapter of another, earlier version of this book and had just turned on my microfilm reader to read the "last" manuscript before finishing my analysis, the statement resurfaced from the depths of my memory and seriously disrupted my concentration. So after a few hours, I turned off the reader and began to write and diagram, asking myself how the first accounts could all be so wrong.

After reading and rereading, checking and rechecking, discussing and debating with anyone knowledgeable enough to have expressed an interest in the topic at one time or another, I got to a point where I had to suppose that the informants and translators were right. If they were correct, what would the fact that the Cuzco was a person tell us about the organization of the empire and the empire itself? Where would the pursuit of the answer to that question lead me? It was a very frightening prospect.[12]

This conundrum and the results of ten intense months of daily and persistent research led me into the depths and labyrinths of library stacks to areas most have rarely seen or thought about; into other people's lives as I pestered them for bibliography on other examples in other times and places of what I was "seeing" and thinking; and into serious but collegial and usually congenial, intellectual confrontations with other scholars and friends. They told me that the archival and manuscript paths I was following would surely lead nowhere. When I began to deconstruct the old and fashion a different vision, they told me that I was wrong, so challenging were my then tentative assertions and overstatements about what I was finding and where the path was leading. They said that if I persisted and published my vision, I would be dismissed, as Pizarro's young interpreters were by Pease and Porras Barrenechea. But I proceeded and, finally convinced of the validity of my inquiry, though fearful of reaction, sent a draft to select colleagues and friends.

This is the story of the second chapter of this book, where I argue that the person of "el Cuzco" was indeed the center or navel of the Inca world. The phrase "el Cuzco" did not solely refer to a place and capital, as usually portrayed in the classical literature. I argue that the Incas had a living center, the person of the Inca or king or emperor himself, who as the navel of the universe—in both the physical and symbolic senses—connected his living subjects to his dead ancestors and ultimately to the sun and moon. His rhetoric and behavior aimed at establishing kinship ties that ideally would connect all subjects to him and his divine lineage and thus to each other.

In Part 2, Chapters 3 and 4, I rethink the way the natives thought their world worked, their cosmology or worldview, the ideological bases of legitimacy and succession of the Incas and curacas, respectively, and the interaction between these two levels of authority.[13] I argue that both the Inca ruler and local ethnic authorities were nexuses between the common folk and the gods and that the ritual and magic, described by the Spanish as infidelities, were some of the many ways of accessing the future and unknown and of legitimizing power. In doing so, I reconfirm Sabine MacCormack's finding that the Inca state-level cult disappeared quickly after 1532. What resisted and survived into the seventeenth and eighteenth centuries was not the master imperial tradition but the ancestor worship, the small or folk tradition, of the provincial peoples.[14]

In Part 3, the ritual and symbolic manifestations of this cosmology and organization are described briefly. Such ritual and public demonstrations and portrayals of the past were ways of immortalizing the leader heroes and great men of the times and of inculcating values of this multiethnic and often conflict-ridden society.

Finally, having argued that cosmology, as a unifying ideology, was an invented and inherited explanation of how and why the universe worked as it did, I expand on the implications of the same. I focus on the idea of community and what it was and what it became. Related to that, I write about identity and how multifaceted, shifting, even fickle, it must have been and how conversion to Catholicism eroded the Andeans' sense of selves. The Incas' grand imperial design was fragile; its degree of centralization was overstated; and the *pax incaica* was a moving and illusive goal, just the wishful memory of a remnant of a once-dominant native elite. In the last chapter, I present some of the lessons that I learned about history and methodology and reflect on the historiography of the topic, including my own.

In short, mine is a contribution in a long line of interpretations, extending from the past into the future. I am not writing a history of the Inca rulers per se. I do not consider the issues and controversies of whether or not there were really more than one Pachacuti or how many Inca kings really ruled. I am more interested in understanding the paradigm, the big picture, and particularly the relationship between cosmology—which I like to think of as software for analyzing and interpreting the world and events—and legitimacy. It is toward a more indigenous vision of the Inca polity, "a less colonized view of colonial times," to quote Gustavo Verdesio, that I strive. This work is an effort to understand the general forms and rationales of peoples at the provincial and imperial levels and their interactions, to reconstruct the world and worldview of persons who have been denied the power of autodescription by heretofore authoritative and, for too long, nearly unassailable sources. Natives for too long had been silenced by the need to communicate in a language that was not their own, with alien concepts and unfamiliar categories. They had no option but to utilize Spanish institutions to defend themselves and their way of life. In reinterpreting the texts, I attempt to shift the paradigm, to decenter the focus from a fixed place to a line of beings and their attempts to forge lasting ties to a disparate number of groups of people with their own gods and identities. Conrad and Demarest systematize the conclusions of archaeologists studying the material record and Andean memories as conveyed by the chroniclers and others to argue that the Incas expanded to conquer land and other resources. They attribute the expansion to a need to amass material wealth by each ruler as a basis for establishing his immortality. I argue here (as I have previously), in contrast, that the Incas expanded to conquer people and that labor was the commodity or resource of primary value. The native belief system masked this attempt and made it palatable to the people from whom the leaders extracted the service by which an individual ruler's wealth was reckoned.[15]

In exploring these themes, I have had to shed multiple layers of my own culturally imposed ways of thinking and innumerable paradigms, values, and assumptions. In some ways, I think the "Spanish," only then being constructed, were closer to an understanding of certain aspects of the native Andean organization than we are. They, after all, imported institutions, such as the encomienda, which was essentially a grant of the power of people and used in a way analogous to the decimal system of the Incas to organize Andean populations. The Spanish did not set off immediately to survey and place boundary markers. For them, the body politic was not synonymous with a delimited country; the idea of an Andean state—or a Spanish state, for that matter—as a unified nation did not yet exist in the sixteenth century. Loyalties were personal. Clientelism defined how society worked. The monarch united the various "kingdoms." Iberians, too, came from a European society where the king and queen had no fixed capital (until the middle of the sixteenth century, 1561, to be exact). A peripatetic, itinerant court was not unusual. And, finally, theirs was a society in which church and state, the religious and secular powers, were tightly enmeshed and interdependent. We are the ones who think of a fixed capital when we read about the place Francisco Pizarro designated as the city of "the Cuzco" in March 1534.[16]

Given the sociocultural, economic, and physical or geographic distance between the sixteenth-century Andeans and us, and my own culturally mediated views, I cannot pretend to have gotten my interpretation right in all respects. Look upon these pages then as an initial attempt to approximate better the past of these Andean people in the sixteenth and seventeenth centuries. This is a start, a jumping-off point for further research, and an opportunity for others to look closer, to reexamine, and to refine. This history, however, consciously manipulates the data at hand to make this one part of Andean history comprehensible and useful to people like me. Never did I imagine that a serious inquiry into the lives and understandings of the "other" was also a deep inquiry into myself.

Part One

SOVEREIGNTY

2 *El Cuzco: A Reconsideration of Sovereignty, Territoriality, and the Inca State*

> Oh Sun! my father, who said let there be Cuzcos and Tambos; let these, your children, be triumphant and plunderers of all the peoples; I adore you so that these yncas your children are happy and so that they will not be subdued or plundered but always be victorious, because for this you created them.
>
> —Cristóbal Molina, el cuzqueño, "A prayer for all the Incas"

Although critical analyses of sources have long been recognized as a cornerstone of the historian's craft, it becomes crucially important in instances in which observers describe foreign cultures.[1] Because the early, firsthand accounts of the conquest era of Spanish America are few in number, their authors' collective views have come to dominate subsequent historical thinking. The Spanish or Hispanicized view of events has become the basis for our own view for lack of an equivalent, contemporary, indigenous countercommentary. Precisely for their monopoly position on first impressions of the peoples of the New World, scholars have become concerned with judging the effectiveness of Spanish cultural filters through which the native world was seen. Philip Ainsworth Means, Raul Porras Barrenechea, Franklin Pease, John V. Murra, and Rolena Adorno are a few of the many scholars who have been active in reconsidering the validity of the information on the indigenous societies of western South America supplied by early Spanish and, thereafter, by Hispanicized native chroniclers.[2] However, even the assessors' own cultural heritage can get in the way, encouraging too-facile acceptance of information at face value. Such technique hinders efforts to evaluate the information on native Americans, especially when their cultures differ significantly from the observer's own. The challenge, then, is to think the (culturally) unthinkable.

Luckily, in the Spanish American case, first-observer or chronicler accounts, very few in number into the 1570s, can, beginning in the 1540s, be measured and balanced against other primary sources, such as administrative and ecclesiastical correspondence and reports and court records. Contradictions within one category of sources can sometimes be understood and resolved after consulting sources of another type. Scholars are then better able to pick and choose among the observers' data, endeavoring to forge new, more accurate consensuses. If such a methodology fails, one must seek explanations and meaning with a reevaluation of the words used, keeping in mind that the significance of terms changes over time.

The following study began as an assessment of conflicting usages of one ubiquitous term from the contact period in Peru and its underlying significance. It should be read as an analogue to Robert Darnton's famous study of a cat massacre in eighteenth-century France.[3] Like Darnton's inquiry, this chapter commenced as an attempt to understand the incomprehensible: why the first chroniclers—those writing in the early and mid-1530s, within days and months of events and first encounters—used the word *Cuzco* to describe a person and not a place, whereas subsequently the word became synonymous with a location and settlement. This perplexing enigma led me to reexamine the concepts of and evidence for empires, governments, and boundaries—that is, sovereignty and territoriality among the Incas, a word that itself is a constructed category first used in the chronicles in the decade of the 1540s, referring to the person and institution that the Spanish described as the native equivalent of a European king or emperor. In other words, my unconventional thoughts about the use of a word, *Cuzco*, led me to realize that Westerners' cultural filters, including my own, were Eurocentric, Christocentric, and so pervasive that they skewed, obscured, and confused writing on the "Inca" empire for generations.[4]

Person or Place?

Since the mid-1530s, Europeans and their descendants have accepted the city of Cuzco as the capital of the Inca empire. The Hispanicized Indian Felipe Guamán Poma de Ayala's famous seventeenth-century map (see Figure 2.1) shows the quadripartite division of the Andean world with the city of Cuzco as its center (shown in Figure 2.2). It was the hub of the intricate and far-reaching highway system, along which walked a seasonal flow of visitors, pilgrims, and produce-bearing human and llama caravans. It was surrounded by a complex hydraulic system that irrigated fields and provided water for household use. Built of magnificent stone walls, it was the ritual focus and sometime home of the once seemingly omnipotent Andean rulers. The gold-plated Temple or House of the Sun was the center of the elaborate ceque system, the sight lines of ceremonial and ritual observance that radiated from it. Sacsayhuamán, often identified as a fortress on a hill overlooking the city, served also as a storage center for the state's reciprocity and asymmetrical redistributive obligations and as a temple. Thus, this city embodied the power that had been the Inca genius.[5]

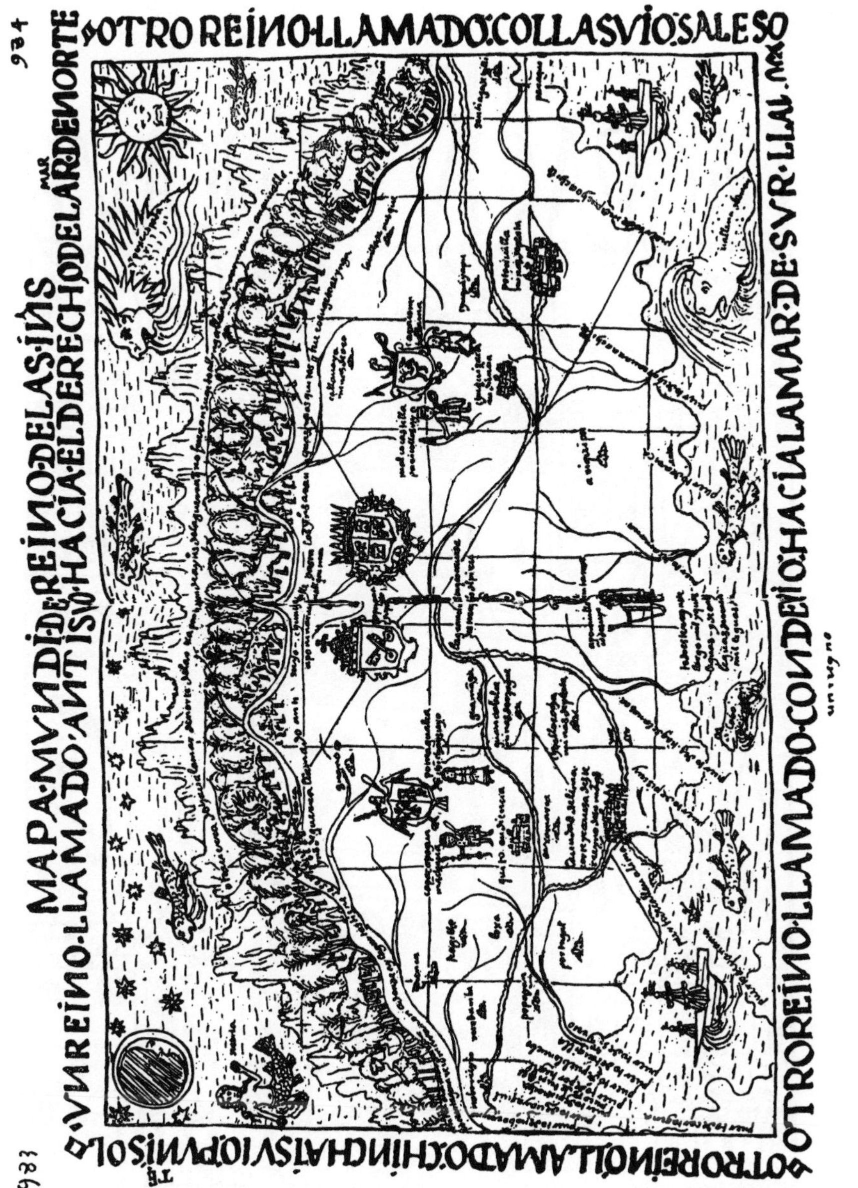

FIGURE 2.1. Traditional view of the Tawantinsuyu. Source: Guamán Poma de Ayala 1613/1936: 983–84.

FIGURE 2.2. The city of Cuzco, showing the Haucaypata and Coricancha. Source: Guamán Poma de Ayala 1613/1936: 1051.

Yet a review of the earliest Spanish documents reveals that observers used the word *Cuzco* in another way. In letters, reports, and chronicles written before 1535, the word referred to a person and not a place. Licenciado Gaspar de Espinosa—whom the chronicler Gonzalo Fernández de Oviedo identified as a judge (*oidor*) of the Supreme Court (*Real Audiencia*) of the city of Santo Domingo and mayor or magistrate (*alcalde mayor*) under Pedrarias Dávila in Tierra Firme—wrote to the king (*Su Magestad*) about Francisco Pizarro's explorations along the west coast of South America even before Pizarro had first reached Cajamarca and met the Inca emperor Atahualpa. In this, one of his periodic letters to the Spanish crown, dated October 21, 1532, and sent from Panama, he related news from the south brought by two ships that arrived eight to ten days after Diego de Almagro, Pizarro's partner, cast off with supplies and reinforcements. The licenciado summarized the crew's news and letters, relating how Governor Pizarro had traveled beyond Túmbez to the site where he founded the Spanish town (*villa*) of San Miguel de Piura.[6] After an enthusiastic recitation of the abundant details on the climate, geography, and population along their itinerary—a summation that reads like a reconnaissance report, and very much like some of Hernando Cortés's first five letters to the Spanish king from Mexico—Espinosa reported that Pizarro heard that beyond Piura "there are two great lords who are brothers who dominate all[:] one who is called Cuzco and the other Tabalizue who are both very different one from the other and they make very cruel war." Such terminology held in a subsequent letter to the king, dated August 1, 1533, where the licenciado related, with a bit of sarcasm and worry in his words, the death of Atahualpa. Here he again referred to a past Inca as "el Cuzco." We know from Cristóbal de Mena's account that "the Cuzco" to whom he was referring here was "el Cuzco Viejo, the old Cuzco."[7]

A few months later on November 23, 1533, Hernando Pizarro, in Santa María del Puerto on the island of Hispaniola—on his way back to Spain from his first encounter with the inhabitants of what would become known later as the viceroyalty of Peru and loaded down with the gold and silver booty of a king's ransom—wrote his own account of the events in Peru in a now-famous and much-quoted letter to the Real Audiencia of Santo Domingo. In his report, he referred to "Atabaliba" as the son "of the old Cuzco and brother of the one who now was lord of the land." He recounted how Atabaliba had spoken of his brother as "the Cuzco, his brother" and how Governor Pizarro asked Atahualpa about "your brother, the Cuzco." He identified houses as "houses . . . of the old Cuzco, father of Atabaliba [Guayna Capac]." The inns, way stations, or resting places (*tambos* or *tanbos*) along the highways were said to have "remained from when the Cuzco passed through that land." There was also talk of the captains of Huáscar's armies who had remained behind with the people (*gente*) "in the town of the Cuzco."[8]

During the next year European demand for detailed news of the events in Peru was met by two chronicles, the first published in April 1534 by Captain Cristóbal de Mena (or Medina), a soldier, resentful of what he considered to be too meager a share in Atahualpa's treasure, given his extraordinary leadership and early command at Pizarro's side. Mena had been a captain under Pedrarias Dávila in the conquest of Nicaragua before Pizarro made him his second-in-command in an early phase of his own expedition and a judge (*justicia*) in the newly founded villas of Túmbez and Piura. Yet he received a smaller share of Atahualpa's ransom than other captains. Mena's account is fresh, spontaneous, crude, direct, and very personal. In it, he used "Cozco" to refer to cacique "Atabalipa's" older brother, Huáscar. He states that after "Atabalipa" was captured, Pizarro found out that "this chief had captured another lord who was called the Cuzco who was a greater lord than he." Further into his short chronicle, he related arriving in the town "of the Cuzco," where the Spanish found "dried images [literally bundles]," one of which was the mummy of Atahualpa and Huáscar's father: "his father the Cuzquo."[9] Throughout, he described Huáscar as "the Cuzco" and Guayna Capac as "the old Cuzco." When describing the city, he used phrases such as "they arrived at the town of the Cuzco." When the Spanish asked a captain of Atahualpa "where the gold of the old Cuzco was," he replied, "in the same town of the Cuzco." Cuzco viejo's gold was in the town of the Cuzco.[10]

Francisco de Xerez, Pizarro's secretary in Cajamarca, wrote to respond to and correct the bias of Mena's version. His description was finished at the end of July 1533 and published one year later. It became the most-detailed, most-read, and best-known official version of those important events up to that time. In it Xerez likewise refers to Guayna Capac as the Cuzco viejo and to Huáscar as the Cuzco, son "of the old Cuzco." In his chronological account, the first reference to what became known as the city of Cuzco has no name and was referred to as "the city where his brother lives." The writer related Atahualpa's boast that he had sent two of his captains to conquer the land of the Cuzco, "and they continued winning all the land up to that city where the Cuzco was." Elsewhere, it is clear that he uses the word as a toponym. And in many places his meaning is ambiguous: "road of the Cuzco"; "they should see the town of the Cuzco, and . . . take possession of the Cuzco."[11]

The use of the word *Cuzco* to refer to a person ended rapidly and abruptly. Pedro Sancho de la Hoz, who became Pizarro's secretary when Xerez returned to Spain, continued the official history of the events in Peru, writing an account meant for the king, which he finished in Jauja in July 1534 while recovering from a leg injury. In it he used the word *Cuzco*, sometimes in an ambiguous way—for example, "the house of the Cuzco"—although most of the time, judging from the word's context, it referred to a place. The reason may be that he wrote his account after the official refounding of the "Very Noble and Grand" Spanish city of Cuzco in March 1534. Yet at the end of his account Sancho still described Guayna Capac as the "old cacique."[12]

As a final note concerning the use of the word *Cuzco* during those early years, Oviedo changed his terminology after interviewing Diego Molina, whom he identified as a young member of Pizarro's expeditionary troop to Cajamarca. Molina told him that Atahualpa was a "great prince." Molina continued, "And some call his father and brother, each one of them, Cuzco; and they, too, are mistaken, because then they were primarily concentrating on gathering money rather than understanding the proper names of each. They did not rightly understand the language, nor was that the purpose of these soldiers."[13] From that point forward, Oviedo wrote that he would use the "proper name" of Guayna Capac for Atahualpa's father and "Guáscara" for his older brother. Diego Molina's information and reasoning became the standard. Thereafter in the accounts and history of the Andean empire, the individual Inca rulers were identified by a proper name.[14]

One naturally wonders whether or not there were some meaning and logic behind identifying at least two Incas, the ruling members of the lineage deemed legitimate from the emic or insider point of view, as "the Cuzco." There are two possible ways of approaching the issue. First, one could dismiss the entire issue as one of miscommunication, as the erudite Porras Barrenechea did.[15] Cross-cultural understanding was undoubtedly difficult, particularly during the initial phase of contact. There existed no bilingual Marina (Malinche) in Peru, as there was in Mexico, to facilitate translation, only several young boys who had been kidnapped off the Pacific coast by Bartolomé Ruiz, his crew, and other Spaniards on previous trips. These boys had learned the Spanish language through their constant interaction with the Castilians. Concepts and ideas were troublesome, as shown in the tense scene in the plaza of Cajamarca on Saturday afternoon, November 16, 1532, where the Dominican friar Vicente de Valverde, through an interpreter, tried to explain ideas about the Christian Bible as the "word of God." Extant testimonies show that these young translators were clearly capable of expressing certain basic terms and of understanding simple information. The fact that they accurately conveyed information to Pizarro about the civil war before the Spanish began the breathtaking ascent into the Andes to meet Atahualpa was proof of that.[16]

Alternatively, if one accepts that native translators were conveying basic information, perhaps the use of "el Cuzco" reflected the standard native practice of not using the Inca's "proper name." Native Andeans assumed successive names during a lifetime—at or shortly after birth, at adolescence, and after an accomplishment or unusual event—in accordance with the characteristics that they exhibited.[17] Authorities had additional occasions to acquire and assume new names. Betanzos reports that conquering captains could use the name of the conquered as their surname (*sobre nombre*) and family name (*apellido*). The Inca was renamed upon ascension to the throne.[18]

The given names of the Inca were not normally uttered, because their personal names, perhaps like those of ancient Egyptian pharaohs or the Hebrew god, were considered too sacred to pronounce, except during ritual circumstances. Garcilaso de la Vega states that "the majesty of his name [referring to Manco Capac], so great and so high, that among them it was considered so sacred and divine that no one dared utter it, except with the greatest veneration, then only to name the king." Cieza states, likewise, that "in public no one dared name his [Huáscar's] name." Instead, they were more commonly addressed by their titles, epithets, or sobriquets, a fact that Diego Molina either did not appreciate or, if he did, did not emphasize enough to Oviedo. According to Guamán Poma de Ayala, Tupac Inca Yupanqui talked to the sacred objects (*guacas*) and knew of the coming of the Spanish (whom the Andeans called viracochas, after their creator god). Thereafter, he was called Inca Viracocha, or the "powerful Inca." Manco Capac was known as Pachacuti, which means "reformer" or "overturner of the world" in the Quechua language. Blas Valera stated that such titles or appellations, should the person possess the qualities and powers inherent in the words, made persons forget first names, "in such a way that in all parts they forgot the first names to call him by these."[19]

Cuzco may have been another such title or term that was, in addition, inheritable between generations by men in the same position. There is evidence that the appellation "Cuzco" was the name or label of the lordship (*señorío*) and that each ruler took that name upon succession to the leadership position of the empire. Xerez reported that Atahualpa, as son of the Cuzco viejo, took the title upon succession, "and as successor to the dominion he is called Cuzco like his father." Such name taking also occurred at the local curacazgo level. Inheritable names and positions might explain why, in contrast to using the standard list of ten to twelve, Father Fernando Montesinos included over a hundred names of kings in his account and Blas Valera identified Pachacuti as both the seventh and ninth of that name. Perhaps names such as Pachacuti and Cuzco are indications of "positional succession" and "perpetual kinship." Such a manner of addressing the Inca may also explain why the local lords of Jayanca appear nonplussed at a question about Guayna Capac in 1540. They did not understand a Spanish inspector's query because the question used the Inca's proper name in place of "Cuzco," his title and customary designation.[20]

Although not defined or simply identified as the city in the early dictionaries by Domingo de Santo Tomás or Diego Gonçales Holguin, the word *Cuzco* is translated by chroniclers in several ways. Garcilaso de la Vega wrote that "Cozco," referring to the city, meant navel (*ombligo*) in the private language of the Incas. Sarmiento de Gamboa, in relating his Toledo-inspired version of the mytho-history of the Incas' origins and specifically the story of Ayar Auca's lithification, stated that in the "ancient language of this valley" the word *Cuzco* referred to "marker [*mojón*] of possession" where the Incas were to "populate and live." An alternative translation from the same source is "sad and fertile." Other authors, both Spanish and native, use the term to mean center, brain, or heart of the universe. The pre-Inca name of the place, Acamama, where later the religious and administrative center was built, was all but forgotten.[21]

But the possibility that "Cuzco" could have been an epithet for the Inca leaves a related question unanswered: Why were there various physical locations identified as Cuzco? Chroniclers stated that Guayna Capac was building another center or Cuzco in Tomebamba: Guayna Capac "settled there [the area of Quito] and named a great city where he was: the city of the Cuzco." Atahualpa wanted to depopulate the southern (city of) "Cuzco" and build a new "Cuzco" in Quito; and Manco Inca constructed a town in the "image of Cuzco," the Spanish related in their chronicles, which he called "Rucquiri." Guamán Poma de Ayala lists other Inca sites, besides these, called Cuzco: at Vilcapampa (or Vilcabamba), Huánuco (Pampa), Hatun Colla, and Charcas. Finally, Cieza identified Incahuasi in the Cañete Valley as another "new" Cuzco.[22]

Analogous evidence from Mughal northern India, Mesoamerica, provincial Andean curacazgos, sixteenth-century England, fourteenth-century Java, nineteenth-century Morocco, and even Spain until the second half of the sixteenth century (1561, to be exact) suggests that the center or what Westerners would call a "capital," was wherever the king, chief, or curaca happened to be. From the mid-sixteenth through the early eighteenth centuries, the Mughal imperial capital was not a single urban center but a series of capitals. These represented foci where the Mughal emperor and his royal household could be seen and venerated by numbers of his subjects as they moved about. A shifting center was characteristic of some chiefdoms in Mesoamerica. Eugenia Ibarra Rojas found for the chiefs of what became Costa Rica that "there where the paramount chief lived was the capital [*cabecera*]." Because local curacas could come from one of several lineages (*ayllus*), each living at a different place, the geographic focus or center could shift with the location of the home of the person in office. Finally, Clifford Geertz reminds readers that Elizabeth Tudor roamed in "endless peregrinations" in sixteenth-century England; that a fourteenth-century Javanese king visited over two hundred localities in an area of ten to fifteen thousand square miles in one season; and that in nineteenth-century Morocco, "the king's throne is his saddle [and] the sky is his canopy." Mulay Hasan's mobile court consisted of forty thousand people. He concludes that for such sovereigns, "motion was the rule, not the exception."[23]

If there could be multiple capitals or various simultaneous or diachronic centers, then the idea that a person and not a place might have been the navel or center of the Andean universe is not such a radical one and makes sense.[24] What made a place a center, albeit temporarily, was the presence of the person called el Cuzco. Zuidema recognized this in 1973, when he states: "In Inca social organization the living king was the center of the universe." Perhaps with this in mind, he also denominates Cuzco, Quito, and Huánuco Viejo as "capitals in the Inca empire." Geertz's article on centers, kings, and charisma supports this conceptualization and develops the idea of multiple centers used by a roving court. He writes of "the symbolic value individuals possess and their relation to the active centers of the social order. Such centers, which have 'nothing to do with geometry and little with geography,' are essentially concentrated loci of serious acts; they consist in the point or points in a society where its leading ideas come together with its leading institutions to create an arena in which the events that most vitally affect its members' lives take place." The Inca was the animating center of the religio-political system. As initiator and benefactor of essential and fundamental rites and ceremonies, it would have been incumbent on him to travel (a royal progress?) to visit his subjects, stopping no doubt at local sun temples, hence, the mention of multiple Cuzcos. Yet in this scenario the center was wherever the Cuzco happened to be, that is, the person was the center of the center. Zuidema again gives evidence suggestive of this fact. He says that when the sun goes through zenith (on October 30 and February 13) in the city of Cuzco, "a vertical pole, a gnomon, will not cast any shadow. It was the symbol of the king himself as Axis Mundi." If this is true, what type of imperial organization might such a personal and movable "center" imply, and how did it differ from contemporary European conceptions of the same?[25]

To answer these questions, even tentatively, requires the rather daunting task of analyzing native concepts of religio-political organization and sovereignty, which were cast in terms of personal relations, and disentangling them from the somewhat more secular and material Spanish ideas and culture embedded even in the language of the conquest. This involves a broad inquiry into the conceptualization of space and territory and, by extension, boundaries and markers, always endeavoring to separate the native from the European. To explore the concepts of territoriality and sovereignty, I have chosen representative examples to illustrate my points. A careful reading of chroniclers' accounts and local-level primary sources helps unwind the twisted and interrelated histories of native and European experiences. The results of my attempts to understand the use and significance of the term "Cuzco" are presented by comparing the conceptual organization of the indigenous empire with the notions of political authority and territoriality of the Spanish invaders and my changing interpretations of the same.[26]

Whether or not the Inca was addressed as "el Cuzco" or later indicated by a proper name, my research leads me to believe that the Inca was the center of a jurisdictional state that was defined and imagined in terms of shifting allegiances, sacred duties, and kinship. This was a jurisdictional state in which the populace believed that the center was a living god who embodied the "cosmological" nexus or locus of power, and whose very decisions and actions might be reflections of divine will, as long as the ancestors favored him. If the Spanish recognized the true nature of such relations, they dismissed them as pagan, infidel, unworthy, and too undistinguished for comment. The rapid breakdown of Inca institutions, above the local level after 1532, and Oviedo's mid-manuscript change in the way the Inca was addressed and described allowed the Spanish to force incompletely understood facts into a European narrative mold. Onto the ideal lineage-centered structure of the colonized, the colonizers imposed territorial conceptions (although this took time).

One Law . . . One Birth

Before 1532, according to Cuzco-centered stories, devout followers of the Inca worshipped, loved, feared, and served him as a living god, direct descendant of the Sun, ruler and emperor of a domain that included this world and the next, the living as well as the dead. Embodying both religious and secular authority, each ruler in his turn was considered by true devotees to be a divinity who brought order and peace from confusion and chaos (*behetría*). Ideal Inca kings promised well-being and were known for their hospitality, gifts, and favors. Sinchi Roca (Ruca), for example, "ordinarily had set a table with full glasses for as many as wanted to come, and always (day and night) they were occupied in dances and music according to their custom, both natives as well as strangers." Cobo writes that the Incas had so much surplus that they worried about how to give it away. Even the dead, the embalmed bodies of past rulers, were adored as gods; offered sacrifices of llamas, alpacas, guinea pigs, corn, and beer; and consulted. The various rulers were cognizant that the basis of this cult, the ceremonials or rituals, and the relative luxury of their court were the people, their loyal subjects. One of their greatest delights, a chronicler writes, was to "know the souls that were under his jurisdiction [*reino*] and how many were being born and added to different age grades." The Inca empire was an attempt to unite ever greater numbers of Andean peoples under "one law" and into one lineage. Eventually, the promise was that being of "one birth," all the peoples under the empire would live in a world of peace and plenty.[27]

This concern with symbolic kinship is a key to understanding the Inca organization and conceptualization of their dominion. Indeed, in the Andes, the Inca did not conquer geography so much as people or nations. Chronicles are full of accounts of how various ethnic groups came to be systematically incorporated under Inca jurisdiction. State emissaries routinely tried to convince curacas or paramount lords—locally known as creators of Indians (*dueños de indios*)—and their subjects to associate and pledge allegiance voluntarily, rewarding such peaceful submission profusely with gifts and privileges. Such may have been part of the history of the Lupaca's nonviolent capitulation to the Inca.[28]

Resistance, in contrast, met unrelenting and unpardoning imperial force. Once having subjugated it, the Incas symbolically and ritually took possession of the ethnic group by making the defeated leaders don ridiculous red tunics with long fringe or tassels; by splashing them with maize beer (*chicha*); and by sprinkling crumbs of maize flour on their heads. A new translation of one victory song, conserved in writing by Betanzos, suggests that they were dressed so as to resemble women, thus symbolizing their failure in battle: "Inca Yupanqui, son of the sun. He dressed the Soras in tassels; he dressed the Soras in skirts. Tanarara, tanarara!" The Inca sometimes made such degraded prisoners parade before his warriors, his captains, and his own litter in a procession that demonstrated worldly imperial success and supernatural backing. Likewise, when triumphant captains returned from the battlefields, amid general rejoicing and victory songs (*chamay wariqsa*), they feted the Inca and begged him to tread on their humiliated prisoners and their paraphernalia—which was later placed in a gallery with trophies of other victories. By doing so, the Inca signaled the subjugation of the defeated and his acceptance of his generals' service.[29]

Unlike the loosely linked confederation of culturally and linguistically heterogeneous peoples subject to the Aztecs (Mexicas or Nahuas, following Lockhart) of Mexico, those ruled by the Inca state were (at least in theory) required to learn to speak Quechua, to worship the Sun and his descendants as gods, and to serve when asked in an attempt to foster unity. Commoner soldiers and their families, if not killed, sometimes were relocated and assigned to perpetual servitude; for an undeniably strong motivation that drove imperial expansion was accessing the labor potential of provincial subjects, whose directed efforts built roads, terraced lands, rerouted irrigation water, and constructed the monumental architecture of imperial centers and shrines.

To facilitate administration and control, the Inca's growing number of subjects were divided into four parts (*suyus;* also *suyos*), translated by the Spanish as kingdoms and dominions (*reinos y señoríos*). All four were collectively referred to as Tawantinsuyu. Most scholars assume that the individual suyus and the Tawantinsuyu were geographic and administrative districts that, according to an early testimony, had jurisdiction or limits (*términos*) that were marked "as they are today." Zuidema has long sought to define the boundaries of each.[30] A 1577 manuscript, published by Waldemar Espinoza Soriano, provides an alternative view of these quarters. In this "Memorial," written by members of the surviving Inca elite, *Tawantinsuyu* was translated and defined as the four lineages (*las cuatro parcialidades*). Their "Memorial" described the suyus in terms of people, by listing the names of native authorities, who represented themselves and "the rest." Titu Cusi uses the term to refer to four peoples, and Santacruz Pachacuti Yamqui equates the suyus with nations. Both Molina and Joseph de Acosta translate the terms as factions (*partidas*) and address the people who composed each. An illustration included in the drawings by Murúa shows the Inca held aloft by four natives, easily distinguished by their dress and decoration as from four separate and easily recognized groups (see Figure 2.3). Guamán Poma de Ayala also consistently depicts only four distinctively attired groups of natives in the hundreds of drawings that illustrate his voluminous letter to the Spanish king, and he writes that the whole kingdom had four kings and four parts. The answer to a 1574 questionnaire on the genealogy of don Diego Saire Tupac Mancocapac Yupanqui Ynga used suyu in the same sense. So does Garcilaso de la Vega, who in one place in his text echoes the definition of *Tawantinsuyu:* "that is, the four parts of the kingdom, or *Incap Runam*, that is vassals of the Inca"; while elsewhere glossing the term as "district."[31]

This demographic or genealogical definition of suyu is consistent with the supervisory structure made up of native officials who communicated information and requests between the center and local societies. The Inca appointed four governors, one for each quarter or parcialidad, often from among his close relatives. Within each quarter, the population was organized using a decimal system. Hernando de Santillán states that each quarter was divided into provinces (*guamames* or *guaniani*) of forty thousand heads of households (*vecinos*). Within these, population units of ten thousand, one thousand (*guaranga*), one hundred (*pachaca*), ten, and even five tributary households were each headed by a local lord (called curaca or *mayco* [*mallco*], lord [*señor*] of vassals). Santillán describes this organization as follows:

> He gave responsibility for each one hundred Indians to a chief [curaca], who was called lord of a *pachaca;* and among each ten curacas of these he chose the most capable to rule and the bravest [*más hombre*], and he made him curaca over the

FIGURE 2.3. A Chinchaysuyu, a Condesuyu, a Collasuyu, and an Antisuyu carrying the litter of Huáscar Inca. Source: Wellington Manuscript by Fray Martín de Murúa, ca. 1615, fol. 67, Getty Museum.

other nine; and the latter was responsible for the nine curacas and their people, and he commanded them, and they obeyed him and were his subjects; this latter was called curaca of guaranga, that means lord of a thousand Indians. And each pachaca appointed an overseer [*mandón*] who helped him when he was absent; and to rule an entire valley where there were many guarangas, he appointed a lord over all called *Huño* [*Huno*], who was governor over all the curacas of pachaca and of guaranga, and they obeyed him as their lord.

Fray Cristóbal de Castro and Diego de Ortega Morejon, surveying the Chincha coastal peoples, wrote that Tupac Inca Yupanqui actually carried out just such a reorganization. Such a structure reflected a primary concern over the administration of bodies, not territory.[32]

A lord's rank in this structure was a direct reflection of the number of his followers. The more persons from whom a lord could expect service, the mark of allegiance and subjugation, the higher his prestige, power, and status. Guamán Poma de Ayala stated about the standing of various native chiefs that "they will gain status if they multiply according to the law of dominion over Indians. And if they [the numbers] decline they [the lords' ranks] will also fall." He continued that a commoner with five sons became a lower-level lord of his progeny (*pichica camachicoc*). Men with ten, thirty, forty, or fifty sons could "settle wherever they might want on empty land and they could be lords over them." Demographic increase, either through reproduction, allegiance, or conquest, brought social mobility. The Inca ruler having, in theory and in practice, the most subjects stood at the apex of this ranked hierarchy, above them all.[33]

The system was imposed on ethnic groups duly incorporated into the Inca's realm. But these decimal divisions, though exact in theory, were only approximate in practice. Although a guaranga, for example, was theoretically equivalent to a thousand households, one witness stated that in practice, "in times of the Inga" the numbers were significantly lower. Groups of varying sizes were doubtlessly adjusted upon incorporation by moving people (*mitimaes*) to other geographic areas for different types of labor or by appropriating some for the direct service of the Inca as personal retainers (*yanaconas*). In some cases, the administrative vocabulary might have been introduced without fine adjustment of the actual numbers of people. The vocabulary facilitated record keeping on mnemonic devices based on colored and knotted strings (*quipus*). It seems particularly important for labor organization and, according to Ake Wedin, military needs; although John V. Murra cautions readers: "To what extent this decimal effort went beyond census practice into the actual administration of the subject ethnic group is uncertain."[34]

This decimal division may have been an administrative shorthand for describing kin groups of various sizes and complexities. The ayllu, the basic local unit of social organization, encompassed relatives who traced their lineage back to a founding ancestor—that is, they were sociopolitical and religious units delimited by kinship, both consanguineous and fictive. They were not geographically defined units as once commonly claimed. These ayllus were combined under lords of increasing rank to form a nested hierarchy, as suggested in the previous quotation from Santillán. As populations grew, junior groups split from the parental group, establishing their own lineages, which developed and colonized unused areas, while often retaining kin and cult ties to their ancestral origins. Thus, the status and power of a lord fluctuated in direct proportion to the population that owed him allegiance—increasing as population increased and decreasing as population fell.[35]

That just such a demographically, subject-based structure defined the extent of Inca strength is provided by Manco Inca's response to two of Pizarro's actions. The first was a request for information on the extent of his Andean domain. Whereas Pizarro might have expected a maplike painting or drawing, showing boundary markers or natural frontiers such as rivers, ravines, or mountain crests, he received instead from the king's agents an account of lords with their corresponding numbers of subjects.[36] The second was his reaction to the granting of encomiendas based on this demographic information. This distribution of native Andeans to the Spanish companions of Pizarro and to Pizarro himself upset Manco Inca, "who a short time before had seen himself as ruler of all the land [he means here peoples on the land] and to see himself deposed of the rulership, being left as the rest of the poor Indians, without luck, only with the promises they made him." He now felt that "he was ruler of nothing, because the Marques [Pizarro] had distributed the land [meaning natives] to encomenderos [Spanish trustees], so that each encomendero would know his curaca and his Indians [*repartimiento*]; he [Manco Inca] was not lord of more than four Indians who served him." More than the continuing Spanish demands for gold and silver, the loss of his sovereignty over his subjects on which his wealth, his position, and his status rested motivated an enraged Manco Inca to revolt and later retreat to Vilcabamba with seventy thousand Indian warriors (*indios de guerra*).[37]

Kinship proved the idiom and cement of growing dominion among the Incas. It was extended by bride exchange to ethnic groups when they accepted the Inca's sovereignty. The Inca gave the local leaders, the curacas or chiefs, gifts of women—from among his "sisters" or "chosen women." Espinoza Soriano reports that Chuptongo, a paramount lord of Cajamarca, for example, received one hundred wives from the Inca in exchange for years of devoted service. Local leaders considered such Inca largesse the highest honor, because many women and offspring bettered the odds that his memory would be preserved after his death. From the Inca's point of view, such gifts of women to provincial lords were, as Tupac Inca Yupanqui is reputed to have once declared, "to sustain their friendship and to keep them from rebelling, disturbing him, and putting him to the trouble of pacifying and subjugating them once again."[38]

The Inca also sometimes married one or more of the local leader's daughters or sisters to build and fortify further alliances and relations. For this reason, the Inca received women from all parts of the empire. Some Incas, such as Pachacuti Inca Yupanqui (Yupangue), were reputed to have had twenty secondary wives from one area of the south alone. Others, such as Guayna Capac, had five hundred from many groups. Most married as many as they wanted. Such liaisons multiplied personal relations geometrically.[39]

A good example of this bride exchange comes from the highland people of Guaylas, studied by Rafael Varón Gabai, Espinoza Soriano, and others. Guayna Capac "married" (*casado a su modo*), as secondary wives, two high-ranking women who were daughters of the lords of the two moieties (Ananguaylas and Ruringuaylas [also Luringuaylas]). Guayna Capac favored both wives, Añas Colque (daughter of Guaca Chillac, leader of "Lurin Huaylla," and Inca Paullu's mother) and Contarguacho (daughter of Pomapacha, curaca of "Jatun-Anan Huaylla," and mother of doña Inés), with gifts of produce and service. The ruler gave Contarguacho, for example, the produce of his herds of camelids and the coca, chili, corn, and other things produced for him by as many as six thousand households. She also enjoyed hundreds of male and female retainers and servants to do her bidding. The Inca used such wives as a tool to ally himself with the Guaylinos and to undercut continued resistance and relieve the humiliation of subjugation. The Guaylinos benefited by increased local privileges because marriage generated reciprocal, if asymmetrical, obligations between the two groups.[40]

The use of marriage to form mutually beneficial alliances and increase the power of curacas also holds in instances where local lords were not favored with an Inca-designated wife. Marriage partners were indexed, according to the size of the group they represented. The anonymous author of a report on Yucay in 1571 informs us of the criterion a lord might use to choose his primary spouse: "And from here there arose [the custom] that the most esteemed woman to marry was the one with the most kin, and not the one who was richest [in the Western, material sense]." Thus, ideally lords chose as principal wife "the one with the most relatives, who brought with her the most friends and people, that was what was most valued, because the house would be larger." Such marriages obligated the female's relatives to support her spouse. But lords took secondary wives as well. Female household workers were called servants (*chinas*), widows (*viudas*), and concubines (*mancebas*) in the sixteenth century. A 1566 manuscript documents that an attendant of a curaca's principal wife became his secondary wife (manceba) and favorite.[41]

Interdependence and gift giving back and forth were also the basis for tribute service. The emperor's periodic trips (*visitas*) to call on his subjects were precisely to maintain contact, negotiate, and request labor to support state endeavors, personnel, and cults; to build and extend the road and bridge network that physically facilitated communication within the empire; and to supply and tend the warehouses and the rest stations along the roadways. Commoners served under their local lords as the Inca or his delegates directed. Labor was the medium and measure of the tax to the state. Subjects expected, in turn, aid in time of drought, famine, natural disaster, or need in general. The Inca ordered supplies warehoused for these and other purposes. In that sense, allegiance to local lord and king was a form of real protection and insurance.[42]

Religious beliefs and state ideology reinforced the kin ties, the joint genealogies, and the mutual, though asymmetrical, economic dependency that tied the led to their leader. Upon incorporation of local peoples, their deities were subsumed into the Inca pantheon, a clear appropriation of ethnic symbols by the state.

> [B]ecause even if the Peruvian kings compelled everyone they subjugated to receive their religion, it is not as if they made them cast aside all of their previous religious beliefs, only those that were contrary to their own; and, thus, they [the subjugated groups] not only kept their ancient gods, but even the Incas accepted them, and had them brought to Cuzco where they were placed among [the Incas'] very own.

Provincial gods were housed near the monarch or mummy of the Inca that had subjugated them and awarded due ceremonial honors and rich sacrifices in accordance with provincial expectations.[43] This was also true at the local level. The 1571 report on Yucay includes the following information:

> This father had his children and relatives who recognized him as such; and if one killed another while quarreling, he was the lord of that body [remains] and of his homestead and of a stone's throw all around, [and even] of a slingshot. This body was very valuable because they cured it and it remained dry like embalmed, and he kept it in his house. And to gain his consent so that they [his relatives] could come to revere him and give him food—which was one of the inanities that they practiced—they became his subjects, like those of his own house.[44]

But worship of the king and the Sun was paramount. The Inca as a multidimensional ruler was simultaneously a political and military leader and the prime mover and head of the state cult—a cult to his ancestors, traced back to their origins, as sons and heirs of the Sun. Intermarriage gave kin status to local lords and, as kin's kin, their followers, thus establishing direct claims to divine protection and aid. A subject's ties, however tenuous and fictive, to the royal genealogy made the worship of the Sun the worship of a common, though distant ancestor, who supplied the legitimizing ideology for Inca authority. They were worshipping a symbol and representative of imperial domination, of the "one birth" ideal.[45]

Thus, theoretically, the Inca's transcendent genealogy and history became the ancestral lore, the past, of the local communities in what Irene Silverblatt has labeled "a flattering, novel, imperial fiction in which kings became kin of those they ruled." Work for the Inca was more than just a tax or tribute; it became a sacred duty to help create and maintain, in some senses, to shore up, the world, all explicitly buttressed by cosmological sanction. The Inca, as head of the state cult and heir of the Sun and immortal god in his own right, claimed and directed the energies of thousands of subjects as mediator and communicator between the living and the dead. Subject labor tasked to build monuments and temples buttressed and aggrandized the religio-political myth on which Inca power, in part, depended.[46]

Thus, because the Inca, or the Cuzco, was the center of a system in which loyalty and obedience were paramount and definitional, the king's authority extended only so far as he had subjects, willing or coerced, to do his bidding. The demographic and personalistic nature of this system was fragile.[47] To maintain it and keep it viable, the Inca himself was obliged to periodically visit his subjects to ceremonially renew personal contact through ritual and the generous redistribution of goods. As his power grew, the Inca felt it necessary to leave a deputy or lieutenant to carry on cult functions, lest while he was away, the people, sensing weakness or a religio-political vacuum, might rebel.[48]

The extent of an Inca's dominion was an expression of his ability to enforce his moral sway, his "one law," to paraphrase Huarochirí informants, over the population of the Andes. Imperiling crises occurred often. When the Inca failed to live up to the expectations of his subjects, oaths of allegiance and loyalty could and did falter and fail, endangering the precarious unity, even the existence, and claim to his power. Guayna Capac faced a serious rebellion for neglecting his nobles while on campaign against the Carangui in the north. Manco Inca's siege of the Spanish city of Cuzco in 1535–36 failed, according to one interpreter, because the delicate balance of reciprocal rights and obligations between the Inca and his subjects had so deteriorated that the soldier commoners abandoned the effort.[49]

It is also possible that the soldiers fighting for the Inca might have concluded that, in light of their failing efforts, the Spanish forces and their god were more powerful than their own.[50] The recalcitrance and rebellion of incorporated groups, military defeat, periodic natural disasters (drought, flood, famine, and plague), and other crises undermined the confidence in the Inca's supernatural connections and ability to appease the gods. When the gods were not favorable, the emperor weakened. In such instances, his claims on labor shrank proportionately and disappeared when expected services of the state failed to materialize. The abundant supplies stored in the local warehouses were the elite's precautionary and farsighted response to surviving such periodic turmoil. But, in each case, the loss of dominance over people and their labor and production was at issue.

To lose sway over a group meant the empire contracted. To dominate a new group meant an expansion. Thus, the empire's human or social frontiers (as I have labeled them elsewhere) were flexible, expanding and contracting, and constantly in flux—even with the rotation that came with the seasons and the variations in the fertility of the fields. Worship of and loyalty to the center indicated the multitude over which a godlike emperor or local lord held influence and labor-taxing jurisdiction. Thus, the Inca "empire," in its starkest outline, was an attempt to incorporate provincial peoples into a gigantic, sun-worshipping congregation or grand lineage through persuasion or, if need be, the force of conquest, legitimized by the belief that the ancestor-gods would provide, if well served. Such an organization, I would argue, is the essence of what has been called elsewhere a jurisdictional state.[51]

Peter Sahlins, in his important book *Boundaries: The Making of France and Spain in the Pyrenees*, describes jurisdictional sovereignty as a relationship between the king and his subjects, a form of administration that gave precedence to jurisdiction over territory, and a system in which leaders ceded or acquired—in war and in diplomacy—specific political jurisdiction and rights to domains, mixing personalistic forms of domination with administrative circumscriptions of district origin. Although this definition was formulated in relation to a long-negotiated border dispute between two western European states that was resolved only in the nineteenth century, I think that jurisdictional sovereignty, characterized "primarily as a relationship between the king and his subjects," best conveys the nature and extent of Inca authority and power. Hierarchical, asymmetric relationships based on mutual dependence and embedded in complicated notions of sacred duty, sanctions, reciprocity, and ritual kinship, all backed up by force, confirmed Inca dominance. At the time of the Spanish invasion and takeover, Inca sovereignty is best described as divinely sanctioned and won jurisdiction over subjects, not over a delimited, bounded, and contiguous territory.[52]

Land Is to Rule

In declaring that the Inca state was jurisdictional, I do not mean to ignore or slight evidence of territoriality, boundaries, and landmarks, but only to put them into historical context and to question standard interpretations of the same. There are three problems in dealing with the topics. First, the discussion is complicated by the problem of unit or scale. There is no consensus among sixteenth-century sources or modern scholars about standard units of analysis. As noted previously, *suyus* and *provinces*, like the less commonly used words *reinos* and *districts*, appear indiscriminately, almost haphazardly, in the sources without definition.[53] Second, chroniclers and many modern scholars alike assume that such entities were cohesive territorial units with physical boundaries, when the personalistic nature of the native state might lead one to expect that the sacred landscape in which people lived and moved would be different from the effective areas of cultivation and settlement and the jurisdiction of various lords.[54] The third problem is philological. The Spanish terms are imprecise, having several meanings. Thus, in the previous quotation about Manco Inca's reaction to the distribution of encomiendas to Pizarro's followers, Betanzos, for example, used the word *tierra* (land) to mean population, making it difficult to distinguish and identify indigenous polities from Spanish impositions and creations.

The hegemonic nature of discourse and the mention of boundaries and markers, not uncommon in sixteenth-century records, obscure the jurisdictional nature of the Inca state.[55] The first chroniclers do not mention boundary markers. Observers were preoccupied with other immediate concerns. Later sources, however, note that human-made markers signaled the farthest points north, south, and east that the Incas penetrated. Cabello Valboa and Santillán wrote that Tupac Inca Yupanqui placed the southernmost markers of his empire (*imperio*) and señorío in Chile. Another example, to the east, is "a piece of marble thrust in the ground of the height of a man" that the natives of Tucumán said the Incas placed there during their conquest "to remember that they had conquered up to there." To the north, Guayna Capac arrived in the Valley of Atres, but because he judged the people there and beyond "poor," he marked his advance and returned south. On this point, González Suárez distinguished between the limits of Inca exploration and the actual extent of the conquest and effective incorporation of subject peoples into the empire. The two did not coincide. The Incas, he noted, explored Esmeraldas, but neither became established there nor exercised influence over the population. Therefore, the markers left by Guayna Capac expressed the limits of exploration, not effective control.[56]

Other markers were said to partition the highland sierras and the coastal valleys and plains. Boundaries of coastal valleys are naturally defined on three sides: ocean on the west and desert on north and south—beyond the reach of the irrigation network. It was on the east, where coastal peoples met highlanders, that potential existed for dispute. Here, the sources indicate that the Inca established divisions between coast and highlands in zones of mixed use. Rostworowski identified such divisions in the Valleys of Lima and Mala (to the south). She thinks that such markers separated lands worked by the coastal people from those worked by the highlanders. This interpretation based on the local record differs in emphasis only from Guamán Poma de Ayala's more general statement that during the rule of Tupac Inca Yupanqui and Guayna Capac, two nobles placed markers between the coast and the highlands to delimit work responsibilities.

Limits and boundary markers of the Indians of the highlands and of the coastal plains, *yungas*, . . . were [ordered] placed by Topa Ynca Yupanqui and Uayna Capac Ynga and of their boundary-makers [*mojonadores*] Yngas Una Caucho Ynga, Conaraqui Ynga, by the royal council and nobles [or principal lords] and authorities of this kingdom, so that there would be limits between the Indians of the highlands and those of the plains. So that each one would fulfill his obligations to the royal authority within his own jurisdiction. . . . From here [the highland people] have to provide service to highland towns [plazas] [and] mines. In the same way, the Indians of Hatun Yunga have to serve towns and mines in the Hatun Yunga.

Note that the demarcations were established to set service responsibilities. The tasks may or may not have included working parcels of land in support of the state cult and officials. Similarly, other chronicles mention limits between ethnic groups to define tasks, such as work on roads or in the mines. Thus, the Inca seemed most concerned with defining work responsibilities and keeping the peace; a corollary, such as marking the point at which climate and elevation made it dangerous for highlanders or lowlanders to pass without risking their health, was secondary.[57]

Chroniclers also report boundaries of provinces and "towns."[58] Betanzos noted that Guayna Capac marked boundaries on one of his inspection trips. Guamán Poma de Ayala, who often writes of rigid Inca laws, wrote that landmarks were set up by order of Tupac Inca Yupanqui to mark "each province of these kingdoms and each people of each ayllu." But here he seemed to be using the words *province*, *pueblo*, and *ayllu* as groups of people and not territorial subdivisions. Be that as it may, punishment for moving human-made markers was torture and, if the offense recurred, even death.[59]

But such provincial and local, artificial boundaries are only occasionally found. Between the coastal valleys of Jayanca and Motupe, natives used the part of the irrigation ditch that they cleaned as a natural limit of their cultivation. Given the desert conditions of the coast, this is not surprising, because artificial watercourses defined the limits of cultivation. It is hard to determine, however, whether or not such irrigation ditches and watercourses, hills, or uninhabited desert drylands (*despoblados*), which Spaniards used to describe valleys or provinces, had the same meaning before the conquest as thereafter.[60]

FIGURE 2.4. The suyus as traditionally depicted, based on the direction of the roads leaving the city of the Cuzco.

Fieldstones or other artificial boundary markers of individual fields, although expected, are likewise elusive until the second half of the sixteenth century unless erected by the Spanish themselves. Native plots were bounded instead by neighboring fields, hills, swamps, rivers, roads, and canals. Such delimitations, at least to the middle of the sixteenth century, seemed sufficient to describe unambiguously the fields in Yucay, the areas around Cuzco, and the lands near Lima as far south as Pachacamac. Thereafter, human-made boundary markers are increasingly noted. A 1555 decree orders officials to give, assign, and demarcate (*amojonar*) fifty *fanegadas de sembradura* (a land measure) to a Spanish vecino of Cuzco, Martin de Meneses.[61]

Historians and archaeologists who have taken the reports of borders and markers literally and tried to find them have had varying degrees of success. María Rostworowski tried to establish the territorial extent of one-quarter of the empire that the Incas called Collasuyu (see Figures 2.1 and 2.4). She premised her remarks on her deduction that the natives had "an apparent need . . . to demarcate space." Despite the fact that the quipu or record keepers (*quipucamayocs*) informed Governor Vaca de Castro (1542–44) that the four suyus were delimited, Rostworowski found no evidence of any such indigenous boundaries in the historical record. The earliest mention of boundaries that she could find came from a 1573 letter from Juan Maldonado de Buendia to His Majesty. All of the mentioned boundaries were natural: "from the river of the said city of Arequipa . . . one hundred and twenty leagues along the coast toward Chile and from the Cordillera of the sierras to the sea twenty and thirty [leagues] in width." To what extent this description reflected native conceptions and practice before 1532 is not addressed. Further compromising her interpretation is that her sources are relatively late and concerned with Spanish colonial control of the native population, for example, a six-folio list of the ecclesiastical organization of Cuzco of 1584; a similar document on Arequipa of 1649; a report dated 1601 over excessive labor exactions; and, the earliest, the above-mentioned letter whose purpose was to report on the resettlement of the dispersed indigenous population to nucleated villages in the southern area.[62]

Another regional study was no more successful. In this case the author, an archaeologist by training, published an impressive, data-filled monograph, trying to establish the territorial divisions of Condesuyu, another of the four traditionally accepted divisions of the Tawantinsuyu. Her analysis rests on the assumptions that, first, the Incas had a territorial order and that the Condesuyu was one territorial unit (although the borders, the author admits, of Inca Condesuyu "cannot be clearly defined"). Second, she assumed that "one or more native towns were granted to an *encomendero* [holder of a native population in trust], and this early encomienda territory was the foundation of the parish and the *corregimiento* [local governorship]." Here, the related assumption is that this "encomienda territory" reflected the area of the original native polity. Although the author recognized that the encomienda was not a unit of land, she argued that by locating the people included in any grant awarded, an "encomienda territory" could be defined. She states that on territories such as these, Viceroy Francisco de Toledo (1569–81) "found[ed] native parishes and define[d] the boundaries of corregimientos." Thus, the author concluded, citing Charles Gibson, that one can re-create the Inca territorial order by establishing the relationship between encomienda, parish, and corregimiento—which by the way, were all Spanish institutions. Last, the author assumed that Andean people "occupied discrete territories" (although she presents data that prove otherwise). All these assumptions reflect current Western constructs better than they describe Andean and early colonial reality.[63]

The concept of encomienda territory is a case in point. Recent research has found that encomienda grants did not often coincide with original precontact indigenous polities. Encomiendas were often dismembered fractions of a larger demographic unit. Too frequently the demands of too numerous conqueror-pretenders forced Pizarro and his successors to split the original polities into two, three, or four units, assigning the paramount lord to one Spaniard; his lieutenant (*segunda persona*) to another; and, if the population were large enough, one or more noble lords (*principales*) to the third or fourth Spaniards on the list of the meritorious:

The Marques don Francisco Pizarro governor who was of this kingdom all the repartimientos [encomiendas] that he made he did not make in one day but in several. . . . it seems that the said Marques did not entrust to all the heads and caciques principales who existed, but to some he entrusted the cacique principal and first person and to others the second [person] and other principal lords were left for others even though these were subject to the principal and first person of the said caciques.[64]

As a result of such fractionalization, curacas, such as those of highland Chucuito or coastal Jayanca, with subjects living at a distance from the rest of their kin—for example, on the coast near the Sama and Moquegua for the former, or in highlands occupied primarily by the Guambos for the latter—often lost control over them, because the Spanish did not early recognize such discontinuous settlement patterns. Pizarro and his successors dismembered native polities by assigning the curaca to one encomendero and the distant colonies to another. Furthermore, subjects of various curacas often lived side by side in the ecological islands of the vertical archipelago. Although this second author admitted finding examples of such overlapping settlement patterns, she usually dismissed them. She explains that creating a territorial base for the encomienda is "admittedly imprecise" and that the boundaries she draws "obscure the more complex pattern of settlement that existed before the reductions were effected."[65] Encomiendas, it must be concluded—as awarded by the Spanish from as early as 1534—did not reflect indigenous territorial conceptions of organization, if they existed at all. The concept of encomienda territory is flawed. Furthermore, neither parishes nor corregimientos were conceived of as discrete and bounded territories when first established. They were created to administer population, as will be shown in more detail later.[66]

Alberto Rex González, also an archaeologist, tried to delimit the geopolitical divisions of Inca Tucumán (northwestern Argentina) by seeking boundaries. He assumed, like his colleague, that ethnic group divisions would neatly correspond to political boundaries. He specifically looked for the geographic limits of the Inca provinces of Quire-Quire, Austral, and Humahuaca, using historical and archaeological sources. He identified the northern limit of the province of Quire-Quire but admitted that its southern frontier is "extremely difficult to establish." Furthermore, he concluded that "the limits of the Inca province of Humahuaca coincide only in part with those of the ethnicity of the same name." Instead, he found peoples of various ethnic groups and economic or military functions living together. The dispersed cropping patterns of the native born and the presence of twenty thousand mitimaes who purportedly defended the frontier of the region complicated the picture.[67]

John Hyslop, likewise, sought to delimit the kingdom of the Lupaca and its seven political subdivisions or provinces on the shores of Lake Titicaca. Like Julien and Rex González, he expected subdivisions or provinces to be "more or less cohesive territorial units." Instead, he found clusters of ayllu members, but also some pueblos and towns subject to the lords of Chucuito living among peoples of other lords. This confirmed the 1567 testimony of the chief don Martín Cari, who listed some of his Chucuito subjects who farmed among subjects of another lord. Hyslop also found colonies of Lupaca living far away in what appear to be multiethnic enclaves. He concluded by questioning whether or not there had been borders between provinces (Chucuito and Acora) and by stating that "it is uncertain whether the Lupaca ever imagined their subdivisions to have well-defined boundaries." He also found that it was difficult to specify boundaries of the Lupaca kingdom itself, especially on the southwest side.[68]

Hyslop's conclusions were confirmed some years later by Gabriel Martínez. Martínez first considered the intraprovincial settlement patterns of the two moities, or halves (*sayas*), of the Lupacas. In contrast to the common belief that people belonging to the upper moiety lived concentrated in the higher altitudes as opposed to their lower-half cohorts who lived in "low-lying lands" (*tierras bajas*), Martínez found that the people of the two moieties all shared a wide area. They lived interspersed in a way that gave both moieties access to lower-lying agricultural lands and higher-altitude pastures. Not surprisingly, the same was true of the ayllus. Family units lived spattered (*salpicados*) and interspersed or interdigitalized among themselves. Furthermore, the Lupaca peoples also had members living in other provinces (Quina and Chapaca). This finding stands in obvious contradiction to Hyslop's original thesis that the Lupaca lived in cohesive territorial units (*unidades territoriales cohesivas*). Martínez concluded that "it is not territoriality but the control of complementary resources through a pattern of dispersion that permits the greatest degree of security given the rigours of the environment." Martínez's conclusions echo Murra's research that held that an ethnic group lived dispersed over a wide area to gain access to a broad range of ecological niches to guarantee subsistence.[69]

Martínez likewise found no precise, "continuous and defined" limits between the territories of Acora and Chucuito. "On the contrary, especially in the northeastern sector, there is such an imbrication of ayllus of one and another 'province' that it is impossible to declare that the ayllus of one do not intrude in the conglomeration of ayllus of the other." He concludes that territory is not the basic and fundamental factor of cohesion or unity of a lineage or an ethnic group. By extension, he advanced the thought that territorial exclusivity does not define interethnic divisions and relations.[70]

Thus, one of the major reasons that unambiguous territorial divisions cannot be found is that ethnic groups—before the Spanish resettlement efforts and, in some cases, for decades thereafter—did not claim or occupy a cohesive, bounded, and stable geographic zone. Instead, research finds overlapping settlement patterns or a pattern described as spattered territoriality (*territorialidad salpicada*), discontinuous (*discontinua*), or scattered towns (*pueblos derramados*). Rostworowski found coastal peoples "mixed up with" (*mezclada con*) highlanders from Paucarcollas, Zepita, Collagua, and Chucuito in the south and evidence that the Pacajes had coastal enclaves in Arica and on the coast of Arequipa. Mercedes del Río and Ana María Presta describe multiethnic enclaves in what became the corregimiento of Tomina Yamparáes (Bolivia). Highlanders and coastal peoples also lived together in the Lima Valley. One witness said that Guachinamo, a predecessor of don Gonzalo, curaca of the Valley of Lima, had "a large quantity of lands and homesteads in said valley in different parts of it but that other nearby Indians and caciques also had lands in the said valley." Julien found "foreigners" among the Condesuyus. Martínez, Hyslop, Pease, and Rostworowski mention islands or colonies of the Lupaca near Moquegua on the Pacific coast and in the province of Cainota on the slopes of present-day Bolivia. Huertas lists the enclaves of ethnic groups (including Chachapoyas, Cañaris, Quitos, Antas, and Quichuas) who lived among the Guamanga. Shared towns (*pueblos compartidos*) can be found as far north as Cajamarca and as far south as Atacama.[71]

In the north, lords of both coast and highlands swore that they had subjects "divided in many parts." A principal and his followers from Casma are recorded as living and working in the Chimo Valley; both the coastal curacas of Copez (Copis) and Controilico had subordinate lords and subjects dwelling in the highlands. The 1540 inspection of coastal Jayanca records over 250 settlements of various sizes within two leagues of the curaca's administrative and ceremonial center and groups of Jayancas living also in the neighboring highlands of Guambos, two days' journey from the sacred precinct of the paramount lord. They were not alone. An eyewitness account of Huaraz in 1558 enumerates peoples living scattered in twenty-four hamlets or compounds, themselves dispersed over a six- or seven-league area: "They declare that they are settled in cold and rugged land, and some in flat and forested land near rivers and that is healthy land." There exist reports of coastal Yunga-speaking peoples in Cajamarca, including one lord of Saña, who reported having nine groups of his subjects living in highland clusters in the 1560s, and another who claimed that coastal Sañas lived dispersed across more than thirty leagues, from the sea inland in 1566. A 1782 manuscript written by the resident priest of Mórrope, Justo Modesto Rubiños y Andrade, reported enclaves or small colonies of Cajamarquinos on the coast. Another analysis of census data of the highland Cajamarquinos reported members of one ayllu divided between a number of different, shared towns and locations. Such a distribution, according to Rostworowski, "did not conform to European concepts of borders."[72]

Such interdigitalized and overlapping settlement patterns reflect pre-Hispanic notions of land and tenure. There was no concept of private property among the Inca and the people they conquered—in the European sense of bounded land, whether used or not, controlled exclusively by one individual or institution until explicitly alienated to another. Andean peoples, like those living in the town of San Ildefonso de Recuay in Guaylas, believed that the earth was sacred and that the landscape had been created by the ancestors and gods. Unworked, naturally occurring elements in nature remained, therefore, open for use by anyone, including people who belonged to different ethnic groups and obeyed distant lords. Natural, unplanted, wild pastures—like the seasonal pasture lands (*lomas*) that appear on the western slopes of the Andes during the occasional rainy season—and the fish, seaweed, and mollusks of the sea—being wild—were open to use by all. Unimproved, uninhabited land was also open, theoretically, to cultivation and colonization by anyone. When population increase or discord mandated the establishment of a new settlement, people moved to empty, unworked land. Recall Guamán Poma de Ayala's statement that new settlements could be established on "empty land [*tierra valdia*]."[73]

Any improvement—clearing a piece of land or building waterworks such as reservoirs and irrigation canals—that required the directed work of labor gave the initiating person or group and subsequent generations of caretakers claims to the land cleared or the land watered. Such rights, in theory, might establish long-term, ongoing use of a particular plot by a given descent group and be the closest native conceptions came to the European notion of private property. Yet here too the principle that unused land is open to anyone holds. If the irrigation system fell into disuse, anyone could clean it and begin to use the land it watered. The same held true for all improved resources, be they irrigated pastures (*bofedales*) or terraces. The improver had use rights for as long as the improvements were maintained and the resource occupied and exploited.[74]

Guayna Capac's efforts at Quispeguanca in the Valley of Yucay exemplify this notion of land and tenure. There, the Inca chose a site with potential, for a natural resource does not become such until it is recognized and developed. He sent in workers, who were identified as both mitimaes and yanaconas, to cut down trees, redirect water, and level the land and terrace hillsides to create agricultural plots. Thus, at his instigation, arable land was created, improved, and populated. Work made the area productive and established his claim to use it for his own purposes for as long as he (and by extension, his royal ayllu [*panaca*] and certain yanaconas) used it. Such is the origin of what historians have called the "private estates" of Inca Guayna Capac.[75]

These Yucay lands passed through stages, which, in their postconquest form, looked to the Spanish like private estates. First, lands were created by terracing, moving rivers, or leveling hills. Then, a permanent or rotating, often foreign-originating, labor force—mitimaes, yanaconas, or mitimaes acting as yanaconas—was assigned to work the land for the developer or his beneficiaries. Yucay lands, for instance, would have been worked to benefit Guayna Capac while alive, and his mummy and lineage after his death. Thus institutionalized, the land would have continued to be controlled indirectly by the benefiting institution or group—in this case, his panaca—for as long as it functioned. After 1532, the dissolution of the empire and its institutions and the rapid substitution of new norms and forms allowed the panacas and/or yanacona occupants of the parcels to claim them as corporate or private property, respectively. If the panaca personnel did not claim it and the yanaconas moved away and abandoned the land, it would have been open for use by anyone and probably claimed by the Spanish as "tierras del Inca" (lands of the Inca).[76]

Huáscar, too, ordered unused lands along the river near Calca, called Gaytobamba (or Caitobamba or Pomabamba), cleared and cultivated. According to the translated testimony of don Diego, lord (cacique) of Quylluay in 1555, the lands had lain fallow for some thirty years. But Tupac Cuxi Gualpa (Huáscar) had the river moved (*se quito el rio de alli*). And "by mandate of the said ynga, after moving the river from there, they planted a field and from then on they planted corn there for the ynga and what was harvested was taken to the cuzco." Like the workers who labored on land for Guayna Capac, many or most of those who worked these lands for Huáscar fled after the Incas were gone: "Once the Spanish arrived here, few yngas came to this land. The said Indians of the said four provinces returned to their lands and these said lands were left empty [and] they have not been planted since."[77] Another example of the same phenomenon occurred in Cajamarca. Tupac Inca Yupanqui had sent peoples "of different provinces" as yanaconas to work for him. After his death, some "Indians returned to their caciques." The Spanish later glossed those who remained as mitimaes.[78]

Bolstering this vision are other lands said to have been the private estates of Inca Viracocha at Caquia Jaquijahuana and Paucartica or of Pachacuti at Pisaq, Tambo, and elsewhere. Farrington points out that some of these estates are "not archaeologically manifest" and "such estates were not claimed in any extensive manner in the early Colonial period by his descendants." Thus, "their exact status as private lands must remain in question."[79]

Working land or maintaining the irrigation system that watered it established rights that the holder could share with others. This long-standing tradition that can be traced back to Manco Capac's time (and probably existed long before) was another reason for such scattered-site tenure and the seeming overlapping jurisdictions among lords. To allow subjects of various lords to work the same resources in a single area was a win-win situation, benefiting the host, his people, and the outsiders, because the host and his subjects received labor or part of the produce. Thus, "Uros of Challacollo came and planted in Cochabamba and in exchange for being allowed to plant they helped plant and weed the fields of the Indians whose lands they were and they brought fodder and firewood and straw for the encomenderos of the said Indians of Cochabamba when the chiefs of Cochabamba ordered and this they did and in this they helped." Rostworowski found that the curaca of Mala, when he needed more labor than his own subjects could provide to clean irrigation canals, "recurred to the neighboring lord of Cosyllo and in recompense [for help] he gave him, for one time [only], some lands so he could plant them." Other examples include Chupachus and Queros, who worked salt pans among the Yalo in 1549; a local lord at Pimampiro (Ecuador), who received several types of service from highland polities seeking access to highly prized coca; and the highland Colla, who worked for lowland groups in return for the same narcotic leaf. Such "resource sharing" generosity also aided in a lord's competition for subjects.[80]

Another reason for the interdigitalization of the population of various lords over a given landscape and lack of a contiguous, bounded territory is mandated labor assignment—either permanent or temporary—and is here exemplified by the history of the Valley of Cochabamba. Records that go back to 1556 suggest that there, too, what modern scholars interpreted as private estates of the Inca were not private or estates at all. The Inca Guayna Capac removed the Chuis, Cota Cotas, and Sipe Sipes from the valley (and assigned them to garrison duty on the frontier at Pocona to defend against the incursions of the Chiriguanos) and in their stead transplanted fourteen thousand Caranga, Colla, Aymara, Soras, and other laborers under their own lords to work the vacated lands. The records show that rather than giving them the land as property or even taking it as his own, the Inca merely assigned people to agricultural tasks, like modern piecework (*tareas*), for which they were responsible. The corn that they planted, cultivated, and harvested had then to be delivered to regional storehouses to support Inca armies. This work was their tribute to the state. After the empire collapsed, their sacred duty finished, all but a tiny number (five or six) of the individuals returned to their families and home base. None made subsequent claim to the land.[81]

A similar situation involves the interpretation of the word *chapas*. Jeanette Sherbondy interpreted the word as lands, private estates, worked by yanaconas of various ethnic heritages to support royal Incaic panacas. She based her views on her definition of an ayllu as a corporate group with a name, a head, and founder, from whom the people of the lineage considered they were related or descended, and with exclusive rituals to care for and honor their ancestors. Ayllu members furthermore thought, she continued, that the ancestors had given them rights to specific lands. This view is contradicted by other historical data, some included in Sherbondy's article itself.

Elsewhere, ayllu members did not have "exclusive" rituals to care for and honor their ancestors. Hernández Príncipe's reports on the traditional Andean religion of the Recuay suggest that one group encouraged, even coerced, "outsiders" to propitiate their ancestors, for protection and privileges, while among them. Furthermore, I find no evidence that ayllus held "rights to specific lands" (in a territorial sense), other than individual fields, or that Incaic panacas held "corporate ownership of their means of production."[82]

An alternative interpretation is that the Inca assigned labor to support the royal panacas, hence the Inca equivalent of an encomienda, on lands that sometimes happened to be located side by side. Sherbondy admits, in an aside, that the word *chapas* "may not have been a unit of land but a distribution of rights to Indian labor: . . . a *chapa* was an assignment of rights to labor for a duty owed to the Inca state, rather than a unit of land per se." I believe that yanaconas worked lands and delivered the produce to the panaca members. When the Inca empire disintegrated, the formal reason for the existence of the panacas as royal corporations or, more accurately perhaps, interest groups of the empire was less important. Because yanaconas as personal retainers had lost ties with their own origins, they were stranded. The common cause they made with panaca members appears to have been a pragmatic ploy to survive the trauma and reorganization of the initial period of encounter. So the pre-Columbian panaca members and yanaconas reinvented themselves as a colonial ayllu or corporate community based on common ancestry or cult with land claims for its subsistence. But the transformation took several decades; only circa 1570 did they make claims for the lands they occupied to Spanish authorities.[83]

A final reason why Inca-period physical boundaries are so elusive is the fact that many of the markers that are mentioned in the chronicles or other sources were, in fact, only so designated and defined after 1532 and then by the Spanish and natives who went along with European assumptions for reasons of their own. The quipucamayocs, a professional group of "rememberers" and record keepers (literally, the keepers of the knotted strings or quipus), who informed Vaca de Castro, for example, described the epoch before the Incas as a time of behetría. People allowed animals to wander past landmarks (*mojones*), giving rise to conflict. Such informants made mojones synonymous with civilization and order—an order then being newly defined and imposed by the Europeans on the basis of private property, fixed and bounded in space. Likewise, Guamán Poma de Ayala mentioned mojones in his chronicle and even drew the mojonadores (pictured in Figure 2.5). His drawing portrayed builders and engineers, not land surveyors. Two explanations for the emphasis given to boundaries in his text are that he wrote a half century and more after the Spanish invaded, and that he himself had by then learned the importance of boundary markers for claiming land within

FIGURE 2.5. Marker makers, building pillars or columns. Source: Guamán Poma de Ayala 1613/1936: 352.

the Spanish judicial system. He was party to such a pending claim before the Spanish authorities of Guamanga while he wrote his long letter to the king.[84]

In fact, I think that aside from common field markers, many of the boundary markers historically identified as such were probably not markers of territory or province, in a bounded sense, at all. Alternative explanations include some purported markers that were, in reality, stone columns used for calendrical calculations (reported by Polo de Ondegardo; by an anonymous author, who wrote in the 1570s; and by the Jesuits in 1608 Cuzco); others that the Augustinians warn should not be confused with "pillars that they erect in parts where there is snow to show the road"; and monuments that were commemorative or symbolic in nature, which reminded individuals of their common group past. Examples of the latter are omnipresent in colonial texts. Some go back to the mythical-historical times of the first Incas. Ayar Oche, one of the four brothers who emerged from a cave at Pacaritanbo, remained as a stone idol at the hill of Guanacaure for all to worship. He would remain there in order to ask "their father the Sun to protect them, increase their number, give them children, and send them good weather." Likewise, another brother, Ayarauca, who had been imprisoned in a cave, cursed the servant who shut him in, lithifying him. Both these stone representations could still be pointed out in Betanzos's lifetime. Elsewhere, the Canas peoples built "a sumptuous guaca" where they erected a stone statue, and where Viracocha, the creator god, appeared.[85]

The records concerning Andean religious practices, likewise, are full of descriptions of places replete with supernatural, sacred significance. The Huarochirí manuscript—believed to be the Andean oral traditions of the peoples of the highland hinterlands of Lima collected by a priest near the turn of the seventeenth century—is full of mentions of mythical-historical figures, some human and some other forms of animal, that lithified and in that guise were still visible when the tales were collected. The stories incorporate physical features of the landscape, such as mountains, irrigation canals, and lakes, into the history of the inhabitants of the area, thus giving them meaning and making them symbols of the group. Hernández Príncipe reported that some of the Recuay peoples worshipped a lake because they believed that it was the origin of their llamas and alpacas (*carneros de la tierra*). Likewise, the peoples of Ocros in 1622 traced their origins back to a consulting priest of the Inca, who remained lithified on the hill called Choque Cayan. Places of origin (*pacarinas*), such as boulders, springs, lakes, and caves, were centers of ritual observation that lent identity to worshipping groups. As such, each was an ethnic identifier, not a territorial boundary marker.[86]

All these have in common the purpose of establishing a marker that had ethnic, religious, and historical significance. Because the Incas had no alphabetic writing, they devised alternative methods to preserve memory. To date, most students of Andean history have focused on the knotted strings of the quipu, which quantified the past as well as preserved other types of information. Another means garnering new respect is their songs. Physical reminders such as certain stones, boulders, mountains, springs, caves, or constructions—all of which marked the location of an important event or sighting—were a third device that imparted meaning or marked a "sacred or ritual geography." Examples of these might even include the Inca wall and painting of the sun on a cliff above the place where Inca Urquo was killed and the guacas where they "venerate and adore [the bodies of their curacas] and they bring them food" so as to preserve "the memory . . . of that cacique."[87]

Together, such places and objects textualized and animated the landscape, converting it into a cosmic and ceremonial space. Each site conveyed a message, embodying the stories of the ancestors and gods for all—commoners and elite—to learn and remember. Such meanings, given contrasting European tradition and values and the continuing efforts to suppress native religion, were lost to Spanish observers. Instead of boundaries, ethnic identity, I would suggest, based on a common cult; a common ancestor; and common language, values, and customs, was vastly more important for cohesion than physically where one lived.[88]

It is undeniable that sovereignty over people gave the Inca uncontested claim on their service and indirectly to the lands on which they labored. For the Jayancas, Chinchas, Guaylas, and Chicamas, the obligations of the subjugated consisted of working land for the Inca and Sun and delivering the produce to storehouses. But, contradicting the Inca-centered political myth, local-level accounts indicate that the ruler did not "take" the land. Local lords recruited subjects to work certain lands consecrated to the Inca as ruler and imperial cult. The lands worked did not remain in the same location year after year. They were moved according to seasonal and annual cycles of fertility and rotational sequences of production and fallow. They did not "belong" to the Inca or Sun as private property; they were not literally "lands of the Inca" or "lands of the Sun." They were in fact rotating pieces of land, sown and worked for the ruler and the Sun as sacred obligation. Despite Spanish declarations to the contrary, the Inca received the produce of labor, a principle consistent with tribute expectations. Land is to rule, to paraphrase the words Walter Neale used to describe India. The Inca was more concerned with subjects than territory, because territory without people to work it was valueless, except perhaps symbolically in the eyes of the other.[89]

The Territorialization of an Empire

The actions of the Spanish transformed the Andean landscape. Juan de la Cosa's map—circa A.D. 1500, the earliest surviving chart showing the

"New World" in global context—and subsequent ones remind viewers that the Spanish claimed possession of a good part of the Indies. The process had begun with Columbus's disembarkation in the Caribbean. Later, with the intermediation and active involvement of a pope, a treaty was signed fixing an imaginary line between Portuguese and Spanish claims. In short, that such measures were codified and illustrated on the early maps, which were "instrument[s] of empire," made clear that the Spanish arrived with imperial goals and a mind-set significantly different from that of native Americans in this regard.[90]

The arrival of Francisco Pizarro on the west coast of South America began the long, slow, halting, inexact, and piecemeal process of territorialization of Inca jurisdictions. Pizarro and his expeditionary force arrived already thinking in terms of domains and leagues. On a previous trip down the coast, Pizarro had sent the pilot Bartolomé Ruiz ahead to reconnoiter and gather intelligence on the land and peoples that he encountered. Armed with the information he gathered and his own observations, Pizarro returned to Spain to negotiate an agreement (*capitulación*) with the empress Isabella for his exploration and conquest. In the very first provision of the document, known as the "capitulación de Toledo" of 1529, Pizarro's future jurisdiction was defined in geographic terms: 200 leagues along the coast from the place the natives called Temumpulla (also spelled Temmipulla, Tumpula, Temunpulla, and renamed Santiago by Pizarro) to the town of Chincha. As the number and wealth of the Inca's subjects became better known and appreciated, Pizarro successfully applied to the Crown to have his jurisdiction expanded from 200 to 270 leagues (granted May 4, 1534); it became known as the Kingdom of New Castile. Later, King Carlos extended his jurisdiction to 275 leagues. Diego de Almagro, Pizarro's partner, was named governor and captain general of the Kingdom of New Toledo on May 21, 1534. His jurisdiction (*governación*) started at the southern end of New Castile and continued south for 200 leagues down the coast of present-day Chile. This did not satisfy him. He felt cheated out of the jurisdiction over the southern ceremonial center. This only further fueled his growing distrust of Pizarro, who he believed had cheated him by not giving him a partner's share of Atahualpa's ransom.[91]

While such jurisdictions were being negotiated and decided in Spain, Pizarro founded cities as the outposts of Spanish civilization. He had established San Miguel in the coastal valley of Piura before reaching Cajamarca. Jauja in the central highlands, although not yet declared a Spanish city, was becoming an important way station. One of his most important efforts in this regard, though, was the refoundation of one of the Inca's southern ceremonial centers as the "very noble and grand" city of the Cuzco ("muy noble y muy gran ciudad del Cusco") on Monday, March 23, 1534, as a Spanish provincial settlement. During that day, as an act of possession, he cut into the wood of the step of the pillory, which he had ordered built in the plaza center, before all assembled. He then proceeded to assign space for the church, before proposing limits of the city's jurisdiction. Pizarro's vague description of these limits included the province of Chinchaysuyu no farther north than Vilcas; the province of Condesuyu (Cuntisuyu) to the Pacific Ocean; the province of Antisuyu (Andesuyu), toward the east; and the province of Collasuyu near Lake Titicaca. He thus set imaginary and very broad limits to the power of the municipal officials that he chose on the following day. On Wednesday, Pizarro exhibited the royal decrees that gave him the power to command and establish European civil and criminal jurisdiction over local Christian and native inhabitants. He subsequently rewarded encomiendas to his followers. By October, the Spanish had measured and assigned each Spanish vecino or citizen a house site. In fast succession, Pizarro proceeded to found the cities of Lima (Los Reyes) and Trujillo, following this procedure and model.[92]

In founding and naming the city and using the names of the four Inca suyus as the limits of the city authorities' official civil and criminal jurisdiction, Pizarro defined and fixed the future use and understanding of such terms. Note that only after the city's rededication as the Spanish city of "el Cuzco" did the use of the term "Cuzco" become ambiguous and forever changed. Whereas the first accounts of Hernando Pizarro, Licenciado Espinoza, and Mena consistently used "Cuzco" to refer to Guayna Capac (the old one) and Huáscar (the young one)—and alluded to their ceremonial center as "the town of the Cuzco" (*el pueblo del Cuzco*)—subsequent writers (such as Sancho de la Hoz and Oviedo) use the phrase ambiguously or increasingly as a place, as in "they brought the gold to Cuzco." By the end of Sancho de la Hoz's discussion, Guayna Capac is identified as the "old cacique" rather than "the old Cuzco." By February 1536, persons outside Peru had begun to describe the native rulers as "inga the cacique" or "the inga lord of the Cuzco." By the early 1540s, Inca (meaning king) was a title of the top native ruler; Cuzco was a place; and the four suyus were geographic designations. By the 1550s, the Inca was a named king and part of an established indigenous dynasty, such as those of Europe. One might speculate whether or not the Spanish capital of Lima originally was named the city of "the kings" to make it analogous to the city of "el Cuzco."[93]

Following Pizarro's untimely murder, the Spanish Crown's earlier decision to exert its control more effectively in the Andes became manifest with the establishment of the viceroyalty and the audiencias. The former defined the extent of a viceroy's power; he held legislative and executive authority and in some circumstances judicial (as president of the audiencia) and military (as captain general) power. He also administered the royal treasury, subsidized and promoted the church, and protected the native population.

The limits of the viceroyalty were vague and frequently changed. At one point the limits were south to the jurisdiction of Chile; north to the coastal region of Paita; inland including Piura, Cajamarca, Chachapoyas, Moyobamba, and the region of the Motilones to the lands occupied by the people of the Collao; and east until encountering the unconquered inhabitants of the jungle. The viceroyalty encompassed the governorships (*gobernaciones*) of New Castile, New Toledo, and four others (Río de la Plata, Quito, Río de San Juan, and Popayán). The outer limits of the early colonial gobernaciones served as the limits of the viceroyalty. These expanded as new expeditions pushed back the frontiers of effective Spanish settlement.[94]

The audiencias likewise established jurisdiction for panels of supreme court justices. Besides serving a judicial function, they replaced the viceroy in case of his death or incapacity and held other duties and responsibilities that often overlapped with those of the chief executive. The geographic limits wherein they exercised these powers were defined and refined several times over the years. Charcas, for example, was created in the mid-1550s, and its members were installed in 1557. Its jurisdiction, which originally extended to a one-hundred-league radius, was later restricted to the governance of Tucumán, the province of the Mojos and Chunchos and "the rest that might be settled in the extension [of land] between the city of La Plata and the city of the Cuzco." In 1568, its jurisdiction was downsized when Cuzco was transferred to the Audiencia of Lima. Further alterations to its jurisdiction were made in 1573. Likewise, the Audiencia of Quito, created by royal decree in 1563, had a jurisdiction to the port of Paita on the south; inland to include the towns of Jaen, Valladolid, Loja, Zamora, Cuenca, La Zarza, Guayaquil, and pueblos or peoples of Quijos and Canelos; on the north coast, the port of Buenaventura and inland cities of Pasto, Popayán, Cali, Buga, Chachapoyas, and Antioquia. Thus, jurisdiction was expressed using population centers and groups and the limits of their dignitaries' jurisdictions and were imprecise and in many places "doubtful" (*dudosos*).[95]

At the local level, the Crown's power was delegated to a provincial governor (*corregidor*). Theoretically, there were two types: a corregidor of Spaniards (*de españoles*), who exercised jurisdiction over the population of the Spanish municipality and its hinterland; and a corregidor of Indians (*de indios*), who was given power over one or more encomienda populations and whose duties included coordinating native religious indoctrination, labor obligations, and tax collection with the local native lords. In practice, one individual often served as both corregidor de indios and de españoles. According to Rowe, Viceroy Marqués de Cañete (1556–61) was the first to experiment with establishing these provincial governorships. Most were unsuccessful. Governor Lope García de Castro (1564–69) revived and extended the plan to control the native population. The corregidor of the

Collao, for example, administered the population of the encomiendas of Asillo, Asángaro, Chupa, Arapa, Taraco, Xullaca, Caracoto, Manaso, Atuncolla, Nicasio, Cavana, Cavanilla, Lapa, Quipa and Pucara, Angara, Ayabiri, and others. Robert G. Keith points out, in an excellent article on the structural relationship between encomienda, *hacienda* (large estate), and corregimiento, that the latter was not, at first, a territorial unit. It was established to administer the encomienda populations of several grants as the encomenderos lost direct control over their charges. Lohmann Villena's detailed study of the corregimiento confirms this fact.[96]

Paralleling this secular organization was the definition of ecclesiastical jurisdictions. Governor Vaca de Castro was responsible for establishing the important Bishoprics of Los Reyes, Cuzco, and Quito (February 18, 1543). These were generally described in terms of jurisdictions over Spanish municipalities and the subjects of specific native lords. At the local level, separate parishes were established for Spaniards (*parroquias*) and Indians (*doctrinas*). Like the viceroyalty, the audiencias, and the bishoprics, neither the corregimientos nor the parishes had specified geographic boundaries when created. Corregidores, as noted previously, had jurisdiction over encomienda populations. Thus, like the curaca's power, the corregidor's power extended in a geographic sense, only to where the native population was settled.[97]

The history of native parishes, ably studied by Fernando de Armas Medina, shows that they also had no geographic boundaries until at least Toledo's time. Armas Medina shows that the roots of what became the "doctrina" originated with the encomendero's explicit obligation to arrange for the conversion of the natives of his encomienda grant. Some encomenderos took this seriously and established churches and contracted priests for this purpose. But before the 1570s, he continued, the jurisdiction of a doctrinero was only a given number of the faithful:

> Of course the limits of the Indian parishes are not geographic, since the territory of their jurisdiction depends on the area occupied by their Indian parishioners, or said in another manner, it is a function of the more or less geographic extension that the Indians of the respective encomiendas occupy, within which those Indian parishes develop. And one should keep in mind that the encomienda never had a telluric meaning, only personal.[98]

In Toledo's time, in remote areas where no doctrinas existed, the viceroy's instructions indicated that the creation of parishes was also a function of population. Toledo's instructions to his deputies read, in part: "Because in Clause 12 of the Instruction . . . you are charged with determining the bases for the establishment of parishes, you should give notice relating to this that the basis will be the reduction you make of the Indians. . . . if you settle towns of 400 Indians or somewhat less, that will be a parish." Thus, four hundred tribute-paying natives, almost always from several ayllus, were required before a parish could be established. The number of households became a proxy indicator for a population's ability to support a priest's material needs and one of the fundamental criteria used by the Spanish to establish the parishes, not any preexisting Inca provinces, encomienda territories, or boundaries as claimed by Julien, Gibson, and others.[99]

Spatial limits and geographic boundaries became feasible and practical after the introduction of the concept of private property. Homesteads, duly measured and mapped, were given out to citizens in and around the Spanish cities. As standard practice, a municipal council gave each permanent householder a plot of land in the suburbs to use as a garden. After the initial founding and in the absence of royal officials, land grants continued to be made by the town council (*cabildo*). In Guamanga, grants were given to Spanish settlers and native lords as early as 1540. Because of boundary disputes among various settlers, the cabildo issued an order to erect boundary markers (*amojonar*) for both house sites and agricultural lands near town within the year. As more Spanish immigrants settled in the cities, the council granted land farther and farther away. Land grants were being made to Spaniards of abandoned land around Cuzco in the 1550s with the order to establish clear boundaries. It took about thirty years for Spanish demand for land to spread north into the adjacent valley of Chicama from the city of Trujillo. Even in the vicinity of Lima, boundary markers of rural lands were still mostly absent in the 1570s.[100]

Natives did not, as a rule, receive individual land grants. Instead, corporate grants were fixed and specified when the native population was concentrated in Spanish-style villages, called reductions (*reducciones*). The reorganization and consolidation of the native population actually had begun in the 1530s as disease, overwork, and mandatory carriage (forced transportation of goods and people for the Spanish) took their toll. As numbers decreased, some natives abandoned homesteads and moved closer to others in an unauthorized attempt to reconstitute community. A principal of the Túcumes testified that there were five principales of the Pácoras in the 1530s. Only one survived in 1570: "For that reason the peoples that they had have been added to the one group that they say is of pacora and they made don Joan pacora who is now cacique[,] cacique of them all."[101]

The resettlement policy (reducción), although discussed and regionally implemented in the 1550s, only began to be systematically enforced in the 1560s and 1570s after the civil wars. Under Toledo's direction, reducción communities, in theory, were to bring together several ayllus or about four hundred households into Spanish-style settlements, organized on a grid pattern, complete with central plaza and lots for a church and town hall.

This policy implied that native peasants abandoned their old hamlets or homesteads, fields, irrigation works, and shrines. In practice, more than five lineages were sometimes concentrated into one reducción, often without regard to patterns of ecological control. The 1540 visita of Jayanca listed about 250 distinct towns, hamlets, and places inhabited by natives within a two-league radius from the residence of the curaca. These were "reduced" to three pueblos in 1566. The curaca of Chicama saw his 14–15 pueblos reduced to 4. The 200 pueblos of the Anan and Urin Yauyos were reduced to 39. In Guamanga, 16 pueblos were concentrated in 7. In Collasuyu 226 pueblos were reduced to 22 by 1573. The 77 towns of the Conchucos were made 5 under Toledo.[102]

Royal instructions mandated that when native populations were reduced, they be either confirmed in their landholdings or assigned new ones if a population was moved more than one league. Toledo's 1570 instructions state:

> Tell the Indians that from now on they will be assigned lands that will be theirs forever; therefore, the Indians should declare what [lands] they have so that they will be left with enough lands for their needs and the extra lands should be given to the nearest Indians that need them. . . . those lands which exceed the needs of both groups [should be given] to Spaniards; . . . execute this [order]; . . . so that the Indians' fixed holdings remain assigned [*señalado*] and marked [*amojonado*], [and] are more than enough and very sufficient [for their needs].

The new towns were to be given three types of land: (1) some entailed for the office of the lords (not their persons), (2) some for the commoners, and (3) some to be held and used communally. And they were to receive "twice the lands that they might need." Thus did the Spanish imperial state mandate the fixation of native occupation, when prior to the order they had been mobile, able to move their sites of cultivation and herding according to the natural rhythms of the seasons and the availability of resources.[103]

Such a reducción and reassignment of lands occurred, for example, in Chérrepe, under Juan de Hoçes, a Toledo-appointed visitor. Another occurred in the central highlands, where members of the ayllu Ahay were settled in San Gerónimo de Copa, more than twenty kilometers (12.42 miles) from their old homes.[104] But the lands granted were sometimes not all in one piece. Judging from extant land titles, these holdings sometimes consisted of several relatively large parcels instead of one cohesive holding. The fishing and farming community of Mocupe in 1712, for example, had four tracts of land: one measuring 423 *fanegadas* (one fanegada is equal to a plot 144 varas by 288 varas [1 vara = 33 inches], or 2.89 hectares, or 7.16 acres); "Colo," with 217 fanegadas; "Levichi" and "Siam," with 108 fanegadas; and "Calcaquil," with 25 fanegadas, for a total of 773 fanegadas. Nearby, Monsefú, at the same time, had three pieces of land: "Potrero de

Alicán," "Chichipe," and "Callanca." These assignments became the basis for a post-reducción identity. The word *llacta* lost its original meaning of guacas and their devotees to translate simply as "pueblo," which took on a territorial dimension and later was referred to as a "fatherland" (*tierra patria* [*pacarisccay llakta*]).[105]

The history of successful reducciones shows that, despite Crown wishes, landmarks to delineate indigenous landholdings were not systematically placed for years to come in some instances. Neither indigenous communities nor the first Spanish landholders show an early preoccupation with exact boundaries. In the sixteenth century, boundaries tended to be the lands of neighbors; natural topographical features, such as hills and rivers; or human-made features, such as roads, irrigation canals, or native shrines. The first formal grants or confirmations of land for livestock stations, which usually date from the 1590s, were measured only in a specific number of fanegadas (between one and twelve, with four as the average size) at a named central site.[106]

This picture held to the middle of the seventeenth century, when boundaries became more codified during the second general visitation to inspect land titles (*visita de la tierra*). Names of irrigation canals, hills, rivers, roads, and native shrines were included, and the number of fanegadas the boundaries encompassed were noted. Only in the eighteenth century did the judge routinely use a cord (*cordel*) of a given length to measure the distance between boundary markers. At that time, too, the royal officials were more prone to insist on permanent boundaries. In one case, the land-title inspector Juan Múñoz Villegas had rocks "of an adequate size" placed under a tree to serve as a boundary marker, lest the tree be cut down and its stump burned. Just such an instance of impermanent landmarks gave rise to a long court case in the same era.[107]

Other boundary disputes erupted over seemingly immutable limits. A problem over the boundaries of Sialupe in the 1780s occurred when no one knew which of several, parallel irrigation canals was the mentioned limit. Not ten years before this, no one in the native communities of Éten and Reque could find a shrine that was a boundary marker, so they had to agree on a new delimiter. Unconcern about precise limits allowed peasants of Éten to move onto lands of Monsefú and graze their animals on pastures of the neighboring hacienda of Collús. The priest of Éten charged farmers of Monsefú rent for cultivating lands that were really their own, an example that shows the general ignorance of the physical extent of native possession. These local efforts to describe scientifically individual and corporate landholdings coincided with systematic efforts to map viceregal domains in the eighteenth century and became the foundations for more exacting modern territorial limits of districts and provinces in the nineteenth and twentieth centuries.[108]

"The Cuzco" as Person and Place

Concepts of sovereignty and territoriality in Western thought have a long history.[109] According to Jean Gottman on whose short book, *The Significance of Territories*, the following synopsis is based, they can be traced back to Aristotle's *Politics* (Book VII), where he discusses the three elements of state: population, government, and territory. About the middle of the fifth century A.D., imperial authority lost its territorial base in the West and became nomadic in practice. Individual and tribal allegiance to a sovereign and the church became the essential framework of social and political structure. Individuals drew their rights from the group they belonged to rather than the place they came from. In the eighth and ninth centuries, throughout Europe, there was too much insecurity and migration of tribes, too many local wars and roaming foreign hordes, and not enough stable authority or law enforcement to give a territorial entity any lasting jurisdictional value. Only in the twelfth century did the defense of the faith lead to a defense of a patria or homeland. Even in the fifteenth century patria or republica, the author continues, may have still been more closely associated with a community of individuals than with a territory.[110]

But the concept of territory was becoming more important, and community began to be discussed in terms of spatial territory at the level of self-governing units claiming privileges of autonomy and jurisdiction. Cities and abbeys required delimitation. Gottman states that "the first major work stressing the sovereignty of the individual state within a partitioned and diversified world was written by a Frenchman [Jean Bodin]," because France had been early in affirming its national individuality. Modern nation-states endowed with territorial sovereignty date from the seventeenth century, but the relationship between sovereignty and effective settlement of territory was not fully established until the eighteenth century, when fixed limits were set to the spatial extent of sovereignty. They outlined its size and location. Territory had become a source of wealth, the location of a taxed population. The history of Spain's territoriality follows this outline. Sahlins's study of the Spanish and French frontier disputes in the Pyrenees mountain district of Cerdanya shows that national boundaries were invented over hundreds of years. This process was not completed until the nineteenth century.[111]

Given this history and the histories of Mesoamerica, Shang China, and Mughal India mentioned earlier, Andean history is not unusual. The native Andean state was jurisdictional, and so was the Spanish until the process of fixing the political limits became practicable. Thus, modern attempts to find fixed geographic boundaries to the empire in the sixteenth-century Andes are anachronistic in the most literal sense of the word. The search for pre-Hispanic boundaries of such major units of the Andean empire as suyus down to those at the province level has proven mostly futile. When archaeologists or historians do find a marker, there is no sure way to determine who placed it there, when, and for what purpose. Many markers probably are not pre-Columbian, and if they were, most no doubt had original purposes other than to fix a bounded and contiguous territory as, say, eighteenth- and nineteenth-century Europeans conceived of one. We cannot expect to find marked boundaries, beyond those of individual fields, in the sixteenth century unless we construct them ourselves, as Schramm found was the case in Bolivia.[112]

Spanish and modern scholars sought a territoriality that did not exist in the minds of the natives. They then invented boundaries instead of accepting the fact that indigenous conceptions of sovereignty, land, and tenure, and their resulting settlement patterns do not conform exactly to modern Western cultural paradigms. The keys to understanding Inca organization at the empire or local level are cult, kinship (both consanguineal and fictive), and labor. With no private property, what the Inca conquered was labor, not territory. Instead of precise boundaries, we find constantly changing ethnic frontiers defined by kinship, personal relations, and loyalties.[113]

There is no doubt that the ceremonial center in the southern Andes denominated by Santacruz Pachacuti Yamqui as "the city of the Sun," with its elaborate monumental architecture and plazas, was the traditional home of the rulers. Bowing to the exigencies of expansion, the Inca had additional ceremonial centers built, which were modeled after the original one, at Quito, Tumebamba, Huánuco, Túmbez, Hatun Colla, and Charcas (Sucre)—complete with sun temple, house of chosen women (*acllahuasi*), ushnu, and royal palace—as dedicated ritual stages within which the Inca could approach and sacrifice to the gods. Such places for ceremonial reenactments of the Inca religio-political foundation myths were necessary, some might even say critical, for introducing and maintaining the uniting imperial ideology and ritual associations among the outlying and scattered ethnicities. Huánuco Pampa, for example, was a ceremonial center, fully equipped for feasting and drinking, so important to foster good relations with locals. The arrival of el Cuzco and his court transformed this location into a focus and destination for sacred pilgrimages where he was the central shrine. His ministrations united diverse peoples—all eager to hear oracular pronouncements and seeking divine protection and deliverance. The first Spanish to describe the southern ceremonial center called it the city of the Cuzco, or Cuzco for short. Guamán Poma de Ayala denominated other ceremonial centers, too, as Cuzcos. They, like the first and most elaborate, had the same function; each became the location of the sacred center and capital of the empire for as long as the person of el Cuzco remained stationed there. Once he moved on, these centers were left (with the one southernmost exception), perhaps temporarily abandoned or minimally staffed, until his return. Such intermittent use may explain why the ritual center of Huánuco Pampa was abandoned after 1532. One can only wonder—as mentioned previously, and despite its association with the Day of the Kings of the Christian calendar in January—if this understanding by the first Spanish on the scene made them originally call Lima the city of "the kings" to associate it in native minds with the god-given power of the Spanish monarchs, and thus make it analogous in status and prestige in native eyes. Suggesting that this is true is a statement by Stansbury Hagar, which holds that the Spanish themselves reproduced some of the features of the ceremonial center of the Cuzco in the arrangement of their own coastal capital.[114]

This story is also a commentary on the history of the history of the colonization process itself. Notice how quickly the native concept of "el Cuzco" as a person was transformed and reconceptualized into Cuzco as a place, a place that Polo de Ondegardo later called a sacred city, a "house and residence of the gods"; a place that Sarmiento de Gamboa called the city of the Sun and of Viracocha; and a site that Santacruz Pachacuti Yamqui called "the lion city." To what extent did the Spanish "filter" filter out native elements? If "el Cuzco" was a person, I must answer the question and conclude, in this regard, "definitively" and "almost completely"—so effectively that to see the native view and understand its rationale means piecing together bits of surviving information from many sources, sometimes only by chance encountered. The perspective of the classic chroniclers in this regard, then, becomes evident.[115]

Part Two

DIVINE RULERSHIP

3 *Kingship and the Gods*

> To better understand which and how many services and taxes that that people gave and tributed to the persons and places to which they were obligated, it is convenient to understand the religion and adorations that they practiced, and the sacrifices and offerings that for this reason they made.
>
> — Licenciado Hernando de Santillán

In Chapter 2 on el Cuzco, I showed how Westerners—both past and present—disregarded, rejected, and misinterpreted information that did not conform to their own cultural paradigms. Instead, they described and configured what they saw to fit their own learned perspective. Thus, they depicted the Inca governing system as if it were a European monarchy. They portrayed el Cuzco, later retitled the Inca, as a king or emperor, similar in authority, bearing, and grandeur to those at the center of the European and Oriental courts of which they had knowledge. By the decade of the 1550s, the many and confusing stories of Andean rulers had been distilled, synthesized, and simplified into one dynasty, in which primogeniture was the preferred rule of succession. Mostly well-born, noble informants filled hours telling, retelling, and explaining how the government—characterized as bureaucratic and highly centralized—functioned, even to the point of enumerating their customs and traditions, which were dutifully transcribed, translated, and frozen into the empirewide "laws" of this preliterate society.[1]

The Nexus

Many Iberian observers who commented and described native practices were much less curious about indigenous religion, considering it pagan and devil influenced. Their early, sixteenth-century reports were shallow in this regard, given their deeply ingrained Christian certainties, intolerance, and self-righteous prejudices born of the centuries-long struggles against the Moors on the Iberian peninsula. In reality, their doctrinal myopia caused them to miss or disregard one of the most salient and important features of the Andean governing system, because religion organized and supported what Westerners might call the secular functions of the state. Religion was a facilitating basis of political and economic power. As the imperial dynamic proceeded, beliefs in the supernatural and feelings of love, respect, and fear of the gods were used to control population and organize tributary workforces. This belief system sanctioned kinship, articulation, identity, and reciprocity. As the Incas pushed ahead, it became the would-be ideological mortar of the imperial edifice. Most early chroniclers and later writers miscast what they observed, perhaps because the theocratic Andean system, centered on the person of el Cuzco, quickly disintegrated; state authority became disarticulated from its demographic base; and what remained of the legitimating ideology was shortly driven underground to be hidden from the sometimes slow and sporadic but eventually relentless and persistent drive to save the native souls and win converts to Catholicism.[2]

Thus, to understand how el Cuzco, the person, could be the physical and ideological center, even the mobile nucleus, of a vast imperial patrimonial and authoritarian structure, one must understand the relationship between the personage and his subjects and the basis for this interaction. In this chapter, I show that the Andean world over which the native elite ruled was ordered by an evolving rationality of its own, but perhaps not original, construction. An ideological superstructure that was an ongoing negotiation between the center and the provincial peoples of the empire imputed divine favor on el Cuzco with its attendant abundance, aid, and blessings. Because a multiplicity of gods and spirits influenced daily life, it was incumbent on all to please and propitiate them. El Cuzco, as son of the Sun, a god incarnate, was the main mover in this regard, serving as the nexus between his kin and tributaries and the divine and supreme beings. People believed that his intercession and ministration brought them material benefits on earth and access to "another world" after death. This function bespoke of his legitimacy. Should his conduct prove displeasing to the divinities, he would lose their favor. Mishap, misfortune, disaster, and even chaos would mark the waning cycle of his rule.

Imperial Cosmology

The religious pluralism that was visible to the Christians in the early 1530s had been under construction for generations. Chroniclers such as the mestizo Garcilaso de la Vega—who spent most of his adult life in Spain and wrote a sympathetic and sanitized account of Inca history and culture—and the Catholic priest Miguel Cabello Valboa—who published an interesting, detailed, and passionate account—described the culture before the

Inca expansion. They noted that each "province," "nation" (ethnic group?), "pueblo" (people, town, or hamlet), neighborhood (*barrio*), lineage, and house worshipped any number of trees, hills, mountaintops (*cumbres*), springs, crags (*riscos*), stones, animals, lakes, piles of rocks, fire, the sun, thunder and lightning, the most brilliant stars, their lords, and their deceased grandparents and great-grandparents.[3] Garcilaso de la Vega explains this plethora of gods or forces, writing that each nation and people had its own deities, because it seemed to them that "only their own god could help them, because the god of others, preoccupied with them, could not help them."[4] Such complex and overlapping, group-specific ideas about the supernatural—multiplied by the scores of chiefdom-level societies in existence at the time—resulted in an elastic but confounding, unwieldy, and probably henotheistic belief system centered around the chiefs and the lineage ancestors. The relative importance of each cult, according to Michael J. Sallnow, constantly waxed and waned as a function of its oracular reputation, the power of the priesthood, patterns of exchange, and political and military fortunes.[5]

In the early, preempire times, the Incas constituted one more of the many small societies in what became the southern heartland of their empire.[6] Religious beliefs were of fundamental importance to the workings and rule of the evolving Inca state. Pease, one of the most dedicated scholars of the Incas, relates that the power of the elders (or philosophers and intelligentsia [*amautas*])—whose responsibilities were religious, magisterial, administrative, and legislative—was based on "religious prestige." They chose the military leaders (*sinchis*), whose military prowess "had an adequate religious endorsement."[7] Pease continues, saying that the amautas and sinchis remained antagonistic until the Chanca war, which marked the start of the imperial phase, when the sinchis gained power over the priests.[8] Although I do not believe that the sinchis and the amautas were two always mutually exclusive groups, it is clear that at any one time the persons in charge of military matters and those who addressed the sacred remained associated and interdependent. The great military strategist Pachacuti Inca Yupanqui and his followers, who took to the field to conquer new ethnicities, thereafter relied on the priests for the beliefs that legitimized and for the interpretation of the signs of the gods' will.

Over time, successive rulers and their advisers expanded, improved, and elaborated on their polytheistic faith and its ritual manifestations. According to Guamán Poma de Ayala's long manuscript letter to the king, the Incas worshipped mountains (*cerros*), caves, and boulders (*peñas*). Manco Capac, the mythologically recalled first human ancestor of the Inca kings, venerated the sun, moon, and other idols. One of his successors, Capac Yupanqui, ordered the idols and guacas fed.[9]

According to Rostworowski, the sinchi Pachacuti Inca Yupanqui, the great reformer and strategist, reorganized native religion once he had defeated the Chancas.[10] With the help of a general council (*concilio*), he systematized the doctrines of the Inca state because he was unhappy with the great diversity of beliefs and disbeliefs that he had encountered among the ethnic groups that surrounded him. Councilors agreed that the Sun should be adored as the paramount god, followed by Thunder and Lightning (*Chuqui Ylla* or *Ynti-illapa*), the Earth (*pachamama*), and the stars, especially the Cabrillas or the Pleiades (*Collca*) and the Southern Cross (*Urcuchillay*). To this end, Pachacuti Inca Yupanqui (see Figure 3.1) remodeled what had begun under Manco Capac as a small, stone house with a thatched roof (*çercado de oro*, which is, literally, a golden fence, circle, or enclosure), aggrandizing it into the House of the Sun with the intention of making it the "center and religious capital [*metropolitana*] of all his Empire." To adorn and embellish the temple, he instructed artisans to make a band of gold a palm and a half wide that was attached to the inside and outside of the building, near the roof. He also designed and built structures to honor the god Thunder and Lightning, and Viracocha, the creator god. Once the temple was finished, he assigned servants to maintain and support the cults of these gods.[11]

As part of this effort, Pachacuti Inca Yupanqui also made the first of three statues of the Sun that is described by Betanzos as a golden figure of a boy, as he appeared to the Inca in a dream before the Chanca war. Calancha estimated in the seventeenth century that it was worth about two thousand pesos, assuming that the Spanish found the original statue (*bulto*). Pachacuti Inca Yupanqui ordered two other images fabricated. One was a depiction of Viracocha Pachayachachic, which Pachacuti Inca Yupanqui placed to the right of the Sun. To the left stood the figure of Chuqui Ylla. Eventually, a golden throne "where, they say, that the Sun used to sit," worth twenty thousand *castellanos*, was housed in the sun temple (*Coricancha*). Ceremonies and rites were further elaborated and embellished over time. All this reinforced the belief in the power of the gods and the Inca's claim to divine descendance.[12]

He likewise institutionalized the worship of his ancestors, which included his predecessors back to his heavenly father, the Sun. Pachacuti Inca Yupanqui disinterred the bodies of previous Incas and gave to their mummified remains masks, headdresses, medals, bracelets, and scepters. In sanctifying these fathers, grandfathers, and great-grandfathers, he put them on benches and celebrated mourning rites in their honor that continued for months. Part of these ceremonies depicted the life of each Inca ruler and concluded with great and sumptuous sacrifices. "This," says Sarmiento de Gamboa, "gave them such authority that it made all strangers adore them, and worship them as gods." Non-Incas regarded them as sacred objects and were humbled by their majesty. People raised their hands in reverence, palms

FIGURE 3.1. Pachacuti Inca Yupanqui. Source: Biblioteca Angelica, Ms. 1551, fol. 80.

facing forward, to worship (*mochar*, to use the term commonly employed in the sixteenth century).[13]

Pachacuti Inca Yupanqui ordered his subjects to worship only the gods he authorized. To weaken other cults and encourage the adoration of his chosen gods and ancestors, he dispatched missionaries to carry his message and teach the new religion, its sacrifices and ceremonies, to his followers.

Several sons, including Amaru Yupanqui, left on extirpating trips, charged with eradicating illegitimate guacas.[14] Thereafter, when an Inca conquered an opposing group, he imposed the imperial cults and specified the manner in which his gods were to be worshipped and how their temples were to be constructed and serviced. Coordinating these efforts were the religious specialists of the sun temple, who kept track of the ceremonies and tendered offerings, and undoubtedly helped elaborate and enhance the legitimizing myths that accompanied the expansion.[15]

Pachacuti Inca Yupanqui, too, preparing for the time when he would join the ranks of his ancestors, "found happiness in leaving memory of himself." To guarantee that his fame persisted after his death, he acted like a god, not allowing people to see him except as a great favor. He ordered that no one should come to behold him without worshipping and bringing something in his hand to offer him. Those who did not want to come to do reverence to his person, like the Ayamarcas, and those who would not submit were to be destroyed so that "no memory [of them] was left."[16]

But this ideal picture of high-handed, unilateral imposition is exaggerated. The aspiration to create a recognized, uniform, and homogeneous belief system eluded the empire builders. In practice, the king usually negotiated the integration or settlement and peace accord with his new subjects. In this regard, Inca religion proved pragmatic and flexible enough to incorporate additional deities into the accepted, officially recognized pantheon as their sovereignty expanded. The Incas claimed to have allowed subject peoples to retain elements of their local religion—to prove their benevolence and altruism—when in fact they acquiesced to local demands to retain their own ancestor-gods, having no other choice given the strong parochialism of traditional and long-standing practice. When the peoples of the central coast became part of the empire, the Incas recognized and embraced the powerful provincial god and oracle of Pachacamac, to be described in more detail later. Likewise, on the eve of the Spanish invasion, the Incas had not only adopted the north coast god of the Chimu, whom their forces had subjugated circa 1470, but were building it a temple, using ten silver beams—each twenty feet long, three fingers thick, and one foot wide—which Pedro Pizarro estimated were worth ninety thousand castellanos.[17]

But the acceptance of provincial gods was subject to conditions and strictures. One requirement for acceptance was that the principal god or guaca of each ethnic group was to be held hostage in a gallery near the Coricancha to serve as intermediary between its followers and the Sun. As the conquest proceeded north, we are told by various observers that the Incas "took each province's idol and they brought it to the House of the Sun in Cuzco, where they had all of them, giving them servants from their same people."[18] Once in the southern ceremonial center, the idols of these and all the subjugated peoples were put in a hall and bountifully honored, but each was chained to an altar with its insignia to show symbolically the subservience to the state of the people it represented. Each year the king ordered these and other provincial guacas brought to a great celebration in honor of the solar divinity. They were taken to the Coricancha and placed next to the Sun and Moon. At the conclusion of the ritual, the Inca gave each guaca clothing and jewels before they and their congregation departed.[19]

Given that these local gods and oracles represented, in many cases, the founding ancestor and event of each ethnic group, this appropriation of ethnic cults incorporated their history into the official imperial epic. Guaca hostage, says Silverblatt, is tantamount to the Inca "taking over the past." But ironically, in worshipping captured images, the provincial ethnic groups were, she continues, "honoring the very symbols of their subordination."[20]

Each cult also had a separate temple situated near the Coricancha where its religious specialists ministered, making the southern Inca ceremonial center truly "the city of the gods."[21] This concentration of local guacas and their attendants also encouraged and facilitated a negotiation of labor and aid between the center and local peoples, which was legitimated by exchanges of gifts and the bestowal and withdrawal of royal favors. No mention is made in the sources as to whether the provincial people also maintained guacas, personnel, and structures in other ceremonial centers. That they might have is suggested by local-level idolatry records showing that curacas maintained several cult and lineage houses in different sites among their followers.[22]

By the time of the European invasion in 1532, the Andeans worshipped a recognized, but shifting, pantheon of gods, deities, ancestors, and spiritual representations, lumped together by the Christians into one generic category of guaca—perhaps because they all represented a vital force or energy that could speak and give answers to questions. For the advice and protection that their forces promised their adherents, they reciprocated, sustaining their cults through offerings and sacrifices. Each ruler could and did rearrange the hierarchy of gods, adjusting his devotion to reward those who had shown him advantage. Not all guacas had equal force, and more important, what vital energy each possessed could be shared and was transferable. Those of highest rank, in society's view, had more energy than those at lower levels. Andeans believed that a person, such as the king, could partake of the power of a guaca that would allow him to escape his normal human capabilities and acquire godlike powers to prophesize, cure, or transform himself into other beings or objects. Assumption of such a supernatural essence was not, however, permanent and unalterable. A person could lose such power by being defeated by someone with more such energy or by committing some transgression, such as by not giving the guacas their due veneration, by not observing some solemn ritual, or by bad-mouthing or cursing a guaca. Thus, one risked sometimes very adverse consequences by flouting the standards of reciprocity or not observing anticipated decorum. Favor could only be regained by penance or retribution to reestablish equilibrium in the exchange.[23]

Although different sources disagree on the relative ranking and, in some cases, significance, of various ancestor-gods and spirits, there is wide consensus in the primary sources that the major deities at the expanding imperial level included celestial bodies, such as the sun, the moon, and the stars; thunder and lightning; the earth; and the sea. There are also references to an overarching creator god, called Ticci Viracocha. Each of these gods had its own cult significance. Ticci (or Tece or Illa Tecce) Viracocha, for example, according to oral and sung tradition heard and recorded by Cieza—an early and fairly reliable chronicler—was said to be a tall, fair man who demonstrated great authority and self-confidence.[24] He allegedly emerged from the waters of Lake Titicaca with great powers that enabled him to realize miracles, such as transforming mountain ranges into plains and plains into high peaks and sierras. He was said to have created humans, the world, the sky, the earth, the sun, and the moon. According to one version, he also governed time: the days, seasons, and years. He therefore was regarded as the people's father and progenitor. Chroniclers write that this creator god had no universally recognized name and could be and was addressed by any appropriate title. Believers called him "Creator of all existing things, Origin of them all, [and] Father of the Sun."[25] Although known by other designations elsewhere and associated at times with other origins (for example, having emerged from a cave [*ventana*] in the southern Andes), the faithful dedicated temples to him where they placed stone statues in his likeness. As Betanzos describes, "In the said sumptuous pagan shrine they placed a large image of sculpted stone almost five varas long and a little less than one vara wide in memory of this viracocha, where these people and their descendants offered much quantities of gold and silver."[26] Most stories conclude with his disappearance into the sea. The name *Viracocha* itself commemorated this, being traditionally translated as "sea foam" and more recently and more accurately rendered as "foam of the water of life" or "sperm," relating directly to his creator role and fertility.[27]

Outshining Viracocha was the Sun. It was the main focus of adoration among the Incas, and the worship of this deity was introduced and imposed on all the persons incorporated into the expanding imperial fold. Three anthropomorphic idols of the Sun existed at the time of the entrance of the Christians into the Andes: the lord Sun (*apu-inti*); the day, daylight, or the young Sun (*Punchao*); and brother Sun (*inti-guauqui*). They were, at times, worshipped as separate deities. The focal point of adoration of these three aspects of the god was the Coricancha, undoubtedly the most sumptuous place in the Andes at the time. When the Spanish entered the gold-plated buildings associated with the Sun, they first saw the golden throne before which the natives sacrificed and then the ancestral mummies—one of which was Guayna Capac, who had at his preserved side a female attendant wearing a golden mask, who whisked flies off his fixated remains.[28] In the first patio was a stone basin (*pila*), where persons spilled maize beer (chicha), saying that the Sun came down to drink there. So great was the reverence for this god that no commoner dared to cross the street of the Sun with sandals on; no noble dared enter the sacred precinct unless barefoot.[29]

Other houses of the Sun had been built among the Inca's subject peoples. One stood in the south on an island in Lake Titicaca, and another was erected among the Hatun Collas. A third, which was painted in rich colors inside and out, was constructed among the once-rebellious, then defeated, Tumbecinos of the north coast. A fourth stood near the temple of the great oracular god Pachacamac on the central coast.[30]

Likewise, chroniclers mention a thunder god that also had at least three aspects: *Chuqui Ylla*, *Catuilla*, and *Inti-illapa*, each with its own representation. Cobo writes that the three images of the thunder god were identical to those of the sun god. Such statements are the basis for Demarest's contention that Viracocha is manifold, encompassing both the sun and thunder deities.[31]

The official doctrine, as depicted by Santacruz Pachacuti Yamqui (see Figure 3.2), taught that these and other deities were related and formed a kinship-based pantheon that explained creation. According to Silverblatt's synopsis, Viracocha, an androgynous divinity, established a gendered, cosmologically ordered hierarchy. The Father Sun and the Mother Moon, his sister, produced the Inca. (See the simplified relationships in Figure 3.3.) The Inca stood at the level of his parents' brothers and sisters: Venus of the morning and Venus of the evening, who together begat the local chiefs. These provincial leaders merited a place at the level of the Lord Earth and the Lady Ocean or Lake or Mother Sea.[32] That such an ideology was accepted at both the imperial and popular levels is evident from the facts that Inca Sinchi Roca considered the Sun and the Moon his grandparents and that Andeans, in general, said that they were children of the gods.[33]

Besides these celestial deities, several other guacas and oracles played an important role in Andean history and government, giving representation and voice to non-Inca minority social groups. Important oracles functioned at Guanacaure (in the southern heartland); at Lake Titicaca in the Collao region; at Aporimac (or Apurimac), twelve leagues from the Coricancha; at Chimor on the north coast, and elsewhere.[34] But the major oracle and shrine, after the Coricancha, was Pachacamac. The word *pachacamac* itself is made up of *pacha* (world or universe) and *camac* (god). The latter is the present participle of the Quechua verb *cama*, which means "to animate."

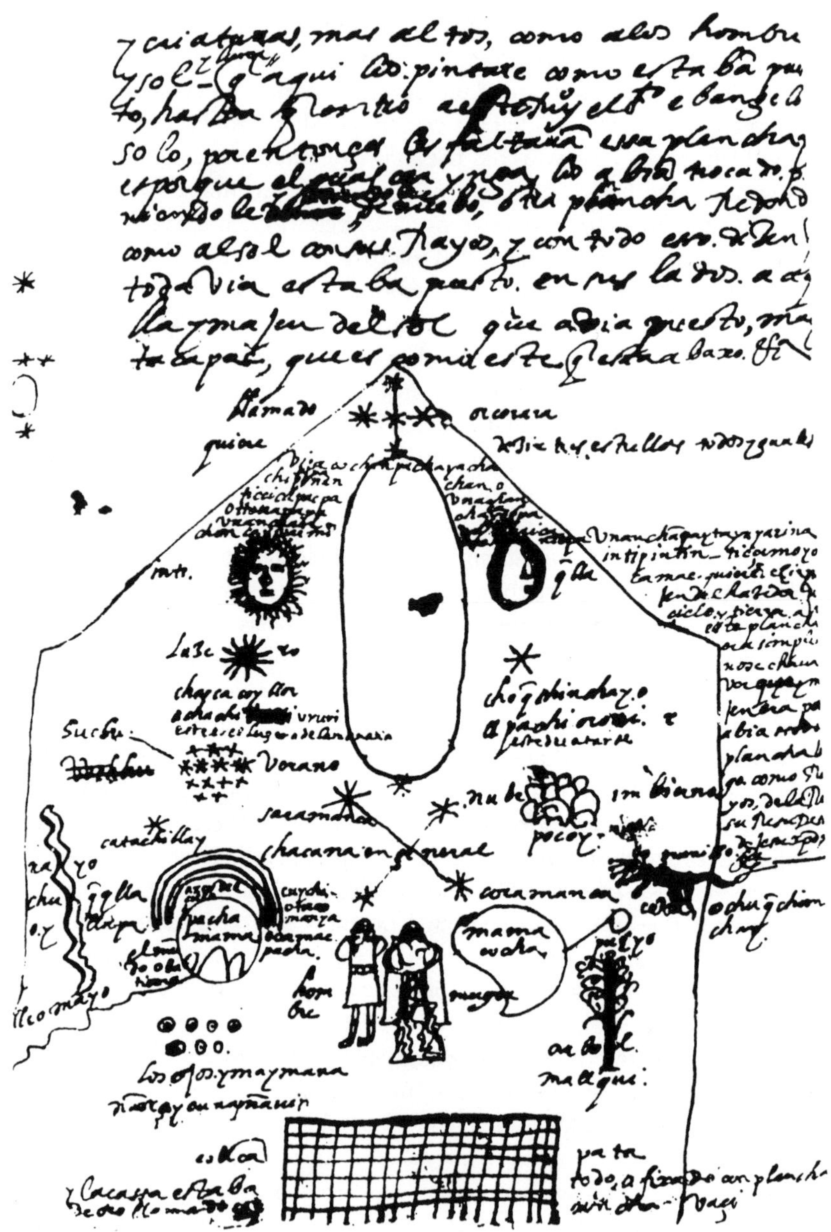

FIGURE 3.2. Inca cosmology. Source: Santacruz Pachacuti Yamqui 1613/1993: 13.

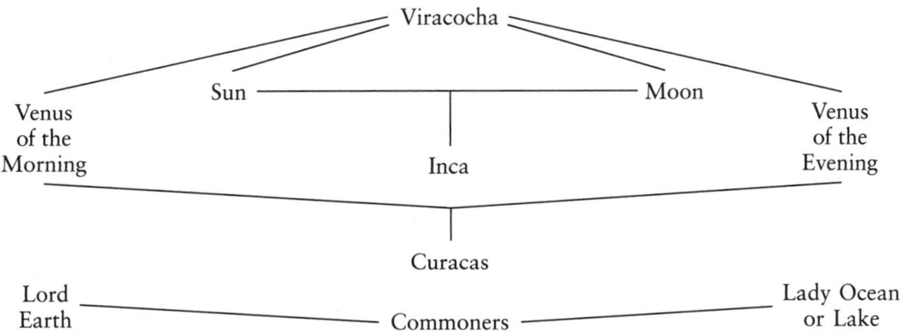

FIGURE 3.3. Diagrammatic depiction of Inca cosmology. Source: Based on Santacruz Pachacuti Yamqui 1613/1993: 13.

As a noun, *cama* means "soul." In other words, the word literally translates as "that which [a force which] gives soul to the universe." This meaning is reflected in the descriptions in the sources of the day. The Spanish were told that Pachacamac was "he who creates and gives life to the universe"; "the lord who takes the earth"; "he who creates and sustains them and creates the sustenance"; "he who animates the universe as the soul does the body"; "creator of the earth"; or simply creator and earth shaker. This coastal oracle also had the reputation of curing illnesses. MacCormack characterizes this "maker of the world" as a two-faced deity who, on the one hand, created and sustained human beings, made the crops grow, and cured disease; but on the other, brought disease and caused earthquakes and the overflowing of the sea. This prophetic force was also considered a brother to the Sun. Some explained the relationship as the Sun giving life to the above (ground), the realm of the gods; Pachacamac "gave form to the things here below" (at ground level). Calancha, too, hints at the relationship between the Sun and Pachacamac, writing that the latter is the invisible god and the former the visible god for all the nations.[35]

To Pachacamac's shrine on the central coast came the messengers of curacas, the curacas themselves, and even el Cuzco, as Mena wrote in 1534, to worship and to petition the priest to consult the oracle on important issues or to answer questions. A priest would enter into the idol's dark chamber for advice or responses. Hernando Pizarro, writing in 1533, records that "they speak with him, and . . . the devil [his Christian perception of the idol] tells them that he is mad at the caciques, and the sacrifices that they are to make, and the gifts that he wants them to bring him." He continues, recording that the oracle was "feared by all the Indians, . . . they think that if one of the devil's attendants asked them for all that they had and they did not give it, they would die soon."[36] Pilgrims traveled over three hundred leagues, bringing gold, silver, clothing (*ropa*), and camelids to offer and sacrifice to this idol. These sacrifices and other presents explain why storehouses formed part of the coastal complex and account perhaps for its huge population, which Estete approximates at twenty thousand in 1532–33.[37]

For those unable to travel so far, this powerful "great coastal god," to use Rostworowski's apt description, had established subsidiary cult centers conceived of as his "children" or "wives." Such holy shrines functioned at Mala, Chincha, and Andahuaylas. Another subsidiary chapel was planned at Chimor during Guayna Capac's reign. Archaeological and historical evidence indicates that Pachacamac remained sacred in Chimor at least into the 1560s, where his likeness was found during the excavation of the temple-tomb of Yomayoguán. His counsel was deemed so important that a portable representation accompanied Tupac Inca Yupanqui on his travels.[38]

Another important shrine and oracle was that of Guanacaure, whose lithified representation, such as those of other historical and mythical personalities, studded the landscape. Andeans remembered him as one of the original Inca brothers who emerged from the caves of Pacaritanbo. His story, as told by Cieza, is that Ayar Oche (Ayar uchu) commanded his other brothers to found a polity. He would remain petrified in stone at Tambo Quiro, the original name of the spot, to pray to the Sun, their father, that they "would attain great dominion." If they sacrificed on his altar, he promised, "I will help you in your wars." For his intercession with the Sun on his siblings' behalf, he implored, "I beseech you to always adore me as god"; "I will be always honored and adored by you and your descendants" as *Guanacaure*, a word that translates as "rainbow" and is associated by some scholars with the thunder god. He remained an intermediary and sacred oracle and purportedly spoke to them again, once before Manco Capac (see Figure 3.4) found the spot where he would remain to build the original stone Coricancha, or "the golden enclosure." He thus became the protector of the dynasty (at least until the time of Pachacuti Inca Yupanqui) and channel of communication with the Sun. Guanacaure's stone-bound image became the hallowed location of major imperial rites of puberty (*Huarachicoy*) for the adolescent elite males who were being inducted into the ranks of the young knights or nobles well past the time of the arrival of the Spanish.[39]

Pilgrimages to other shrines and oracles located throughout the empire, such as on mountaintops, in caves, in trees, or at lakes, were common. As noted in Chapter 2, these shrines and sacred places textualized the countryside, imbuing the geography with common historical and religious associations and significance. Some of these spots represented the pacarinas of the ancestors and the local sociopolitical group.[40] Molina, el cuzqueño, explains that "in memory of their founder, they made and named idols for each and every one of his gods, and thus they adored and offered them

FIGURE 3.4. Manco Capac Inca. Source: Guamán Poma de Ayala 1613/1936: 86.

sacrifices of those things that each nation used." Mythico-historical accounts are divided on the pacarina of the Inca kings. Some stories say that the Incas believed that they emerged from caves at Pacaritanbo; others state that their origin could be traced to Lake Titicaca, as will be retold in more detail later.[41]

Of lesser importance were the unusual objects and the finest, largest, most beautiful, or representative examples of an object in a class that Andeans also respected, cherished, and glorified. They worshipped corn and other food products, camelids, their chicha, and even the water that was its base. Also considered sacred were any disfigured individuals.[42]

Cabello Valboa sums up this hierarchical and polytheistic religion, saying that "they had idols and prayers for each necessity."[43] The multiplicity of gods and the rites and ceremonies that attended them structured the actions and thinking of every inhabitant on, one might reasonably speculate, almost every day of his or her life. Molina, el almagrista, gives us an idea of the pervasiveness of their religiosity.

> Every time the Indians chewed coca they offered [some] to the Sun, and if they were near fire they would throw some in by way of an offering, with much reverence and each time they approach some high snowy and cold mountain pass, they have there as a shrine and place of adoration and sign a great mound of stones, and in many parts they place many blood arrows [*saetas*], and they offer there whatever they carry . . . and others pull out their eyebrow hairs and eyelashes and they offer them with great reverence; and they have the custom of walking through there very quietly and they do not dare talk, because they say that if they speak that the winds will get mad and they will send a lot of snow and they will kill them.[44]

Like devout adherents of most of the world's religions, Andeans worshipped these deities and spirits because they believed that the deities had power to affect and did affect the lives of the living, for better or worse. They revered the idols that represented their gods and the spirits of the ancestors as their "creators and from whom they expected all good things and happiness"; they believed that the ancestors watched over their descendants and played an active and crucial role in the world of the living. This is a topic that deserves more attention and will be discussed at length subsequently.[45]

Legitimacy

Anchoring this supernatural pantheon to the ground was the oft-repeated belief that the Incas were sons, direct descendants, of the Sun. The dead kings, their bodies preserved as mummies (malquis in the highlands, *munaos* on the coast) or represented as statues, these somewhat mythical ancestors or "binding agents" (to borrow a phrase from Farrington), were protecting divinities who symbolized the link between the Sun and the sacred and the living, the past and the present. Death in this society was considered merely a passage to another life. Thus, when a ruler perished, scores of subordinates either committed suicide or were killed to accompany and serve him. One chronicler reported that when Tupac Inca Yupanqui died, many beloved personal retainers (*yanas*), lords (pachacas), women, and servants were buried with him to dote upon him in the "other life." When Guayna Capac succumbed to measles or smallpox, an entourage of a thousand sacrificed courtiers and domestics accompanied him into the next world. Burial goods included vessels, adornments, and rich clothing, much of what was imagined would be needed in the beyond. Likewise, his house remained functional, full of kin, aids, and servants so that they could care for and feed him, because they expected the dead to be resuscitated and need then all of these household items.[46]

The embalmed bodies and statues of previous rulers were worshipped from at least the time of Pachacuti Inca Yupanqui—who, as mentioned previously, institutionalized and systematized the cult to his ancestors and prepared himself for such reverence after his passing—through the time of the Spanish invasion and after Inca rule ended. Like Pachacuti Inca Yupanqui, Guayna Capac, once invested with power, went to visit the remains of past kings, where he heard attendants sing the stories about the deeds of each. When he called upon the house of his grandfather Pachacuti Inca Yupanqui, for instance, he stayed for a month holding great feasts and making sacrifices to his image. Before leaving, he assigned his grandfather's bulto servants from the Soras, Lucanas, and the Chancas peoples of Andahuaylas—the first groups he had subjugated—and instructed them to settle in the valleys near Cuzco and bring what they raised to the Inca's house. After Guayna Capac's death, Huáscar, in turn, sent a noble (*orejón*) to Tomebamba to offer sacrifices before his image. Likewise, though Tupac Inca Yupanqui's mummy was burned in 1533 by Chalcochima, one of Atahualpa's generals, his followers preserved his ashes and his idol (*guauqui* [*huauqui*, *wawqui*, or *huauqui*]), or Cusi Churi. They were found years later in Calispuquio, where the natives had continued to offer sacrifices and veneration. Polo de Ondegardo eventually sent the ashes of Inca Viracocha, which had been put in an urn and worshipped, and some other Inca mummies to Los Reyes in the time of the Marqués of Cañete (1556–61), where they were placed in a yard, or corral, of the Hospital of San Andrés "so that the Kings' vassals will no longer adore them."[47]

In public rituals, the dead grandfathers and kindred (*deudos*), symbols of dynastic perpetuation, were also remembered and celebrated. Select persons entered the temple, prayed to the Sun, and brought the dead rulers out on litters, in order according to their antiquity and age, amid singing and dancing servants. In the plaza, their devotees lit wood fires before their images to burn food offerings, and they, in turn, feasted with them. The communion continued with offerings of chicha. The living toasted the dead, and the beer that was not consumed was dumped onto a stone in the middle of the square. These activities in the plaza (*Haucaypata*) sometimes attracted crowds of thousands and continued day and night. Besides these dead kings, close family members, like their sister-wives (*coyas*) (see Figure 3.5), were to be loved, adored, and served as well as feared, obeyed, and respected. Sancho reports seeing ten or eleven life-size golden statues of females. He writes that "they venerated them as much as if they were ladies of the world and alive, and they dressed them . . . and they adored them as goddesses, and they gave them food and they talked with them as if they were women of flesh."[48] Accordingly, ancestor worship in its many forms had become a major focus of el Cuzco and his court by the sixteenth century. Previous kings and queens were considered participants in the social structure of the living, and their worship played a major role in maintaining the reigning sovereign's legitimacy, majesty, and awe in the eyes of the populace. As we will see later, it also provided Andeans with a basis for a common but precarious, tenuous, and short-lived identity.[49]

It was in this context that the person of el Cuzco, as next in line, held sway and directed the evolving, complex, and flexible, religio-political system that organized and controlled the numerous ethnic populations of the empire and regulated economic production and exchange. He, like his ancestors, was believed to be a guaca, a sacred object, a god-king and divinity, the Capac Inca (or *sólo señor*), where capac meant rich, "not in material goods [hacienda], . . . but of soul, of gentleness, piety, clemency, munificence, justice and magnanimity and will [*deseo*], and works to do good to the poor. . . . It also means able and powerful at arms."[50] Julien, who wrote a paper on the meaning of the word and concept of capac, sums up her findings by saying that Inca capac status was, quoting Betanzos, "very much more than king"; it marked them, she continues, "as uniquely powerful beings, similar in concept to supernatural beings like the Sun."[51]

The reigning Inca was acknowledged as son of the Sun, and he acted and was treated as such.[52] In life, the Inca's bearing and conduct already bespoke his sacred status. Eyewitness accounts of the first face-to-face meeting between the Spanish and el Cuzco at the hot springs of Cajamarca in late 1532 noted his mannered regal austerity. He acted and was displayed as a bulto. Surrounded by women, el Cuzco sat on a low stool or throne (*dúo*, *duho*, or *tiana*) behind a sheer cloth "that they covered him with, so that no one could see him, because they had the custom some of these lords of not being seen except on rare occasions."[53] He showed no emotion. Like the scenes in the plaza, where spokesmen literally put words in the mouths of the mummies

FIGURE 3.5. The first coya, Mama Guaco. Source: Guamán Poma de Ayala 1613/1936: 120.

of past emperors or the great regional oracles of the empire, a delegate standing beside Atahualpa responded for him when an answer to the translated Spanish queries was required. An eyewitness writer describes the scene. The Inca's "face was so serene and his composure so serious, that he did not want to respond a word to what they said to him, but one of those lords who was next to him, responded."[54]

The following day, servants swept the ground before his litter was carried into the parade ground of Cajamarca, like the mummies of his ancestors were carried into the Haucaypata when their presence was needed on a ceremonial occasion. The Inca did not walk; he was carried, seated on a litter. Like a god, he sat to order the world and maintain harmony and equilibrium. People believed that, like Viracocha or Pachacamac, if he walked, there was danger of an earthquake, a landslide, or a volcanic eruption. On the November 1532 afternoon that he encountered the full force of Pizarro and his followers, the Inca, as a guaca, was being carried along a ceremonial causeway among as many as fifty thousand soldiers, singers, and musicians and being adored as he passed. His public world was a ritual.[55]

Like the rigorously restricted access to the idol Pachacamac and other such idols, an audience with the Inca was rare. Cabello Valboa wrote that it was a crime to look at the ruling monarch. Cieza recalled that if a cloth (*paño*) was lifted on his litter and bystanders actually saw his person, "they let out such a great outcry that it made the birds fall [from the sky]"—an obvious exaggeration, but his point is well made. Most persons had to approach the ruler through a subordinate. Under extraordinary circumstances when an audience with the king was allowed, those admitted had to enter the sacred precinct barefoot, carrying a burden on their back, "back to the lord" having first "revered him, what they call '*mochar*.'"[56] Betanzos describes an actual scene. When a messenger approached Huáscar, the messenger raised up his clasped hands to the Sun and said, "Oh, Sun, oh Day, give light." Then he bowed his head and bore a burden on his back. Barefoot and with his eyes on the ground, he paid his respects to the Inca by raising his hands and saying, "Oh, unique king, lover of the poor and son of the Sun." This was the accustomed way to pay respect to the emperor when a person appeared before him.[57]

On the rare occasion when the Inca showed himself publicly, he dressed as a god, resplendently, sometimes covered in gold, symbolizing his intimate association and ability to communicate with the Sun. In his battle against Atahualpa and his generals, Huáscar dressed in rich clothes and gold accoutrements: "he ordered to be covered with some polished sheets of gold."[58] He must not have realized, as his foes did, that such splendor in the sunlight of the Andean day would "wound the eyes" and mark him as an easy target. Similarly, when Atahualpa's litter entered Cajamarca, the Spanish were astonished; even the members of his accompanying retinue shone in the sun as they marched into the plaza. Pizarro wrote that "they wore so much gold and silver that it was astonishing how much it shone in the sun."[59]

His efforts to appear godlike also explain why the king dressed in ethnic costume and, because his own hair was cropped short, donned wigs in imitation of local style when he periodically visited provincial people. This practice probably reflects the story that, according to Molina, the "Creator of all things" fashioned the "peoples and nations" that inhabited the Andes out of clay, painting the costume, clothing, headdress, and hairstyle on each. The living identified with their progenitors and ancestors by imitating their clothes and hairstyle: "And thus each nation dressed itself and wore the same costume that they dressed their god in." If we recall MacCormack's discussion of the meaning of the word *pachacuti* (upheaval, or the world turns), each Inca brought on a new epoch. One title of Atahualpa, for example, was Ticci (Ticsi) Capac or original ruler, he who began the world afresh. She states that "an Inca's accession could thus be understood as a return of the world to its origins." The fact that the elect wore traditional costume and wigs in imitation of local style, especially on the initial visitation after coming to power, could therefore be interpreted, in one sense, as the personification of the people's founder, ancestor, and guaca. In this regard, the Inca was honoring and respecting ancient ethnic tradition, especially when he danced and worshipped with them, but the charade was also another way of equating him to the divine and asserting that he was an element of their past and a symbol of unity.[60]

As a child of the Sun, the person of the Inca, his statues, and images were worshipped and revered as gods: "Sacrifices like those made before the statue of the Sun were made before them." Some of the Incas were said to have statues made that were considered their "brothers" and "predicted the future and answered their questions." After Atahualpa's investiture, he had a statue made, called brother of the Inca (*Incap guauqin*), that incorporated his nail clippings and hair. It was placed on a guarded litter and then sent to the provinces where his captains were "so that the peoples of the subjugated provinces could render obedience to that statue in place of his person. . . . They performed many and great sacrifices and served and respected this statue as if the very person of Atahualpa were there."[61]

Thus, the Inca became part of the greater imperial pantheon, an articulating point of contact; a link between his celestial kin, the mummified remains of his ancestors, and his earth-bound relatives and followers; and between the supernatural immortals and living humans. Only the king could drink with the Sun, as its immediate representative on earth (see Figure 3.6). As such, he was a mediator between opposing "levels of the world," between the sacred world and the profane world. As the center, the Inca communicated

FIGURE 3.6. The Inca drinking with the Sun. Source: Guamán Poma de Ayala 1613/1936: 246.

with the "world above," where the celestial gods lived (*Hanan* [*Hanac*, *Hanaq*] *Pacha*); and the world here (*mundo de la superficie*), where humanity lived (*Cay* [*Kay*] *Pacha*).[62] His status as guarantor of cosmic harmony was epitomized by his ability to drink chicha and communicate not only with the Sun but also with other guacas and mere mortals.[63]

As guaca, as supreme religious authority of the official cult of the Sun, and as the Sun's kin, messenger, lieutenant, and spokesman, the Inca was said to be omnipotent. His power was said to be omnipresent. As the personification of sacred force, who even spoke a sacred language (*lenguaje divino*), he was said to be capable of changing form, as Atahualpa was rumored to have done, escaping from the hold of Huáscar's forces by turning into a snake and going underground.[64] He was like a god in that, it was said, he made sterile countryside fertile by establishing order, building or repairing infrastructure, and/or relocating inhabitants. He, as the embodiment and delegation of the creator's supernatural power, ordered monumental architecture such as Sacsayhuamán, and communities such as Chinchero, built. As all-knowing, ceremonial leader, he signaled the passage of time and determined when the earth was ready to be planted. And in keeping with the role of a benevolent and protective god-king who wanted to increase his "republic" and conserve it, he also guaranteed subsistence by sending food and other necessities from the storehouses, as needed, to stricken peoples. He also cured. Like a god, in short, he could be the font of hospitality, benevolence, and life, especially in periods of crisis.[65]

Pease thinks that the Inca, as a guaca, could negotiate with the other gods over such matters as the conquests as well as the form of organizing the population. But if negotiations broke down and he encountered resistance, he became the prime mover in conquering and punishing as a warrior king. Retribution was moderated by the Inca's ideology of enlightened self-interest that encouraged leniency, rather than wrath, because numbers of subjects and access to their labor counted. Ideally, he strove toward harmony. Theoretically, his goal was to become, in time, the real or fictive father of the subjects over whom he ruled. He articulated different groups through ritual marriages, which simultaneously established the bases of reciprocity and redistribution. Thus, kinship with his sacred person united diverse groups, ordered the polity and society into a common lineage under one law, and helped establish the bases for an all-encompassing common identity and memory.[66]

This personified religious focus and its related beliefs and practices were essential to ideologically unify a dispersed, multiethnic population and legitimize the Inca's overarching power. In the highlands, "All had the same beliefs and rites and ceremonies, and they adore the Sun. . . . All this cold region adores the Sun and his son, the lord of the land, who also is called Son of the Sun."[67] To be part of the empire was to be kin to a god, to be incorporated into the sacred hierarchy. A person's status reflected the closeness of this relationship. Inca genealogy was a "banner of their collective identity," of their "Incaness," as put so well by Frank Salomon.[68]

Thus, the Inca epitomized the Andean worldview: the ancestor gods could and did affect the outcome of events and could advise on choices and decisions. Their dogma, values, and practices explained the universe, rationalized the subordination of local ethnic groups, and enabled the rulers, one after the other, to assume the central and all-embracing mandating function. The establishment of a link through the Inca to a divine order headed by the Sun allowed the Incas—either in the person of el Cuzco or as an ethnic group itself—to impose their sociopolitical order and precepts on others and thus to secure their hegemony. The cult of the Sun became an instrument of political unification.[69]

Inca claims to divine origin were validated, supported, and manifested in various ways. The first, and perhaps least important way, which played only a supporting and subsidiary function, was their use of verbal communications and forms of address. When the Sun was mentioned, the king said "our father the Sun," not only as a means of veneration and obeisance (*acatamiento*) but as a reminder and reinforcement of his claimed descendance. Similarly, when individuals were privileged to approach the king, as mentioned earlier, they made adoring gestures to the Sun and then revered the Inca through words ("Oh, child of the Sun, loving and kind to the poor") and deed. Upon their approach, they placed gifts or sacrificed camelids before him with great deference, as befitting the offspring of a deity.[70]

A second, and perhaps more important, means to the same end was to create a history that legitimated their domination. Two predominant versions of origin myths served this purpose. One stated that various numbers of Inca ancestors emerged from caves at Pacaritanbo (see Figures 3.7 and 3.8), and the other linked their origin to Lake Titicaca. In general, the first states that the Andean peoples lived in an uncivilized, disordered manner before Inca ascendancy and domination. The Sun took pity on them and created one to four pairs of brothers and sisters, depending on the version one reads, and sent them from the sky to earth to teach others his ways.[71] At the hill of Guanacaure, they saw that the signs were good for exploring and selecting a place to settle down. Manco Capac, a leading character in the tale, looked "at the flight of birds and in the signs of the stars and at other portents full of confidence." He concluded from these signs that he would be a founding father of all the Incas. Manco Capac "asked the Sun with great humility that he favor him and help him in the new settlement that he wanted to make and turning his eyes toward Guanacaure hill, he asked the same of his brother, who he already accepted and revered as god. He and his family eventually made a new settlement in what today is the Valley of Cuzco with the consent and help of the natives of the region."[72]

FIGURE 3.7. Tambotocto depicted on the coat of arms. Source: Guamán Poma de Ayala 1613/1936: 79.

FIGURE 3.8. The Inca and the coya worshipping at Tambotocto. Source: Guamán Poma de Ayala 1613/1936: 264.

The credulous locals, so the origin myths continue, identified them as sons of the Sun because, according to Cieza, "Their presumptuousness was so great that they planned to make themselves the only lords of the land." They "were so conceited and of such grand feats . . . that as a result, when the Indians adulated them, they addressed them . . . Oh very great lord, son of the Sun!" More realistically, he writes that they were valiant, gallant, and fierce captains from "some people of these regions or come from another part of the Andean highlands." They conquered and won the sovereignty that they had. This concurs with Sarmiento de Gamboa's claim that "they made the people believe and fear them, and hold them to be more than men, even worshiping them as gods." Cabello Valboa's version explains that they came to dominate the very rustic, unsophisticated people of the area by making and wearing unusual clothes covered with gold and jewels. The Incas hid and at dawn appeared, he says, thus disguised, making the people believe "that they had come from the Sky and that they were sons of the Sun and his messengers." No one knew where they came from; their dress was different and of such majesty (*de tanta magestad*). People were easily persuaded that the Incas were divine. People "received them as secular and spiritual Kings and Lords."[73] Garcilaso was more pragmatic:

> I can guess the origin of this prince . . . Manco Capac, . . . he must have been an understanding, prudent, and wise Indian, and he understood well the great naivete of those nations, and he saw their need for doctrine and instruction for everyday life, and with finesse and sagacity he imagined that fable to increase [his] esteem, saying that he and his woman were children of the sun, and that they came from the sky, and that their father had sent them to instruct and do good to those peoples; and to give credence to his tale, he probably assumed the form and dress that he wore, particularly the large ears of the Incas, that for sure were incredible to those who had never seen them . . . and the favors and honors that he conferred on his vassals confirmed the fable of his genealogy, the Indians firmly believed that he was the son of the sun come from the sky, and they adored him as such.[74]

The other version of the myth substitutes Lake Titicaca for Pacaritanbo but follows the general outline of the first. Garcilaso de la Vega, however, adds and paraphrases the reported civilizing charge that their father, the Sun, gave them. His words express their legitimating ideology. They were ordered to teach the people to adore the Sun

> so that they would give them precepts and laws so that they could live as humans with order and civility; so that they would inhabit houses and towns, would know how to work the lands, cultivate the plants and corns, raise the livestock and benefit from them and the fruits of the earth, like rational beings, and not as beasts. . . . When you have reduced those peoples to your service, you will rule them with reason and justice . . . [as a] merciful father toward his young children, . . . imitating and copying me, that to all the world I do good, that I give them my light. . . . I warm

them. . . . I generate the pastures and cultivated fields; I make the trees fruitful and the livestock multiply . . . to provide for and help, as sustainer and benefactor of the peoples; I want you to imitate this example like my sons, sent to the earth only to instruct and benefit these humans. . . . I . . . name you kings and lords of all the peoples that you thus will instruct with your wisdom, deeds and government.[75]

These fabricated stories were sung, conveying the significance of the past into the present. Cieza said that the quipucamayocs sang their songs so that "the people upon hearing them would be motivated and understand the past in other times." Yet Thomas Abercrombie reminds us that most of these story-songs were probably more important as descriptions and validations of social hierarchy and political relations than as histories in the Western sense. That is, they were less an account of the past than propaganda, consciously manipulated and retold to fit individual, ethnic, and imperial ends.[76]

Whatever the details of the stories—and these conceivably were altered to accommodate the political realities and the audience—the Inca let it be known that he was the sole son of the Sun. And "with this title, he made himself adored and he governed so strictly that no one challenged him; his word was law and no one dared disobey his word or will."[77]

A third way to reinforce the Incas' kinship with the divine was by their claim to be capable of interpreting the will of the gods. Santillán states their propagandistic message: "And their lords and authorities were careful and vigilant to make their subjects and those who they wanted to subjugate understand that they were more than men and that they knew supernatural things and that they talked with the Creator of all things, and that they had more communication with him than other people, and that they were children of the Sun." One way they did this was by expounding on the meaning of omens, signs, and dreams. From the heroic time when Ayar Oche turned to stone to remain a constant conduit for his earthly family with the Sun, the appearance of a rainbow was considered a good omen that all could see. The Incas and their astrologers, who studied the heavens to predict the seasons, could also forecast the occurrence of lunar and solar eclipses. Both promised danger.[78]

In other words, the imperial elite had the knowledge and science to read both good and bad signs in the sky. The Incas did not think that these foretold ordinary occurrences; they invariably signaled uncommon and grandiose occasions. Francisco Pizarro, for example, saw a green sign in the Cajamarca sky, which saddened Atahualpa because Guayna Capac had seen a similar color in the heavens before his death. Atahualpa died within two weeks. Other signals simultaneously presaging and reinforcing the fear of impending doom and disaster for the Incas appeared in the reign of Guayna Capac. Calancha records that while Guayna Capac ruled, a bird appeared at a ritual near the Coricancha and indicated that sacrifices would end. A comet was seen there for many days in the east. There also appeared a pyramid of fire. Santacruz Pachacuti Yamqui adds to this list, citing the silence of Guayna Capac's dead father to his appeal for a second wife; sky signs meaning blood; a midnight vision in which a million or so were to die of a pestilence; and the story about the messenger who brought a locked coffer, like Pandora's box, that when opened by Guayna Capac released something similar to butterflies, which carried measles and infected the Inca and great numbers of his followers.[79]

The Incas read the signs and consulted the guacas before undertaking new enterprises (see Figure 3.9). Before Tupac Inca Yupanqui set out for Chinchaysuyu, he sacrificed and burned animals to worship the Sun and seek favorable indications for his expedition and visitation.[80] He also used a sorcerer or great necromancer (*antarqui*) to help decide whether he should tour islands off the coast. Only after getting positive indications did the Inca embark. Such practices continued after the Spanish arrival. Saire (Sayre, Sayri, or Sairi) Tupac, when negotiating his surrender and retreat from Vilcabamba, said "that it was necessary to consult with his gods on the issue." The counsel advising Saire Tupac set one roadblock after another for his surrender.

> [Finally, in 1557] everyone agreed to make the sacrifice (according to their custom) to ask the Sun, and the earth, and the rest of the Guacas for an answer: and so in the morning they ordered that that day all fast and no one light a fire while the answer was pending. All the captains climbed to the high mountains, accompanied by the Inca with his trumpets, and preceding him the Priests: for whom they have great respect and give total obedience. In their ceremonies to the Sun, the earth and Guacas, the priests asked them to declare if the proposed exit would end well. Once done and interpreting the signs, the Priests said that the Sun, the land, and also their Guacas, had replied that the exit would be happy and beneficial; because to all their questions they had answered yes: the answers had been negative to questions about the exit when previously asked. . . . This done the trumpets blew signaling the descent from the mountains, everyone proceeded with great happiness.[81]

For ordinary predictions and judgments they relied on the interpretation of their own dreams and the divining rituals that they practiced. These rituals, which were one of the many ways to assess the will of the guacas, were used to determine succession, to foretell the outcome of battles, and even to predict "the length of a life." The Incas consulted male and female divining specialists (called *Guacarimachic*, meaning persons who make the guacas predict the future), who practiced arts that had been handed down since predynastic days. One type of specialist (called *ayatapuc* or *malquipvillac*) talked to the dead. Other practitioners prophesied by using coca, tobacco, or other herbs. Cabello Valboa reports that during the reign of Mayta Capac (the fourth Inca according to Cabello Valboa, Sarmiento de Gamboa, and Guamán Poma de Ayala; the fifth Inca according to Betanzos), the witches and wizards (*hechiceros*) (see Figure 3.10); diviners (*agoreros*);

FIGURE 3.9. The Tupac Inca Yupanqui talking to the Huacas; the Inca asks about the past and the future. Source: Guamán Poma de Ayala 1613/1936: 261.

FIGURE 3.10. A sorcerer. Source: Guamán Poma de Ayala 1613/1936: 277.

clairvoyants (*adevinos*); palmists and chiromancers (*quiromânticos*); augurers and soothsayers (*aruspicios*); sorcerers, fortune-tellers, and conjurers (*sortilegos*); and bewitchers (*maleficos*) were much esteemed, valued, and celebrated for their ability to communicate with divine forces and access their wisdom.[82]

Such practitioners helped carry out divining rituals, one of the most common of which was the *calpa* or *callpa*. The Quechua word itself means a force of the body, spirit, or soul; or the vigor or energy to work and act. During this ceremony, humans gained access to the power and wisdom of the ancestors. In the course of the solemnities, a divinity answered questions put to it by a priest or religious specialist, such as who might win an upcoming battle. In the case of an Inca succession question, as will be detailed later, the divinity consulted was the Sun himself. In the calpa, as depicted in Guamán Poma de Ayala's drawing (Figure 3.11), the lungs and entrails of a purified camelid or the organs of birds were removed and inflated. The interpreters looked at the lungs and heart for "omens" to determine whether the successor would be spirited and valiant. Then they burned the organs and ate the meat. This was one way that the god participated in the everyday life of the community.[83]

The Inca could also communicate directly with all the idols, guacas, and oracles of the empire. Mayta Capac was said to be able to speak to the bird and oracle *Indi*. While in the town of Urcos, Atun (Hatun) Tupac Inca saw the vision of the god Viracocha, who announced his future and told of great and wonderful ventures; thereafter, he became known as Inca Viracocha. Another example occurred when the oracle Pachacamac asked Guayna Capac to take it to the Chimu so that it might be worshipped even more than these coastal people idolized Viracocha. Visions and dreams where a god spoke and prophesied also were attributes that distinguished among the sometimes many male offspring of the king as a future contestant for power. To Tupac Inca Yupanqui, Inca Viracocha's youngest son, there appeared a vision of a person in the air, like the Sun, consoling him and animating him for battle. From the apparition, he understood that he would subdue his enemies and be greater than any of his ancestors. It was said that Tupac Inca Yupanqui begged something from the Sun; he talked with him as he would to a family friend. Generalizing from such reports, Ziólkowski believes that the "election" of a successor to the role of Inca was through such a "direct contact" with the Hanan Pacha, in the form of a vision or a dream during which the future sovereign communicated or "conversed" with the gods. This "divine election" was then confirmed by the priests.[84]

The commoners were said to believe that through such consultations and transmissions, the ancestors supplied their leaders with special knowledge that was unavailable to most. Inca Mayta Capac predicted the civil wars

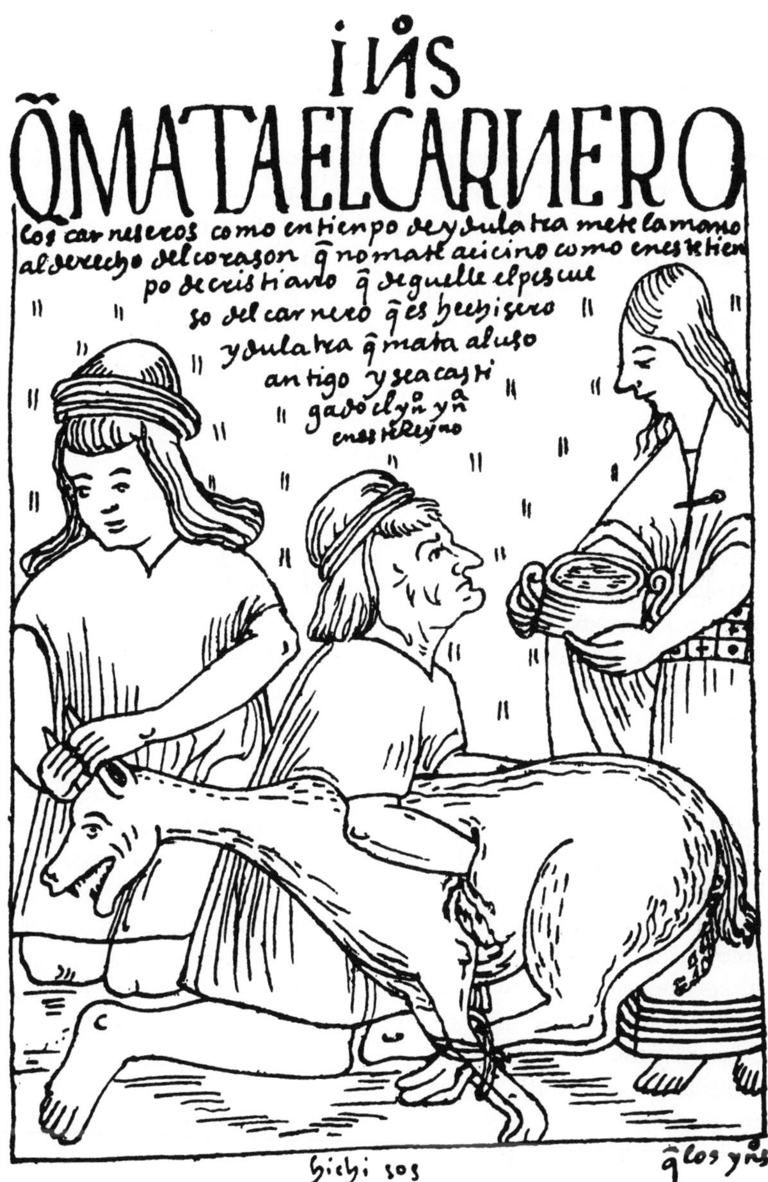

FIGURE 3.11. The calpa ceremony. Source: Guamán Poma de Ayala 1613/1936: 880.

that divided the Andeans in the sixteenth century. Just before death, Tupac Inca Yupanqui predicted a crisis, or pachacuti, after Guayna Capac's days, caused by the arrival of "a white, bearded and very tall people with whom they would fight and in the end would serve." [85] Guayna Capac's knowledge of this prediction made him predisposed to accept the landing of the Spanish as the return of the gods. Guayna Capac may have learned of the Spaniards while in Tomebamba in 1515, two years after Vasco Núñez de Balboa and his companions "discovered" the Pacific Ocean and approximately ten years before his death.[86] While there, he heard of strange and never-before-seen beings who came by boat along the coast, making inquires. Garcilaso de la Vega suggests that the intelligence was accepted because the news dovetailed with an old story: "The news of that ship gave him much pause, remembering an old prediction that the Incas had, that after a number of kings, strange and never-before-seen peoples would arrive and take away their suzerainty, and destroy their government [*república*] and religion." [87]

Oracles and signs confirmed the veracity of the news. Antonio de Herrera reports that one oracle responded that "when a Volcano erupted in La Tacunga, a strange people would enter the land from a distant region, who through war would subjugate these provinces." Pedro Pizarro also reported that Apurimac spoke to foretell the arrival of the Spanish, advising the Andeans to consume all, so that they would have nothing to give. And toward the end of Guayna Capac's life, bad omens appeared, including an eagle that was attacked by hawks and died in the Haucaypata; and a moon, ringed in red, black, and gray, which the diviners of the realm interpreted as a bad sign, predicting that the Incas and their empire were doomed.[88]

Regardless of how Guayna Capac gained access to the news, he presented it as privileged information to which he alone, in his sacred capacity, had knowledge. Thus, while in Tomebamba, just prior to his death, Guayna Capac summoned his relatives, captains, and curacas and told them that he knew "from his oracles" that the monarchy would end with the twelfth king. He also told them "that they should expect that very soon after his death other foreign lords would arrive to conquer this Kingdom, and destroy the natives, their religion and the cult to their idols would end." He concluded by telling them to obey and serve them because the invaders' law would be better than their own. They were not to resist with arms; they were to give them assistance (*socorros*), grants and gifts (*dádivas*), and presents (*regalos*).[89]

Likewise, other Incas summoned the representatives and custodians of guacas of the empire to consult on local matters and the outcomes of conflict. Such consultations were useful to the head of state, because by interrogating the priests and guardians of these guacas, he could keep abreast of the occurrences, concerns, perspectives, and interests of powerful sectional establishments.[90]

There were two additional oracular aids and avenues into the unknown future. First, each Inca had an idol (*guauqui*), that accompanied him and "predicted outcomes and gave answers." Manco Capac, for example, chose the bird Indi as his guauqui. Pachacuti Inca Yupanqui chose Lightning as his, because it had appeared and spoken to him in a desert place and given him a two-headed serpent. While he had the snake with him, he believed nothing sinister could happen in his affairs. Second, there were the illustrious Inca ancestors, the mummies and bultos of previous rulers, who represented ancient authority and also spoke and answered questions through their spokesmen in the Haucaypata, where they were daily fed and offered drink.[91]

At times, the guacas refused to respond or answered in an adverse and unexpected manner. Guamán Poma de Ayala relates that Guayna Capac wanted to "speak" with all the idols and guacas of the kingdom. When asked a question, none wanted to reply. So Guayna Capac ordered that they be broken and destroyed. He spared only the most important idols, like Pariacaca, the Sun, and Moon. The same fate awaited the oracle of the Guamachucos, Catequil. Atahualpa arrived and ordered a great sacrifice in its honor atop its hill before asking it "what it knew about his good fortune and success." The stone oracle displeased the king with its answer, predicting that Atahualpa would be defeated by the Christians. So he called it an enemy spirit and personally decapitated both the idol and its spokesman. He then ordered it dismantled, smashed, burned, and destroyed and its hilltop location leveled. Molina, el almagrista, notes that "his revenge did not leave a single wizard in all the province alive."[92]

Divination was a precarious art. The prestige and reputation of oracles that predicted wrongly plummeted. Annual evaluations of each guaca's credibility and capabilities determined the type and amount of the sacrifices and offerings to be made. Cieza states that the gifts to each guaca were analogous to the Christian tithe and a type of ingratiating and deserved donation. To those whose predictions proved incorrect, "the next year they were not given any offerings, instead they lost prestige." When Guayna Capac was sick, a message was sent to Pachacamac to ask what to do to restore his health. Pachacamac replied that if Guayna Capac was exposed to the sun, he would survive; instead, he died. It had also predicted that Huáscar would win and that Atahualpa would kill the Spanish. As a consequence of these erroneous predictions, Atahualpa accused Pachacamac of lying. He became disillusioned with the oracle's false indications and ceased believing its pronouncements. Once the oracle's counsel had been discredited and delegitimized in the Inca's eyes, he rejected him as a god. This reaction explains why Atahualpa allowed the Spanish to sack the sanctuary and foreshadows the crisis of legitimacy that followed.[93]

A final means of supporting the idea that the Incas were embodied gods, sons of the Sun, and sacred rulers without peer was the perpetuation of the stories that the successor, in the final analysis, was the choice of the Sun himself. Legitimacy was not based on European concepts of Christian matrimony, monogamy, and dynasty; it was the Sun that conferred the mantle of acknowledgment and history on the successor. The record of successions is confusing because it is clouded by Spanish assumptions and attempts to organize the details to fit European categories, preconceptions, and models. What is known for sure is that succession could be a tense time, full of palace intrigue, drama, assassinations and death, and chaos and anarchy as deliberations took place and elite factions jockeyed for position in the elaborate fiction that the Sun chose the heir to the throne of the empire. According to the chronicles, after a king died, his death was (ideally) kept a closely guarded secret and not disclosed to the general populace for at least one lunar month (*una luna*) to give the priests time to divine, to consult, and to listen to the lobbying of the panacas—the royal descent groups with a common male progenitor—whose main purpose was to perpetuate the memory and worship of one of the Inca rulers. As such the panaca constituted a spiritual community or congregation and acted as an interest group. During this era, an interim ruler was chosen from the lords, and it was expected that all the Inca's sons and the high lords of the kingdom would do penance and fast.[94]

But the sons could be a problem. Each Inca, because he had sexual relations with many women—the coya (often his sister), as well as innumerable consorts and concubines, the daughters and sisters of local lords—left dozens of potential heirs. Although the Spanish would have us believe that primogeniture was the favored succession rule, Rostworowski believes that all sons of the Inca had accession rights and could aspire to power.[95] A review of Inca succession shows that primogeniture was rarely or uncommonly observed. In fact, there was no single prescribed way that the heir was selected; there was no single, universally followed law of succession.[96]

A variety of factors were considered in choosing a successor. One undoubtedly was the desire of the Inca himself, who according to the chroniclers, nominated his heir before death. His predilection may have reflected his respect and/or affection of the heir's mother, be she a coya or another woman. It also undeniably reflected the potential heir's qualities, such as strength, virtue, moderation, affability, and high-spiritedness. The individual designated or elected, ideally, would be "the most able and sufficient" among the candidates (a principle that held at the curacazgo level as well).[97]As early as the puberty rites ceremony (*Huarachicoy*, *Huarachicu*, or *Horachico*), the adolescent boys were watched to see who could run the fastest and who demonstrated other signs of ability and bravery, that is, who was "most apt." Age alone was not a major determining factor. Andean society did not keep track of ages by Christian calendar years, but rather by broad categories, the age-grades mentioned earlier.[98] Circumstances and expediency, no doubt, were also considerations. But along with these worldly factors were others—namely, the individual's ability to communicate with the gods and the will of the gods, which reflected political calculations and preferences of the elite factions, especially the conspiracies of the panacas.[99]

The Sun's will was manifested through divination. Once a candidate was named or advanced as a favorite, he entered the temple to sacrifice to the Sun (or if he was too young, sacrifices were made in his name). Then, he was subject to judgment by the Sun through the calpa ceremony.[100] The ritual was carried out by prominent religious specialists, after having been subjected to intense lobbying by interest groups at court. For example, when Guayna Capac fell ill, he was asked to name his successor. He named Ninan Cuyoche (Cuyochi), though still a child, subject to a favorable calpa divination. If the divination was not favorable, he named Huáscar as second choice. The first divination ceremony for Ninan Cuyoche, performed by Cusi Tupac Yupanqui, the chief steward of the Sun, was inauspicious.[101] Therefore, a second young camelid was opened. The lungs and certain veins were examined, and they also proved contrary and ominous for Huáscar. Guayna Capac died before naming a third candidate, so here an oracle, the voice and will of the Sun, decided between the two options. Huáscar was selected and installed.[102]

Although details differ, there is one commonality in most of the tales of succession: the successor is ultimately designated by the Sun.[103] Thus, despite the fact that Pachacuti Inca Yupanqui's defeat of the Chancas—which Patterson places in the 1430s—gave him great power and control over many people to the extent that he successfully staged what amounted to a coup against his father, Inca Viracocha, he was still subject to solar sanction and approval. He offered a great sacrifice in the Coricancha, after which the Sun was asked who should be Inca: father or son? The oracle of the Sun or, as Sarmiento de Gamboa opines, "perhaps some Indian who was behind to give the answer," designated Pachacuti Inca Yupanqui.[104] At hearing this verdict, all those present prostrated themselves before Pachacuti Inca Yupanqui and cried out, according to Sarmiento de Gamboa, "Ccapac Inca Intip Churin" (sovereign lord child of the Sun) or "Indi Churi" (son of the Sun). The next day, the nobles accompanied Pachacuti Inca Yupanqui to the Coricancha, where the Sun's golden statue was found to be holding the headband and crown in its hand, as though freely offering it. Pachacuti Inca Yupanqui made the customary sacrifices, and a priest placed the red-fringed headband (*masca* [*maskha*] *paicha* [*pacha* or *paycha*]) on his forehead and the scepter (*suntur paucar*) in his hand, with great ceremony and reverence. Both were visual representations of his divine election and power. Witnesses of the enthronement then called him Intip Churin Inca Pachacuti, child of the Sun, lord overturner of the earth. Thus did the Sun participate in the determination of who was then to be "son of the Sun." [105]

Once seated on a low golden stool and equipped with the symbols and insignia of his new authority, he was worshipped by the people from afar. Subjects pulled out their eyebrows and eyelashes and blew them toward the god-king as an offering. Others offered handfuls of coca leaf or a white feather, a symbol of obedience. He, in response, presented many gifts and celebrated the event with feasts. This procedure and ceremony became the model in the following investitures of Tupac Inca Yupanqui and Guayna Capac.[106]

Divine Wills

Thus, Andean society believed that the ancestor-gods—both celestials and malquis—were active and accessible and that they sometimes played a leading part in the lives of the living. The Sun was conceived of as the head of an extended celestial family, which included the Moon and the stars, the ancestors, and the ruling king. In acknowledging the Inca as lord and guaca and accepting marriage alliances, provincial leaders and their followers were accepting the tenets of his rule and a reciprocal relationship between the living and their ancestor-gods. Each contributed to the well-being of the other and the stability of the cosmos.[107]

The fate of the living reflected divine will. According to tradition, Manco Capac set the precedent when, on his deathbed, he announced that as a divine ancestor "from the sky he could care, favor and aid them in all their necessities." He, like his descendants, guaranteed "life and health and food." For such reasons, Manco Capac's representation was adored as a god, son of the Sun, and offered many sacrifices of camelids, guinea pigs (*conejos caseros*, *cuyes*), birds, corn, and other foodstuffs on a continuing basis. He was praised as the "lord of all the things that he had left" and for his perceived ability to benefit the living in many ways.[108]

Continuing participation in the daily life of the living took other forms. In peacetime, Inca mummies, as representatives of their panacas, gave (or withheld) permission for marriage for members of the Andean nobility. In wartime, their statues and representations were carried into battle for supernatural support and psychological advantage. Thus, Tupac Inca Yupanqui took his guaca with him to suppress the revolts and pacify the Puquinas and Collas after Pachacuti Inca Yupanqui died. Likewise, when the news reached Guayna Capac in Cajamarca that the Chiriguanos threatened Cuzco, he began to draft people for the war that was sure to come. To oblige and motivate those convened, "he ordered that each nation bring with them the major god of their land that is the idol that they most attend." Sarmiento de Gamboa gives some specific examples when he describes the king's sending a captain south with the guacas of "Catiquilla" (Catequil, according to Albornoz; Lightning, according to Arriaga) of the Cajamarquinos and Guamachucos; of Curichaculla of the Chachapoyas people; and two others. They were sent "with many devotees of the guacas." Eventually, the threat from the Chiriguanos subsided and the army disbanded, each group taking its guaca home with them.[109]

As another example, a mutiny was stopped by the timely intervention of an ancestor. Custom dictated that a king feed his militia while on campaign. Guayna Capac, in the field in the north, gave out rations to his troops every ten days. However, he skimped on supplies for his orejones, distributing necessities only monthly, which were deemed far from sufficient, to the point that the orejones felt unappreciated and neglected and their king looked ungenerous, even niggardly. Discontent grew until the orejones announced that they were retreating to the south, taking the image of the Sun with them.[110] The spokesman proclaimed that "we want to take with us the sun our father because we swore and professed his protection and custody." As the orejones prepared to leave, other infantrymen decided to follow. In the face of this massive desertion, the priests of the Sun brought out the statue of Guayna Capac's mother dressed in mourning clothes and pulling out her hair (*mesando sus cabellos*). Her impersonator, in a female voice, first implored and then finally persuaded the nobles to stay. To change their minds, she promised them clothing and sandals. She called them her sons and reminded them that she was their mother. Persuaded, the troops decided not to be disobedient to the sacred descendant of Manco Capac. Their insubordination fizzled once they felt themselves "content and well-paid." An open-handed and liberal distribution of food and clothing followed.[111]

To curry favor with the ancestor-gods, the Inca worshipped them, just as the living revered, in turn, the Inca. To propitiate their forefathers at the appropriate times, they danced, sang, and presented sacrifices. Some rituals and ceremonies were designed to beseech the ancestral gods for help. Others were planned to maintain favor and make the Incas prosperous, lucky, and blessed before "all who had been born," and, finally, to thank and reciprocate for favors granted. Thus, after Pachacuti Inca Yupanqui defeated the Collas, he returned to the heartland and sacrificed the Colla Capac, their supreme ruler, to the Sun. But offerings need not always be human.[112]

On a daily basis, it was sufficient to feed the gods and ancestors to keep them content. Molina, el almagrista, in describing the Coricancha complex, explained that the chamber where the Sun's image sat was located just past a cornfield made of gold. Inside the chamber there were twelve forked poles (*horcones*) of white silver, so large that two men could not embrace them. There they placed the corn that they offered to the Sun; "they said, that he should eat and drink." Sometimes, the idol of the Sun would be carried to the plaza and placed on a painted stool covered with feathered mantles (*mantas*). There, too, he was fed. In like manner, the Cuzqueños fed the mummies of the dead Cuzcos. In 1533, Mena was told that "still even though he is dead they follow his orders as fully as if he were alive: and thus they give him drink and they pour that wine (chicha) that they are to give him there near where the body of the old Cuzco [Guayna Capac] is." Similarly, life-size figures, made of gold and silver, of women had servants who attended and fed them as if they were alive. In fact, both women and men arrived to serve the cult of the dead, of their own free volition, "each one to the dead person they wanted." Food production and preparation were undoubtedly part of their tasks. The caretakers that Guayna Capac assigned to Manco Capac and his grandfather Pachacuti Inca Yupanqui likewise guaranteed that they would be fed and maintained.[113]

Andeans believed that if they did not serve and feed their ancestral mummies, the guacas would suffer hunger and roam the land. Cataclysm and disaster would follow. Natural disasters, drought, frost, earthquakes, pestilence, famine, and defeat in war showed that the ruler had displeased the ancestors and forfeited his divine mandate. He had become ineffective. He and his leadership had been supernaturally repudiated.[114]

In addition to failure to fulfill their responsibilities to the gods, desecration, too, invited major misfortune. Thus, when the Spanish saw that the Coricancha was plated with gold, they set about removing it with a copper crowbar (*barreta*). The Cuzqueños refused to help in this endeavor, "saying that they would die," and so they would have under the old regime—not from the ire of their ancestors but from their human representatives and spokesmen. In another case, soon after the Spanish arrived in Pachacamac, the region suffered an earthquake. The inhabitants fled, interpreting the tremor as a sign from Pachacamac that the deity was mad because they had allowed the Spanish to approach and contaminate sacred space. They imagined that all were to be destroyed.[115]

Thus, Andeans believed that the Inca's ability to satisfy and appease the dead influenced the success or failure of his reign. Like the oracles whose power and reputation waxed and waned with their prediction accuracy, so too did the fortunes of the various succeeding rulers. Peace, victory in war, the absence of killing frost, plentiful rain at the right time of the year, health, and fertility were just some of the signs that reflected to all the favor and continued support and acknowledgment of the ancestors and the Sun of the Inca's actions and behavior. Like his earlier counterparts in eastern Asia, he enjoyed what the Chinese called the "mandate of heaven." According to Anello Oliva, Andeans believed that after the ritual of initiation, the king became invincible: the Inca could not be defeated. In Atahualpa's case (and disregarding whether or not it really happened), his divine status was revealed after he, disguised as a snake, escaped Huáscar's imprisonment. Thereafter, having had a vision in which Inca Amaru Yupanqui appeared to him and assured him of solar support, he never lost another battle (*no vuelve a ser vencido*) against native forces. The opposite, however, was also true.[116]

Given these beliefs that the ancestor-gods could and did intervene in human affairs, and myths that recounted that a new age was sometimes initiated after one god defeated another, it is not surprising that war had strong religious overtones. It confirmed continuing supernatural approval of the victor and was often perceived as a ritualized rivalry between guacas and gods for hegemony. In fact, to test their strength vis-à-vis their neighbors, guacas were said to initiate and even encourage power struggles, promising victory to their congregations.[117]

To capture or destroy a lord and his guaca demonstrated that either the victor's god was stronger than those of his foes or, should victor and foe both appeal to the same god, that the victor held the god's favor. Santacruz Pachacuti Yamqui relates an example of the former case. He writes that a guaca, Cañacuay, advised his adherents to murder the king Pachacuti Inca Yupanqui. The attempt on his life motivated the Inca to retaliate. According to the account, Cañacuay then sent a fire to prevent the Inca's advance and a snake to consume his soldiers. The Inca appealed to the gods of the sky and earth with "affliction and tears." They obliged, sending an eagle to destroy the snake; thus, the Inca's supernatural supporters were proven to be stronger than the guaca of his enemies.

An example of the latter goes back to the death of Pachacuti Inca Yupanqui. Soon thereafter, several ethnic groups, including the Collas, revolted. Tupac Inca Yupanqui, the successor, accompanied by his guacas and idols, went to fight them. The conflict stagnated with an estimated 120,000 of the Inca's troops surrounding the Collas. The siege lasted three years, during which time the Collas made human and other sacrifices to the Sun. The Sun's spokesperson (*tata*) told his followers that the deity promised good hope (*buena esperança*). This message motivated the Collas to fight without fear, as if the war was already won. Meanwhile, the Inca too had been worshipping (*cantando*) and asking for victory. Eventually, this face-off ended when the Collas' generals were apprehended, humiliated, and skinned. Their guacas were destroyed and thrown into a lake—to erase memory once and for all. For such reasons, it was said that the guacas trembled before the Incas and feared them.[118]

These precepts about war and supernatural sanction explain three key conflicts in the history of these Andean kings. The first goes back to the Chanca war. The standard interpretation, alluded to in part previously, emphasizes that Inca Viracocha and the heir apparent, Inca Urquo (Urcon), abandoned their palaces and retreated to Caquia Jaquijahuana in the face of an imminent Chanca attack. Inca Viracocha's youngest son, then called Inca Yupanqui (before he added "Pachacuti"), remained to defend the Incas and their followers from this threat to their sovereignty. Sometime before the attack, Tupac Inca Yupanqui had a vision in which Viracocha Pachayachachic (according to Betanzos; but later identified as the Sun), to whom he was praying, promised him victory, and so it was. After his father subsequently refused to accept the triumph and acknowledge his accomplishment, Inca Yupanqui deposed him (by some accounts), was confirmed as king in the Coricancha, and took the name Pachacuti Inca Yupanqui.[119]

A recent and innovative analysis by Ziólkowski adds the religious underpinnings to this incident. He concludes that the war started and was won as a consequence of the Inca's communication with Viracocha Pachayachachic. Among the more than two hundred other lords in the area that called themselves Capac Inca or lord and king, was Uscovilca, the leader of the Chancas, whom Sarmiento de Gamboa and Albornoz both describe as a guaca. He decided to challenge the pretentious assertion that the Inca was a god.[120] The Chanca leader demanded obedience. As a consequence, Inca Viracocha and Inca Urquo fled. Inca Yupanqui decided to stand and defend their sovereignty and the ceremonial center, called at the time the "city of Ticci Viracocha Pachayachaci." His vision promising victory gave him the confidence to meet the enemy in hand-to-hand combat. When subjugation was not forthcoming, Uscovilca decided to "test their strength" and attack to try to vanquish the Incas through battle. Uscovilca was martyred in the attempt. The Inca claimed Uscovilca's surviving subjects, stating "that he had won them in a good war," and following accepted custom, required "that they should well-serve and obey that Emperor whose people had conquered them." These acknowledged and served him.[121]

Just before a second armed encounter, Inca Yupanqui rather fatalistically boasted to a Chanca emissary that Ticci Viracocha gave victory "to whom he wanted." After the final Chanca defeat, he deposed his father and took the title of Pachacuti Inca Yupanqui Capac Yndi Curi (change of time [or reformer], King Yupanqui, son of the Sun) or Intip Churin Inca Pachacuti (son of the Sun, lord, turner of the world). When confronted by those who demanded to know the secret of his success, he identified the god in his vision as the Sun: "According to the splendor [*lumbre*] that he had seen that must have been the sun and when he approached him and the first word that he said: son do not be afraid . . . thus his followers thereafter called him son of the Sun." Subsequently, he was confirmed by the priests of the Sun in the Coricancha.[122]

At this point, Pachacuti Inca Yupanqui, the great innovator, began his religious reform. He elevated the Sun to the highest position in the state pantheon. It had predicted his victory, favored him in the contest against the Chancas, and given him legitimacy as the new ruler. This reordering meant the demotion of Viracocha, Guanacaure, and other gods to lower levels, where they would wield less power and receive less attention. Guanacaure, as related earlier, had designated Manco Capac the founder of the dynasty; and its priests, according to Ziólkowski, had served this role until Pachacuti Inca Yupanqui's coup. Thereafter, the Sun chose the king, gave power, and bestowed legitimacy. It is then that the Temple of the Sun was remodeled and a new image of the Sun, the Punchao, was installed. Hence, Punchao supported and legitimized their succession and conquests.[123]

Victory proved the favor and support of the gods for the king, a posture that some contemporary Spaniards seemed to have understood. Rafael Sánchez-Concha interprets Licenciado Hernando de Santillán, suggesting that "the inca is not just another cacique, he is a monarch tied to the Creator of all things, synonym to name God, and who gives him the right to conquer the rest of the peoples. . . . without divine favor one could not govern." Gose believes that "the test of a king's divinity was whether he could hold and expand his realm." I agree, as long as by "realm" he means hegemony over people and not jurisdiction over land or territory exclusively. In the lifetime of the king and those of his followers, this divinity or favor was periodically tested and reconfirmed. The defeated became subjects of the victor and (theoretically) accepted the new, more powerful deity as their protector and became adherents of its cult. In this sense these conflicts were not just duels between men or kings; they became cosmic struggles between guacas and the sacred forces they represented, and the contests took on the cast of holy wars.[124]

The religious angle, so ignored or deprecated by the first Iberian chroniclers, also helps us comprehend the internal dynamics of the fratricidal civil-war battles between Atahualpa and Huáscar and gives credence to Sarmiento de Gamboa's claim that there were always two candidates to compete or fight openly for capac status. A close reading of contemporary accounts indicates that in this fraternal war both Huáscar and Atahualpa claimed celestial descent and tried to win the support of their ancestors to find victory on the battlefield. As soon as Huáscar was selected, he, his mother, and sister, Chuqui Huipa, began a ritual four-day fast, which prepared them for the inauguration ceremonies. Then Huáscar celebrated the posthumous triumph of his father and, by way of legitimizing his succession, joined Guayna Capac's generals in standing on the dead Inca's spoils and prisoners of war. But this gesture did not win the support of all royal Inca lineages. There was conflict even within his own panaca over his succession. The mummy of Tupac Inca Yupanqui, his grandfather, reportedly refused to give its consent to Huáscar's projected marriage to his sister. Relatives of Atahualpa's mother, who descended from Pachacuti Inca Yupanqui, backed Atahualpa's claim.[125]

Matters did not improve. As Betanzos, an Atahualpa partisan, informs us, Huáscar was allegedly a drunk, an iconoclast, and a promiscuous rogue. He insulted his mother and threatened to take support away from the panacas, saying that the dead did not eat. In this very politicized atmosphere in which Huáscar challenged and promised an assault on the dead and their elite lineages, Atahualpa confronted his brother, initiating a ritual war between the two siblings, who both claimed to be the divine favorite. The outcome of this competition and conflict would determine who merited the ancestors' aid; who would be selected and inaugurated as the champion and next god-king, the incarnation and personification of the Sun; and who had the mandate of heaven.[126]

Hence, as the tides of war turned against Huáscar, he looked for "consolation" from his guacas, especially Guanacaure. He offered great sacrifices, presented offerings, and ordered fasts. Subsequently, he asked his consultants to beg victory from the statues of the Sun, Pachacamac, and Thunder. He wanted to know what he should do to "appease the creator." After all these efforts, danger signs continued to appear around him. But the diviners, to console him, told him that if he himself went into the field, he would win a victory over his enemies. Huáscar understood how important were penitence and sacrifice to appease the wrath of deities that must have been offended. As Atahualpa's forces approached, Huáscar looked for divine relief as the head of an infantry composed of Charcas, Collaos, Chucuitos, Condesuyus, and Antisuyus. Initially, Huáscar's armies won a battle, as predicted. Upon receiving the decapitated trophy heads of his enemies, Huáscar is reported to have said they represented the "first-fruits of the gifts that Pachacamac promised to my fasts and fears." So emboldened was he at this sure sign of divine favor that he dressed in gold to go into battle himself. So brilliant was he in the sun thus attired that he was easy for Atahualpa's generals to spot and unseat. At that point, "the battle began to weaken," his army disintegrated, and Atahualpa's forces ended victorious.[127]

Likewise, Atahualpa interpreted victories as the gods' approbation and blessing. Cieza reports that after defeating and deposing Huáscar, the young Cuzco (*el Cuzco joven*), at the battle of Quipaypán, Atahualpa, said that "his gods fought for him." His northern followers, recognizing this, adored and praised him in loud and joyous voices, crying, "Long live Ataualpa our lord Ynga, the Sun his father give him long life, and the earth permit him to tread upon it, a long time, and help him irrigate it with the blood of his enemies, and saying these things they pulled out their eyebrows, and eyelashes, and they flung them toward that direction, as a sign of sacrifice." Thereafter, the traditional nobility in the south assembled by ayllus and kin groups (*parentelas*) at a place called Quibipay Pampa to render obedience to and worship an effigy of Atahualpa oriented toward the north (where his person remained). His statue was revered and obeyed, like his person. They called the statue of Atahualpa "Ticçi Capac," lord of the last ends of the earth.[128]

At this juncture, the Spanish invaded, raiding and looting as they moved south. The earliest accounts attributed divine status to the Spanish. Natives, such as the Tallanes of the north coast, thought the Christians, coming from the sea, were messengers of Viracocha—perhaps because, in part, they seemed to be inaugurating a new era. In an anonymous text dated 1576, it is reported that Guayna Capac told Atahualpa that the yet-to-be-identified Spanish were viracochas.[129] Calancha reports that when the fat and ferocious-looking Pedro de Candia went ashore at Túmbez on the second voyage, "The Indians, surprised at his person, looked upon him as a god . . . appearing to them as no ordinary animal, or a superior enemy. The Indians believed that Candia was the son of the Sun, or come from the sky, and they took him to their Temple of the Sun."[130] The natives venerated him.[131]

Elsewhere, the Spanish were identified as children or kings of the sea (*hijos de la mar*, *reyes del mar*) and messengers of the Sun or of Ticci Viracocha. Because the Spanish were considered gods, the natives brought them gifts or sacrifices. In Túmbez, the Spanish received camelids, gold and silver beads (*chaquira*, a highly prized commodity), clothing, and several boys, because the locals thought the Spanish ate human flesh.[132] People offered eyelashes and eyebrows, which they blew in the air right in front of the Spanish. Atahualpa ordered that they be given servants and food. In Cajamarca, a translator introduced Pizarro, saying "that he came by command of God," probably confirming the natives' first assumptions. Later, Estete reports that the Spanish were given camelids, perhaps for sacrifice. When the Spanish arrived in Pachacamac, the people walked from all parts of the realm to see them, bringing gifts of gold and silver, just as they had come previously on long pilgrimages to the oracle's sanctuary bringing presents. Likewise, as Hernando de Soto and the soldier Pedro del Barco traveled south into the heartland while Atahualpa was a prisoner, the credulous gave them gifts and adored them as gods, at least until they showed themselves to be men, described as "weak of resolution, subject to lascivious tastes."[133]

Don Gonzalo Zapayco, a noble (principal) born in Atun Larao (Yauyos), testified in 1573, when he was more than seventy years old, about how he first heard of the arrival of the Spanish and native impressions of these strange apparitions. His words show how the natives interpreted what they saw and the fantastic, otherworldly aura that soon cloaked the arrival of the Europeans.

Soon after the ships on which the Marques don Francisco Pizarro and the rest of the Spanish entered Payta[,] it was said in all these kingdoms that certain bearded people had arrived in some houses floating on the sea [shown in Figure 3.12] and that they had landed and founded a town in the Valley of Tangarara [San Miguel de Piura][;] and a few days later other news arrived in this province of the Yauyos people[,] where this witness is a native and resided[,] of how those men who had come from the sea arrived at the tambo and Valley of Cajamarca and that there they had routed and taken prisoner the Inca Ataualipa[;] and that this news made all the natives of these kingdoms marvel in general of how so few men coming from the sea had done so much to take prisoner and defeat such a great lord as was the said Atabalipa who brought warriors in such quantity against his brother Guascar Ynga[;] and[,] soon after hearing what he has declared[,] messengers arrived of said Ataualipa Inga who was prisoner in the said Valley of Caxamarca with his order to all the caciques of this province of the Yauyos that they gather all the gold and silver they could in whatever form they had, even if it should be women's jewelry[,] and that they bring it quickly to the said Valley of Caxamarca where he was prisoner. . . . those men who had taken said Ataualipa prisoner brought some sheep in which they inserted themselves and that with one breath they ejected fire and they killed many Indians even though they were far away from where they were and that with the tail [*cola*] they cut a man in half and that those sheep ate gold and silver.[134]

Pizarro and his followers contributed to these fanciful stories by spreading rumors designed to reinforce native perceptions of the Spaniards' godlike qualities. Pizarro made the natives think that the horses were immortal; that they ate gold and silver (something that appeared likely, in the first era of encounter, given the metal bits they had in their mouths); and that the poitrel or breastplates (*pretales*) of bells made them stronger and fiercer. His captains, too, planted similar disinformation in native minds. Captain Alvarado, for example, addressing the people of Puerto Viejo, declared explicitly that Pizarro ("a very great and good lord") was the son of the Sun (*hijo del Sol*).[135] Pizarro later acted like the incarnation of the Sun when he "made a lord of that son [Manco Inca] of Guainacaba because he was a prudent, vivacious youth, the most senior there, . . . to whom . . . the right of lordship belonged."[136]

When Atahualpa heard news of the Spanish arrival from the cacique of Cajamarca, he recalled that Guayna Capac had gotten a similar message, but then the strangers had gone away. This time, he "was certain that the prediction of his father was now coming true." He rejoiced that these beings, whom he identified as messengers of Viracocha, had arrived in his

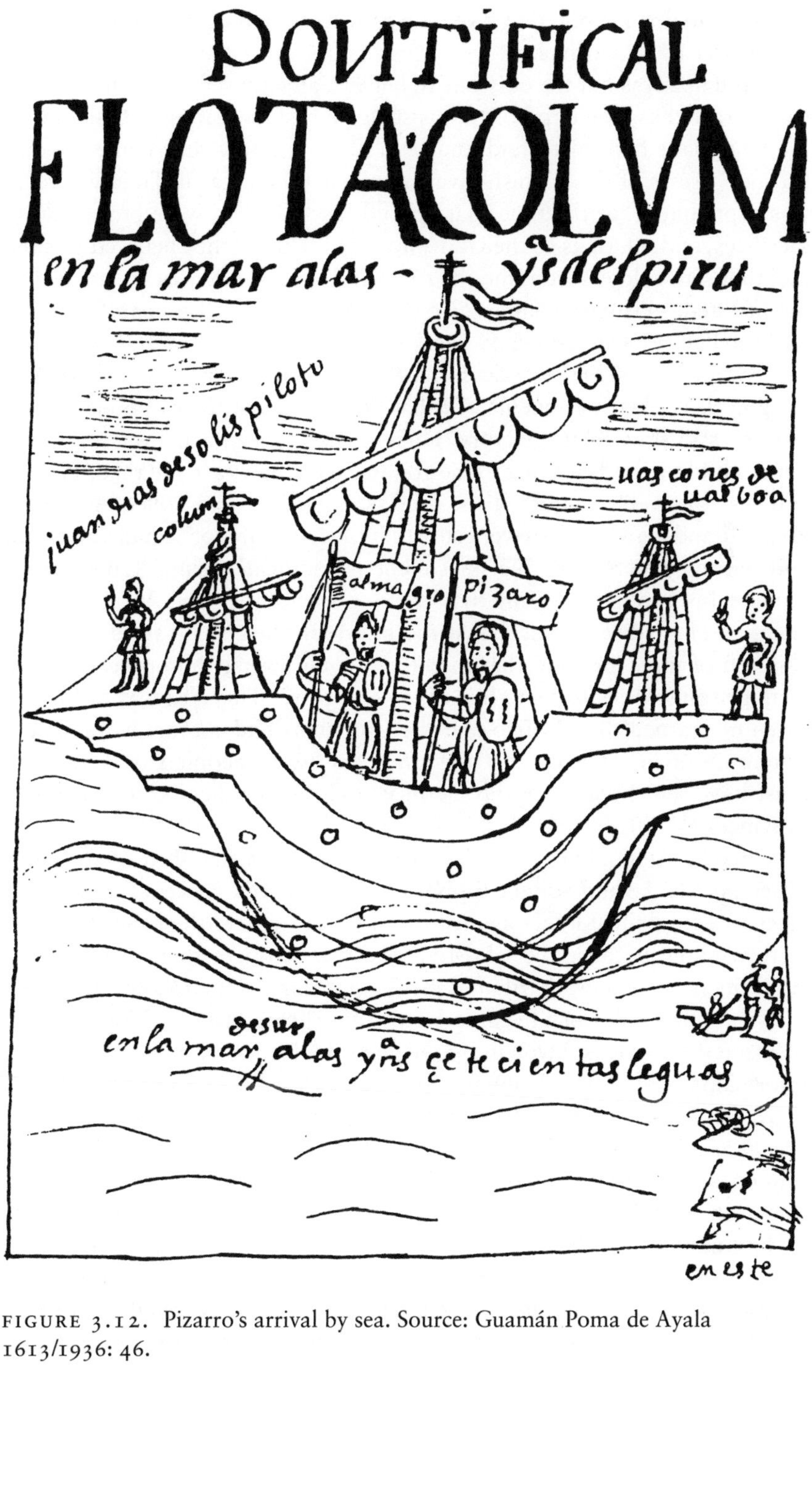

PONTIFICAL

FLOTA COLVM

en la mar alas yns del piru

juan dias de solis piloto

colum

almagro

pizaro

uascones de ualboa

en la mar de sur alas yns cetecientas leguas

en este

FIGURE 3.12. Pizarro's arrival by sea. Source: Guamán Poma de Ayala 1613/1936: 46.

time. Atahualpa proposed to give the Spanish safe passage, obedience, gifts, and service as viracochas.[137]

Atahualpa was not the only one to believe, albeit briefly, that the Spanish were viracochas, come to bolster his struggle.[138] Huáscar also thought that the Christians arrived to find and help him: "I know they come looking for me." News of the Spanish invasion reached Huáscar in Jauja where he was a prisoner, "at the time that he and his followers were busy making sacrifices, and offerings to the God Viracocha that . . . they believed was the idol that sent soldiers from the sky to defend against offences and to avenge the insulted." Primary sources give the reasons for such preparatory ceremonies before war. Andeans sacrificed birds of the *puna* (high, cold, windswept plateau in the Andes mountains), camelids, and dogs "to weaken the guacas of their opponents . . . that the Huacas of their opponents lose power" and thus ensure victory. Huáscar had just finished offering these items, children, and clothing to the god when the news arrived that "Pizarro and his followers conquered the land, taking lives and collecting gold." Huáscar and his aids "were very sure that the God Viracocha had sent them, and that they were from the skies come to vindicate them." Calancha rephrases his thoughts succinctly: "Having heard the God Viracocha his clamors, He had sent him, that without a doubt he and his followers were children of this God, and that thus they would avenge him, releasing him from prison and restoring to him his sovereignty." This idea was confirmed when he learned that Pizarro and the Christians had captured Atahualpa. Therefore, it made sense that the strangers "were people that Viracocha must have sent because of the sacrifice." This assessment spread into the provinces.[139]

Whereas Atahualpa's victories over Huáscar had confirmed to native observers that he had "divine support," the Spaniards' success and victories at this stage of the conflict against the Andeans upheld the belief that they were winning because the Christian god was stronger than their own.[140] Andeans became temporarily resigned. According to their expectation and the customary rules of the game of warring spirits, they had lost, so now they and their guacas, "won in a good war," had to serve. In fact, Betanzos's informants related that Atahualpa was predestined for failure. He, accordingly, foreshadows Atahualpa's defeat with the story of his split ear, interpreted as a bad omen. The fact that the king could not end the Spaniards' raiding and looting probably undermined his political control and cast doubt on his role as effective religious intermediary. Likewise, the incident at the Guamachuco oracular shrine presaged his overthrow. These facts and the early belief that the Spanish were gods seems to be an explanation or an excuse for the Inca's failure to overcome the Spanish, as weighty, effective, and convincing in its explicative power as the more common explanations for the relative ease of Spanish conquest, such as technological superiority and disease. Defeat was given a transcendental interpretation: the ancestors had abandoned the Incas or they were no match for the Christian god.[141]

The arrival of the Spanish complicated a conflict between two rivals for divine status and converted it into a conflict between the partisans of the Christian god and the congregation of Sun worshippers. "Dios" or God had intervened on the Spanish Christians' and their partisans' behalf and vanquished the guacas and the Andeans.[142]

The Andean witnesses might have recognized the pattern from their mytho-histories, which recalled the passage into a new age following the defeat of one god by another. Manco Capac had founded a new era. Multiple Cuzcos had predicted just such a cataclysm. Disease, which had killed Guayna Capac and devastated the Andean population before 1532, brought havoc and psychological uncertainty and announced that another cycle was being initiated. Andeans in the 1520s and 1530s were experiencing a pachacuti, a cyclical destruction and restoration of the world. With this realization and the anxiety that it must have caused, most organized opposition ended. Natives abandoned many Incaic ceremonial centers. Only intermittent, sporadic, and guerrilla-like resistance continued until the revolt led by Manco Inca. During Manco Inca's siege of the Spanish villa of Cuzco, the natives thought that burning the church would defeat and destroy the Spanish God: "The Indians really wanted to burn down our church, that, they said, that if they burned it, that they could kill us all." But this effort failed. Some say that the Andeans did not even seriously try to defend themselves "because they believed that the invaders were sent by the god Viracocha." This mirrored the Spanish belief that God had destined them to find America and thus convert the heathen and save their souls.[143]

Thus, in cosmic struggles such as these, victory at arms was commonly construed as the favor of the gods. Such successes led Pachacuti Inca Yupanqui to boast to the assembled lords that "they could see that the Sun was on his side." To celebrate the defeat of the Hatun Collas, Pachacuti Inca Yupanqui had a Temple of the Sun built there, and he sent word of his triumph to his followers to tell them to offer great sacrifices to the Sun and other guacas—as if to thank them for the victory.[144] In the conflict between the Sun worshippers and the Christians, both shared a faith in the religious underpinnings of their power. Victories were constant renewals and confirmations of divine favor that gave each faction the confidence to continue the struggle and sometimes win.

Alternatively, adverse news was a sign that the Andean ruler was losing or had lost favor. The news that his forces had retreated from the battle against the Caranguis caused Guayna Capac "great pain, and this was not so much for the loss of his brother and followers as for being on the verge of having his name and reputation fall into an irremediable namelessness and eternal opprobrium." After Manco Inca gave up the siege of the city of Cuzco and lost to the Guancas in their second encounter, he told his followers that he was no longer their lord; he gave up and retreated, telling his followers that they should return to their fields and serve the Spanish. His actions and words showed that he thought that he had lost his divine mandate and the support of his gods, his ancestors, his allies, the purported source of his authority and power. He had been reduced to the status of *atisca*, which Cristobal de Albornoz, an ecclesiastic from Cuzco who probably wrote in the 1580s, defined as a defeated guaca or one that had lost all or part of its power. The populace "did not value" such defeated gods. Andeans believed that deities had a force, the calpa, which they could and did pass on to their successors and worshippers. They could also lose it when defeated. Álvarez writes that "when they entered their battles, the army carried their [g]uacas with them to be aided by them, and when one side fled defeated, they said that the [g]uaca went defeated." Thus, to the reasons that Manco Inca's siege of the Spanish city of Cuzco failed must be added cosmological beliefs.[145]

The ideas that the gods favored one side or the other and that claims of divinity were manifested and proven on the battlefield explain why, when the natives were winning, they fought on strongly. At the first signs of weakness, they fled, abandoning the pursuit and defecting, or changed sides. "These Indians are characterized by one thing: that when they are winning they are all devils, and when they flee, they are wet chickens, and as here they wanted victory, seeing us retreat, they pursued it with great valor." In the war against the Chancas, "upon seeing their principal guaca in enemy hands, they lost their courage and started to flee followed closely by the Inca's troops." Analogously, a defeated god was one with diminished power. Once Atahualpa had been taken prisoner by the Spanish, despite being housed in the local Temple of the Sun, his subjects were slow to obey. "Because he was a prisoner," he told Pizarro, "the Indians did not follow his orders." His vassals, Indians, captains, and high lords of his kingdom abandoned him and did not serve him. He had to order them not to flee, to come and serve him.[146]

Thus, in such struggles as these, success bred power and brought the potential of more victories; whereas failure initiated a crisis of confidence, the questioning of success and the legitimacy of the power wielding, which, should it continue, would lead to a turning point that assured final disaster. Any one Andean ruler succeeded until he failed. To capture a lord and hold his guaca was to assert that your god was stronger than the other or that you had the god's favor. At such a time of realignment and juncture, another lord could rise up and claim divine sponsorship, as did the chief of Charcas,

Catari Apasca, in 1537–38. As the proclaimed new son of the Sun, he led the Collaguas and Lupacas into battle at the Río Desaguadero against Hernando and Gonzalo Pizarro, only to fail. Meanwhile, the Spanish believed their god had given them victory.[147]

These ideas about spirit wars between guacas did not disappear when the Inca was defeated. They are echoed anew in the information on the native rebel movement called the Taqui Onqoy of the 1560s. One informant states that

> in the said visitation the said Canon Cristobal de Albornoz found a new sect that was planted all over the land among the Indians and natives that is called Taqui Onqoy, and the basis of it was the generalized Indian belief that all the guacas of the kingdom, all those that the Christians had burned and destroyed, had resuscitated . . . and that these had united to give battle to God Our Lord, who they already considered defeated and that the Spanish of this land would end quickly because the guacas would send illnesses to kill them all, all of whom were mad at the Indians because they had become Christians, and if the Indians did not want sicknesses to befall them or death but health and the increase of their goods they had to repudiate Christianity . . . and they were not to use Christian names nor eat nor dress things of Castilla believing that God was powerful for having made Castilla and the Spanish and the foodstuffs and the things that there they raised, and that the defeat of the Indians and the reduction of this kingdom by Marquez Pizarro was because God then had defeated the Andean guacas, but that now all had resuscitated to give him battle and defeat him.[148]

The Power of Cosmology

The realization that religious ideology or cosmology played such an important underlying and foundational role in the history of the Incas and the success of their government and rule leads to several implications and conclusions. First, cosmology provides the framework and legitimizing ideology for the political economy, which was based in its simplest form on asymmetric reciprocity and redistribution. It justified the rule and elite status of members of one southern Andean ethnic group. Their genealogical fiction promised membership in a divinely favored and privileged kindred. It also provided for the establishment and enforcement of customary law, which guided behavior. To be part of the solar cult's congregation or the constituency of this one expanding, southern state theoretically guaranteed (in the long run) peace, prosperity, access to sumptuary goods, and basic foodstuffs in times of need. If taxpayers worked to feed the gods, they, in turn, would be fed. It was a situation where a growing "us" contrasted sharply to the outsiders, the unbelievers, the foreigners, the "them."

Second, the flexibility of this constructed cosmological system allowed subject peoples to maintain their customary allegiances and loyalties, to continue the worship of their own ancestors, as long as they also revered the imposed imperial ones. The king demonstrated his power, in part, by controlling and supervising the service of the guacas among all his subjects. He fed them and showed them generosity.[149] To demonstrate his prophetic aptitude, the Inca questioned the guacas. Their answers were his way of learning about the concerns of his provincial and non-Inca followers. Thus, the incorporation of local ancestral gods provided the Incas with listening posts and sources of intelligence at the heart of major ethnic groups. He thus could gauge the pulse (the support or resistance) of various subject ethnic units. Inca queries gave the adherents of these sectarian cults the, sometimes dangerous, opportunity to voice their opinions and concerns, albeit in a coded, (sometimes) ambiguous, and ritualistic fashion. To be too blunt, to displease, might invite the wrath of the more powerful with a correspondingly swift eclipse or even the destruction of the source of local abundance.[150]

But this cosmological flexibility proved to be a fundamental failure of the Inca design. The late fifteenth and sixteenth centuries were times when the Inca state was in the process of consolidating recent gains and incorporations. The Inca attempt to impose an unfamiliar language (on non-Quechua speakers) and unaccustomed credos on local ancestor worshippers was a means to foster a new, broader identity, a sense of Incaness, to make the newly subjugated accept the one-law and one-birth ideal. The Inca was not strictly replacing one belief system, just augmenting, enlarging, extending, and redirecting the traditional local one.[151]

Yet the attempt to graft imperial ideology onto a more parochial one served, in some cases, to clarify and strengthen a local counter-ideology, because the acceptance of the graft implied consent to an expanded notion of selfhood and a rerouting or redeployment of labor. The Inca promises of potential economic rewards, hospitality, and added security were insufficient to offset the hesitance to accept supernatural additions and substitutions and compensate for the expected contributions to the economic base of the victorious group. Especially in the north, where the Cuzco's hegemony and induction into the larger whole were recent, this endeavor to instill personal confidence in the new slate of ancestor gods was fragile and incomplete. Provincial peoples clung to their more comfortable beliefs in their founders and loyalty to their kindred. There was resistance to the loss of autonomy and the imposition of a new identity from without and above.

Thus, "before a first Cuzqueño military expedition," the priests and people of Guaylas and their allies resisted.

> They revolted and convoked one ethnicity with others, putting aside their particular interests to support a common defense; and thus they gathered and responded saying that all wanted to die before receiving new laws and customs and adoring new gods, that they did not want, that they were fine with their ancient ones, that

belonged to their ancestors, known for many centuries, and that the Inca should remain content with what he had tyrannized, because with religious zeal he had usurped the dominion of all the curacas who he had dominated.

The war was difficult and almost lost, but the Cuzqueños eventually defeated the defenders of local gods and freedoms. A number of their captured priests were marched south and defrocked, and a new priesthood was sent to instruct the provincial members in the ways of the solar cult. This coalition of local peoples resisted too because of the recently imposed obligations—military and labor service. In conquest and wars between polities, as noted previously, "it was customary that conquered subjects had to plant corn, coca, and chili pepper fields and deliver the harvest to their conqueror."[152]

In some cases, local counter-ideologies were muted only temporarily. Reluctance to accept and resistance to the Inca ideological fiction crystallized in the innumerable revolts, which erupted at perceived unstable points in the Inca trajectory. One dangerous period was the time when the Inca and his armies were engaged at other fronts. Thus, under Tupac Inca Yupanqui, "a large part of this kingdom had rebelled," while his armies were conquering Chile. There were other troublesome times during the uncertain interregnum periods between the death of one incumbent and the installation of his successor. Tupac Inca Yupanqui feared revolt of the Collasuyus and Antisuyus after his father, Pachacuti Inca Yupanqui, died. When Pachacuti Inca Yupanqui passed away, the Antis rebelled again. To forestall provincial rebellions during months the locals might deem a period of imperial weakness, non-Inca peoples were notified only after a new king had been recognized.[153]

In addition, under Guayna Capac many provinces had risen, "realizing that as sons of the Sun they had ruled them depriving them of freedoms that they had had, holding them in much submission, and they saw them as mortal men like them. . . . they rose up each day and they rebelled." One might speculate, based on the last statement, that the cosmological fiction propagandized through officially controlled state channels had been exposed as a hoax and a fraud. Other reasons why revolts were always menacing include the fact that "they were not attentive to anything but robbing and spilling blood, they did not put garrisons in the towns that they conquered," and when they did, the troops stationed there were "harmful and vicious with the women."[154]

These battles for themselves and their ancestral spirits added to the construction of identity. Benedict Anderson shows that "all communities larger than primordial villages of face-to-face contact are imagined." Those in the north may be connected to those in the south, whom they never see through the Inca and the elasticity of genealogy and clientelism. In the Andes, boundaries of sometimes fragmented social groups were defined by kinship (real, imagined, or constructed) plus religious adherence. Guacas were symbols of common origin and collective identity. Anderson says that "in the older imagining, where states were defined by centres, borders were porous and indistinct, and sovereignties faded imperceptibly into one another. Hence, . . . the ease with which pre-modern empires and kingdoms were able to sustain their rule over immensely heterogeneous, and often not even contiguous, populations for long periods of time." [155]

But the notion of identity was dynamic and complex because of the polytheistic and flexible nature of the Andeans' supernatural allegiances. Individuals might identify and ally with one native lord and the associated ancestors of his ethnic group yet also be expected to adopt a wider identity in the face of an extraethnic "other." Although these individuals were the subjects of the Inca and worshippers at the ceremonials of the Sun, the Moon, and the imperial malquis, they were also subjects of the ethnic curaca and devotees of his local progenitor. If we multiply these consciousnesses and affiliations by the number of guacas in the pantheon, we see that a person's allegiance would be divided, overlap, and even potentially conflict.[156]

In short, the Inca expansion had proceeded too rapidly. The generals trounced and advanced without completely winning over and soundly indoctrinating the last group that had been annexed and inducted into the Inca fold. Bonds and allegiances fostered by reciprocity and redistribution did not hold. Provincial peoples recently injected into the imperial lineage constantly tested the Inca's purported divine legitimacy. The ties between the various ethnicities were few. The mechanisms for transmitting imperial ideology to the provincial subjects were weak. There seem to have been few state missionaries, and although in theory the shared fellowship of the Inca solar cult superseded local ancestor worship, in practice, the first allegiance of traditional leaders and shrine attendants was to their local guacas. The fragility of royal propaganda was compounded if ethnicities had not experienced the benefits of being solar-connected. They may not have enjoyed the benevolence of the personification of the Sun when it counted most, when they were in dire need of help due to earthquake, frost, drought, or the ravages of an El Niño cycle.[157] Such failures highlight and underscore the fact that expansion and domination by persuasion, force, or threat of force were easier and faster than changing people's minds, allegiances, and adherences; or that consent is more powerful, in the long run, than force. This is one factor that helps explain the Incas' short-lived regime.[158]

MacCormack's conclusion that the Inca religion faded so quickly in the hinterland after 1532 shows how shallow their religio-political myth's acceptance had been outside the southern heartland. The Inca gods diminished with the state. The people reverted to the worship of their own vigilant, life-sustaining ancestors in the provinces, especially the more isolated ones. Local religion persisted, surreptitious and concealed, of necessity, under the care and feeding of the curaca, as will be shown in the next chapter. Romero relates that in Vilcabamba, ancestor worship continued into the 1570s. Elsewhere it still existed in the eighteenth century.[159] Ironically, local peoples recouped political and religious independence only to be newly subjugated by the Christians, who baptized them into another cult, which was reinforced by missionaries and secular priests. Surely, this must have confirmed the native people's belief in the cyclical nature of their lives.

To overcome such provincial predilections, forestall discontent-signaling insubordinations, counter the image of a weak state, and consolidate power—especially after the death of his predecessor—the incoming god-king made periodic visitations, accompanied as he traveled by idols, figures, and guacas, including the statue of the Sun. His legitimacy was introduced, constructed, and reinforced through ceremonials and action. He stopped at provincial ritual centers, such as Huánuco Pampa, to display hospitality and bestow favors and largesse; to meet, engage, and confirm curacas and reconstitute relations with these provincial leaders; and to renegotiate terms of service and organize work projects. Hence, there was a need for ceremonial complexes built on the model of the original throughout the empire.[160] Such regional centers and royal progresses were attempts to ingratiate himself with his subjects and, more important, to reinforce belief systems, "to recast the Inca cosmos," or to establish a "new Tawantinsuyo." Such customary and repeated efforts amounted to the reestablishment of the empire in each reigning generation and emphasizes the personalistic and patrimonial nature of the imperial base.[161]

Thus, state and local affiliations and loyalties were conceived in religious, not strictly secular administrative and political, terms. The state was more a congregation of occasionally like-worshipping individuals than a political constituency of friends, allies, and interest groups. The Inca visited where he was acknowledged or sought to be recognized as overlord and sovereign. The king's ability to know through divination and to influence through prayer and sacrifice the will of the ancestral spirits legitimized the conceptualization of political power in his person. Protection against danger and fruitful harvests was thought to be made possible by his sacrifices and the rituals he performed. People who benefited from the cult were part of the theocratic polity, where one danced before and sang to the gods as part of worship.[162] Religion, politics, and kinship were metaphysically fused in a state where people, not place, were the basis of a monarch's power. The Inca, to use Frazer's concept of a divine king, stood at the center of a cosmic and social order that was controlled by magic. The government rested on control of population, but authority in this case rested not on election by the people but on election by the sacred (through their spokespersons).

4 *To Feed and Be Fed: Curacal Legitimacy and Cosmology*

> Ancestor lords creators of foodstuffs irrigation canals and springs you who have cultivated fields receive this offering that your children give you so that there might be good harvests and good food.
>
> Father Huari, eat this, drink this, so that there might be bountiful fields, that there might be good harvests, to avoid suffering.
>
> —Seventeenth-Century Native Prayers

Plagues, comets, and other harbingers of trouble—and above all, the resounding defeat of the Incas by the Christians (retold in Chapter 3)—made manifest to the native Andean peoples the revealed truth that the gods ultimately governed and determined the fate of the living. The forces of the Sun and his celestial family were no match for the Christian god. In this context of disarticulation, disaccreditation, "destructuration" (to use Nathan Wachtel's term) of the ancient imperial regime, and of loss, provincial Andeans continued the worship of the ancestors of their kin, confident that their own antecedents, who shared their bloodlines and represented their origins, would be more sensitive to their quotidian needs.[1]

Cosmology and Legitimacy

Therefore, in this chapter I focus on the roles that the ancestors played in the lives of the provincial peoples they represented. In many ways, the local malquis' participation in and impact on local lives was analogous to that of the celestial powers and royal mummies in the Coricancha and Haucaypata on the fate of the divine kings and the empire as a whole. The form and functions were the same; the scale, of course, was different, though proportionate. The spotlight accordingly shifts to the fixture of Andean history at the local level, the figure of the paramount lord or curaca, the leader of a group of people who acknowledged common ancestors, and his orchestration of the cults of these progenitors.[2]

I am not the first to write on the curacas. Scholars have studied this ubiquitous personage in several ways. Some students have focused on individuals, such as don Gonzalo of Lima or don Juan de Collique. Others have highlighted curacas in one region. Succession has been another topic of interest. Recently, Martínez Cereceda has published on the insignia and characteristics, material and otherwise, of these chiefs. Guillermo Cock Carrasco, Franklin Pease, Karen Powers, and this author touch on the "wealth"—understood etically and emically, respectively—of these leaders. Others concentrate on the exercise of a chieftain's political power—his duty to serve as spokesman and champion of his subjects, his roles as guardian of tradition, his service as a font of justice, and his power over life and death.[3]

My contribution will build on these studies but offer a focused, analytical vision of how provincial peoples conceptualized the curaca's roles and his legitimacy both before and after 1532. As noted previously, to European and Western eyes, the most visible role of the traditional, pre-Hispanic curaca was as a representative and administrator of his people.[4] In Spanish chronicles, early encomienda grants, and colonial administrative records, this chiefly personage appeared as the key figure in the management and allocation of subject labor and access to natural resources. He expedited his people's work on ancestral fields, at the seashore, and in the mines to produce goods that he could redistribute or send the Inca. His executive skills materialized visibly through the well-being and number of his subjects. In return, they worked to support his household and activities. Thus, the native leader was locked into a mutually dependent relationship with the led. Those curacas who lacked the wisdom, interpersonal skills, and executive ability to guarantee surplus production to satisfy obligations to the state and to provide hospitality and be generous to his followers did not fulfill local reciprocal expectations and were deposed as being incapable of rule or "por ser incapaz." Another, judged more likely to live up to corresponding commitments, took his place. Such obligations explain the curaca's apparent and well-documented administrative and material basis of power and the most obvious meaning of Guamán Poma de Ayala's oft-repeated phrase "good government" (*buen gobierno*).[5]

His important ceremonial roles, which were tied in large part to ancestor worship, served concomitantly as both enabling and manifestation of his heritage of power and legitimacy. These ritual roles included a duty to serve the larger community, a group that from the Andean perspective included the departed. I will argue that their material well-being convinced his followers of their lord's supernatural support, although to many native peoples the spiritual was so tightly enmeshed with the material that to divorce the concepts is to misrepresent their understandings. Like the emperor, the local curaca was responsible also for maintaining cult traditions.[6]

His intermediation with the ancestor-gods assured his followers health, fertility, and subsistence. Long after 1532, certain native peoples still held that without the love and favor of the ancestors neither the curaca nor his clients and kin could hope to live comfortably and without disease or disaster. Abundance and well-being reflected the spiritual forces and validity bestowed upon local leaders by their progenitors. In comparison, as at the imperial levels, disaster was attributed to the curaca's incompetence or transgression. Thus, integral to the basic and manifest material basis of legitimacy was a closely linked, but less obvious (to Spanish eyes), spiritual component, which explained, rationalized, and justified the curaca's status as an acceptable bridge between his followers and their antecedents. This analysis brings into focus the undeclared and silent, but emically understood, meaning of Guamán Poma de Ayala's phrase "buen gobierno" and expands its connotations for non-Andeans from its material and secular associations. It rounds out and completes its intended implications, restoring its spiritual dimension. Thus, the addition of the cosmological overlay deepens our understanding of the bases of legitimacy in native society.[7]

This analysis of the curaca's role in the ancestor cults at the lineage and community levels relies primarily on locally generated sources. Most early chroniclers neglected local polities, so preoccupied were they with the challenge of describing and understanding the socioeconomic and political structure of the empire their imagination designed. Most included little detailed information on curacas and curacazgos, and then only in passing. Because there are few equivalents to the chronicles for local histories, I therefore use local-level manuscript sources, most particularly records of Crown inspections, reviews of malfeasance in office (*residencias*), detailed résumés and witnessing of individual services to the king (*probanzas de méritos y servicios*), and various and sundry records generated by judicial and administrative institutions. Important additions to these are the reports of early missionaries, especially the Augustinians and the Jesuits, and the records of the extirpation of idolatries (*idolatriás and hechicerías*). Information on the purported survivals of Andean religions begins to appear within a decade of contact. It becomes more available with each successive ten-year span. Unlike the sources on the Inca state, a good portion of which are early (that is, before 1570), the bulk of the detailed material at the local level, which actually gives voice to individuals, comes from the seventeenth century. Their use can be justified by the fact that this facet of native culture is relatively conservative; and my goal is not to separate native survivals from Spanish introductions but to glean from the records the outlines of their cosmological visions. Many of these sources reflect the Catholics' purpose of "knowing" the adversary (personified by the devil to many peninsular Christians), so that it could be extirpated or eliminated. Ironically, it is in these records of alleged and overstated wrongdoing (from the Spanish point of view) that the voices of individual natives as protagonists of history are heard most clearly.[8]

The purpose for which these documents were generated led to exaggerations and biases similar to those found in the chronicles. Whereas the chroniclers often magnified Spanish military accomplishments to impress the king and the Council of the Indies with the commitment, audaciousness, and valor of the conquerors and first settlers, the distortions and hyperbole found in idolatry records had different aims and audience. Some records read like a scorecard, recording how many guacas and malquis were uncovered and destroyed among each ethnic group, without much effort to understand their significance and associations. Large numbers were meant to impress and advance ecclesiastical careers. The underlying reasons for the effort to weed out practices labeled pagan and infidel and associated with the devil, in some cases, were the directives and pleas of a fanatical archbishop and the parallel self-interest of the extirpators. Although most reports on these investigations pick up the tint of a Christian filter, they are nonetheless welcome additions to the other sources for the detailed descriptions of persistent practices, beliefs, and values that they provide.[9]

We are indeed fortunate to have these, because as Father Bartolomé Álvarez stated in the late 1580s in his recently found and published *Memorial*, the parish priest who tried to correct or eliminate the surviving indigenous practices among his parishioners was condemned vociferously, avoided, or even worse. A manuscript in the Archbishop's Archive of Cuzco tells the story of a priest who was rejected and ultimately deprived of his position by the locals, who continued to dance, sing, drink at, and worship a nearby mountain (cerro). Priests and their assistants were also aware of the danger that they might encounter if they pushed too hard for compliance to the introduced Christian doctrines or otherwise meddled in the sacred realm of the natives. One energetic priest wrote of his fear of returning to the church of Cochamarca after he tried to uproot traditional practices in 1621. He said that the natives hated him and refused to go to mass. They stoned his assistant and surrounded his house with the intention of burning it. Both subsisted solely on eggs for fear that the natives would poison them with other food. In other instances, thoughts of murder were not out of the question. The people of Guamachuco killed Marcos, the translator for the Augustinians, for revealing their secret religious practices to the fathers (*padres*). MacCormack reminds us that circa 1680 the people of Atun Yauyos planned to murder the parish priest so they could follow the rites of their pre-Hispanic religion with more freedom. Millones writes of a curaca in Ayacucho a few years later who was accused of killing a priest who had died "bewitched" (*hechizado*).[10]

In contrast, the lenient priest with a live-and-let-live attitude, who looked away and closed his eyes to these survivals, was loved and respected. This dilemma led to the priest's connivance to ignore, excuse, or dismiss. Álvarez continues, saying that investigative reporting was difficult also because the natives were very good at hiding their beliefs and practices. The fact that native religion, albeit changed, survived indoctrination and intermittent persecution into the seventeenth century and beyond shows how deeply rooted, conservative, vibrant, resonating, and strong were these local legacies.[11]

Faith of Our Fathers

Like the Incas, the provincial peoples the Spanish encountered had a slate of gods that they claimed as their progenitors. As in pre–Pachacuti Inca Yupanqui times, each ethnicity, each moiety, and each lineage had its guacas, leading sometimes to the bewilderment of the Spanish. It would be both tiring to list and tedious to read a full accounting of the deities or guacas of all the polities and lineages for which information is available.[12] Therefore, examples of the foci of worship of a sampling of ethnicities will suffice to show the diversity and depth of their beliefs and how these changed over time.[13]

Miscellaneous references describe the variety of indigenous beliefs and practices in the mid-sixteenth century on the coast of what became the viceroyalty of Peru. Pedro Pizarro wrote that in Puerto Viejo in the far north, the inhabitants adored stones and idols of wood and, by mandate of the Inca, the Sun (*por mandado del Ynga, al sol*).[14] Coastal peoples also worshipped stones that Marco A. Cabero called guardian deities (*dioses tutelares*, or *alecpong* in the local Mochica language). The worship of these stones, particular to each lineage and representing their first and founding ancestors, explains in part why, despite significant contact with Spanish travelers, many coastal peoples still did not take communion in 1561.[15]

A related practice that generated much comment was human sacrifice. The Túmbez, according to Juan Ruiz de Arce, sacrificed Spanish prisoners to their gods during the first months after contact. Their neighbors, the Tallanes, offered small children to the ocean and the moon, which, in contrast to the Incas, they believed were more powerful deities than the sun (see Figure 4.1). Further south near Trujillo, Father Álvarez reported that a natural "calamity," which the natives attributed to punishment "for the interaction that they had . . . with Christian things, and because they have cut down somewhat on the ancient and usual sacrifices," led to ritualized murder. To appease the wrath of their ancestors, these coastal peoples kidnapped a noble child, a native of the highlands, who had been taken to Lima to serve a Spaniard. When the moon came out on an indicated night, they hit the lad in the head and sprinkled his blood on the face and head of the

FIGURE 4.1. Sacrifice of the Chinchaysuyus. Source: Guamán Poma de Ayala 1613/1936: 266.

lords and natives in attendance. After dancing and singing, they gave his life to the moon.[16]

These sketchy references are greatly enhanced by the earliest systematic report on native religion that was written by Augustinian missionaries to the Guamachuco people. They reported that in the 1550s, their charges worshipped a creator, called Ataguju, who made the land and sky and ruled from above. He created two guacas: Sagad zabra (Sugad-cabra) and Vaungrabrad (Uciozgabrad), who were responsive to prayers for the health and fertility of both humans and livestock. Ataguju also created two servants, who were equated with the saints or thought of as intermediaries (*intercesores*): Uvigaicho and Vustiqui. They could be approached for children, camelids (sheep, *ovejas*), corn, and necessities.[17] The natives also worshipped Catequil, of Chapter 3 fame, the local equivalent of the thunder god and a famous oracle, which had been destroyed by Inca Atahualpa. So important was Catequil that after Atahualpa departed, pieces of the original idol were recovered from the river where they had been discarded, taken to a house where they were dressed, and subsequently moved to a cave in the mountains. At mid-sixteenth century, the Guamachucos still worshipped its hilltop location despite the missionary presence.[18]

The remainder and most significant portion of this Augustinian report reads like a catalog, listing the names of guacas and describing their powers—for example, Llaiguen for water, Guaillo for help spinning thread for fine cloth, and Casiapoma for war. Some were worshipped specifically by one group (for example, Quispeguanayai, son of Catequil, by the Cumbicos [makers of fine wool cloth] for good dyes). Others were worshipped by seven or eight lineages or might have an extraregional following and be a pilgrimage destiny, such as Llaiguen. The Augustinians end their narrative by writing, almost boastfully, that they had found three thousand idols, a way to distinguish themselves from their rivals, the Dominicans and Franciscans, who "have not worked much and uncovered many idols."[19]

Padre Álvarez's *Memorial*, which covers the decades of the 1570s and 1580s, is equally self-serving and informative. He bases it on over ten years' experience living on the altiplano near Lake Titicaca but excuses his relative lack of detail, blaming it on the dissimilitudes and secrecy of his parishioners. He says that "the Indians cover up one for the other; the curacas and principal lords hide them for their own ends and work so that nothing can be known." He apologizes for his own failures at conversion, complaining that "the Indians are complete unbelievers . . . even though some are baptized." They resist calls to attend mass, he continues, and are not Christians.[20]

He exaggerates when he says that "from the sky and moon below there is not a thing that they do not adore. . . . There are no things that they do not adore, and all the things that they adore they adore out of fear that they have of the things that they adore." In this vein he continues, writing that they worship the sun, moon, and stars, at least the first of which was an Inca imposition. Natives also celebrated and adored the thunder; the rainbow; and agricultural products and animals, such as the condor and the puma. But the principal veneration, he admits, was reserved for the guacas, stone figures of rulers or principal men, the people's ancestors. Each people and each ayllu had its guacas, some placed atop the highest, hardest-to-scale peaks, so they would be out of reach of the Spanish. They worshipped the surrounding hills and mountains because their guacas were there or because their ancestors spoke to them or frightened them there. Guacas were portable. They moved when the group moved and were carried into battle for support and strength against their enemies.[21]

A 1613 report centered on the Huachos and Yauyos is much more detailed and explicit on the persistence of native tradition. Here the author writes that the natives "have not been well catechized and taught the things of our faith, nor have they lost their ancient rites and native ceremonies of their huacas and advisers (*villacs*); instead, given the little preaching and teaching of the clergy, they have increased their faith in idolatries and superstitions." The excuses given are that there are only two missionaries to preach to the people of the nineteen named towns, which are "surrounded by high and towering mountains"; the towns are dispersed and distant from each other; and the roads from one to the other are bad. Furthermore, whatever the Catholic priests said was contradicted by the native authorities and kept hidden. The natives were portrayed as fanatical in this regard. They believed that if they revealed their secret religion to the Spanish, the natives would be punished with hunger, disease, and death, or perhaps, even worse, they would be condemned, shunned, or murdered. A curaca principal was poisoned because he had converted to Christianity and no longer believed in the traditional gods. Two other native lords and practitioners were killed for revealing their ancient practices to the Spanish.[22]

Nonetheless, the insistent and unrelenting missionaries were able to learn the names of the native gods: Pariacaca, Tambraico, Auquichanca, and his son Cuniavillca. These drew adherents from as far away as Cuzco and were celebrated regularly four times a year. Besides these, each town had a principal guaca (*cuncahuaca*), which was likened to a patron saint, and each ayllu and parcialidad had a lineage spirit and symbol (*ayllu-huaca*). There were several types of other gods, called *chancas*, *mayhuas*, *canllamas*, *ingas*, and *pichiges*, which were named without elaboration, except to say that they were inherited from one generation to the next. They also revered guacas of the fields (*chacra-chomas*, *saramamas*, and *inga-mamas*) and others that they found unattended on the roads, crossroads (*encrucijadas*), or deserts because their ayllus were extinct. These last were thought to bring good fortune to a lineage. They also venerated rivers, springs, irrigation canals, colored birds and llamas, corn, and thunder and lightning.[23]

As the Augustinians and Padre Álvarez point out, a major part of their religion focused on the ancestors, especially on the mummies of their authorities, which were considered guacas. They stole their buried bodies from the parish churches and took them to the ravines, passes (*quebradas*), and crags (peñas), where they idolized them day and night for days, leaving them at the end of the festivities with a great amount of food and drink. Thereafter, these cherished spirits and fonts of energy, who received offerings of clothes, silver, livestock, and food, and who had persons dedicated to their service, advised their adherents through their religious specialists.[24]

About ten years later, another priest, Licenciado Rodrigo Hernández Príncipe, visited the Recuay. He was the third extirpator to approach them in the never-ending colonial pursuit of evidence of persisting idolatrous practices. The first such priest was Fray Francisco (Cano?), who found and burned their idols and mummies circa 1551; the second was don Fernando de Avendaño, who did the same some two or three decades later.[25] Hernández Príncipe scolded the Recuay for having hidden their idols and malquis from his predecessors and having continued their worship. He called the apostasy a common malady (*mal común*), because whole lineages were involved and united in the veneration and reverence of these forces. He recognized one reason for their secrecy: "The son that knew feared his father and grandfather, and the latter feared the principal lords and head of the town; who, out of fear that someone might discover their idolatry, concealed the beliefs of the community, so that as a consequence nothing was ever revealed not even in the penitential act."[26]

He says that his investigation faltered at first, until a few of the Recuay realized their error and began to reveal their secrets, especially "the surname of their own huacas that they all usually took as last names." He subsequently learned that the two moieties each had a separate creator god. The Llacuaz livestock raisers adored the thunder god (or lightning, *el Rayo*) in its three manifestations—Llíviac, Thunder; Námoc, his father; and Uchu Llíviac, his son—"from whom all these llacuases Indians pretend to descend."[27] The Guari farmers worshipped the first settlers of the region and, ultimately, the sun. Some of the Recuay whom Hernández Príncipe interviewed talked of guacas principales "that the Inga gave them." But in the early seventeenth century, these appear to be of minor importance.[28]

In contrast, the malquis or ancestors figure prominently in his reports. The ayllu members that he interviewed provided him with the name of their founder and (often) his origin or pacarina.[29] The Recuay were prodigious in recalling the names and kinship ties of these ancestors as far back as eleven generations. For example, the commoners of Ocros began their genealogy

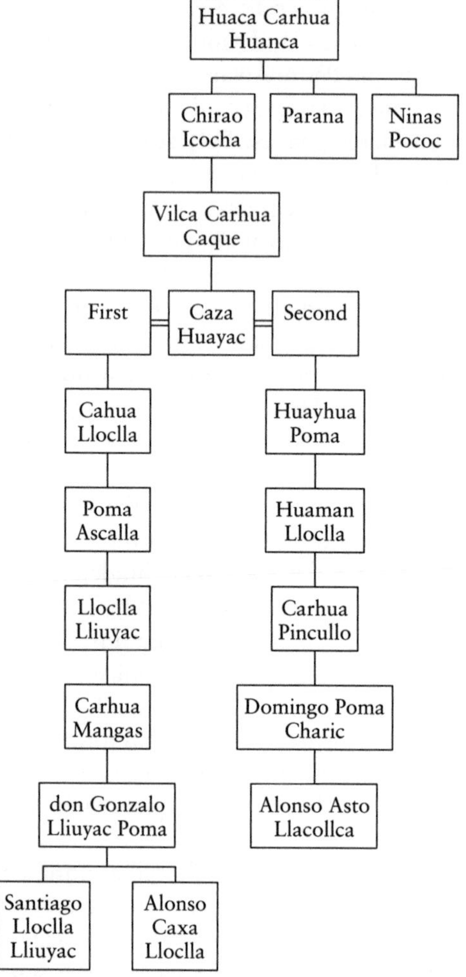

FIGURE 4.2. Genealogy of the natives of Ocros: descendants of Huaca Carhua Huanca. Sources: Duviols 1986: 465–67; and Hernández Príncipe's account (1621–22/1923).

with the Huaca Carhua Huanca and recited the names of his descendants into the early seventeenth century (see Figure 4.2). Carhua Huanca had four offspring, three of whom were named. Chirao Icocha, his third son, begat Vilca Carhua Caque, whose son, Caxa Huayac, left two sons from two different women, who each left sons, grandsons, and great-grandsons. The first to be baptized was Caxa Huayac's great-great-grandson, Domingo Poma Charic. His son, Alonso Asto Llacollca, was a minor local lord (*camachico*) in 1621, despite his baptism and Christian name.[30] His cousin, don Gonzalo

Lliuyac Poma, was the first of his line to accept the Catholic religion. His grandson (not shown in the genealogy chart), don Pedro Montalao, was the sacristan of Ocros at the time of Hernández Príncipe's visit.

Huaca Carhua Huanca's fourth son, Ninas Pococ, begat at least three sons, each of whom left numerous descendants. Their three lines are traced through as many as six more generations, noting who was the first to be baptized, and sometimes their purported role in their ancestral rites. The great-grandson of Hasta Caque, Ninas Pococ's third son, was a man named Luis, who was accused of being a practitioner (hechicero) of the old ancestral religion. Several generations later, a descendant of another one of Ninas Pococ's sons, don Gonzalo Poma Caque, is described as a "penitential" during Avendaño's visit.[31]

Interestingly, the lords of Ocros traced their descent from a different progenitor, Caha Yanac, sometimes also identified as a stone called Ocros. Members of his line can be followed in Hernández Príncipe's narrative for eight generations (Figure 4.3). Among those who are mentioned most is the lord Caque Poma, who sacrificed his daughter Tanta Carhua as a human sacrifice (*capacocha*) and received (or was confirmed in) the curacaship from (by) the Inca in return. His son Condor Capcha was the baby of the family and grew up to be a hechicero. His generation was the last to live in the time of the Inca kings; their offspring witnessed the coming of the Spanish. Don Rodrigo Caxa Malqui was baptized in Cajamarca in 1532 and governed for the Spanish. After his death, his cousin, don Juan Rimay Chahua, led the lineage. He was followed in the leadership position by a grandson of don Rodrigo, don Juan, who governed at the time of the Hernández Príncipe visit. In 1621, a cousin of don Juan, Francisco Lloclla Taccachin—a descendant of Nauin Mangas, the brother of cacique Caque Poma, and uncle of Tanta Carhua—was a priest, hechicero, and adviser (*consultor*) of Caha Yanac, despite having been baptized. He could recall the names of the religious specialists who had preceded him in worshipping their ancestors for at least nine generations back.[32] Hernández Príncipe found the whole ayllu, under the direction of Francisco Lloclla Taccachin, still actively worshipping the pre-Hispanic cacique Caque Poma and his son Poma Suntur, who had died in a battle in Pisabamba in the time of the Inca. Genealogical information on service to the king provided by don Gerónimo Puento, cacique of the people of Cayambe in the 1570s and 1580s, and material in the sources on La Barranca and Cajatambo in 1611–13 also show that lords came from a designated lineage different from that of the commoners. The separate origins of lords and commoners are also confirmed in myth (recall the creation story about Ataguju). Such genealogical data provide evidence of a persisting, sacred, indigenous historical tradition, what Thomas Abercrombie has aptly labeled "pathways of memory," based on ethnographic research in Bolivia.

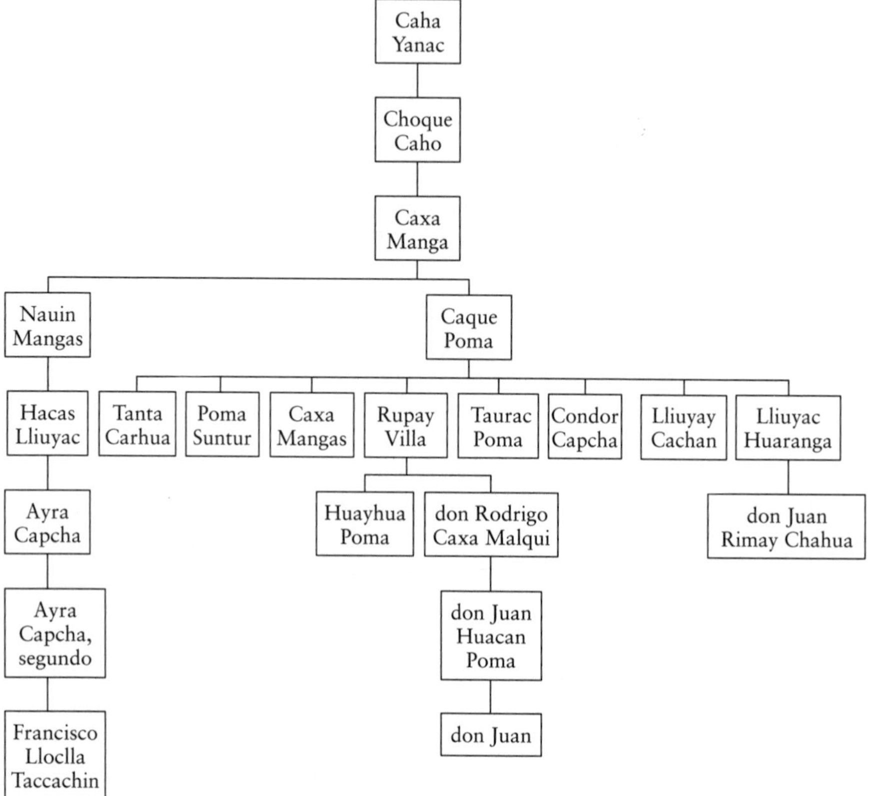

FIGURE 4.3. Genealogy of the lords of Ocros: descendants of Caha Yanac. Source: Duviols 1986: 465; and Hernández Príncipe's account (1621–22/1923).

Recitation of such genealogical traditions by the lords identified pretenders and candidates and established the right of their lineage to rule.[33]

In two places nearby, the extirpator found the actual mummies of the malqui founders, sitting in a cave or cavern on a raised platform, surrounded by other dead members of the kindred. The natives had hidden the bodies of their founders when the first visitador, Fray Francisco, had arrived in the middle of the sixteenth century. Hernández Príncipe found these mummies in the kindred's secret burial place on top of the mountain called Racian. He described the scene thus: "They were seated with majesty, with their crowns and their silver bracelets, although their clothes were rotted, and within sight of the sacrifices of llamas and guinea pigs and their altars where they burned incense to them." Another burial chamber was in the old town (*pueblo viejo*, or original, pre-reducción ceremonial center) of Urcon.

All the said infidels, the founding great-grandfather, grandfathers, fathers, and uncles of the caciques and governors [of] don Pedro Ventura, were in the old town [pueblo viejo] of Urcon, within an ancient fortress, in the vaults and tombs [*soterrados*]; so built and covered in thorns, . . . that it appeared impossible to find them. The cacique [Caque] Poma, so renowned and respected, was seated in the middle of them on his stool, [dressed in] a shirt of finest wool and covered with metal plates. Empty vaults awaited his descendants.[34]

Special devotion was given also to the capacochas. The Recuay remembered Runa Curi and Anco Ripay, two children without blemish, who had been sacrificed to the thunder god in a pact meant to guarantee the friendship of ayllus in the area. Likewise, the ayllu Urcon and those who could see her burial place from the surrounding hills paid homage to Tanta Carhua, the young maiden daughter of the cacique Caque Poma, whom he sent to the Inca as a human sacrifice. She returned, distinguished, to be interred alive on a high mountain peak with silver jewelry, jars, and small pitchers, which had been gifts of the emperor god-king himself. For this capacocha sacrifice, Caque Poma was "privileged" by the Inca with a "stool" and the señorio, as mentioned previously. Tanta Carhua was revered as a guardian of her people, who continued to feed her some seven decades after Fray Francisco found her tomb. At the time of the Hernández Príncipe visit, the caciques worshipped her and consulted her through religious specialists: "The caciques her creators communicated with her and adored her through the medium of a wizard," giving her a voice and role in their lives. Hernández Príncipe's informants recalled other capacochas sent to such distant places as Huánuco Viejo and Quito, in addition to the Temple of the Sun in the south.[35]

Besides these ancestor cults, each ayllu or group revered other guacas for specific purposes. Chaupis ayllu, for example, honored Lake Querococha, from which they believed that they had emerged. Another ayllu praised a lake from which they believed their llamas originated. Potters venerated clay pits called Sañomama, to ensure that their vessels would turn out well. The guaca Huaslla, embodied in "a warty stone without features," was revered "for their foodstuffs." There were certain guacas that more than one group celebrated. The pachaca of Allauca worshipped the "gran huaca" of Murpa that also counted as its devotees the Cochapitis and the Cotoparacos. All the Llacuazes worshipped the thunder god. For some rituals, both moieties would congregate to celebrate and commune, for example, before the start of the rainy season.[36]

Hernández Príncipe quantifies his activities and findings in an appendix. During his stay, he identified more than two hundred native ministers; more than one hundred malquis; thirty-two human sacrifices; forty-six principal "huacas"; and innumerable other minor idols, stones, aborted fetuses, and bodies of twins and breach-birth babies, who were held in special regard.

He also cataloged the paraphernalia of ritual, including silver, gold, and copper ceremonial vessels; and ritual vestments, some of which were made of *cumbi* (fine wool, usually referring to *vicuña*).[37]

The most revealing information on the Andean religion, driven underground by the Spanish, comes from the middle years of the seventeenth century, when the voices of local inhabitants appear in the record. Although in translation and solicited at times under duress, their testimonies provide the most genuine and intimate record of their beliefs and rituals. One example comes from 1660s Chancay, an area immediately north of Lima, where one would expect less of the traditional belief system to have survived, given the proximity of the region to the Spanish capital and the continuing interaction of the Chancay with Europeans.[38] Yet the members of ayllus, sometimes called derisively "worshippers of guacas" (*guacamochas*), still venerated the bones of their ancestors and named stones and hills. For example, Tomas Acauchanca, a native of the town of Oteque, annex of Yguari, and of the ayllu Chinca, confessed, after yielding to torture, that the wife of the governor of the polity, doña Graciana, had hired him (*lo mingo*) "to worship at a rock whose name he does not know but [he knows] that the site where it is located is called Yacancopa because it was the ancestor of the ancestors of the said doña Graciana and that she told him that he should ask to be given planted fields and she also asked him to ask that the Indians be respected." He offered the guaca coca and chicha as a sacrifice, with these words: "Father since the time of the ancients you have supported those who are your children[,] the casiques[;] assist this one too, who continued to rely on you[;] and fix it so that he will be respected by all the relatives and those who are of good blood and that he have good harvests and have with which to live."[39]

As in the past, each ayllu had at least one ancestor in common, often addressed as in the preceding prayer as father or "father of families." Thus, when asked about the religious services at the hill Villcacoto, Tomas Acauchanca feigned ignorance, stating that he did not know because it was of another ayllu. Another witness, likewise, had not seen the mummified remains of another group's progenitor, explaining that "they do not want to call them to said sacrifice because it is the custom among idolators that the particular ancestors and dead bodies of one parçialidad do not belong to or serve outsiders."[40]

The information gathered by the extirpators in Cajatambo at midcentury shows similar general patterns.[41] Persons worshipped stones (*guancas*) or stone idols, especially when they represented the founders and origins of the group. Pedro Ripa, a confessed religious specialist, worshipped one he named "Lubiac," saying that it had come down from the sky. The idols Corcuicayan and Capacvilca, guacas of the ayllu Quirca, were said to have originated on the coast in ancient times. They competed for power, each creating springs from which the lineage still irrigated its fields. Being wise and of almost equal strength, they became friends. When they died, they turned to stones that were acknowledged with sacrifices of guinea pigs. Another group worshipped a spring as the mother or creator of the water and the stone that represented the spring's maker. Thus, Bartolome Chuchucondor testified in the town of San Pedro de Hacas on January 29, 1657, that his father, Christobal Caxa, showed him and his brother, Gonçalo Pomalloclla, a stone "Sumacguanca," which stood near a spring (*puquio*). The stone was described as the puquio's "owner" (*dueño*), because "originally he was an Indian named tupinguailla who they say . . . created that spring."[42] Some of the Llacuaz revered certain snow-capped peaks for the same reasons.[43]

The mummified remains of some of their founders still existed at mid-century. Thus, before mentioning "Sumaguanca," Bartolome described how his father, who had always lived in the gardens (*huertas*) of Eruar—which were five or six leagues from the town of Hacas, next to the Barranca River where no priest had ever arrived "because of the rough roads"—had shown him and the rest of the members of the ayllu the malquis. The malquis "had been and were the first conquerors and founders and were the first to plant fields and gardens[;] and the principal ancestor[,] who is in one of the burial structures[,] is called maiguaicaxamalqui[,] who they say was the first Indian to bring the first coca of the people of Quitai[;] and he planted it in the said gardens[;] and in another tomb are six ancestors guaris that his father told him were the first to open the irrigation canals." The mummified body of (don Rodrigo) "Caxamalqui," the ancestor of the curaca of the town of Ocros (Cajatambo), who was baptized by the Spanish and governed for them, remained viable in the 1640s (he is shown in Figure 4.3).[44]

But the ancestors who were remembered best and longest, whether their bodies had been preserved or had been replaced with stone idols or other objects, were the ones featured in story-songs. To highlight just one example, all the natives of the lineage Cotos worshipped Coya Guarmi and her brother, Condortocas, who came from the seacoast to the west to support and benefit (*por amparo y bien*) them. The people of the Cotos ayllu of the pueblo of Mangas worshipped these siblings because the lineage believed that they all descended from this one incestuous couple. Several witnesses testified that Condortocas was the creator or soul (*camaquen*), malqui, and first founder (*primer progenitor*) of the community: "A dead body . . . was the ancestor and spirit of don Alonso Callampoma from whom the said don Alonso and all the proceeding curacas and the rest of the Indians of the lineage Cotos descended and that all worshiped him."[45] Coya Guarmi took the form of a "small jug and they have it clothed in tunics and mantas and pins and *tinpanas* [chipanas? (rings or bracelets worn on wrists and ankles)] of silver with necklaces and earrings and beads." At celebrations, they sang their history:

> They worship the idols with dances and drinking and he witnessed especially that . . . the said Don Alonso [and others] danced with the said coca and maize beer and all the people of his lineage imitated him with little drums. . . . they were dancing and singing these words in their language: machapita y camur canqui Cusi cayan man Llaclla cayan man pisarcutan man Lucma huaritahuan pacay huatauan canqui Coya huarmi panaquiuan—that in Spanish translation means according to their tradition that this ancestor Condortocas and his sister Coya guarmi came from the sea and they arrived and rested at the plain of Cusi and in the plain of Llaclla and in the place near where today is called Pisarcuta . . . and later they rested at a site called Calta quenca which is located between the road to Mangas and Pahas where they offer and sacrifice guinea pigs.

The song was not just a myth. The extirpating priest, following the geographic clues in the lyrics, located malqui Condortocas's body. Coya Guarmi's remains, in contrast, were never found. The ayllu Cotos had hidden her, and none would reveal the secret. The predominance of such local cults resulted in strong and persisting identities, which underscores the difficulties the Incas must have faced when trying to overcome them to aggregate peoples and forge imperial allegiances.[46]

Capacochas were another element of Cajatambo ancestor worship. Don Christobal Hacasmalqui, a lord, sacristan, and confessor (of his ayllu), being deposed in the Pueblo of Hacas in 1657, testified that

> always . . . they have worshiped and venerated until today and accept as an ancestral tradition that the said idol ticllaurao [the idol that was common to the people] was a principal Indian of the Hacas people and he represented them before the ynga and that said ynga ordered the said ticllaurao to offer him a human sacrifice upon his return to his people . . . and they offered it to the sun who was the father of the ynga and the said ticllaurao offered the human sacrifice at the place called ñabincoto next to the idol yanaurauc.

He continued to sacrifice there yearly. The minister, Hernando Hacaspoma, showed the extirpator two additional capacochas that had been offered to the Inca and the Sun and were also still adored in 1657.[47]

Celestials were mentioned much less frequently—by fewer than twenty witnesses in four different Cajatambo towns between 1656 and 1658—and then usually in response to the extirpator's leading questions, indicating again their relative unimportance to religious observance of this (and, by extension, other) ethnicities in the middle of the seventeenth century. When queried, they supplied few details of their worship and no indication of their representation. In their confessions, they mentioned no specific sacred places of worship and no specialized ministers.[48]

There are some known exceptions. One is from Chancay, where local witnesses admitted that, besides the bones of their ancestors from whom they descended, they actively worshipped and sacrificed to the Sun, the Moon, Thunder, the stars, and an idol that had once been the Sun's priest, long since lithified. A second comes from Guaylas in 1611–13; another from Huamantanga in 1656, where the Sun is invoked in divination. When their worship is acknowledged, it is because the Sun is "father and lord of All the Guacas" or the universal creator.[49]

Despite the Catholic Church's persistent conversion efforts, the Cajatambos continued these traditional practices into the eighteenth century. Records published by Juan Carlos García Cabrera show that in 1725, they still venerated their ancestors, either as malquis or as stones and idols. Whole communities worshipped together, though each of the faithful asked the guacas individually for what she or he needed through the priest. Like their parents and grandparents, they prepared themselves for this by fasting and doing penance "to keep the said idols content."[50]

This sacred panoply of the provincial peoples contrasted with that of the Incas. At the imperial level, the celestials (who were, according to their religio-political myth, also ancestors), the malquis—here referring to the representations of their ancestral god-kings—and other sacred things, including the major oracle gods of the ethnicities, were worshipped, in that order. The Recuay, Chancay, Cajatambo, and others inverted this hierarchy. Most important to them were their ancestors, their malquis and capacochas; next came sacred places and other holy things; and, last, often mentioned as an afterthought in the mid-seventeenth century, were the Sun and the "principal huacas" that the Inca imposed on them. One native expressed their priorities succinctly, saying that "what is their principal object of veneration are their ancestors in first place and in second their stone idols and household gods and in third place the sun moon venus and the two small stars that they call chuchucoillur and the seven stars that they call oncuicuillur." The criteria for ranking was perceived closeness of kinship and responsiveness to the needs of the group doing the celebrating.[51]

In these records, guaca, guanca, and malqui are often used interchangeably, leading to confusion. This confusion occurs especially when the reports are shallow and data are presented in a scorecard style, or when the mention of the gods is random or haphazardly and unsystematically included in the records without the god's history, mythical paths, and cultural contributions—that is, without a historical context. However, the testimonies of these extirpation inspections, when considered chronologically, suggest how the objects of worship shifted over time in a process that was neither constant nor lineal, and how the malquis became guancas and guacas and eventually associated with crags and mountaintops, some of which appeared humanlike in form (see Figure 4.4). It is only in the first systematic reports on native religion that the ancestors and the major guacas are not associated. This may be the fault of the missionaries' tentative language skills and the fact that they dismissed the native stories of the past as pure fiction.[52] Later, testimony indicates that the people originally worshipped the mummified remains of their founding ancestors. To the frustration of the extirpators, their often-jealous efforts to burn mummies did not usually uproot and end ancestor worship. As their bodies were destroyed or otherwise lost, the preserved remains of the forebears were replaced with stones, idols, masks, and other objects. In San Francisco de Otuco, the native catechist and assistant (*fiscal*) Andres Chaupis Yauri testified in 1656 that the large stone idols that people worshipped—named Carua Guanca, Llacssa Guanca, Cari Guanca, and Guarse Guanca, and located above the town of Caruapampa—represented the first Llacuaces that came from Titicaca. They were "Indian conquerors who came from Raco Cayan and Picho Cayan . . . and they turned into the said stones." He did not say what happened to the bodies of the ancestors. Assuming that they were once real individuals, like Condortocas and Coya Guarmi, when the flesh disappeared, it was replaced by stone or another material. Pedro Sarmiento testified in 1657 that when the stone idols Yanayacola and his or her brother Carua Yacolca (or Caqui guaca) were destroyed by Father Avendaño, they were replaced, not with other stones but with masks that their lord Anton Pacari—himself already dead in 1657—ordered made and put in their stead. "This lineage has always worshiped him and this witness accepts the tradition that in ancient times in titicaca the guacas who were live Indians were distributed throughout the provinces and the two said idols came to stay in this place of yanaqui and there had children." Or ancestors might spontaneously turn to stone upon death to perpetuate their memory and power.[53] Villagómez confirms this transformational process, writing in 1649 that the natives worshipped high hills, large stones that previously had been men.[54]

Thus, the association, at least at first, was not forgotten; guacas in a variety of forms were openly identified as progenitors, some of whom had lithified. These, to survive the campaigns of extirpation, were hidden and moved to caverns and caves, some on the highest surrounding peaks, to prevent their discovery and destruction by the Spanish. One native admits that "it is well-known and everyone of his lineage knows that when the gentleman Bishop don Fern[an]do de Abendaño visited they immediately hid the ancestor mummies and they have them hidden until today which they showed caratupaico-malqui pomaguaraca-malqui chaupisguaracamalqui and llacsapaicomalqui all of which are in their tombs and burials and this witness and everyone of his lineage have always worshiped them." As the elders died, memory faded and terminology became imprecise. Malquis

FIGURE 4.4. Veneration of a mountaintop by Collasuyus. Source: Guamán Poma de Ayala 1613/1936: 270.

became idols, guancas, and guacas. By the late seventeenth century and on into the eighteenth, native peoples were reported to be worshipping stones and mountaintops, and the significance of these was thereafter either forgotten and lost or not mentioned (see Figure 4.5).[55]

This process is best illustrated by Duviols's analysis of the myths of Apu Llibiac Cancharco, the legendary Llacuaz hero—man-god, founding ancestor, and sinchi—"the dazzling great flash of lightning" (*el gran relámpago deslumbrante*), also known as Yanaraman. Surviving stories about this man-god told that he was the son of Thunder and had been deposited on a hill named Raco. Another myth stated that he originated from the snow-capped mountain of Yarupajá. His children, also called Llibiac, were likewise considered men-gods and sinchis. They traveled west with their troops looking for places to settle. They came upon the Guaris of Otuco, whom they subjugated. Colonial extirpators had assumed the tales were myths, but in the course of their investigations, they found a cave in which a mummy of "Llivia Cancharco" sat "with his *huama* or crown on his head, dressed in seven fine wool shirts that the Indians say that the ancient inga Kings sent and presented him." Years later in 1724, the natives still worshipped a stone idol with human characteristics, named Apu Llibiac or Apu Llibiac Cancharco. This sequence shows the persistence of ancestor worship and how a living cultural hero's story and image were preserved and transformed over the centuries. It also provides us with an explanation of why mountain peaks are often equated with ancestral gods and worshipped as if they represented or were the god himself into the late twentieth century.[56]

This progressive shift in terminology and association underscores again the fact that native Americans were worshipping themselves—their own past heroes, their forefathers, the superior among them. They attributed to these individuals herolike qualities and supernatural capabilities that over time turned into sacred attributes and godlike feats. Provincial people believed that the guacas were real persons and the living were literally their children.[57] Guacas and people were kin, united by genealogy that many recalled in their songs as they danced. Thus, aside from the Incas' ancestors, the Sun, Moon, and stars, to whom most felt only tenuous links, local peoples were actively related to their ancestors and their cults. Licenciado Hernández Príncipe realized this and informed his superiors that "the llachuases [of the community of Ocros in 1621] pretended to be children of Thunder-Lightning and these and the Sun were their objects of worship. The founders [llactas, Guaris] pretended to be descended from the huacas and their origin is from them and not from Adan and Eva and for this reason they are convinced that God Our Lord made the Spanish and they were made by their huacas." The household and personal gods (*conopas*, or *dioses penates*—stone representations of foodstuffs and animals, used for propitiatory purposes) were also believed to be

FIGURE 4.5. Antisuyus worshipping ancestors on a mountaintop. Source: Guamán Poma de Ayala 1613/1936: 268.

gifts of the ancestral spirits. Sometimes they are described as the servants (*criados*) of the guacas, just like the saramamas are sometimes identified as the wives of the guacas. They were venerated as much for their innate power as their divine origin. Thus, even through these very numerous, more personal gods, the native peoples were worshipping the power, vitality, and energy of their forefathers. In sum, one might say, perhaps at the expense of overgeneralizing, that the basis of local Andean religion, as at the imperial level, was ancestor worship.[58]

Rites and Roles

Local curacas, in whom ideally were concentrated traits of kindness, wisdom, diplomacy, pragmatism, courage, charisma, and responsibility, were the heirs of the awesome vitality of the ancestors, as the genealogies diagrammed previously graphically illustrate. So, too, were the outsiders, appointed to their positions by the Inca. They brought along extralineal genealogical linkages, perhaps to the divine king's own through gifts of chosen women. Others, perhaps of undistinguished birth, had proven themselves "brave" (*valientes*) in battle, thus showing the favor and power of their ancestral gods. Regardless of the terms and circumstances of their ascension, all, in fact, were considered living representatives and proof positive of the credibility and viability of their belief systems.[59]

Manuscript sources include references to the election of local authorities from among their lineage and noble peers. We can only guess at the reason for the choice and unstated meaning of the word *election* in these circumstances. Local ceremonies, analogous to the Incas' calpa rites, were used to answer questions and foretell the future among the people of Huarochirí in the 1560s and 1570s; the Chancas in 1599; the Huachos, Yauyos, Guancavelicas, Chinchacochas, Julis, Checras, Barrancas, Guaylas, and Conchucos in the early seventeenth century; the Recuay in 1622; the Checras in 1647; and the Cajatambos then and at midcentury. Ancestral input and approval (*aprobación*) was sought on such diverse issues as the truthfulness of the speaker, the names of children, the identity of suitable marriage partners, the reasons for a sickness or death, the outcome of travel, the timing of planting and harvesting, the location of a lost or stolen object, and the decision of whether or not to wage war. Cobo writes that "their use was common and very frequent so that nothing important was started before they determined its success with the wizards and fortune-tellers." Therefore, it is logical that such rites were used to consult the spiritual founder of the group when it was time to choose a new leader from among the contenders, at least until the Spanish began to meddle in succession. In fact, references, the most direct of which is reported by Antonio de la Calancha, suggest that ancestors were consulted as part of the process for choosing a curacal successor: "The master [Calisaya] uses oracular revelations that reveal the will of the gods, the same that gives succession legitimacy, reserved for 'the most loved and those who are the most responsible.'" Undoubtedly the elders were aware that such practices ran counter to Christian teachings, and for that reason they were usually kept hidden.[60]

Native testimonies indicate that inauguration imbued the curaca with supernatural force (for example, to change shape and travel through the air) and the weighty authority of divinities of the past, once he sat on the stool of office (the tiana or dúo, literally, the seat of power) during the investment ceremony.[61] (The investment ceremony will be described in Chapter 5 in great detail.) It is only after "enstoolment" that the chosen successor was capable of receiving the vital energy of the ancestors (referred to as the *camaquen*) or, to paraphrase a modern informant, "the breath of life" (*el soplo de la vida*).[62] The word *camaquen* has several meanings, including "soul" and "effective, powerful animating or sustaining force," and is associated with the concept of *camac*, another word meaning "divinity" or "guaca." The curaca accessed this camaquen either by communicating with it or by being possessed by it. Hernando Hacaspoma, a priest of the town of San Pedro of Hacas, confessed that having made sacrifices before his malqui, he entered a state of ecstasy, "deprived of his senses and within himself he heard the said ancestor speak," answering his questions. Elsewhere, he stated that the camaquen entered his heart and possessed his body.[63]

Thus did the forefathers condition the curaca's right to rule and command by endowing him with moral authority. After his investiture and enstoolment, the paramount lord was worshipped like a living god or an individual who was recognized to be in a position to become an honored ancestor someday. His ascension as heir and direct participant in the power of the divinity implied the acceptance of the heavy responsibilities of communicating, mediating, and arbitrating between such supernatural forces and his followers. At the juncture of heroic and genealogical history, to paraphrase the well-chosen, illuminating, and cogent words of Saignes, he, thereupon, was entrusted with assuring the continued flow of this vitalizing energy that guaranteed (*vela*) the fertility, reproduction, and continuity of the group. This capability put the curaca in a special category of beings that could make the potentially dangerous personal contact with the sacred and mediate between humanity and the supernatural. He thereby maintained the equilibrium of the local universe.[64]

For these reasons, the enstooled curaca was likened to a priest, worshipped by most, and accepted as the embodiment of a spirit by many. A curaca like don Juan Calchaquí, a paramount lord who lived in the southern altiplano in Puna (what is today northwestern Argentina) in the 1560s, was held to be a guaca: "They accept him as a guaca and nothing is done in the land without his order." Río's study of Tapacarí also found evidence that the local curacas "were guacas worshiped by their peoples, through which they activated and created their collective identities and ties." In his chronicle, Las Casas explains that commoners venerated "the Lords they had had because they had governed them gently and tranquilly; and thus little by little they came to the opinion that they were more than men." He also writes: "They accepted their Lords who had governed them well and justly and with love and gently and who benefited their peoples, as more than men, and little by little they came to esteem them as gods and to offer them sacrifices and come to them, invoking them for their needs." Thus, to quote Las Casas, they made "of men gods" (*haciendo de hombres dioses*). Martínez Cereceda's analysis of emblems also shows a strong possible equation between guacas and curacas. Elsewhere, duly enstooled curacas were likened to "kings." Although we have no sure indication that pre-Hispanic curacas married their sisters, the anthropologically indicated theoretical definition for godly status, the accepted sacred aura of such personages is consistent with the image of that of the old-style "creator of Indians" described in documents from the 1560s on the north coast. Sources also indicate that local paramount lords, like the Inca, gave wives to their followers.[65]

Commoners and lesser lords alike acknowledged his supernaturally sanctioned authority and showed their respect, obedience, and reverence to the seated figure by kissing his hand; by embracing him; by cheering and otherwise showing their approval; and by raising their hands above their heads and making a kissing or smacking noise with their lips—the traditional pre-Hispanic way to show reverence.[66]

The sacred status of a lord is found in a wide variety of sources, from myths of the Huarochirí, for instance, to concrete statements of eyewitnesses. Molina, el almagrista, wrote that "all the lords of the land, no matter where they were, made people worship them in life and in death." Pedro Sancho relates that Pizarro named a new lord so that his subjects could worship and obey him. Cieza states that "the native chiefs of these [coastal] valleys [like Jayanca] were reverenced by their subjects, and those who survive still are so." In 1567, during the inauguration ceremony of the curaca of Cajamarca, Dr. Gregorio González de Cuenca, the royal inspector and judge of the Real Audiencia of Lima, ordered a participant

> to bring a stool and he made the said don Al[ons]o Chuplingon sit and after he was seated he ordered the said principal lords who were present to worship the said don alonso chuplingon as a sign that they accepted him as lord and caciq[ue]. In keeping with the order each of the said lords worshiped the said don Alonso Chuplingon as he sat on the stool in recognition of his status as their cacique and natural lord.

Such reverential attitudes toward what was considered imbued with sacredness are not surprising because even secondary wives of the Inca, such as Contarguacho, the provincial wife of Guayna Capac from the Guaylas peoples, were venerated (*reverenciada*).[67]

Thus, the curaca was not just a secular ruler, charged with managing human resources for production and survival. As heir to the sacred and invested with ancestral force, he was the fulcrum and focus of traditional rites. As such he took responsibility for maintaining (and protecting, after 1532) local cults. The second Concilio in 1567 acknowledged strong indigenous resistance to the overtures of Christianity supported by curacas. The caciques served as ringleaders of resistance among the Guaylas in 1611–13. And not just the paramount lord was involved. The whole hierarchy of ethnic authorities (curacas, caciques, and lesser lords [camachicos or *hilacatas*]) was associated and directly linked to the hierarchy of gods. The weakest authority, perhaps the person with the least seniority and the fewest adherents, advocated for his antecedents. The paramount lord, himself part of the sacred lineage, defended, in turn, the principal guaca, and so forth.[68]

Later in colonial times, despite Spanish prohibitions, risks of severe punishment—which sometimes included whippings, torture, jail, exile, and privation of office, as well as threats of the same—these local-level chiefs acted as the heads of traditional Andean religion of their ayllus (or parcialidades) and wider communities of followers. Calancha reports that, in general, they "commanded their idolatrous practices." In the town of San Francisco de Mangas, before the priest Bachiller Bernardo de Noboa of the parish of San Pedro de Ticllos, Miguel de Harta Beitia accused the curaca and governor of the town, don Alonso Callampoma, of worshipping the mummy of his forefather, Condortocas, and his sister. (Don Alonso Callampoma identified himself as a segunda persona [literally, second person, or second-in-command, after the curaca or paramount lord] of the town with a title from the royal government, a collector of tribute, and head of the ayllu of Cotos.) Miguel de Harta Beitia described what he saw at the times when they worshipped the pair or when the ayllu(s) gathered to celebrate Roman Catholic religious holidays, such as Corpus Christi or saints' days—which, in reality, were thinly disguised festivities dedicated clandestinely to their ancestors, of whom they had asked permission or license to conduct the festivities in the first place.[69] Another contemporary testified in the town of San Juan de Machaca:

> He saw that before the Corpus and Saint John the Baptist celebration the said wizards approached the standard bearers and they would ask for offerings of llamas[,] guinea pigs[,] coca[,] animal suet[,] and maize beer to offer to the ancestor[;] and ask their license to celebrate said festivities[;] and he always saw that they always gave

them [the permission] and they would hold them [the festivities][;] and they returned saying that they had already been granted the license although they had been maddened at first and they had not wanted to grant permission[;] and they also had asked them to multiply the food and drink so that they had enough for all the guests[;] and in the same manner the day of the celebration[,] they spilled a little of the first gourds of chicha given to the elders[;] and[,] to this witness in the plaza[,] and gave coca as sacrifice to the said idols[,] saying[:] "lord grandfathers receive this offering"[;] and that night they went and walked throughout the settlement from house to house dancing with little drums and drinking[;] and at the house of the standard bearer[,] they spilled some of the maize beer that they were given[,] saying lords[,] eternal fathers[,] spirits [*yayas auquisllari*] do not get mad for all these celebrations and rejoicings are not done [to honor] the God of the Spanish nor to their saints[,] but for you.

Lords such as don Alonso led the festivities to prepare and escort deceased community members to their final resting place, to begin planting and harvesting, and to roof or reroof houses. Thus, "on all the days of corpus and roofing and reroofing of new houses [don Alonso Callampoma] orders brought the idol of Coya guarmi . . . and in the house the said curaca dances pagan dances [*cochas*] in her honor."[70] They sang the song, quoted earlier, which recalled the exploits of Condortocas and his sister, as they danced through the streets toward Calta quenca, the site where the mummy bundle of the first and the representation of the second were normally kept, to make offerings of coca and chicha. On these occasions, don Alonso was accused of appearing attired in impressive ceremonial garb: "The said Don Alonsso dressed himself for this end in a fine woolen shirt[;] and on his arm he puts a silver bracelet[;] and on his head a headdress[,] decorated with a silver half moon[,] pagan adornments[,] and clothing that ministers of idols wear to carry out their rites and worship." A contemporary, don Alonso Ricari, likewise dressed in ancient costume (*vestidos antiguos*) and multicolored sandals (*ojotas de muchos colores*). He also kept "a club called a *champi* and three fine woolen shirts and other clothes in which he dances with the rest of the Indians when they sacrifice and at the festivities they make [in honor of] the said idols." Such costumes contrast markedly with the more modest dress of the other religious specialists, who typically only wore a shirt of fine wool, maybe a bracelet, but no headdress. The clothing of don Alonso Callampoma and don Alonso Ricari, by comparison with others, were the most elaborate and opulent, another indication of their prominent priestly roles in the events.[71]

Not only did the lords of the various towns and ayllus in the region set the dates, lead, and participate in the rituals and observances, but they, like the Inca, made certain that their followers did likewise. In fact, local chiefs appear to be the biggest promoters of such gatherings—ordering that certain ceremonies be held and being present at them. Don Pablo Guaman, principal and camachico of the town of Hacas, ordered his subjects to worship the malquis and instructed them in the proper form of adoration. Likewise, don Christobal Pomalibia, another principal and camachico of the town of Hacas; don Alonso Ricari, principal, camachico, and religious specialist of the town of Otuco; and Juan Chuchu Liviac, principal of the town of Santo Domingo of Pariac, directed, sometimes through the public crier, the local population to prepare for and attend specific rites and ceremonies. This included gathering and contributing sacrifices for burnt offerings. At the appropriate seasons, such as at planting (*Pocoymita*) and harvesting (*Caruamita*) times, and at Corpus Christi, don Alonso Ricari is said to have ordered "the making of the maize beer and the sacrifice of the llamas and the invitation of all the Indians for the said celebration." When the priest questioned Ysabel Llupay Vilca, who admitted to being a practitioner of traditional religion, she stated that when she confessed her assembled neighbors twice a year, and when she divined the future, Ricari was always present. In blaming Ricari for the idolatrous practices then under attack, another witness, perhaps in an effort to avert his own blame, said that "all this is caused by the said Don Alonso Ricary because he encourages it and attends to all [the details][;] and at the drunken feasts he and his wife and children are the first to dance." Leonor Asto Cuyo agreed, saying, "Don Alonsso orders and attends all the religious festivities." She remarked that he also attended funerals and the rituals on the first anniversary of a dead person's death.[72]

In colonial times, native lords did not act alone. They were aided by religious specialists, whom they sometimes appointed and ceremonially inducted and confirmed, and generally favored.[73] Polo de Ondegardo remarks on this practice in the sixteenth century. Among the Cajatambos, lords allowed religious specialists to board in their homes and exempted them from tributary service: "And so that they would serve the said idols Cuia guarmi and Condortocas [don Alonso] has appointed and deputized ministers and he exempts them [from tribute service]. . . . he shelters in his house Domingo Nuna Callan[,] Pedro Rimay Chagua[,] and Biolante Quillai so that they can serve the said idols." Don Alonso was said to keep them with him always: "He supports them in his house and he always has them with him." According to Sebastian Xulca, don Alonso allowed Domingo Nuna Callan ("whose infamous name is sayco" [*por mal nombre llamado sayco*]), an elder of the Cotos ayllu and a "wizard dogmatizer of bad reputation," to stay in his house "for bad ends" and exempted him from tribute labor (*mitas*) as his professional record keeper (quipucamayoc). Pedro Rimay Chaua ("infamously known as siratinti") and Biolante Quillai were "ministers of . . . ydols" who carried sacred objects to celebrations and memorials from their resting or burial places, cared for the idols, collected corn and distributed it to maidens to make into chicha for ritual offerings, danced at the gatherings, performed sacrifices, and sometimes engaged in activities meant to foretell the future.[74]

Don Alonso was not the only lord who named such religious specialists. Pedro Rimay Chaua confessed that Pedro Achahuaranga, his brother and a principal, had chosen him as minister of certain ancestors. Likewise, Francisco Yacalhua of the ayllu Cotos admitted that "Don Diego Atachahua and Francisco Gomes principal lords and lower-level lords of the lineage Tamborga and of the lineage Cotos . . . named and ordered this confessor and they appointed him as a minister to serve the idol Hucas Canpuri that is at the site of Vampac [and] idols and ancestors called Capcha Rurai Maichachin that are at the site of Nauin Rara." Atachahua, before his death, also named Garsia Morales of Cotos ayllu as another minister of the idol Hucas Canpuri.[75]

One witness suggested that high-ranking native lords inducted or confirmed newly appointed religious specialists. Juan Flores confessed that two religious specialists who served don Alonso Callampoma named him to attend the ancestors (malquis) of his ayllu Tamborga "in front of the curaca Don Alonso." He was then admonished to keep silent about these practices or be punished by being sent to serve (a mita) in a textile mill (*obraxe*). The Archbishop of Lima, don Pedro de Villagómez, added that some religious specialists were elected by other holy men. Yet, the chosen "who they judge to be the best for the purpose" is accepted with the acquiescence and approval of the curaca and caciques. These chosen practitioners of the ancient faith took no action in this regard "without consulting their caciques."[76]

Local lords requisitioned and gathered offerings, and with or without the help of the recognized specialists, personally sacrificed to their ancestors. Don Christobal Pomalibia, for example, "made the crier announce the offerings." Domingo Tantayana, principal, mandon, and scribe of the local cabildo, ordered everyone of his ayllu to obey the holy men in this regard. "He made them gather the offerings . . . for the idols and ancestors" and "they collect and give the requested offerings." Failure to comply might result in a scolding or a whipping. On another occasion, after three days of dancing, the curaca made offerings of silver.[77]

Responsibility for the support of cult practices also implied the maintenance of the religious infrastructure and production of sacrificial goods. Local lords saw to it that ceremonial structures, where subjects gathered to worship and burn offerings of coca, llama lard (*sebo*), corn, guinea pigs, and chicha, and to dance and sing, were repaired: "All the curacas are and have been and have had the said responsibility on pretense that it is a house of the curacas saying that said house is communal they maintain it to worship and fast." They also oversaw the planting of cult fields: "Publically through the voice of the crier the said curaca ordered that the fields of vintin dedicated to the said idols since ancient times be planted with the pretext that they were for the community." Products of these fields, such as maize, became ritual offerings: "Don Christobal pomalibia prinsipal lord and lesser lord and Domingo tantayana[,] Christobal tanquis[,] Pedro caico also lesser lords ordered the people to make the beer and plant the field for the said ancestors."[78] Lords also kept llamas for ritual purposes.

This information from the central Andes is consistent with other data from the region and more fragmentary and earlier data from elsewhere in the Andes. Documents from the Archivo Romano de la Compañía de Jesús report secret rituals as early as 1561 that included the worship of ancestral bones (*huesos*) as well as peaks, types of divination ceremonies, and sacrifices. Somewhat later, Toledo's deputies and inspectors of 1572–73 mentioned ceremonies—which included *taquies* (story-songs preformed in dance) and dances (*bailes*)—outside the tombs, in people's houses, and at other sacred structures. Viceroy Esquilache complained of the persistence of such rituals in 1619. Like their Inca counterparts, native lords on the north coast possessed festive garb and symbols of power for such occasions. In sixteenth-century wills, they listed rich clothing of cumbi, litters, trumpets, ceremonial drinking vessels, crowns, headdresses, feathers, bells, and beads.[79] Grave goods like silver vessels, silver and gold crowns (*diademas*) and medallions (*patenas*), and silver trumpets suggest that these same objects were used in pre-Hispanic times for similar purposes. Local lords of Túcume, Moro, Tecap, and Lurin Ica also kept camelids (*carneros y ovejas de la tierra*)—almost certainly for sacrificial obligations to the forebears. Llamas were also kept to offer in the central and southern highlands. Guamán Poma de Ayala, in depicting a llama used as a burial offering on the coast, suggests that such sacrifices were pre-Hispanic in origin.[80]

Finally, a court case about looting the guaca (in this case, a pyramid, palace, or tomb) Yamayoguán (at Chan Chan, near the city of Trujillo) in 1558–59 contains information about bones and wool figurines splattered with blood at the site, which were interpreted by the Spanish as offerings to the ancestors ("their grandparents and ascendants"), which the local curaca, don Antonio, admitted were buried there. Yamayoguán was a "shrine and guaca where in ancient times they used to worship, give offerings, honor and adore with their conjuring and ceremonies . . . and thus it seems to be that that guaca and shrine, even though it is an ancient place on the surface of it, there appear many bones of children and camelids and wool and other signs of sacrifices." Native witnesses in this case insisted to the Spanish that if the guaca were violated and the ancestors disturbed, all would perish. Such an equation between not worshipping the ancient gods and sickness and death is likewise found in the annual letters from Jesuit missionaries.[81]

Thus, the chiefs acted as the leaders of local Andean religion, taking responsibility for worship in general, the direction and instruction of religious specialists, the maintenance of sacred space, the collection of offerings, and the organization of the labor necessary to continue such practices. They acted as, and were recognized as, priests of the local cults. In 1638, don Pedro Liquitaya, curaca of Atacama La Alta, had to flee after being judged and condemned to death as "the high priest of idolatries." Don Alonso Ricari, according to witness Pedro Mena, "dressed himself . . . in ancient clothes[,] sandals of many colors[,] and a golden headdress on his head after which they adored him as a priest of the said guaca." Pablo Cura, a principal, diviner, and famous curer, a native of the ethnicity of Guaylas, was a priest (*sacerdote*) of the idol called Aina.[82] Another don Pablo (Guaman), a principal of the colonial town of Hacas, is likewise identified as a "minister of idols." Jan Szemiński's research pushes these seventeenth-century observations back a century by concluding that every curaca and native leader had some priestly traits. The Franciscan B. de Cárdenas reported the same to be true in early seventeenth-century Charcas. Frank Salomon suggests that the role continued. In eighteenth-century Andagua (Arequipa), the head of a "family" functioned, he found, as chief priest to the ancestor shrine of his group.[83]

To Feed and Be Fed

The motivation behind this active orchestration of the ceremonies, sacrifices, and offerings to the ancestors and idols was the generalized Andean belief that the ancestor-gods (1) had been the common beginning of the group and, therefore, represented their origin; (2) had been the first to settle down in the area; (3) had been the first to plant a piece of ground; (4) had been the first to bring important crops to the area; (5) had been the first to build irrigation canals; and, in general, (6) had exerted an ongoing and beneficent influence on the day-to-day life of the earthbound living.[84]

On the first point, the lords and commoners of Cotos ayllu, who worshipped Condortocas and Coya Guarmi, did so because they considered themselves descended from them. Members of other ayllus worshipped their malquis or hero-guacas for the same reason. A Jesuit report from 1614 stated that the people of Andajes still worshipped Llibiac Cancharco: "Having been the first cacique of that province . . . he was the creator of the human species, he was the one who gave life, he produced all the plants and the corns, he gave rain, the only creator of all the necessary foods needed to conserve human life." They continued to carry the mummy of Llivia Cancharco, "anointed as the custom of the fathers dictated, from one city to another and presented him the most precious offerings." When not being worshipped, the body was housed in a "shrine" (*templete*, *sacrariolo*).

[The body was] on top of a mountain, with a crown of multi-colored feathers on his head, the front of which was decorated with a half moon of pure gold, with little precious chains around his neck, completely covered with six fine woolen and embroidered cloths. He was covered on each side by a cotton gauze curtain sent as a gift from the Inca kings of Peru, together with the rest of the things, more or less 200 years ago and it looked so white that it seemed to have been woven yesterday or three days ago.

Four years later, the practice continued: people of Cajatambo worshipped the mummies of their "pagan progenitors, heads of their lineages." In 1620, the priests R. de Ávila and J. de Cuevas found the preserved body of the founder of the people of Huanchor, who was their principal god. The ayllus of Quirca and Canta of the pueblo of Hacas revered their progenitors, Corcuicayan and Capacvilca, respectively, of coastal origin. One member of an ayllu said that "these mummies were the first progenitors of this lineage of Julca Tamborga." Some malquis were old enough to be considered the founder of several related lineages and of the ethnicity itself. Thus, "all the people worshiped the said stone because they say it was the first Indian who founded the ethnicity."[85]

Elsewhere, natives confessed that the malquis were the first to settle in a place or to bring crops to the area. The witness Gonsalo Lloclla revealed this point as he recited a traditional prayer before his Catholic interrogators: "Marca parya lloclla who is his ancestor take this offering as the first person to plant this field and you have the energies to help us have good harvests." Another invoked the ancestors with these words: "Receive this offering that I make to you ancestors who founded this town and chose this site to build a house."[86]

Ancestors were said to exert influence over the health of the group as a whole, over the abundance of crops, and over life and death. Health was uppermost on the mind of Biolante Sira, of the ayllu Chacos, when she confessed "that she went to the site called Camachirca where Coillar malqui was burned and there she sacrificed to said malqui Coillar with coca and maize beer saying Coillar malqui give these my eyes health." Juana Ancaguato of Arapaio ayllu propitiated a malqui for the recuperation of her husband when he was very ill. Don Pasqual Haro of Cotabambas sacrificed to placate the spirits to prevent the death of his wife. Hernando Condor Yncachi, of Julca Tamborga ayllu, did likewise to the malqui Rao Lliuyac to ward off sickness or plague (*no diese enfermedad*). Don Juan de Mendoza, cacique and governor of Chaupiguaranga Lamas, sacrificed twice for the health and life of his son, don Alonso. So did Fernando Carua Chin, of the town of San Pedro de Quipan (Huamantanga), who prayed and sacrificed for the health of his godson. When a plague of measles and smallpox threatened, people pleaded in prayer to the ancestors that the diseases would spare their lives.[87]

Others sacrificed to the ancestors for fertility—of the women and of the fields and waters. It was believed that Coya Guarmi could affect women's reproduction. If Coya Guarmi was not worshipped, a woman "would not have daughters or sons." Some participated to guarantee the fertility of the fields—abundant crops and supplies of food. Alonso Chagua confessed that he sacrificed to a malqui "so that his fields would increase that year." Las Casas mentions that people of the mountains worshipped their ancestor gods "so that the gods would give them the fruit of the land"; those of the coast, "who usually are fishermen, so that their nets would be full of fish and they would be guarded from the dangers of the sea." [88]

In general, the inhabitants of the Andes believed that the good things they enjoyed were gifts of the ancestors. Properly propitiated, they served as their guardians, protectors, and advocates. Their intervention assured life and reproduction. They appointed the curaca, subordinate lords, and religious specialists who led and carried out community worship in honor of their forebears and traditional forces to ensure their health, well-being, and the reproduction of their people. As the Inca was venerated as the link between humans and the celestials, so the old-style curacas and, after death, their bodies and images, were recognized as mediators between human and superhuman societies. Although the status and power of the principal curacas had diminished considerably between the first half of the sixteenth century and the middle of the seventeenth, many continued to play a leading role in clandestine religious observance that was meant to show respect and maintain reciprocity with the ancestors as loci of sacred power. They siphoned off surplus production to continue to feed and clothe them as if they were still alive. Las Casas writes that "if he was a principal lord or person, all the people and their neighbors would gather . . . at the feast[,] the chair or stool where the lord used to sit was present, and if the deceased was a King or principal Lord, there was an image in the same seat, and, if not, his clothes were there. They also placed food before it as if he being alive would eat." One native informant explained that they brought food and drink to maintain the souls of their old ones (*maiores*) who were in limbo (*en el limbo*). Souls of the ancestors were summoned and celebrated with food and drink. It was incumbent on the survivors to provide for them, because "so many Indians have died, they no longer qualify for a piece of planted field larger than the fingernail of a hand [in the next world]." The description of the burial site of Caque Poma, the much-recalled cacique who lived under and was appointed or confirmed by the Incas, who sacrificed his daughter to the Sun, and who had directed his subjects in building an irrigation canal, suffices to suggest the elaborateness of some ancestor cults.[89]

As the extirpators observed, often in frustration, ancestor worship was ubiquitous and difficult to suppress. If a Catholic priest burned a malqui or destroyed an idol, the natives gathered the ashes or its pieces or made a new representation of the spirit to worship, because the body was believed to have a spiritual presence that remained after death. Thus, "Anton pacari overseer and lord of this town of Hacas and Raucallan great wizard and dogmatizer . . . ordered made two wooden masks called guasac so that they could adore and worship them instead of the burned idols." They sacrificed to them, in the same place where they had been, even when their original physical presence was gone, "because even though their souls had departed they lived." Though burned, "the soul of the said idol lived and came down to the sacrifice and received it." Additional evidence shows that burning idols did not stop veneration, because "making the said sacrifice the said idols would come down and hear them." Gareis relates that Albornoz thought they had to destroy idols in front of their devotees to end their adoration. But native priests started cults of "sons" (*hijos*) of their annihilated gods and their worship continued.[90] This suggests that the locus of divinity lay not in the object or representation itself, but in the spirit, soul, or vital force that it represented, the essence of superhuman power. The material objects were symbols of group and community solidarity and power, and of the heroic past that was meant to instill pride. Veneration could continue because the stone, idol, or representation was only a material object where the deity "came in the form of wind to receive the offerings." Perhaps for this, often unstated, reason, in some of the records from the Cajatambo in the middle of the seventeenth century, the words *camaquen* (meaning soul), *malqui*, and *guaca* are used interchangeably.[91]

Whatever their form and wherever found, they continued to speak to their followers, advising them on the future and the proper course of action in life. Caque Poma was buried with "two great wizards named Villca Rique and Machuay Caque who were his advisers. . . . the caciques consulted these dead through the wizards." With the help of alcohol or drugs, the living could receive oracular responses to their questions and directions on how to proceed. Villagómez states that

> when they talk with the huacas they usually are unconscious or suffering the effects of the Devil who makes them dumb when he speaks to them, or drunk on strong chicha that they drink when they want to communicate with the huaca. . . . In the lowlands from Chancay north, the beer that they offer the huacas is called *Yale*, and it is made of zora [jora (malted corn)] mixed with masticated corn, and they add powdered *espingo* [a hallucinogenic plant], and they make it very strong and thick, and after sprinkling some on the huaca, the bewitched drink the rest, and it makes them crazy.

The priest Hernando Hacaspomas, presumably under the influence of such drugs, made sacrifices so that the malqui Guamancama—described as a nephew of the idols Caruatarqui Vrao and Ticlla Vrau, the progenitor of the ayllu Chacac, a son of Libiac and a creator of humans, and, in sum, a "great and powerful Lord"—would answer his queries:

Having made sacrifices he embraces the said idol and he entered another trance and he said that the soul of the ancestor and idol Guamancama ratacurca came into his heart and told him what he was to do in that business that he had consulted with him[,] and in the same way that he gave him his answer[,] this witness came down to the people and he told all the principal Indians and the rest of the community what he had been told by the said appo [great lord or superior judge] and yayachi [confessor] and they acted as he said.[92]

In another place, we learn that malqui Guamancama "made them [humanity] increase in numbers and he guarded the planted fields and he gave the Indians silver and estates and he responded telling them what they were to do." Other malquis or their idols "until the Spanish arrived at Cajamarca, gave responses to their children, the men and the heads of their native lineages that today exist in this land, but then they agreed and determined that to survive it was better not to give public audiences and responses to the Indians[; but] instead to hide somewhere where all the priests would know." In sum, through the intercession of the curaca, the living-dead were accessible and continued to play active roles in the lives of their earthbound descendants. In the 1580s and 1590s, a dignified canon and vicar-general of La Plata, Diego Felipe de Molina, reported similar oracular activities "in every town." Drugs were part of prophetic rituals in Chachapoyas in 1612. Other communication with the divine (labeled as the "Devil" by the reporting Jesuits) is also documented for the Guancavelicas in 1613.[93]

For the lords themselves, perhaps, the most important motivation for their leadership in this respect was their inherited belief that the ancestors bestowed authority and legitimacy on them in the eyes of their followers. The constructed belief in divine sanction, the ability to make contact with the forces of the "other world" and manipulate and placate them, legitimized traditional authority and the exercise of power. Lords or would-be lords often sacrificed llamas (one of the most valuable of the items used for offerings) to please the ancestors in return for power. Those who already occupied office asked for continued wisdom and ability to govern. The governor Juan de Mendoza came to the pueblo of Hacas, sacrificed a llama, and addressed his subjects as follows: "I am your casique governor[;] let us make this sacrifice and pour this llama blood on this land so that I will know how to govern you and that I might govern in peace and tranquility and all will live in peace and tranquility." Like doña Graciana, mentioned earlier, another wife of a camachico and mayor of the town council (alcalde mayor), made sacrifices for the same reason: "so that the Indians will love and obey me." Don Christobal Pomalibiac sacrificed to be "respected . . . and obeyed by his Indians." Don Diego Julcaguaman, of Chilcas, sacrificed for the same purpose. He declared that he "sent this people a llama and other things to be sacrificed to the guaca caruatarquivrao so that he might give him good ability to rule [*manderecha*] his lesser lords and so that the Indians might obey him."[94]

Those who sought authority also needed supernatural favor. On another occasion don Juan de Mendoza sacrificed, with the help of Hernando Hacaspoma, so that his son "might get the position of casique and governor that the said don Juan de Mendosa possessed"; so that he "might succeed in entering the said government"; and so that "when he came among his people the Indians might come to love and obey him and would receive him as their governor."

Don Juan Caxa Atoc's entire future as curaca depended on winning a court case against don Diego Taparaco. Therefore, he and a certain number of his followers sacrificed to the malquis:

> He ordered each one alone and all to go to a shrine called Rauriñvca that was where their grandparents were buried and that they bring the guaca offerings [*muchca*?] as they did for that purpose[;] they took a llama and all the rest of the things that they use to make their [rites and ceremonies][;] before they went to do this[,] all the said Indians went and with them the said don Juan Caxa Atoc to a river and where the waters meet all confessed . . . and after that they went to make the said veneration that was done in the name of the said don Juan Caxa Atoc[,] who said to this said witness that he was already almost the winner in the court case over the curacaship with don Diego Taparaco[;] and in order to know how to govern and command his Indians well[,] he made the said veneration the same way that his parents and grandparents had done and did when they had differences about their rulerships and those who wanted to govern well.

He expected that "when he was curaca and finished with the court case he would know how to govern well his Indians imitating as he imitated his ancestors and did as they had done." Likewise, don Juan Gonsales, native of the parish of San Juan de Lampian, allegedly "had ordered them [two women] to make charms to have a good outcome in his court cases and be released from prison where the corregidor had put him in order to take away his government . . . because all the charms are aimed at and meant to culminate in positive ends in the court cases and this is more common in cases among the principal Indians over the casicasgos."[95]

The lords used the belief in supernatural forces to legitimate their right to rule. They reinforced the idea that the ancestors could and did judge their behavior and affect their own claims on power. Their roles as lawgivers and judges, their right to sentence their own subjects to death, if necessary, came from their antecedents.[96] As long as the ancestors were pleased and experienced no hunger, the lords felt secure and self-confident of their powers. The absence of natural disasters indicated that the ancestors were content.

The prestige of the curaca increased. Attraction and recruitment of additional followers became easier.[97]

Failure to tend and respect their ancestors, Andeans believed, brought catastrophe. If remiss or negligent in the obligations to the usually benevolent and life-sustaining ancestors, they could and did turn malevolent, it was believed, capable of sending hunger, disease, disaster, death, and misfortune to visit a lord's people. The ancestors could curse. The guacas of the Huachos and Yauyos threatened their devotees when they spoke. If their sacrifices were poor (consisting only of coca, chicha, *mullu*, *paria* ["that are colors of the land," dyes?], and guinea pigs), "he told them that they were lax in his service and he would not speak to them, or appear, and he would send them work and pestilences." In Cajatambo, some years later, the witness don Christobal Pomalibiac, a principal of the town of San Pedro de Hacas, stated that "if we do not adore the idols guacas and ancestors and other things to which we make sacrifices . . . he would die a bad death." Hacaspoma, a wiseman, holy man, and curer—who spoke with the idols and ancestors, and "who was consulted by all the peoples"—declared, in an obviously self-serving manner, that if they did not adore the ancestors, all the Indians would be consumed. Without sacrifices to the ancestors, "they would lose their planted fields and food and they would eat dirt." These statements are consistent with others made in the sixteenth century on the north coast, where native peoples feared that if the ancestors grew upset or were disturbed, the living could lose all or all would perish.[98]

Drought, hailstorms, deluges, and frost that destroyed crops; plagues; canal system breakdowns; or other natural disasters signaled that the ancestors were hungry and thirsty, that they were displeased for perceived ritual neglect. For such "sins," the ancestors withdrew their support and favor.[99] Villagómez stated that the Andean peoples "understand that because of their sins the ancestors and guacas are angry and for this reason they get sick."[100] Such problems were blamed on the religious negligence or ineffectiveness of the curaca. Misfortune signaled that the ancestors were displeased and in a wrathful mood. The lord had failed in maintaining consensus and harmony among the living; he might not have observed strictly his sacred obligations; therefore, he was no longer capable of ruling and maintaining the balance and order of society. In a few documented cases, feckless curacas committed suicide. In others, in the face of prolonged drought or devastating flood and the perceived impotence of their lord to appease the ire of the ancestral spirits, to neutralize their curses, and to convince them to reverse the negative influence, the lord would be doomed. His subjects might shun him first and then desert, abandoning him.[101]

Commoner response to natural disasters was to seek "protection" of another lord and his gods. The rains and floods on the north coast of 1578 left adobe houses ruined, their roofs collapsed; stored food and seeds rotted; and domestic animals drowned or dead. Fields of cotton, corn, and vegetables were uprooted and washed away. Irrigation canals became clogged with brush and silt. The dampness and humidity also brought plagues of crickets and worms. Native farmers fled. The Lambayecanos deserted to their neighbors, the Callancas, to find corn. The Pacasmayos, to the south, declared that "we go to plant distant lands and where we do not normally plant nor are the lands of so much benefit." Such withdrawal of support and corresponding attitudes, which attributed hardship and struggles to sin and ancestral anger, may explain why natives would not obey don Juan Tacsitarqui, their sick lord in 1568—disease and troubles being a manifestation of divine disfavor. Likewise, a candidate for the chieftainship (cacicazgo) in 1693, Piura was judged to be disqualified for the "impediment of poverty and age," a sure sign that he needed to go to rest with his forefathers and let another more vigorous person assume the role. In fact, Zuidema states that the Inca's well-being was deemed a proxy for the health of the empire. This seems to be true for the provincial peoples as well.[102]

In extreme cases, the lord was judged spiritually incompetent and responsible for great natural and social catastrophes. He might then be deposed, forcibly removed from office, and murdered. Legend recalls how the perceived misconduct of Fempellec, for example, brought on thirty days of ruinous rains on the north desert coast. His priests and principals, blaming him for the perceived divine outrage and its consequences, drowned him for the transgression, in a sequence of events that recalls the workings of the ancient Chinese concept of "Mandate of Heaven." Rostworowski documents further examples from the north coast where curacas (even those recently "elected" by their peers) who were judged incompetent, or who otherwise angered their followers, were condemned by public opinion and killed by their subjects. Also on the coast, in 1532, as Pizarro and his band made their way into the area, the Lambayecanos rose up against their curaca, Xecfuin Pisan. They beat him, breaking his arms and legs, finally leaving him to burn in his tent (*toldo*) as he slept, because, according to one version, he was going to go to receive and befriend the Christians. Nearby in the same region, Xancol Chumbi, the curaca of Reque, soon after first meeting the Spanish made unreasonable demands on his people. Such violation of established custom and taboos provoked his murder, perhaps to right the wrong and preserve the system.[103]

Curacas continued to be executed by their followers during colonial times for threatening the well-being of all by being unfaithful to the ancestral forces. The Jesuits reported that a curaca of the Guancavelicas who did not observe the ancient rites and worship the ancestral spirits died of poisoning in the early seventeenth century. Spalding calls attention to the communal stoning of a curaca of the guaranga of Carampoma (Huarochirí) in the early eighteenth century for the suspicion that he would inform authorities of their secret ritual activities. The same was true among the Pacajes in 1543 and other peoples of the altiplano. Thus, to fail to live up to traditional ritual norms of the ancestors, the lord must be sanctioned and punished, because his actions—bad or good—affected the whole group.[104]

It appears, in sum, that traditional chiefs served as intermediaries not only between the Incas (before 1532) or the Spanish (after 1532) and their subjects, but also between the earthbound living and the living-dead.[105] They apportioned a part of their subjects' labor to raise the products or elaborate them for offerings to satisfy the appetite of the gods in periodic memorials and rites. They, in other words, were feeding the ancestors, expecting that the departed members of their family and lineage would, in turn, favor them with good weather, growing conditions, and health so that they could continue to feed themselves; reproduce, attract new devotees, and grow in numbers; and otherwise prosper. The people of Chinchaycocha sacrificed to and fed the mountain named Raco "so that he could give them food." Interestingly, when a witness, Antonio Ripai, an elder Nava, was asked if the guacas really ate the food that was left as offerings, he said that "they left it there but that when they return they found nothing." Thus, the lords were responsible for the welfare of their people (both living and dead)—not only in the secular world but also in the supernatural realm. The relationship was a reciprocal one that can be summarized as "to feed and be fed."[106]

Because local lords served as religious functionaries and intermediaries between two realms, the material and the spiritual, they were themselves worshipped (*mochado*) when they sat on the stool or throne of office and assumed authority as described earlier. Martínez Cereceda asserts that they were considered sacred: "The kuraka himself (. . . after being inducted and not his person) was perceived to be sacred." A lord understood his responsibility for maintaining the good reputation of all those who had preceded him in the position, for should he perform his duties well, his followers would continue to honor and celebrate him and his predecessors in song.[107] He and his progenitors would be remembered as immortal and honored ancestors.[108]

Local inhabitants were convinced that their traditional religion was the right one for them. The elders, ministers, and authorities warned their relatives to worship their malquis, not the Christian god, because, to quote the eloquent Hernando Hacaspoma (in 1657),

> in these times this witness instructed and taught the people that they should not adore God our father nor his saints because they were guacas and spirits of the Spanish and they were some painted and golden sticks and they were silent, they did not

give answers to the questions asked by Indians as did their idol guamancama and other idols and ancient ancestors who when consulted and given sacrifices reply to their questions[;] and that the god of the Spanish does not give anything to the Indians[;] and they should not adore him but adore their ancestors and guacas because they give children, planted fields and the rest[;] and although the Bishop burned some mummies and idols[,] they should be adored and given sacrifices because their spirits are alive[,] they are immortal and they come to the sacrifices made by their children.

A whole chorus of religious specialists and other practitioners confessed to such advice. One said that he talked to the god Luviac and others "who had told them not to adore the Christian God and not to confess that they adored the guacas." Juan Chuchu, testifying in 1656, said that he had ordered "that they not adore God but their idols because they had been their grandparents and ancestors." Ysabel Llupay Vilca, a declared dogmatizer, confessor, and preacher (*dogmatisadora confesora y predicadora*), told the extirpator that she "had preached to them not to adore the Christian god and not to marry because the Christian god would not give them what they needed nor food[;] only the guacas and ancestors would." Catalina Caxa Tanta confessed much the same thing, telling her listeners "that they not adore the Christian god but the spirits and ancestors because the latter are the ones who give them food[,] clothes[,] water[,] and planted fields and not god." Hernando Chaupiscon in 1657 added that

this witness preached to his lineage and to the Cochillas people not to adore god our father nor the saints[;] and [he taught that] they should comply with but not take the sacraments sincerely because he said it was a trick and that the Indians should adore their ancestors and guacas that they had in the old towns and in their fields and sacred spaces [stone altars, *cayanes*][;] and that the Spanish likewise had their guacas and spirits in their churches[;] and that the Spanish guacas did not give them food and belongings[;] only their guacas ancestors and progenitors did.[109]

Many Andeans took the warnings seriously and held this to be true. They knew that if they neglected those who came before, they would lack the necessities of life and would die, like the notorious example of don Rodrigo Caxa Malqui, who suffered two years and died a terrible death after he helped Fray Francisco extirpate and destroy guacas. The guacas, people said, had made him suffer and "die with difficulty." Therefore, his successor, don Juan Rimay Chahua, resurrected the old religion: "He ordered the revival of idolatry in all this land." Crosses were destroyed, and the ashes of guacas were preserved and worshipped to avert such suffering and misfortune. Such sentiments echoed the beliefs of previous generations of central Andeans. The Jesuits reported that the people of Andajes in 1614 believed that "they would not go without punishments, those who abandoned the idols for Christ would remain ruined all the year waiting for rain, the plants would be lost, and the same people would starve to death." Andeans left statements, as early as 1565, to the effect that not to worship the traditional gods would bring death.[110]

They had proof that what their elders, lords, and religious specialists told them was true. Had not the main altar of the church of Huacra been hit by lightning and burned? Had not the guacas declared that they had sent the lightning strike to punish the lying Spanish? In Cajatambo, neglect promised the extinction of the ayllu, with the loss of their chacras and food. Without proper memorial sacrifices, they would be condemned to eat dirt (*comerian tierra*). Did they not know that all the descendants of the malqui Chinchai "had been consumed"? Had they not seen all of Alonso Marques's children die, one by one, because he had neglected his forebears?[111]

Legitimizing Legacies

Spanish and Hispanicized native accounts stress the material bases of the curaca's role and legitimacy. In return for access to natural resources and protection, the people would work for him. He rerouted some of this labor to support the Inca before 1532 and an ever-mounting percentage to maintain the Spanish after 1532. In some cases, service to the Spanish became oppressive and abhorrent to the commoners to the point where the colonial lord's hegemony seriously eroded. The Spanish state, recognizing his dilemma and the competing demands on his resources, provided him with the means and limited support to carry out his colonial functions. To Spanish eyes, his leadership role and accommodation to colonial demands became both necessary and sufficient conditions for his acceptance. To be welcomed by the Europeans meant assuming the guise of a Christian and acquiring the material possessions that symbolized position and influence, and guaranteed sufficient liquid assets to subsidize tribute arrears of commoners (see Figure 4.6). This undoubtedly also gained the goodwill of certain of his dependents. Genealogical respectability was a plus. But many a lord's manifest acceptance of Spanish values and his efforts to amass riches marked an overt shift in motivations and behavior that was more apparent than real.[112]

Administrative ability, political ties, proper genealogical alignment and depth, and sufficient wealth to ease his subjects' colonial responsibilities, in and of themselves, were necessary but not sufficient to Andeans. To traditional native peoples, the bedrock of power and legitimacy remained the acquiescence and favor of the ancestors. They believed that the right and ability to be their leader depended on a candidate's perceived promise to be able to mediate between the realm of the ancestors and their own. This continuing idea, though constructed and inherited from one generation to another, forced the colonial curaca to become the proverbial Janus-faced

FIGURE 4.6. A colonial curaca of one thousand households. Source: Guamán Poma de Ayala 1613/1936: 745.

go-between. To guarantee the support of his kin and clients, the traditional lord continued his mediating role in the rites and faith of the forefathers, refusing to completely compromise the cosmological underpinnings of his power.[113]

Some of the confusion and debate over these issues of lordly power and legitimacy can be traced to the conceptual categories used by Westerners as opposed to those of non-Westerners. On the one hand, European observers describe and interpret the foreign in terms they understand. The majority of Spanish observers dismissed ancestor worship as the pagan practices of defeated peoples. Their understanding of what they observed can be attributed to the language they used, their terms of analysis, and their ethnocentric perspective and cultural filters.

Andeans, in contrast, did not use the same system of classification and reference. To their way of thinking, the ancestors were integral partners and players in their society and wider spiritual community. They had left the resources to the living. Life ebbed almost seamlessly into death and another alternative existence. The curaca (the political force) as the divine (religious) mediator between the two realms (material and spiritual) mobilized the labor (social and economic) of his followers to fulfill their obligations to the honored and respected departed. In this holistic vision of existence, as young cared for the old, so the living cared for their past antecedents, who had favored them in the present. Thus was created a reciprocal, recurring relationship that was repeated generation after generation, creating community and identity.[114]

Part Three

THE PRACTICE OF COSMOLOGICAL POWER

5 *Rites of Rule*

> At midnight the women who were there went with the said Hernando Hacas Poma crying and shouting through the streets and the men stayed with the deceased all of whom said that these honors were made for their principal lord and curaca so that he would have something to eat in the other world.
>
> —Confession of Andres Chaupis Yauri, Pueblo de San Francisco de Otuco, August 15, 1656

The religio-political ideas and notions about the sanctity and centrality of the Andean ruler and chiefs and their roles as intercessors between the profane and the sacred were omnipresent. They were seen in their insignia of rank and clothing. They were heard repeatedly in the myths that Andean folk recalled and chanted. They were evident in the rituals they performed and in the monumental architecture where these took place. Taken together, the myths and ceremonies and the locations where the latter were staged represented reinforcing, tangible texts that, in the absence of writing, served to establish mental paradigms of proper behaviors and, ideally, to reinforce feelings of fit and solidarity. Redistributive activities that invariably were part of certain recurring public gatherings motivated the following of the various authorities to do what had to be done in the hope of guaranteeing survival, if not fertility and prosperity, and of warding off evil.

State Theater

The Europeans, on whose eyewitness accounts we now heavily rely, recorded myriad details of the symbols and rituals that they saw in the ceremonial centers of the empire. They described how the gods were displayed. One of the representations of the Sun, the ancestral god and golden idol of the Incas, was positioned centrally in the Coricancha, seated on a long bench or throne (*escaño*) of gold, worth twenty-thousand castellanos. When on public view, the idol was carried out of the temple on a litter and onto a seat, which was covered with a vividly colored feathered mantle, to the main square, surrounded by a "court" composed of the mummified remains of its purported descendants, the ex-rulers of the expanding Inca realm. Representations of local provincial gods that were in the southern ceremonial center were kept together in a gallery, where they were honored, invoked, and propitiated. At the local level, authorities orchestrated what amounted to a provincial version of the grandiose tradition that surrounded the Inca. There, malquis and idols were also seated on stools and carried on litters when moved, sumptuously attired and crowned in gold. All were routinely and periodically offered libations and food as part of the continuing and reciprocal commitment between the present and the past.[1]

Thanks to the chroniclers, readers also have early, detailed accounts of the mystique and majesty of the living persons and courts of the Inca and curaca. Europeans recorded the awe inspired by their processions: they passed, seated regally on stools atop painted, bejeweled, and befeathered litters. Aloof and detached they rode, in practiced imitation of the gods. Observers described their fine tunics and mantles—made of vicuña or bat fur or feathers—some appliquéd in gold and decorated with colored designs that, even today, inspire scholars to contemplate and study their meaning. Some left accounts of the pomp and pageantry attending them, of the thousands of retainers who accompanied the Inca, and of the scores of dignitaries who surrounded the curacas on pilgrimages and visits—even years after the first encounter, after the initial glory had faded.[2]

But even the most astute eyewitnesses who wrote about what they observed failed to understand completely or acknowledge explicitly the meaning of the symbols, the parades, and the rites that they were privileged to know. Those who might have seen and understood rarely commented in detail on how the symbols and settings reflected the Andean worldview and their notions of legitimacy, propriety, and order. To outsiders, these events might be pleasing and entertaining, but also puzzling, strange, and certainly antagonistic to Christian beliefs and teachings.[3]

Interest in native religious beliefs and practices grew over time, but often outsiders were too quick in their judgments. They dismissed the fables and dogmatically (and nervously) asserted that the religiously inspired but foreign rituals were frightening evidence of a feared devil worship. The many native ritual practices and ceremonies that they witnessed represented the "enemy's" deviousness, misguidance, dangerous temptations, and superstitions, which must be rooted out and replaced with the worship of the one, true Christian god, who had delivered the Iberian peninsula back into the hands of the Spanish and had now bequeathed a large portion of the New World to them as well. Because of their own ethnocentric certainty and religious jealousy, which served as a convenient excuse to the world for this new imperial enterprise, they devalued and dismissed native ritual as paganistic claptrap, a waste of time and resources. Their doctrinally asserted self-righteousness blinded many to the significance of these native religio-political practices. In ignoring indigenous ritual and persecuting practitioners, they were naively attacking the legitimizing and organizational bases of the Inca polity and the native sense of self.[4]

As mentioned previously, the public life of Andean leaders—both imperial Inca and provincial curaca—was one of ritual and display. This pageantry was not haphazard; it was pregnant with conscious and unconscious meaning for those brought up in the culture, who were informally schooled in the import of the symbols and familiar with the stories and songs involved. Emblems of rank included stools or seats; litters (*andas*, *guandos*, and *rampas*), upon which both gods and authorities rode; trumpets and musical instruments; sunshades or umbrellas (*quitasoles*); elaborately decorated beakers (*queros*); festive garb—especially fine shirts of cumbi, jewelry, and headdresses; feathers; and the ubiquitous but seldom-mentioned clowns that were attached to both the imperial and local courts. Each of these was imbued with culturally defined values and significance. They conveyed messages about prestige, acceptance, and inviolability. The tiana symbolized divinely granted authority to order the world. The provincial authority's litters, fine shirts, jewelry, and drinking cups were usually gifts from the Inca and, as such, represented his bestowed honor and mutually recognized obligations.[5] In addition, Inca queros and other effigy pots and ceramics were often decorated with propagandistic iconography that highlighted and illustrated origin myths and fables and stereotyped the meanings of popular ceremonies. Symbols woven into textiles (*tocapos*) were redundant conveyors of rank and rule.[6]

These visible markers were featured and explained in myths that were sometimes told and often sung. For example, one of these stories from the north coast, related by Cabello Valboa, regarded the cultural hero and progenitor of the rulers of society, Naimlap. This myth mentions the symbols and personnel attending the king, thus serving as a model for the "court" of a lord. Naimlap, so the story goes, arrived on the north coast on wooden rafts (*balsas*).

> He brought with him many peoples who as their captain and caudillo they followed, although those who among them were most important were his forty officials, like for example, Pita Zofi who was his trumpeter or player of some large conch shells, that were highly prized among the Indians, another Ñinacola who took care of his seats and litter [and, by extension, his bearers and escort], and another Ñinagintue who was in charge of the drink of said Lord like a Botiller, another called Fonga sigde who was in charge of spreading the powder of marine shells on the path that the Lord was to tread; another Occhocalo was his Cook, another had charge of the unctions and colors with which the Lord painted his face, he was called Xam muchec[.] Ollopcopoc was in charge of the toilet of the Lord, another principal lord, much esteemed by his Prince was called Llapchiluli, who made shirts and clothing of feathers, and

these persons (and an infinite number of other officials and men of importance) adorned and authorized his person and dynasty.[7]

Trumpets made of conch shells, litters, stools that functioned as thrones, and colored powders made from pulverized seashells were some of the mentioned insignia of the invading lord. Drinking cups, effigy pots and other ceramics, and face paint were also important markers of rank and status that reinforced legitimizing beliefs.

Ceremony summarized the Andean peoples' worldview in a succinct fashion. It transmitted traditional knowledge from the past and represented the constructed, legitimizing cosmology that undergirded the rule and strength of Andean leaders. The rituals converted past events and myths into paradigms. Pease believed that "the relations of the Inca conquests that the chroniclers heard were in reality stories of a ritual [and] in that way the past remained stereotyped." Ceremonies represented an effective means to communicate power relationships and social order in a preliterate, multiethnic, polylinguistic, and growing polity.[8]

Song lyrics that accompanied dancing were performed on many ritual occasions. Such pageantry recalled the coming and the feats of the malqui progenitors; they retold and reenacted the story of common origins and basic cosmological forces. The superhuman attributes of cultural heroes were portrayed at such periodic cult reunions amid a display of hospitality that symbolized the scale and concern of the ancestors. As people danced and sang, drank chicha, and ate the meat of the sacrificial animals, these dramatizations entertained and diverted. All the while, the devout absorbed the ideological underpinnings of the imperial system and structure and celebrated their history and being. Such religio-political ceremonies were designed and arranged to create consensual acceptance of their subjection among the dominated and to foster common identity. This proved more effective than naked force in effecting the unity of the disparate and distant peoples of the empire, although not everyone passively accepted with the same conviction the forced cohesion of an ideology advocating the one-birth, one-law ideal. The Incas did not have a professional, full-time army or a constabulary to impose their will. Thus, they relied on the ceremonial teachings and spectacle to provide the information necessary to reproduce society and maintain continuity. Religion and myth, the cultural components most resistant to change, reinforced collective identity and conveyed moral authority, especially to those being newly inducted into the service of the state. They were the essence of ideological control.[9]

It is my purpose here to describe and analyze briefly selected ritual events of the Andean people to demonstrate how state "theater" validated hierarchical relations and served ideological ends—as propaganda for the reigning power structure at various levels. Following Martínez Cereceda's pathbreaking and masterful analyses, my interpretation of ceremony will focus on the investitures and progresses of both imperial and provincial lords. These were designed to impress, to teach, and to control behavior. They perpetuated the lessons of the power of the past and the promises of the future; they welcomed and rewarded partisans; and they excluded outsiders. I will also analyze funerary practices to explore the transition from life and this world to the "other." Though ancestor worship was slated for extinction by Spanish ecclesiastical mandate as early as 1551, the funeral—with its recitation of the deeds of the ancestors and history of the group and its visitation of the places the deceased had frequented—continued to remind people of the interdependence of the living and the dead and of the link between the sacred and profane into the middle and late eighteenth century. In so doing, it justified and reinforced the traditional belief system and status quo (and, in colonial times, sometimes marked identity and served as a statement of resistance, defiance, and continuing communal existence).[10]

Succession and Investiture

The Inca bragged, and official propaganda reiterated, that the Sun had no other son and that the Inca had no other father. The emperor had been begotten by the gods. As the son of divinity, he was capac, the only, unique, supreme, or singular lord, a being without equal. As descendant of deities, the Inca was dignified as the Indi Churi or son of the Sun. "With this title he made himself adored and he governed with a firm hand to such a degree that no one challenged him." His word was law and no one "dared to go against his word and will." Such statements of divine origins, although exaggerated, sum up the message that the investiture ceremony was constructed to convey.[11]

As suggested in Chapter 3, there was no single prescribed and always-followed way that a successor was chosen. Choice, divine confirmation, and subsequent acknowledgment and inauguration were phases of a process that would have begun, in theory, as early as the puberty rituals, or even before. There seems to have been a preference for one of the reigning Inca's sons, but even named favorites, often products of divine incest, were not always the ones who eventually filled the office. The candidate was subject to supernatural accreditation by divination in the calpa ceremony, through which, in theory, the Sun exercised veto power over the proposed human candidates. But this ceremony, and the sometimes intense lobbying and jockeying for power of the factious panacas and ambitious contenders for the role of Inca that preceded it, were probably not public. In fact, news of the secret conclaves that often followed the death of a sovereign were kept from the masses, especially the people of the provinces, until a successor had been duly designated and presented. Keeping succession wrangling and infighting secret helped to prevent factions at the political center from dividing the wider populace and avoided diluting the supernatural trappings of kingship.[12]

Two examples of the investiture ceremony and the events leading up to it will suffice as examples. In terms of realpolitik, they represent a range of variation in the ideal succession process, including the possible intrigue and murder that sometimes influenced the choice. The first example shows the peaceful passage of power from father to son while the former lived. The second illustrates the extent to which politics and ambition could distort the ideal and the accommodation necessary to maintain uninterrupted rule and the semblance of order.

Legitimation of power, as one of the most important of the ceremonials, if we speak of them individually, became grander and grander over time as the renown and strength of the imperial system spread and increased. Pachacuti Inca Yupanqui, so instrumental in prescribing procedure and establishing precedent, set the standard that was followed into the colonial era. When Pachacuti Inca Yupanqui fell fatally ill, he identified two possible candidates as heirs. Pease reports that Pachacuti Inca Yupanqui originally named Amaru Yupanqui to be his successor. But Amaru Yupanqui was judged inept to manage the military aspects of sovereignty, because he had lost several armed contests, a sure sign of divine disfavor. So, in the presence of the statues and idols of their divinely begotten lineage and the nobles in the House of Coricancha (the monument to their ancestors), Pachacuti Inca Yupanqui named another son, Tupac Inca Yupanqui, as Inca-elect. The real reason for Amaru's divestiture, says Pease, was a contest for power between various elite factions. Tupac Inca Yupanqui triumphed in the long run. The announced public excuse was the logical one: "The Sun, father of the Incas, had withdrawn his support of the prince Amaru in favor of Tupac Inca Yupanqui."[13]

The Inca presently ordered a fringe of gold to be placed in the hand of the image of the Sun. After Tupac Inca Yupanqui made his obeisance to his father, the Inca and the rest of those present rose and assembled before the Sun's representation, where they made their offerings, including the capa coche. Then they sacrificed to the new Inca, Tupac Inca Yupanqui, and beseeched the Sun to protect and support him, to make him so that all would hold and judge him to be a child of the Sun and father of his people. This done, the oldest and principal orejones presented Tupac Inca Yupanqui to the Sun, took the fringe from the hand of the image, and placed it on his forehead. He was declared Inca capac and seated in front of the Sun on a seat of gold, garnished with emeralds and other precious stones. He took an oath to be obedient to the Sun, to not mistreat the lords of the realm, to work the fields of the Sun, to defend his sovereignty, and to look after the welfare of his followers. Seated there, he received the befeathered, multicolored staff of office, some golden cups (*tupa cusi napa*), new sandals (*oxotas*), and other insignia of his acquired rank and station. Those assembled kissed his feet and then raised him, seated on his stool, onto their shoulders in parade as the next god incarnate.[14]

All this was kept quiet until the Pachacuti Inca Yupanqui, his biological father, ordered that the news be made public. At one point, Pachacuti Inca Yupanqui instructed his sons to serve their brother, Tupac Inca Yupanqui. Amaru Yupanqui came before him and fell facedown to the earth, adoring him, offering sacrifices, and acknowledging his obligation to obey. Eventually, Tupac Inca Yupanqui left the House of the Sun on his litter, surrounded by the idols of the Sun, Viracocha, other guacas, and the mummified figures of the former kings. At the Haucaypata, he accepted white feathers from those present as symbols of obedience. Pedro Pizarro, an early eyewitness, described such a scene on another occasion:

> All the lords gathered on the plaza and the one who was to be elected king Capac in the middle, seated on his stool, the lords got up one at a time: first the nobles, and then the lords of the rest of the peoples and their subject Indians, and one by one they approached the lord, barefoot, carrying small feathers in their hands: they turned their palms toward the face of the lord, venerating him and they waved these feathers in front of his face, and they gave them to a man who was standing next to him . . . and . . . they burned them. They swore likewise by the Sun raising their faces to it and by the Earth, to be loyal to him and to serve him and to do whatever he ordered.[15]

It represented, according to Sancho de la Hoz, a "sign of vassalage and tribute, and this is ancient custom among them since this land was conquered by these Cuzcos." These feathers represented obedience (*en muestra de obediencia*) and perhaps a symbolic contribution in recognition of el Cuzco's dominance.[16]

Once the Inca was installed and invested, great public ceremonies with songs and dance were held, and more great sacrifices were made to assure that the new ruler would be favored and blessed. Only then was word sent to the general populace, ordering the local lords to come to swear him obedience and offer him their gifts. People worshipped him, plucking out their eyebrows and eyelashes and blowing them in his direction as a very personal offering. Others offered him handfuls of coca leaf.[17]

When Pachacuti Inca Yupanqui sensed that death was near, he called all his sons together and divided his jewels and wardrobe. Then he made them plow furrows in token acknowledgment that they were vassals of Tupac Inca Yupanqui. He gave them arms to fight for their brother. Next, he sent for the orejones and Tupac Inca Yupanqui, telling his heir that he left him "great nations" and charging him with keeping and augmenting them.

He counseled his heir to care for his subjects so that they would serve him. He advised that relatives be named as his advisers. He died after expressing his hope that no living person might "raise his two eyes against you." In other words, he wished that the ritual chaos that could accompany the death of a divine ruler would be avoided. In this case, Tupac Inca Yupanqui was then reinvested with the fringe and insignia of sovereignty before being carried to the Haucaypata, where the people were ordered to come to serve him—to show him respect and obedience as emperor and make obeisance to him as capac or king.[18]

In turn, when Tupac Inca Yupanqui died, perhaps by poisoning, he left many sons—born of his sister, the coya, and other women. Cabello Valboa writes that although Guayna Capac had "more right" to succeed, Tupac Inca Yupanqui named Capac Guari, son of a consort and concubine, as heir. The coya or an uncle of Guayna Capac intervened, claiming that the secondary wife—deemed a witch by some—had poisoned Tupac Inca Yupanqui. She was therefore executed, and her son was either killed or exiled with some servants to Chinchero. Even so, the other designee, Guayna Capac, had to enter the Temple of the Sun "so that he could be chosen by the Sun his father as king Capac Apo Ynga. In the three times that they entered to sacrifice he was not called; on the fourth [try] he was called by his father the sun and he said Guayna Capac. Then he took the crown and . . . thereafter they obeyed him."[19] Thus did the Sun, ostensibly, allow the backers of Guayna Capac to predominate over those of his half brother Capac Guari.[20]

The elements that are important here are the divine election or confirmation symbolically made by the Sun and the bestowal of the insignia of power that signaled the passing of sovereignty from one generation to the next. To onlookers, the new ruler emerging from the sacred sanctuary of the Coricancha had been touched and empowered by the divine. Who could doubt that the celestial ancestors had given him power? No candidate was acknowledged and worshipped as having made the passage from mere human to divine status before receiving the imperial headdress. The "crown" (mascapaicha) represented the acceptance by the Sun of the next ruler and the initiation of his divinity. According to the chroniclers, who sometimes equated it with a royal crown, the first element to meet the eye was a brilliantly red (*carmesí*), fine wool fringe suspended from a golden plaque, straws, or bugles (tubular beads), which hung across the forehead of the Inca—in the shape of a trapezoid—to just above the eyes (see Figure 5.1). Pedro Pizarro remembers that it was sewn onto and suspended from a *llauto*, which consisted of a multicolored braid or woven headband—about half a finger thick and one finger wide—that was wrapped several times around the head to the width of a hand. In the mascapaicha "was concentrated the monarchical majesty of the empire." Taking the fringe (*tomar la borla*) was

FIGURE 5.1. The mascapaicha on the heads of the Incas. Source: Guamán Poma de Ayala 1613/1936.

equivalent to being crowned; this signaled the point when the person assumed a new divine identity, assumed a new name, and officially took his sister as his mate. Coronation was consecrated with the blood of hundreds of children between the ages of four and ten.[21]

The mascapaicha was a powerful symbol. Juan Larrea deconstructs its meaning. It invoked memories of the mythical times of the Ayar brothers and sisters and the arms they carried. The headband represented a weapon that Mama Guaco used: a long rope with a stone or piece of gold attached, which could be slung about in battle or used to ensnare the wings or legs of birds or other animals. In later renditions of the piece, the stone was replaced with a blade in the shape of an ax. Thus, upon seeing the symbol, a person would be reminded of the ferocity with which an irrepressible Mama Guaco swung this weapon. She is described as a cruel, terrorizing, and masculinized woman with magical power to contact and talk to the dead. She was thought to have disemboweled her adversaries and smeared their blood on her face. The message was that even the women of the Incas were ferocious and valiant; they could and would easily, without second thought, use the weapon to impose their will. The fringe represented a bloody blade, an explicit threat to anyone who might dare challenge the collective will of the elite. The smaller headdress of the crown prince, which consisted of a yellow fringe, represented the still unused blade of the untried future leader. Because triumph in battle was one of the signs of the Sun's favor and Amaru Yupanqui had been judged incompetent in this sphere, I conclude then that he was deemed unsuitable, unworthy of wearing the mascapaicha, and for this reason was never invested.[22]

So potent a symbol was the royal fringe that duplicates were given to royal messengers to carry. Those seeing the sign would recognize the emissary as high ranking, backed by the full power of the state. Guamán Poma de Ayala depicts an Inca representative (an *alcalde de corte*) who was sent to arrest an important provincial lord, Apo Cullic Chaua of the Chiccay ayllu of the Cajatambos, for rebellion and treason. He carried an authenticating mascapaicha on his staff as a symbol of his legitimate purpose (see Figure 5.2). In contrast, a low-ranking officer received the sandals or coca bag of the emperor as an authorizing symbol of his mission and task (see Figure 5.3).[23]

Sitting on the tiana and receiving the paraphernalia of rank and office were also important. The golden tiana studded with precious jewels blinded in the sun and symbolized the location of the center of the empire. The description of this stool makes it taller and more elaborate than others, representing the higher status of the ruler. Other emblems of his place in the sacred universal hierarchy included his large earplugs; his royal tunics, which bore distinguishing designs; his mantles; and the imperial staff. This ritual assemblage was completed with a pair of drinking vessels (quero or *aquilla*) of gold, silver, or metal: one from which to drink and one from which to offer drink, usually to a god, such as the Sun. Only after being thus equipped was he hoisted onto the shoulders of his attendants to be carried eventually to the great plaza and imperial stage, accompanied by the Sun and the mummies of his forebears for all to laud and revere. Estete saw the mummies displayed, seated on seats and carried on litters, in 1537. Once in the plaza, each noble, in order of his importance, presented the Inca with a white feather as a sign of obedience.[24]

FIGURE 5.2. A messenger with mascapaicha insignia. Source: Guamán Poma de Ayala 1613/1936: 342.

FIGURE 5.3. A messenger with sandals and coca bag. Source: Guamán Poma de Ayala 1613/1936: 344.

The symbolism here is one of hierarchy, superiority, and service to a superior being. In a society in which most persons sat on the ground and the height of tianas symbolized the rank of its possessor (see Figure 5.4), the Inca sat taller and higher than others and, therefore, was both literally and symbolically above everyone else. While riding on his litter, which will be described later in more detail, he remained at rest with movement all around. According to the origin myths associated with Viracocha, Llasac (of the natives of the pachaca of Urcon), Pariacaca (of the Huarochirí people), Tutayquiri, and Guari—all Andean gods analyzed by Martínez Cereceda—after wandering about, sat in high places, such as on mountain peaks, when they ordered the world. At rest, the Inca resembled the hero-gods of the past: inscrutable, august, stoic, and capable of good or evil. If properly served, appeased, and nourished, he became a creator and protector. The presentation of white feathers signaled the acknowledgment of this uncommon status and his ultimate acceptance by the members of the royal court. It symbolized the consensus that there sat the divinely chosen and inspired leader, the successor man-god and patriarch, the center of the realm, wherever he went.[25]

FIGURE 5.4. A tiana. Source: Field Museum, Chicago, acc. no. 2832.

His new name or title represented his transformation from human to divine. The marriage of the Inca to his sister, which immediately followed, confirmed the divinity of his blood and lineage. Such a marriage guaranteed that his successor's blood, should that person be the offspring of the prescribed incestuous union, would be unpolluted by any deemed inferior. A wife from any other group was beneath his status and dignity and imperiled his position as the ultimate wife giver.[26]

The monumental architecture that served as backdrops and stages for such rites conveyed supporting and legitimizing messages. Embedded in its silent structure was an explanation for the status quo. The buildings surrounding the Haucaypata, for example, represented metaphorically the divine genealogy and celestial ancestors of temporal authorities. The discussion on architecture follows Isbell's analysis and paraphrases his argument. At the apex of the plaza—shaped like an inverted U—was the Quishuarcancha, a group of structures dedicated to Viracocha, the androgynous, bisexual creator god (see Figures 5.5a and 5.5b). There, at the center of that side of the plaza, was the Cuyusmango (Cuyusmanco, Cuysmanco, Cuismanco), which repeated the form of the three-sided plaza. Gonçalez Holguin described it as "the council hall or chamber of Justice of three walls

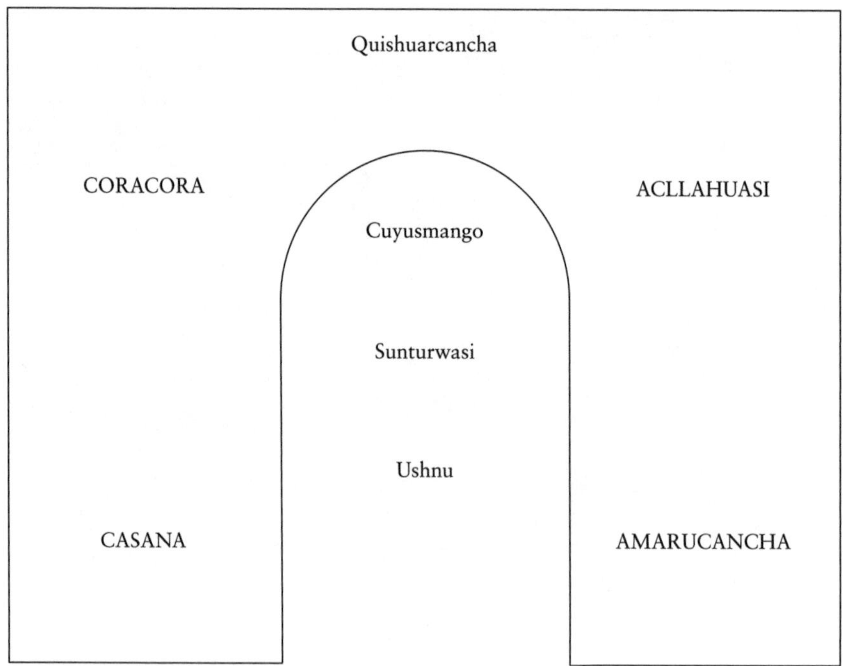

FIGURE 5.5A. Diagrammatic representation of the Cuyusmango.

FIGURE 5.5B. Cuyusmango. Source: Guamán Poma de Ayala 1613/1936: 329.

and one open." To the right of the Quishuarcancha (looking out) were two buildings, the Coracora and the Casana, where scholars, philosophers, and poets resided and instructed noble youths. They were identified with masculine activities. On the third side were the acllahuasi—a repository for chosen women (*aclla*) dedicated to the Sun—and the Amarucancha—the enclosure of the great serpents, associated with the Sun, soil, and agriculture. This side of the U was considered feminine and associated with fertility and reproduction.[27]

Within the U-shaped enclosure of the Huacaypata were two additional structures. The Sunturwasi, a circular building that was the focus of some rituals to the Sun, lay in front of the Quishuarcancha. The mummies of past emperors were assembled and fed there. The last structure was the ushnu, a stepped pyramidal platform where the Inca sat, above the spectators, to watch proceedings and deliver justice (see Figure 5.6). Once seated upon the ushnu platform, the emperor was at one with the cosmic axis and "partook of the spiritual power and wisdom it embodied." Both of these structures were points of contact between the living and the dead.[28]

Isbell shows how this stone creation exemplified, manifested, and revealed the cosmological model drawn by Santacruz Pachacuti Yamqui, presented as a drawing of the Coricancha (see Figures 3.2 and 3.3). The line drawing is enclosed in a U-shaped line, open at the bottom. At the apex is the creator Viracocha. The figures on its right (looking out) are masculine: the Sun; and Venus as the morning star, called "grandfather" and associated with the stars of the summer sky and lightning. Next is "Lord" or "Father" Earth with mountains, mediating rainbow, and seven circles called "eyes of abundance." On the left are female figures: the Moon; Venus, as the evening star, called "grandmother" and associated with clouds of the winter sky; and a feline linked to hail. Below is Mother Ocean or Lake and a tree branch (called *mallqui*), which signifies ancestors. Directly below Viracocha stand a man and a woman. Isbell writes: "They are apparently the descendants of the cosmogenic kinship chart and represent the new synthesis of the parallel axes and descent lines in human marriage and procreation. The position is analogous with that of the Sunturwasi and the Ushñu which bring together the human and spiritual worlds."[29] He concludes that "the inverted U-shape of Haucaypata clearly communicated a great deal of information and is a form composed of essential relationships with a meaning intimately associated with the acquisition of spiritual power by humans in the real world through contact with other realms." The Haucaypata and other such ceremonial areas constituted "stage[s] upon which symbolic, ritual communications took place, employing a configuration of forms, relationships, and meanings." Together they projected a cultural code that made the dominant identity manifest. Thus, the ushnu and the U-shaped ceremonial spaces of

FIGURE 5.6. The Inca seated on his ushnu. Source: Guamán Poma de Ayala 1613/1936: 398.

countless religious centers from the equator south represented the center's power, ordering, and creative ability in a tangible, easily recognized way. The historical messages of such grandiose and majestic architecture often overshadowed and countered the local belief systems.[30]

Similar ceremonies and the same complex of ancient symbols and attributes marked the apotheosis of local lords. Primary manuscript sources reveal that successors to the office of paramount lord and his lieutenant, the segunda persona, were sometimes named by the incumbent before death. If the incumbent died without expressing a preference for a successor, a council chose the individual most fit for the position.[31] These candidates were then subject to being named or confirmed by the Inca. Because power was personalistic, marked by oaths of loyalty and subject to periodic renewal, it is not surprising that the Inca would want to somehow screen local authorities to guarantee fidelity, obedience, and service. Contact with the Inca also conferred local prestige on the ruler. He usually received gifts that buttressed his power among his people, such as women, fine clothing, drinking cups or beakers, a stool, and the right to be carried in a litter or hammock.

Descendants recalled such presents and privileges long after the fact. Thus, in a dispute over the cacicazgo of Lampas, one witness presented by don Alonso Curipauca was don Juan Bautista Fernandez, who, despite the Spanish last name, was a bilingual principal—born in the town of Santiago de Andapirca (province of Tarma). He insisted that not only was the pre-Hispanic lord (Curipaucar) named by the Inca, but that "the Indians carried him on a litter[,] a privilege that the Inca had granted him for the services he had rendered him in the conquests." He also testified that "he saw in the house of said Don Alonso Valverde [the grandson of the pre-Hispanic lord Curipaucar] the said litter." This litter existed into the 1670s and was seen by at least two more deponents. Even more numerous are the cases of the Inca presenting the local lord-elect with his stool.[32]

All throughout the Andes, among the Asillos, Ayabacas, and Catacaoenses, possession of the tiana, especially one given by the hand of el Cuzco, was tantamount to dominion. In a succession case, one party in 1588 is described as "don diego canqui direct successor and heir of the stool of said cacique prinçipal"; and as such he could "govern and command the Indians of his lineage of the said hurinsayas [of the community of Caquingora]." In Simbal, possession was given to don Pedro Xulcaguaman, described as follows:

> He took the said don pedro xulcaguaman by the hand and[,] as a sign of possession[,] he walked with him in the public square of the said town[;] and he made him sit on the stool as ancient custom of the caciques dictated (see Figure 5.7)[;] and he ordered all the principal lords of one hundred households [pachaca] and the rest of the said Indians of the unit of one thousand households [guaranga] [that] they salute him

FIGURE 5.7. A tiana. Source: Hearst Museum, University of California, Berkeley.

[*le hagan la benia*][;] and they embrace him and they obey him and respect him as their cacique[;] and in compliance with the order of the said lieutenant[,] the said caciques of pachaca and the rest of the Indians acknowledged his authority [*hicieron la benia*] and they embraced the said don pedro xulca guaman . . . without any objection.[33]

Litigation from 1568 between don Juan Apoaguaman (also written as Guaguama and Aguaguama)—cacique of the parcialidad of Jequetepeque—and don Juan Puemape—the native leader of the people who served the encomendero of Pacasmayo—regarding who was the rightful curaca of the people concentrated in a north coast valley also indicates the significance of dúo or tiana possession. The representative of don Juan Apoaguaman complained:

Because the said principal lord puemape has sat on the seat and sits on a stool and[,] as it is prohibited of such lesser lords and overseers[,] that which he has done and does in disrespect of the said caçique and going against the obedience that he owes the said his caçique and against that which His majesty has ordered[,] that there be no more than one principal leader of each repartimiento [encomienda] who he has ordered to be obeyed by the principal lords and Indians of the repartimientos[,] to the said caçiques belongs and is incumbent the dignity of the said stools and[,] by having the said principal lord puemape said stool[,] the Indians of the said valley are scandalized and they roam about frightened and withdrawn and in great discord.[34]

He continued by asking for an order that the "stool seat" be taken away from the said Puemape. He should be ordered "not to use it nor have it nor sit on it because he has never before now had it nor because of his ancestors does he succeed to such an honor." Only the cacique, don Juan Apoaguaman, should be allowed to sit on the dúo.

Pedro Alcos (or Alcop), a native witness called to shed light on the situation, related that "the said don Juan puemape goes about with a stool as a cacique principal never having had one in all his life and for that reason no one obeys the said don Ju[an] caçique." Another witness, don Pedro Peygo, a subject of the cacique principal of Jequetepeque, also testified:

> The said don ju[an] puemape goes about on a stool as a cacique principal[;] as a consequence[,] the valley and Indians of it are very disturbed and they do not obey the said don Ju[an] cacique as their cacique principal and everything goes along in such a way that it is necessary to remedy it by ordering that they recognize who is the cacique[,] because as they see that there is another with a stool they do not obey the cacique principal.

A third witness, Pedro Cunmach, subject of the cacique of Jequetepeque, summarized the problem: "The said puemape goes about on a stool and for this reason the Indians of the said repartimiento are disturbed." Thus, sitting on the dúo symbolized equivalence with the divine mandate. The fact that two rivals sat on such seats "disturbed and disquieted" the people to the point where they would "not obey the said don Ju[an] as cacique principal." In this case and others, as late as the 1790s, sitting on the tiana was tantamount to rule.[35]

Recognizing this, viceregal authorities, when issuing titles to Andean lordships, prohibited others from sitting on the stools. Viceroy Toledo's title of the curacaship to don Juan Tacsitarqui in 1575 stated:

> And you will sit on a stool as is custom among the rest of the caciques and principales of this kingdom and you will not consent for whatever reason that any Indian whether it be the second person or the cacique of pachaca or of a lineage or another that they have the stool or sit on it unless he be a cacique principal who has my title and provision as such.[36]

The rank of the lord determined the size, decoration, and material of the stool of office. Whereas the Inca's ceremonial tiana was of gold and more than a forearm (*codo*) high, a paramount lord's tiana was made of painted wood, half a forearm high. A cacique of guaranga sat on an unpainted wooden seat less than two palms high. As noted in the last chapter, Chuplingon sat on a stool before being recognized and worshipped as the next leader of the seven guarangas of Cajamarca. Similar ceremonies mark the accession rituals of the lords of many ethnic groups even into colonial times, as shown in Table 5.1.[37]

Once seated, they were universally respected, served, worshipped, and obeyed. Myths recalled how the founding ancestors traveled across the Andes. Movement was dangerous and associated with chaos. When the founder rested, he usually sat on a raised place. It was only when at rest that he was able to create, order, and rule. Arriaga relates that Andeans worshipped the places where their guacas sat down or rested. Contemporary testimony describes how, once the lord was seated, those present raised their hands above their heads to praise him. The smacking sound made by air

TABLE 5.1
Investiture Ceremonies

Date	Place/Group	Position	Source
1532	Caquingora (Pacajes)	Governor or cacique principal	Rivera and Platt 1978: 104, 113
1568	Cajamarca	Curaca	AGI/AL 128, n.p.
1575	Copacabana	Segunda persona	ALP/1691, c. 35, exp. 16, fols. 31v–32
1578	Charancane	Cacique principal	ANB/EC 1605, exp. 2, fol. 9
1585	Simbal	Cacique de guaranga	ART/CoAG, l. 266, exp. 3068, fols. 21–22v, 41v–43
1589	Catacoto y Caquingora	Cacique principal	Rivera and Platt 1978: 118–20
1592	Calacoto y Caquingora	Cacique principal	Rivera and Platt 1978: 120
1593	Soras	Segunda persona	BNP/A371, 1594, fol. 31
1593	San Blas	Cacique de parroquia	ALP/EC 1691, no. 530, c. 36, exp. 13, fol. 1v
1594	Guaylas	Cacique	ANP/DI 31, c. 622, 1597, fols. 11v–12, 57, 71v
1596	Collurqui	Cacique	BNP/A379, 1596, fols. 30–30v
1598	Guamachuco	Cacique de guaranga	ADT/CoAG, l. 266, exp. 3068, 12-November-1604, fols. 11v–12v
1602	Charancane	Cacique principal	ANB/EC 1605, exp. 2, fols. 27, 29v, 106
1604	Yungas mitimaes of Guamachuco	Cacique de guaranga	ART/CoAG, l. 266, exp. 3068, 12-November-1604, fols. 1v–2
1620	Jauja	Cacique de ayllu	BNP/B1087, 1629, fols. 93v–94
1626	San Blas (Cuzco)	Cacique de parroquia	ADC/CoO, l. 8, c. 11, 1626–31, fol. 2v
1648	Marcavelica (Piura)	Cacique	ARP/Co, l. 8, exp. 117, 1655, fol. 6v
1649	Jauja	Cacique de ayllu	BNP/B1087, 1629, fols. 28v–29v
1657	Lamay	Cacique principal	ADC/CoO, 1.17, no 348, c. 7, 1664, fol. 5v
1658	Larecaxa	Cacique	ANB/EC 1686, exp. 34, fol. 9v
1662	Chayanta	Segunda persona	ANB/EC 1686, exp. 11, fols. 5–8
1666	Ayabaca (Piura)	Principal	ARP/Co, l. 17, exp. 320, 1693, fol. 94v
1667–69	Masari	Cacique principal or gobernador	ANB/EC 1673, exp. 26, 4v, fols. 33–34

(*Continued*)

TABLE 5.1
(*Continued*)

Date	Place/Group	Position	Source
1676	Guachucal (Pastos)	Cacique	Calero 1997: 37
1696–1705	Guancane	Governador	ALL/Pra-36, caja 449, 1715, fols. 10–12, 13v–14v
1710–11	Catacaos (Piura)	Cacique or segunda persona	ARP/Co, l. 22, no. 432, 1711, fol. 22
1747	Guancane	Cacique gobernador	ALL/LB-581, caja 269, 1784, fols. 4v–6v
1784	Guancane	Cacique interino	ALL/LB-581, caja 269, 1784, fol. 21
1790–91	Guancane	Cacique interino	ALL/LB-581, caja 269, 1784, fols. 17v, 19
1792	Asángaro	Cacique	ALL/Pra-170, 1792–98, fol. 1
1795	Guancane	Cacique	ALL/LB-581, caja 269, 1784, fol. 27

escaping pursed lips in the act of mochar may, Martínez Cereceda suggests, represent the wind that is associated with many guacas. This wind might symbolize the transfer of vital energy—the breath (*aliento*) or puff of wind (*soplo*)—from the gods to their representative on earth, the transfer of sacredness and divinity, with the attendant duty to save society from the chaos of the interregnum period. This ritual transfer of power between the sacred and the profane gave the lord the legitimate right to sit and order, rule, and judge his followers and the ability to communicate directly with the divine.[38]

In colonial times, signs of worship and rejoicing followed this ritual. Some of those present approached individually to embrace the lord or otherwise humbled themselves before him. In the pueblo of Lamay, near Cuzco, don Pasqual Curimanya (also Corimaya) took possession of the office of cacique principal and governador when "he sat on the stool[;] and once seated there many male and female Indians of this said town arrived[,] and they embraced him giving him signs of delight and happiness acclaiming him as their cacique and Curaca with rejoicing to the sound of flutes and other instruments." Likewise, on March 17, 1602—farther north in the town of Daule, near Guayaquil—in the plaza and graveyard of the church, where most of the people had gathered for mass, possession was given to don Pedro Serena.

He took Don Pedro serena the legitimate son of Don Martin y quia cas [also Yqui yacas] by the hand . . . and sat him on a wooden stool in the middle of all the Indians and they gave him possession of the cacicazgo principal of this town. . . . and the said Don Pedro serena understood and he took his seat on said stool and he allowed himself to be respected, revered and saluted by the governor, the mayors and their lieutenants and lesser lords of the town who were present all of whom obeyed him and acknowledged him as their principal lord.

Thus, at the local level in a society in which everyone but the lords sat on the ground or squatted, it was not the fringe or the tunic that was so crucial to the recognition of authority. A stool, and in later colonial times, a seat or chair, served that purpose. It symbolized the dominion of a lord. Without the stool or chair, one had no recognized authority and would not be obeyed. According to tradition and myth, a lord, like a god or the Inca, had to be seated before he could order his world.[39]

Local lords were also distinguished by the use of ritual paraphernalia. Besides the stool, clothing, and painted or metal drinking cups, musical instruments—especially trumpets, drums, and flutes—were part of a lord's regalia.[40] Another symbol of status and rule were headdresses. In a long court case that was appealed and brought before the Royal Audiencia of Lima, one litigant used a helmet (*murrion*) that had belonged to his great-grandfather, along with one "bamboo pole" (*palo de guaiaquil*), as proof of his right to succeed. (Note the helmets decorated with the mascapaicha in Figure 5.1.) This murrion had been presented to a Jesuit extirpator of idolatries, don Juan de Arançiaga (or Aranzeaga), during his inspection trip, by don Juan Curipaucar, who was cacique of the town of Santo Domingo de Guacta. Curipaucar identified the helmet as one that "according to their ancient custom Don Fernando Curi paucar [who according to witnesses was lord during the time of Pedro de la Gasca (before 1549)] his great grandfather used." The "Guayaquil cane" (*caña de Guaiaquil*) served as "an insignia of his royal blood when he was carried on a litter by his Indians." He noted that the second pole could not be presented as evidence because "it had been eaten by moths." Both warrior helmet (*murrion guerrero*) and caña de Guaiaquil, as well as the litter, are mentioned by the same Aranzeaga in a letter of 1675 about Jesuit missionizing authorities in the central Andes. This represented an innovative defense, one made necessary after Viceroy Toledo ordered many documents that proved the legitimacy of curacal succession to be burned.[41]

Processions

It is not surprising that in a society in which authority was embodied in individuals and in which personal relations defined the extent of a leader's power, a ruler would have to travel to visit his people, the majority of whom lived dispersed widely over the countryside, at least until the Spanish reducción policy was implemented. Like the gods and their representations who were moved about on litters, so were the Incas and curacas carried on the shoulders of their followers. Vivid eyewitness accounts describe the entrance of a seated Atahualpa into the plaza of Cajamarca. Pedro Pizarro described the attendants surrounding the king's litter. He estimated that two thousand natives, who swept the road, preceded him. Others sang as they danced along. Squadrons of soldiers walked on both sides of the road. The procession moved slowly, covering half a league in three hours. Fernández de Oviedo described the scene (see Figure 5.8):

> And before him came a squadron of Indians dressed in colorful, checker-board liveries. These went along removing straw from the earth, and sweeping and cleaning the path, and putting down cloths. Behind them came three squadrons dressed in another way, all singing and dancing; and then came other squadrons of many people with arms and medals and crowns of gold and silver. Among the armed ones came Atabaliba on his litter, all lined, inside and out, of parrot feathers of many colors, so well placed the feathers, that it appeared that they had sprouted there.[42]

Murúa adds detail, describing Atahualpa's litter, which had been specially brought from Cuzco, as "of finest gold, whose seat was a plank of the same and on top was a valuable woolen pillow adorned in rich stones." He also mentions that the Inca was surrounded by "the most principal of his captains, of the caciques and lords of the provinces who came with him, some on foot and others on litters which were granted as a great favor to the most important of them." A local source from Yauyos contained testimony about the cacique principal don Diego Ynga Mocha of the Allauca, who was in Cajamarca in November 1532. When he and his retinue moved about, "they brought everything they had with them." Another witness to these events, Hernando Curi Huaranga, stated that, because he was traveling with Atahualpa, "his lord," he and other lords "brought the best they had."[43]

Other chroniclers described how the Inca moved on other, less serious occasions. Cobo describes it in the following way:

> Every time he traveled, and many times within a settlement, he was carried on the shoulders of Indians on some rich litters lined in gold; and it was a particular favor and honor to carry it. When he went on the road, he went accompanied by nobles, who were warriors who guarded him and gave him authority. In front of his litter were two to three hundred bearers of the *Lucanas* nation, who had as their occupation to carry him, dressed in livery, who rotated as they tired and they went along cleaning the path where he would pass.

Guamán Poma de Ayala adds, "When the ynga leaves to go about with his footmen and helmets and standards and trumpets and flutes and dancers and singers and he takes along nude Indian Chunchos as ostentation and lordship and he leaves on his litter with his wife, thus he leaves to fight."[44]

Like the gods recalled in myths, the Inca did not walk (see Figures 5.9 and 5.10). He visited his people carried by bearers (*hamaqueros*), who in

FIGURE 5.8. Atahualpa confronting the Spanish in Cajamarca. Source: Guamán Poma de Ayala 1613/1936: 384.

FIGURE 5.9. A litter (*quispiranpa*). Source: Guamán Poma de Ayala 1613/1936: 331.

FIGURE 5.10. A litter (*pillcoranpa*). Source: Guamán Poma de Ayala 1613/1936: 333.

Cajamarca, according to Calancha, were all caciques. Martínez Cereceda's exhaustive analysis of these processions suggests that they clearly represented the center—a seated center—when all others were on foot. The Inca was a reposed and calm nucleus surrounded by movement. When the king traveled with his wife, he represented their androgynous center and origin. Even after the death of the Incas, bearers carried their mummies on litters to the festivals, "singing the things that he did in life on the battlefield as well as in the city."[45]

These customs held true many decades after first contact. Quipucamayocs reported that Paullo Tupac Inca traveled with four thousand native servants. About fifty years after the disintegration of the empire, Rodriguez de Figueroa arranged a meeting with the Inca Titu Cusi Yupanqui of Vilcabamba in the name of the Oydor Juan de Matienzo to negotiate the end of hostilities. His account describes the Inca's entrance into the theater that had been built for the occasion. The Inca was preceded by messengers who announced his approach. Then the Inca entered at the front of a small contingent of about five hundred, including twenty or thirty women who brought up the rear. He was accompanied by his closest advisers and personal attendants: by a mestizo; two orejones with two halberds; a governor (Yanque Maita) with his retinue of fifty or sixty; a camp master (*maestre de campo*) with a following as large as Maita's; and two captains (Vilcapari Guaman and Cuxi Poma), each followed by fifty or sixty men. The last captain's retinue consisted of fifty Antis (presumably from the jungle lowlands). They carried bows and arrows, instead of lances that were carried by the others, and were declared to be cannibals. He was also accompanied by flute music and the sound of trumpets.[46]

This order suggests that the Inca stood for civilization (at the center), with decreasing amounts of order and power the farther away from that center one went (see Figure 5.11).

Thus accompanied, the Inca remained the center, higher than all, and serene amid the movement of the music, dance, sweeping, and other hubbub that surrounded him, as in the eye of a storm. Martínez Cereceda explains his immobility as reminiscent of the seated or still figures of the gods, who were usually seated when they ordered, reordered, or restored balance to the universe. Such a stance represented order among movement, change, and even chaos and destruction.[47]

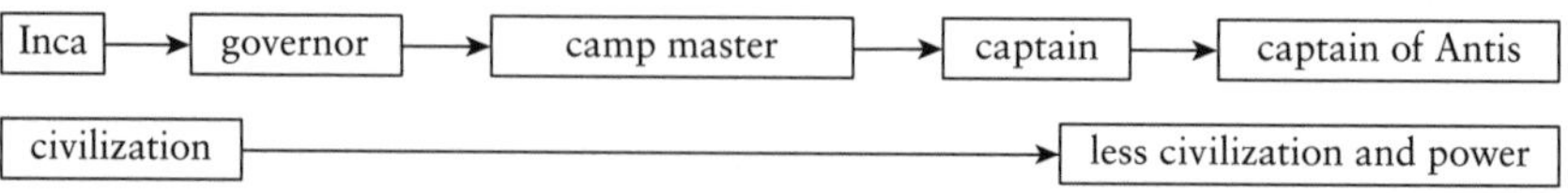

FIGURE 5.11. The Inca as civilizing center.

His dress consisted of a tunic of the finest textile, complemented by a small breastplate made of many-colored feathers and topped with a medal (*patena*); a golden shield; and a handheld staff. Around his calves were feathered garters (*cenojiles*), and around his ankles were wooden bells. He wore a feathered headdress, a feathered necklace, and a feathered mask (*mandul*), which also set him apart.[48]

Similarly attired and surrounded, but most probably with thousands rather than hundreds of attendants and troops, the Inca in his heyday traveled from one House of the Sun to another, located in the various ceremonial complexes that were built as his sovereignty expanded. There he made contact with the local lords, dispensing maize beer and other tokens of his generosity and hospitality, acknowledging their merit and reinforcing the personal bonds of loyalty through which the empire was governed. Such occasions were events at which he granted favors and women and asked for help and service. So important was his elevation that even under attack in the plaza of Cajamarca in November 1532, the Inca's bearers refused to allow his litter to touch the ground. Others replaced those disabled or wounded. Everywhere he went, people worshipped him as a god.[49]

Among some ethnicities, as important as the tiana was the possession of a litter, an extraordinary sign of royal favor and indulgence. Only certain provincial lords who had license of the emperor could travel on a litter on the shoulders of bearers (*en andas y ombros de indios*). Pizarro suggests the great honor that such a singular privilege and concession meant when he described Atahualpa's procession into the plaza of Cajamarca in November 1532: "Likewise accompanying him was the lord of Chincha, on a litter, that resembled his own, a thing of admiration, because no Indian, no matter how important he was, could appear before him if not with a burden on his back and barefoot."[50]

The Marqués de Cañete issued a writ (*provisión*), dated February 1, 1556, that prohibited the use of hammocks. Enforcement was haphazard until the 1560s, when royal inspectors arrived to implement such provisions. But to walk would have been the ruin of a lord and a sign of loss of legitimacy and power. Santiago Guamán, a cacique principal of the people of Guamán, who were concentrated in the coastal valley of Moche, stated, "I am a cacique and I have under my command a quantity of Indians who not seeing me with more authority than they have I will be considered of little importance by my Indians walking like them on foot." Therefore, lords petitioned for exemptions. Long thereafter, their relatives recalled their forebears' use of hammocks and litters as proof that they were esteemed and privileged by those living under their traditional order. In the records of a court case about the curacazgo of Characane (also Charassane), testimony recounts that in the time of Guayna Capac, Arecapa Quequi (also Quique or Quiqui) was the cacique principal of the natives, who later would be reduced to the pueblo of Characane, and many more people in those valleys. He had been appointed (*puesto por*) by the Inca, and they called him the "great curaca" because he "went about like an ynga on a litter [guando] on the shoulders of Indians and thirty Indians ordinarily carried him." Guando probably was the notary's rendition of *huantu*, or open-air, wooden litter. His son (Hayaua; also Hayaba), who sided with the "ynga of the cuzco against his brother of quito," died in battle. His son (Coarete), who succeeded by order of the Inca, also "went about on a litter on the shoulders of Indians." Possession of such an insignia was used in colonial times as proof of the right to succeed to office. One witness, Vasta Saro chate, a commoner (*tributario*) of the ayllu Curua, argued that "because the ancestors of the said don Ju[an] tome were caciques and carried on a litter he has the right to succeed to the said cacicazgo principal of this said town."[51]

Local sources suggest that, after the disintegration of the Inca empire, use of litters proliferated quickly among provincial lords—even though many had never had use of them before 1532—and served as important status symbols years later. Bearers carried the hammocks of Millamisan (a principal of Jayanca) in 1540, and of don Juan de Collique until his execution in 1566. Don Martin, lord of the valley of Pacasmayo, stated in 1566 that "for many years I have ridden on the shoulders of my Indians." In another case, don Fernando Ayavire y Velasco—cacique principal of the nation of the people of Charcas and, specifically, of the repartimiento of Sacaca—petitioned the Crown for privileges, stating that "in the time of the ingas and before them my parents and grandparents were lords with litters who were carried by one hundred Indians of the nation of the Charcas [people] who number ten thousand."[52] Farther north, don Pedro Angasnapon, curaca of the seven guarangas of Cajamarca, and his wife were also carried on litters. In a 1582 document made by his son, attesting to Angasnapon's services to the Spanish king (*probanza*), one of his hamaqueros—then about sixty years old—testified that "when the said don P[edr]o went to visit his peoples he took with him the said cosaua nunchipac his wife[;] they carried her in a hammock with many trumpets like an important lady." The testimony of Juan Tantaxulca, cacique of the repartimiento of Chacalla, also related how Condorguacho, a wife of Guayna Capac and "lady" of Guaylas, was revered and carried on a litter.[53]

Lesser lords also enjoyed the privilege. Fifty bearers allegedly carried the segunda persona of the Soras, don Antonio Auque Paucara, on a litter in the precolonial era. The litter and his stool were both presented before Spanish royal officials to prove his status. Lesser lords (of a guaranga, for example), such as Xulcapoma (who ruled the guaranga of Ichota in the time of Tupac Inca Yupanqui) and Melchior Caxaxas (of Chontal in 1563), rode in a hammock, which was probably one step down from a litter. In fact, witnesses equated "having and possessing the said lordship" with having a "stool and hammock."[54]

When local lords moved about in procession, like the mummies of their ancestors and el Cuzco, they were surrounded by retainers. Pedro Pizarro reports that cacique Tumalá of the island of La Puná "was usually accompanied with much singing and dancing." A witness testifying in a court case involving the hereditary lords of the Valley of Lima said that the ancestor of Guaqui Chiamo "was a great lord" precisely because "he saw him go about with a large retinue of Indians."[55]

Absence of a retinue greatly diminished a lord's ability to rule. One corregidor subverted the authority of a cacique of Jayanca, don Francisco, in the early 1570s, by not allowing him to be accompanied by his usual twenty or thirty escorts: "Usually the said cacique went about accompanied with more than twenty Indians." He ordered him "not to be accompanied with more than two servants." As a result, "since then the said Indians did not want to obey him nor follow the orders of the said cazique or principal lords nor municipal authorities." This story was also confirmed by several witnesses, most notably don Martin Çerquen, an eyewitness and official of the pueblo of Lambayeque. In his defense, the corregidor presented a Spanish witness who claimed that his order was not to delegitimize the curaca but to alleviate his subjects from such a seemingly onerous task. If this is true, the statement is testimony to the incomprehension of some Spanish of the sociopolitical and religious traditions of native culture in 1582, a full fifty years after first contact.[56]

The making of ritual rounds was an indispensable obligation of any lord who wanted to retain or build a following. In fact, in 1566 one young pretender to the cacicazgo of the repartimiento of Moro and Quisquis argued that he was old enough to take over his rightful position from his cousin, the interim governor: "I am now an adult man and I am of age to visit my Indians and go from one town to the next."[57] The Chimu lords—don Pedro Ocxaguaman (cacique principal), don Goncalo Guamán, don Martin, don Francisco Chumbinamo, don Diego Chinmis, don Felipe, don Hernando, and don Christoval (his nobles)—identified themselves to the Spanish in 1566 with these words: "We are caciques and we have Indians to command and visit."[58] The lord of the people concentrated in the Valley of Chicama asked for a license to continue to ride in a hammock, arguing that he needed to "go from settlement to settlement visiting" his people in 1566. His neighbor to the north, don Juan de Collique, petitioned Dr. Cuenca in 1566 for the right to continue to be carried in a hammock to visit his many hamlets and towns spread over more than eight leagues, including some towns on the seacoast. Don Christobal Yacopoma, cacique of Lampas, continued visiting his people accompanied by attendants through the middle of the seventeenth century.[59]

Curacas often maintained structures, referred to as houses or residences in Spanish, in several places to facilitate such visits. Testimony indicated that don Pedro Angasnapon kept houses in various places among his people at the time of the Spanish invasion. Don Melchior Caroarayco, who succeeded him, listed six houses in four locations in his 1565 will. Similarly, in the time of the Inca, don Antonio Acopaucara, a cacique and segunda persona of the parcialidad of Anansoras, had houses in the towns of Soras, Acomsora, Morocollas, and Vilcasguaman, in the province of Vilcas; in the city of Guamanga; and in other towns and agricultural sites.[60]

Material from Cajatambo and Charcas suggests that the lords moved from house to house for ritual purposes. Mercedes del Río reports that the lords of Tapacarí had houses "where they went to celebrate, with singing, dancing and drinking, their clandestine rituals. . . . The houses of both men were, then, their huacas and the place where the strength of their ancestors was concentrated, to whom they could pray . . . that is, the soul of their dead to whom they should worship so that they would be generous with the living." The idolatry reports and trials of the first half of the seventeenth century attest to the fact that many ayllus maintained houses in the pueblos viejos for sacred ceremonial purposes. These houses were dedicated to their ancestral heroes and served as storage for the corn from the fields that were tilled in their service and honor (*dedicada[s] para dichos ydolos*).

Bilante Quillai—a minister of the idols Condortocas and his sister-wife, Coya Guarmi; and an assistant to the curaca of the town of Mangas in Cajatambo—testified in 1662 that the curaca identified the house to the Spanish as a structure belonging to and used by the community. By using the word *house*, he led the Spanish into thinking it was used for secular purposes, when, in fact, the house was where the witness and others worshipped their idols for two days "with their dancing [and] fasting in a pagan way without eating salt nor chili pepper [and] staying away from their women, even if legitimate, the first night . . . and the said house they have pointed out saying that it is for communal use." Thus, in this ancient house (a storehouse [*kullqa* or *colcu huasi*]), the descendants and adherents of the cult fasted, worshipped, and stored the corn from the fields they cultivated under order of the curaca. In 1619 the Ocros people took the dead to the "place of their huacas that they call *zamai huasi* that means place of rest." The existence of such structures recalls the Inca requirement of all of the provincial peoples to maintain a residence near the Coricancha for ritual visits. This may have been a practice common to all the major centers of imperial worship, making them into temporarily inhabited temple-towns.[61]

To have multiple structures for ritual purposes was not extraordinary. The ayllu Chamas of the pueblo San Francisco de Mangas in 1662 also maintained a "house of ancient times on pretense of it being of the community where also they worship [the idol Auca Atama] and store the corn." Gonsalo Lloclla of the ayllu Casas testified that year that "all the rest of the lineages of the town of Mangas . . . fast a lot and worship in the houses that all the lineages of this town have dedicated since pagan times for the service of their ancestors with the title and with the pretense that they are communal houses." He then cites specifics: the ayllu Caiau Tamborga held their rites for the malqui Ynca Villac in the house called Pilco (pilca) Cancha (or Pillana); the ayllu Julca Tamborga maintained two houses called Caian Huasi and Carua Sansal "for the same purpose."[62]

The house Carua Sansal fronted on the plaza of the pueblo and was "dedicated to the service of the said idols [the ancestors Pomachaua (Poma chahua) Tunsuvilca (Tunsu vilca)]." More specifically, the house "is dedicated[,] since ancient times[,] to the idol Yacalva[,] son of the huaca Quilli and Ianca[;] Yacalhua was the father of four sons [and] ancestors called Pomachaua[,] Tunsuvilca[,] Nuna[, and] Rupai from whom descend all the lineage." There all the members of the ayllu worshipped their malquis, according to Ynes Carhuayaco of the ayllu Tamborga: "They fasted five days without eating salt nor chili pepper for the festivities of Corpus and Saint Francis and these venerations and fastings they did to [honor] their ancestors Pomachahua and Tunsu Vilca and for his sister Llanca Anaco." Afterward, according to another witness, Bartolome Quispi of ayllu Julca Tamborga, "they make them offerings of camelids and guinea pigs and suet and coca and corn and all of the lineage gathered to make the said adorations." Another member of the ayllu Tamborga, Francisco Poma Guaranga, admitted to taking offerings of wool and money to the same house for the malqui Llanca Anaco.[63]

The ayllu Cotos, the lineage of the curacas of the pueblo of Mangas, also had a house called Mahacuta (or Mahacuchu), located next to the church bell tower, "that was dedicated to fasting and worshiping the said idols [Condortocas and Coya Guarmi] since ancient times and in it was a storeroom where they stored the corn that they harvested from the field called vintin dedicated to the service of said idols." In 1663, other people of Mangas admitted having such houses in the pueblo viejo and described them simply as "temple of said idols." In the same year, the people of San Gerónimo de Copa dedicated another such ancient house to their malqui Xulcapoma, "who was the *marcaioc* [founder] and first settler of the town."[64]

Sometimes these houses were disguised as houses of a saint instead of being attributed to communal use. Thus, a witness from the pueblo of

Mangas, Domingo Hacha Ricapa, admitted that the community had a large house "that was with the title and with the pretense that it was for the Saintly Virgen or for his community where they fasted and made said offerings." In reality, added witness Domingo Hacha, it served as a cult center for the malqui Auca Atama, "who is the principal idol and ancestor of this lineage Chamas and that of Ananis to whom these two lineages worship and to the idol called Vrpai Vachac because it is said that he came from the sea with Auca Atama his son where he has his origin and birth and that said Auca Atama has four sons who they also worship and adore called Nauin Tambo Poran Tambo Cunquis Xulcas Paryasca."[65]

But lest the reader be seduced into imagining a twenty-first century residence, typically sufficient to house a nuclear or extended family, a more detailed description of the house of the ayllu Chamas is supplied by the extirpator of idolatry Licenciado Bernardo de Noboa. He reported what he saw at the pueblo viejo of the said ayllu:

> They discovered a great simulacra and temple of pagan times that had a little plaza and many small rooms all around[;] and in the middle[, there were] three tombs walled with stones[;] and we dug in and opened the middle one and found the idol called Auca Atama that was a dead pagan body who the Indians of this lineage and the lineage of Ananis worship for being their first progenitor and conqueror and founder of that people[;] and they opened and dug into the two tombs next to it and found four ancestor mummies called Poron Tanbo Cunquis Xulcas Pariasca . . . who they said were children of the said ancestor called Auca Atama[;] and at the sides of said ancestor in some small niches like little chapels they found four family idols [*conopas*] one in the form of a stone person called Nauin Tambo, and another named . . . Oncol Tambo.

Nearby, "on the outskirts of said town," they found another "old ruined house[;] in a little niche[,] like a small chapel[,] they found three family idols . . . and below . . . a simulacra and temple with a patio in the middle and rooms all around[,] and in them little niches[,] like little chapels[,] and in the middle of the said patio[,] having dug[,] they discovered an ancestor idol called Cargua Copa that was bones of a pagan conopa." In the little chapels (*capillitas*) or niches were found fifty-one conopas representing corn, llamas, potatoes, and coca.[66]

> And close by, above the site was a large, roofed house with a storeroom dedicated to the service of said idols in which all the male and female Indians of the town gathered and fasted in the pagan fashion. . . . and in said house they kept four large jugs and three small ones in which they kept the beer. . . . and in the little ones the minister of the idols took beer to offer to all the referred to idols and later . . . two leagues from the town on a mountain called Punchau Cayan [altar of the Sun] they found an idol called Vrpai Guachac which had the form of a little dove . . . to which all the Indians of these two lineages of Chamas and Nanis worshiped saying

that the said idol Vrpai Guachac was the mother of the idol ancestor called Auca Atama.

Thus, these houses that represented stops on the circuit of ritual peregrinations of the curacas and lords were part of repeated ceremonial complexes, the pueblos viejos (or *ñaupa llactas*), that the colonial reducciones were, in part, built to replace. Some of these houses, which also served as mausoleums, were decorated. Such monuments documented the power and dignity of the dead, as did the ritual spaces and ceremonial buildings of the Incas.[67]

As they moved about, they were surrounded by servants and followed by women, who carried and dispensed chicha. To eat as a guest of another was to confederate and accept future obligations of service. The curaca of Cajamarca, don Pedro Angasnapon, was accompanied by trumpeters and other musicians and women, who distributed chicha and corn: "When she accompanied her husband to his settlements they carried her in a hammock with trumpets along with her husband and all the concubines went with her[,] serving her[;] some carried chicha and gourds of food to give them to eat." Such women were indispensable cogs in the smooth-running enterprise of state and in maintenance of the illusion of generosity. Undoubtedly for that reason, the witness Maria Caxadoca—a native of Guzmango in 1573—noted that as they passed, onlookers pulled out eyebrows and eyelashes and blew them at their lord as a sign of ongoing respect and adoration. This was consistent with their beliefs that their lord was invested with divinity.[68]

Last Rites

Funerals for the dead were designed to canonize the deceased by celebrating his or her life and to prepare the body for a continued and active presence in the world of the living. According to sixteenth-century accounts, the very active Pachacuti Inca Yupanqui redesigned the funeral ceremonies that were prescribed and followed into the early colonial era. He ordered the body or bulto of Inca Viracocha to be paraded about his settlement on a litter to the slow, mournful beat of drums, followed by his insignia and arms, in front of fully armed and equipped soldier-citizens as if he were reviewing the troops. Bearers carried his image to all the fiestas, "making [both] the Inca's lords and the rest of the lords respect well his person as if he were alive."[69]

Behind, bare-breasted women wearing black sashes (*fajas*), "crying and wailing," their heads shaved and faces blackened, whipped themselves as they walked. These and others, also with ash-darkened faces and heads and carrying drums, spent a week together searching for the deceased ruler in all the customary places. They even spread cinders and ash all around the late king's house, hoping to see his footprints or evidence of his presence.[70]

This practice continued into colonial times. After Pizarro ordered Atahualpa garroted on the central plaza of Cajamarca, many of his followers, a sister, and other women hanged themselves to go to serve him, saying that "when the great lord died all those who really loved him would bury themselves alive with him." Two sisters remained. They walked around "weeping loudly" with drums, singing songs that recounted the accomplishments (*hazañas*) of their husband. They went where Atahualpa had usually been, calling him, looking for him in all the corners, slowly. When they did not find him, their weeping grew louder. In fact, Pizarro notes the following example:

> It was customary among these Indians that annually widows cried for their husbands, and the kin, carrying his clothing and arms ahead, and many female Indians carrying a lot of beer behind, and others playing drums and singing about the deeds of the deceased, proceeded from mountain to mountain and from place to place where the dead being alive had gone, and when they tired, they sat down to drink and rested[;] they began again to cry until all the beer was gone.[71]

The body itself customarily became an object of veneration throughout the realm. The eviscerated and embalmed body was made into a bulto, which was generally placed in the Coricancha to be worshipped with those of his forefathers. People of the empire offered solemn sacrifices there. After Guayna Capac became king, he asked permission of the Sun to travel to all the haunts of his late father, all the way to Cajamarca, to mourn, feed, and sacrifice to him there. This may have been a way to turn these sites into holy monuments and fonts of sacredness for his father and points from which to disseminate stories and myths of his deeds and accomplishments, while coincidentally establishing his own personal ties with local inhabitants. To mark the Inca's death in the collective memory, people feasted and drank until inebriated and received gifts of wool and clothing from the common stores.[72]

What Guayna Capac did for his father, Pachacuti Inca Yupanqui did for all the previous kings. In fact, if one can believe Betanzos, Pachacuti Inca Yupanqui formalized ancestor worship. He ordered that a mummy be made of all the dead Incas. He then "ordered certain very elegant wooden benches made, that were finely painted and decorated with many multi-colored feathers." This done, he ordered that all the bultos "be seated on the benches . . . to which all were ordered to revere and reverence like idols and likewise that they should make sacrifices to them as such."[73]

The Inca institutionalized ancestor worship by providing for the upkeep of their memory or cult, giving them houses, livestock, and servants. He put these latter to work producing for the dead. They were to feed them morning and night and sacrifice to them. He instructed them to make up songs "that would be sung by the chosen women [mamaconas, acllas] and retainers with the praises of the deeds of each one of these lords in his day." At festivals and celebrations these songs had to be sung "in order and in concert starting with the first song and history and praise of Mango Capac and that likewise the said mamaconas and servants went along saying how the lords had come to power until then and that that order was what they would follow from then forward so that in this way there would be memory of their ancient times."[74]

To resurrect the memory of the dead kings, Pachacuti Inca Yupanqui may also have invented the use of the mascapaicha, to associate them with their mythical origins and instill fear. Betanzos reports that "he ordered when he ordered them put on the benches that gallant feathered crowns be put on their heads from which hung golden earrings and this done he ordered that they likewise have placed on the forehead of each of these images some metals of gold." He was motivated to do this "because he understood that the same would be done to him after his days."[75]

At Pachacuti Inca Yupanqui's death a new ritual was first carried out at his direction. After he died peacefully in his sleep without pain, his body, at his request, was placed in his compound at Patallacta. A golden image (the Inti-Illapa) was positioned atop his body, and a bulto made with his hair and nails was carried on a litter to the Haucaypata to be among his forefathers on important occasions. When he was thus transported by members of his lineage, they sang an oral advertisement of his greatness. Then, all his subjects were required to make solemn sacrifices so that he might go to rest with his father, the Sun. After this, they feasted and were given wool and clothing. This largesse was to celebrate his death. To eat and drink at the deceased ruler's expense was perhaps a departing promise of help and care in the future. It established binding, mutual obligations—to feed and propitiate in return for fertility and protection.[76]

Finally, as mentioned previously, Andeans believed that death was a transition to life in another place, where they would eat and drink as on earth. Because they held these opinions, it was customary practice to bury the dead ruler with pages and servants, who were to continue to serve him in the afterlife. Males were interred in the antechamber, females in the treasury. Companions of a dead chief for whom there was no room in the tomb made holes in the fields that were cultivated for him or in places where he used to hold festivals; and there they were buried, thinking that their chief would pass by these places and take them in his company to do him service. Those who did not go with him were charged with supplying (*socorrer*) the deceased with necessary offerings in the future.[77]

The descriptions of the death vigils of subsequent emperors add details to this general pattern. Death of a ruler was shortly followed by mourning and crying, which sounded like "the quiet cooing of the Doves." This generally was the beginning of a grieving period that lasted "days" (in the case of Guayna Capac) or many months (in the case of Manco Capac). Then, the dead king's bulto was paraded and displayed in public places. It was adored as a god and offered llamas, guinea pigs, birds, and vegetable sacrifices as food. This series of events held true at the time of Guayna Capac's death (see Figure 5.12). The embalmed, wrapped body was carried on a litter toward the Coricancha with other guacas and his wife. Along the way, men and women lined his path, crying and wailing as "they went along collecting peoples wherever they passed to enter in the Cuzco as a Universe." There he was mourned anew with laments and sacrifices. Eventually, he was buried with one thousand to four thousand persons (depending on the source) "of his house" who would accompany and serve him in the "other life," much treasure and jewels, and fine clothes. People feasted and drank until drunk from the royal stores to honor and adore their deceased ruler.[78]

It was on such occasions that the quipucamayocs were called to sing the stories of their lives. In Guayna Capac's case, it was ordered "that all the lords of the Cuzco would enter the plaza and there they would cry and crying say in a loud voice his most famous deeds in constructing the city like in subduing and acquiring lands and provinces under his jurisdiction." This was capped by the capacocha sacrifice of a thousand children, who were buried in pairs where he had stopped on his travels. People believed that they would find and serve him. This ritual was followed by a general ten days of mourning by all the people under his sway (Figure 5.13). The entire procedure—the embalmment, mourning, parading, adoring, sacrifices, and feasting—was meant to lionize the deceased and mark his transition from life to afterlife, from which, it was believed, he could still intercede on behalf of his progeny and their people.[79]

A year later, another rite to commemorate the anniversary of the death marked the deceased's conversion to the status of divine ancestor. On the first day of the festivities, men and women, their faces painted black in mourning, left the city to go into the surrounding hills and to the lands where subjects of the emperor planted and harvested. All went crying and carrying his clothes, adornments, and weapons. When they arrived at the places where he had stood, sat, or passed, they called out to him in loud voices to ask him where he was and speak to him of his deeds. Each one described the possession that he had in his or her hands and told him how it was used or what he did with it when he was alive. This they repeated for fifteen days, dawn to dusk. After they finished these narratives, they called him in a loud voice. The most important lord answered, saying he is with his father, the Sun. Then, they answered this call, asking him to remember them, send them good rainstorms, and take sickness from them and any evil that might befall them.[80]

FIGURE 5.12. Guayna Capac. Source: Guamán Poma de Ayala 1613/1936: 112.

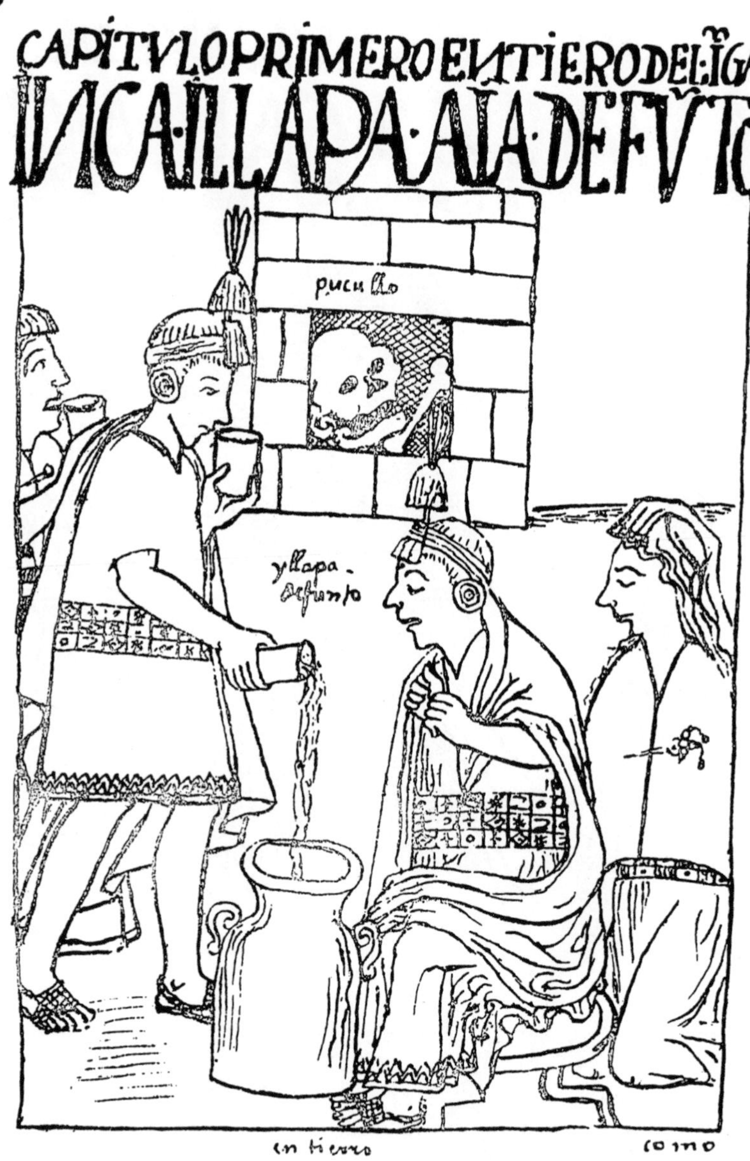

FIGURE 5.13. An Inca burial. Source: Guamán Poma de Ayala 1613/1936: 287.

A story-dance was staged after these first two weeks. In it, four disguised and unrecognizable men dressed in costumes of feathers appeared in the plaza, each with ten elaborately dressed women tied to him by a long cord. While the women remained on the sidelines, the men, two on each side of the plaza, grimaced at each other and ventured forth around the square, still tied to the cord, which the women would slacken as needed. A little girl, who represented a woman, fed each man coca from a gold or silver bag as if in battle; simultaneously, a little boy held a bola (*aillo*) in his hands, which he dragged on the ground, representing an enemy in battle. The women represented the man's will. When the cord was long, he acted like a "free man"; when short, his will was tied and he could do little. When they became tired, two squadrons of soldiers appeared, representing the two moieties (*Hanan* [upper] and *Hurin* [lower]) of the Cuzcos, to do ritual battle in the plaza. Hanan Cuzco won, signifying the successes of the deceased. This ritual battle was followed by mourning—loud crying, weeping, and shouting in which were related the victories and grandeur of the emperor. The third scene of the ritual was played by two squadrons of women dressed as men, complete with male headdresses, shields, and halberds. While the women danced around, a few men circulated among them with slings in their hands. These men may have represented the dead Inca and his forces among huge armies of cowards, who acted like women.[81]

This ritual then made reference to the dual-division, or moiety system, of social organization and the four lineages, or nations, of the empire, as well as to the great battles that had been fought and won to ennoble his name and grandeur of his line. This may have been representative of the other comedies and tragedies orchestrated by the amautas, which often harkened back and reenacted the origin of the Incas and Sun worship; the triumphs of the emperors; and, after 1532, the ruin of the Incas, including "the omens and admirable signs that in the sky and air were seen before they took his [Atahualpa's] life."[82]

After these performances, the emperor ordered that all go to wash away the mourning. Then they gathered in the plaza, bringing all the garments and possessions with which they had grieved for him. These they burned. The sacrifice of thousands of camelids in the plaza and surroundings, in the houses in which he had slept or stayed, followed. In addition, children were buried for him in the places where he frequented. He ordered that all his gold and silver table service be buried or put in his houses. His body was then wrapped and kept in his house, where all could worship and feed it as if it were still alive. He was thus deified and transformed into a sacrosanct being akin to a Christian saint.[83]

Such state theater and grandiose last rites were scaled down for the death of a provincial lord. At a lord's demise, the lesser lords and supporters mourned together. Cabello Valboa reported that "when a paramount lord or lesser lord or one with many relatives dies, it is astonishing the wailing that they make for him, and the howls and songs of praise [*endechas*] that you hear around the body, and there are male (and female) Indians specialized in this occupation, who paid with gifts go there to spill vain tears, and recite verse." Women cut off their hair,

> and with drums and flutes they went out with sad sounds and singing to those parts where the deceased used to enjoy himself more often to cause listeners to cry. And having cried they offered sacrifices and superstitions. . . . And after doing this, and some of his women killed themselves, they interred them in the tombs with their treasures and not a little food . . . and even now it is generally customary that before they bury them they cry for them four or five or six days or ten, depending on who the deceased is. Because the greater a man is the greater the honor they do him, and more sentiment is displayed, crying with great lamentations, and with painful music: saying in their chants all the things that happened to the deceased when alive. And if he was valiant they carried him with these tears recounting his deeds. And at the time they put the body in the tomb, some of his jewels and clothing are burned nearby and some are buried with him.

This done, the women of the ethnicity who were still alive and other servants departed. As in the imperial rituals, some of them held in their hands the lord's arms; others carried his headdress; and others his clothes. Finally, others bore other items, including the tiana where he sat. They walked to the beat of a drum played by a native who led the procession, crying as he went. All repeated sad and painful words: "And thus they go reciting sad verses [*endechando*] all around most of the town: telling in their songs how the man lived while alive; and other related things." Such ceremonies and universal mourning expressed their ties to the deceased and the unity and cohesion of the group.[84]

The material record corroborates the ethnohistorical accounts. Cieza includes a generic statement about such burials after mentioning one held in the 1530s or 1540s in Ica, on the coast south of Lima, which held burial goods worth fifty thousand pesos. He describes the burials as follows:

> [There are] magnificent and tall tombs adorned with flagstones and arches, and they bury with the deceased all his trousseau and women, and service, and much quantity of food, and not a few jugs of beer or wine that they make, and his arms and ornaments. . . . And with the lord they put his treasure and many live women, and other persons who were his good friends when alive. And thus from what I have said it was the general opinion of all these coastal Indians and even those of the highlands of this kingdom of Peru that the souls of the dead do not die, but that they always live and they gather there in the other world one with the others: where . . . they believed that they rested, and ate and drank, which is their major pleasure. And being sure of this they buried with the deceased their most beloved women, and their most

intimate servants: and finally all the precious things, and arms, and feathers, and other personal ornaments. And, mimicking imperial practice, many of his relatives[,] because there was no room in the tomb[,] dug holes in the fields of the deceased lord: or in other parts where he used to take his pleasure, and celebrate: and there they entombed themselves: believing that his spirit would pass by those places and he would take them in his company for his service. And even so[,] some women to serve him better and so that he would appreciate their service more: appearing to them that the tombs were not yet ready, they hung themselves with their own hair, and thus they killed themselves.

This still held true in 1545–46 when a great lord of Jauja died. His followers interred alive with him a great number of women and servants. Archbishop Loayza's prohibition of this practice in 1545 suggests that this was one of the last instances of this type of mass suicide and ritualized murder done in the guise of sacrifice; but lineages were still burying people with their lords in 1571.[85]

Cieza gives additional details about the last rites of the people of the Collao. When a native died, relatives and friends cried and wailed for many days. Secondary wives of nobles shaved their heads. Relatives contributed food and drink. Before the body was buried, camelids were killed, and "they put the entrails in the plazas that they had in their apartments." The blood was sprinkled on the face of the dead, and the lungs were used as a means to communicate with his spirit. During the days of mourning, corn was brewed into chicha. The amount of chicha was an index of the respect and honor of the dead person. "Once the brew is made and the camelids are dead they say that they carry the dead to the fields, where they made the tomb: accompanying the dead body (if he were a lord) were most of the people of the town." Nearby they burned ten or twenty camelids, a greater or lesser number depending on who the dead person was. And they killed the women, children, and servants who were to be sent with him. These, some llamas, and utilitarian goods were buried with the body: "interring (according also to their custom) some live persons." After interment, all the people who attended the funeral returned to the deceased's house to eat and drink, leaving every once in a while "[to go] to the plazas that are made next to the lord's house: where in a choir, as they by custom do, they dance crying." This lasted some days, at the end of which time the poor were given food and drink.[86]

An even more intimate glimpse of the same type of funerary ritual, in Cajatambo, is provided by provincial testimonies. Last rites customarily lasted five days and, according to Huertas, were sometimes therefore called the fifth sunrise (*pisca punchao quinto amanecer*), the time necessary for the soul to leave the body and say good-bye to family and friends. During this period, the living pondered "his qualities and virtues" and repeated the most important events or actions of his life, singing sad verses to the sound of the flute. The rites commenced with the washing and preparation of the body. Proper embalmment guaranteed that the corpse would not be destroyed by worms but would last, dried two or three hundred years.[87] Gold or silver was placed in its mouth, hands, and other parts of the body. The body was enshrouded (*amortajado*) in wool of many colors and dressed in a full-length, sleeveless garment (*cusma*), and a mantle (*manta*), which was placed on the body's head (see Figure 5.14). In Cajatambo, the body was placed in a seated or squatting (*en cuclillas*), flexed position with legs crossed and drawn up to the chest; the hands were placed up against the cheeks. This pose resembled the fetal position and may have signified preparation for a rebirth. Once prepared, the body was placed wherever the person had actually died. At this point, should the deceased be a chief, his attendants would commit suicide or be killed to accompany him.[88]

Food offerings were made before the body. If the relatives could afford it, one or more llamas were killed, stabbed "on the side of the heart." The blood, which one witness described as "the drink that they give to the deceased," drained into some dry gourds (*mates*) to be splattered on the body's head, hands, and feet as an offering. The best pieces of meat—the ears, the eyelids, and the feet—and llama fat (suet or *sebo*), guinea pigs, coca, and black and white corn, were thereafter burned. The smoke of these items, described as incense, carried the essence of this soul food (*mircapa*) to the dead, while blood and chicha were splattered repeatedly on the body's face. Meanwhile, the entire community was invited to congregate at the dead person's house; they sat down before him to drink and eat llama meat.[89]

At midnight, a religious specialist of the ayllu interpreted the llama's entrails (liver and lungs), sprinkling more blood on the deceased, to ascertain if the sacrifice was acceptable to the dead. On July 25, 1656, the witness Andres Chaupis Yauri, fiscal (assistant to the church or religious brotherhood [*cofradía*]) of the town of Otuco, described the divination process: "They blow through the *taranquin* that is the windpipe or gullet and the lungs swell like a bag [*odre*]."[90] If little pockets appeared, it was a sign that the deceased or the malquis and idols were angry, so it was necessary to "make amends [*desenojarlo(s)*]." As appeasement, the relatives of the deceased contributed more offerings to be burned so that the officiant could communicate with the deceased to ask about the reason for his ire. After sprinkling the face of the dead with llama blood, the minister made him speak (*ase que abla con el*). The minister might report back to the assembled that the person was sad and had died because he had sinned. Or the ancestors were mad at the deceased because he had not honored or celebrated them and did not adore the guacas. Alternatively, those assembled might be told that they had sinned and would soon die if they did not adore their guacas and malquis. The same fate awaited those who did not remember the first anniversary of

FIGURE 5.14. A Chinchaysuyu burial. Source: Guamán Poma de Ayala 1613/1936: 289.

the deceased's death. If displeased, the dead could and would curse them so that they would be poor and their labors would be wasted. In such circumstances, the relatives offered more sacrifices to the malquis and idols.[91]

Hernando Hacaspoma, a native practitioner testifying in the town of San Pedro de Hacas in 1657, elaborated:

If in the lungs appear little bags like little bladders that they call *guarcos* in their language[,] this witness told the relatives of the deceased that the deceased was mad because he ate and received the offering with garcos and all those of his lineage [father, mother, sisters and brothers, and wife, according to Chaupis Yauri] would die shortly[;] and said relatives gave this witness offerings of guinea pigs, coca, suet, corn, beer, and blood of a llama that they had killed[;] and this witness made a sacrifice of all this[;] burning it before the deceased and sprinkling the face with the said blood and beer[;] and later he talked and asked the deceased[,] in the presence of his relatives[,] if they would die shortly[;] and the dead gave an answer[;] and he said that he had died because he had not adored and worshiped his guacas well and his idols and ancestors[;] and when they fasted and confessed[,] he did not do as he was ordered by his wizards [*magsas echiceros*][;] and he broke the taboos[,] eating salt and chili pepper[,] sleeping with his women[;] and he did not honor his ancestors and dead[,] and that they would die very fast if they did not honor their ancestors and relatives and adore their guacas and keep the fasts and make confessions[;] and later the said relatives gave this witness the referred to offering so he could make the sacrifice to the ancestor idols and guacas[;] and they confessed[;] and they fasted anew and all that night[,] before the deceased[,] the invited ate of the dead llamas and drank and they got drunk.

They also danced to the sound of little drums (*tamborcillos*).[92] On other occasions, Chaupis Yauri of Otuco related (in 1656) what the deceased had told him:

He [the deceased] got mad so that they would not forget him and thus with this he would not die[;] instead they would not forget him when he was in his house or tomb with the food they left for his soul[—]two kidneys of the llama[,] baked potatoes[,] *parpas* of multi-colored corn [maize *arguay*] on a string were hung from his neck and a fist full of coca was placed on his chest on the side of the heart and they rubbed the blood of a llama in his mouth and on the palms of his hands and the soles of his feet.[93]

The night was spent singing and dancing to "gladden the guaca" (*alegrar la guaca*) and to appease the deceased's soul. At the first crow of a rooster, while the men stayed with the corpse, the closest relatives took the manta from the deceased's head and other pieces of his clothing to cover their own. Carrying some staffs, pieces of llama meat and hide, a container of llama blood, and a pitcher of chicha, the religious specialist and other ministers of idols, all the other women of the town who were there, and the relatives with their heads covered went out into the streets. They walked the avenues and the plaza of the settlement, sprinkling the llama blood and chicha on the walls so that the soul of the dead could drink, while crying and wailing—the ancient way (*al usso antiguo*). They shook their heads, calling to the deceased, telling him how sorry they were that he had left and how they remembered him; telling him to accept the food and drink so that he would not go hungry or thirsty into the other life; asking him not to be angry and curse them from the other life when he went to rest. They asked where he was, how they could find him, and how he felt. Other witnesses report that they called out, asking why he did not come to see and console them, was he in a good place, and was he happy. They also sang a song in Quechua, which, loosely translated, means: "I understood that you were there on your plain where you usually sat [but] you were not there." This procession lasted until dawn, when they returned to the funeral for more dancing and rites.[94]

At daybreak, the cult minister or a relative cut locks of hair from the back of the head and clipped the nails of the deceased. These were kept in a gourd in the tomb (*machay;* ideally a cave) or another secure place for the ceremony marking the one-year anniversary of his death. The attendants remained with the deceased until noon, when the body was placed in a net (*aulla*). It was then carried on someone's back to the sometimes elaborately painted machay of their ayllu in the pueblo viejo to "mocharle." Others went along to the interment site, where they again sprinkled the mummy bundle with more llama blood and chicha. Chaupis Yauri explained that "the sprinkling of blood was to enable the souls to pass across the bridge of Aychay Chaca and Guaroy Chaca Cunas Chacharas that are on the other side of this bridge where they say go the souls of the said dead." They offered additional guinea pigs (*cuyes*) and burned sebo on a ceramic or stone brazier or altar (*callana*). This mircapa was the "viaticum that he was to take to the other world." When they left the body in the machay, they returned home to dance to the sound of drums for hours and hours. Witnesses agreed that the machayes remained open so the bodies could be stored, viewed, visited, and venerated, and served as the sites for the ceremonies that all the natives of the region performed for their dead (see Figures 5.15 and 5.16).[95]

As the name of the funerary ritual suggests, the interment of the body in the machay was the end of the cycle of birth and death that began at the pacarina. It represented the latest addition to the ancestor cult that started when the mythical founding malquis settled in the area. The bodies of the dead, which often numbered in the hundreds and could be identified by the living by name and kinship relation, represented the tangible history of the group. The ayllu originated in the pacarina. The life of its members ended at the machay. Thus, the pacarina and machay were united, to paraphrase Mary Doyle, in the cyclical conception of the universe in which life was a continuity and a constant re-creation. All the ayllu would again be reunited in the Upaymarca, the next world, whereas rituals transformed the departed into a source of new life and protection (see Figure 5.17).[96]

FIGURE 5.15. A Condesuyu burial. Source: Guamán Poma de Ayala 1613/1936: 295.

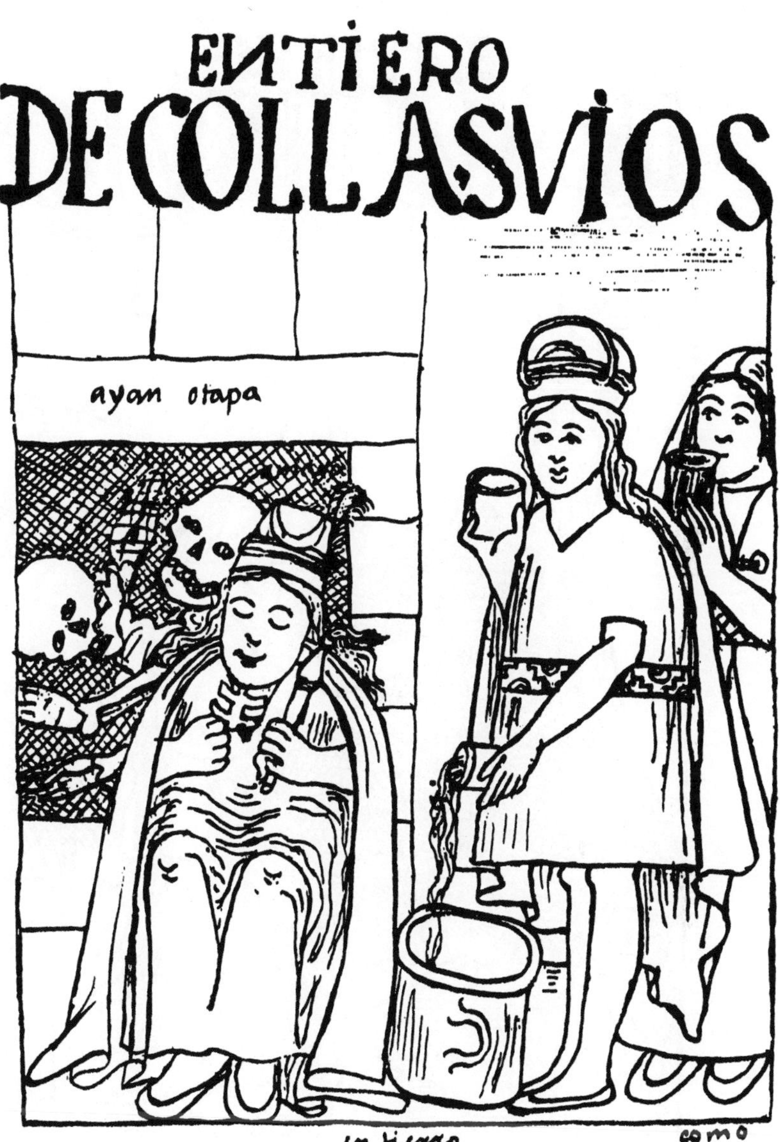

FIGURE 5.16. A Collasuyu burial. Source: Guamán Poma de Ayala 1613/1936: 293.

FIGURE 5.17. An Antisuyu burial. Source: Guamán Poma de Ayala 1613/1936: 291.

Andeans believed that the soul visited his family for five nights to eat food offerings. On the night of the interment at the machay, the relatives began a fast and did not dare sleep the entire night. They kept this wake because, according to Juan Guaraz, a lesser lord (*camachico* or *kamachikuq*) of the town of Santo Domingo de Pariac, "they say that if one sleeps the soul will come and it will kill or punish with illnesses taking away fields and food." Each of the five nights, they burned the available coca, suet, corn, potatoes, yams, yuccas, beans, avocados, fruit (lucumas), peanuts, new potatoes (*papas nunas*), and guinea pigs as incense in the place where he died, saying that the soul came to eat and that this practice prevented the dead person from returning to claim his clothes and hair. With these provisions and chicha, the soul was able to cross the bridge of Achacaca and go to rest in the other world.[97]

To check to see if the deceased's soul had returned, they spread ashes about the house and patios. If the relatives saw in the ashes footprints or other telltale signs of a bird or other animal (such as a rooster, fox, or goat) or an insect, they interpreted it as a sign that the soul had visited—to eat and retrieve his hair, nail clippings, and spit (*escupido*). Those in the house, upon seeing such signs, swiped the walls with their mantles and checked all the corners, saying, "Go because this house is no longer yours because we have already offered what we are going to give you" and "The soul should go to its tomb and origin from where the sacred grandparents and ancestors came out[;] that that house is no longer his."[98]

At the end of the five days, the relatives of the deceased took all the clothing to be washed in the river with parpa, the powder of a white stone (*pasca*), and white cornmeal. The house was swept, and the straw and hides (*pellejo*) of his bed and old rags that he had used were burned outside the town. At the end of this rite natives believed that the soul of the deceased would no longer visit the house looking for his hair, nail clippings, and spit (*racchanta que es lo que a escupido*). These rites also guaranteed that the deceased "should have something to eat in the other world."[99]

Cieza suggests that the last rites were similar elsewhere, although the position of the body and the burial structure might differ. For example, in the Collao, bodies were enshrined in *colcas* that looked to him like little square, sometimes two-story towers, roofed with either straw or tile, with their door facing east toward the sunrise (see Figures 5.13, 5.14, 5.15, and 5.16). Next to these structures, they sacrificed, burned offerings, and sprinkled blood of young camelids (*corderos*) and other animals. In the region around the Coricancha, the dead were interred seated on their tianas and clothed and adorned with their best clothes. In Jauja, the dead were wrapped in a hide from a freshly killed sheep or camelid and kept in their houses. They carried the bodies of their lords on litters periodically to visit dispersed settlements with great pomp and ceremonial circumstance, offering them sacrifices of camelids and even children and women. In the region of "Chinchan" [Chincha or Chan Chan?] on the coast, the dead were put on beds made of cane (*barbacoas*). In many coastal valleys, great walls were built near the foothills of the Andes. In these, each family and lineage had its established place for burying its dead, behind closed doors. These structures, Cieza reports, were called guacas.[100]

The rites on the one-year anniversary of the death took a very similar form. In some cases, the deceased was taken out of the machay and dressed in a new shirt (*camiseta*), manta, and cusma. Then the relatives sacrificed a llama, and the blood and chicha were offered to the deceased. Sebo, coca, and white and dark maize were burned before the mummy bundle, and many cuyes were killed. Kin explained "that the said deceased eats it all." While the offering was made and the cuyes killed, the officiant examined the llama's liver and lungs. If they were full of blood and black, the malqui was mad and the participants could expect punishment and sickness. To appease the spirit, each adherent was to "worship with all his heart and tears and laments." White livers were signs that the spirit had accepted the sacrifice and was not mad. Prosperity would reign. The relatives drank chicha until intoxicated and feasted on the llama. They also danced different dances for the dead, while the closest relative carried the mummy on his back and danced with him one day and one night. When finished, they put the body back into the machay and returned to their homes, where they danced to the sound of the little drums all day and night.[101]

Again, the best single description comes from the fiscal of Otuco, Andres Chaupis Yauri:

> And likewise he has seen that the said wizards[,] to put on the said end of the year celebrations[,] went to the dead in their tombs and returned[;] and they said that it was already time to make them because the God Libiac and the guacas had the deceased under their feet constrained[,] suffering[;] and that they give him drink because the dead had planted fields[,] and he had left food[;] and[,] saying this[,] that they take all that was necessary for the end of the year [ritual][;] and later they made three or four fanegas of chicha[;] and they cut up and burned the meat of llama—feet and the ears and hairs of the eyebrows—before the deceased so that he could stop the suffering he was in[;] and on this occasion they dressed him in a new full length garment [*cusma*][;] new sling [*guaraca*][,] manta[;] and on their backs the relatives carried him and they danced . . . and all this they always did in the door of the tomb an entire night[;] at dawn they did another that they called *cunay*[:] everyone holding their hands they give five rounds and then they go another five rounds the other way[;] and to the lead sorceress[,] they give a leg of a llama who carries it on her back during the whole dance[;] and returning to the tomb they go singing *pariac yay* and they fast the said five days.

People believed that during the year after the deceased's death, the soul suffered and wandered. It is during the next year, after the anniversary ceremony, that the soul reached the next world of rest and delight.[102]

Elsewhere, the ceremony was simpler. Relatives retrieved the hair cuttings and nail clippings from the machay or their houses and used them to represent the deceased. In the dead person's house, they placed them on a pile of his clothes—usually a relatively new mantle—and they honored him, inviting the entire community, slaughtering one or more llamas, and making quantities of corn chicha. They ate, drank, and danced all night to the beat of their drums. At midnight the officiant sprinkled chicha and blood on the hair and burned suet, coca, white and dark corn, cuyes, powders from certain pulverized precious seashells (such as *Spondylous* [*mullu*]), and white pasca powder as a sacrificial food offering. This was done so that the dead would not suffer in the "other life" and could cross the hair bridge separating this world and the next. He could then go with his mircapa to rest in his pacarina "from whence came his ancestors." Thereafter, all the invitees drank, ate, danced, and sang "in their pagan manner" the entire night.[103]

Hernando Hacaspoma explained the purpose of this ritual of the first anniversary of a death (*cabo de año*):

> It was the tradition of his teachers and elders that the dead when they died were one year suffering in this world[;] and after the year and honoring them and sacrificing to them[,] they went to rest to their pacarinas[,] to the upaimarca[,] that was located in titicaca and yarocaca the birth place of the sun and of the Thunder[,] that is Lightning[,] and that to go to this upamarca the soul passed over a bridge [called] achacaca that is a bridge made of hair[;] and so that they do not fall into the river and it sweeps them away[,] they made the sacrifices involving hair.[104]

Thus, this ritual and the sacrifice of dogs to guide the soul helped it pass over the very narrow hair bridge on its way to the "world of the dead" "from whence came [its] ancestors," to rest and "to see[,] live, and be" with its grandparents, relatives, and friends. The consequences of forgetting this rite were that the souls of the dead would be hurt, unhappy, frustrated, and hungry. The dead would curse their relatives, bringing on the premature death of their kin. Despite the prohibition of such practices by the Concilios Limenses of 1567 and 1582–83 and the Sinodos of 1613 and 1639, they continued into the late seventeenth century.[105]

In colonial times, Guamán Poma de Ayala names November as the month to celebrate ancestor cults, whereas Polo de Ondegardo indicates that it was the month of December. At these times, the living exhibited their ancestors publicly, renewed their clothing and feathers, fed them, and danced before them. They placed them on litters and paraded them through the streets (see Figure 5.18). The ancestors, according to Aguirre Palma, were considered

FIGURE 5.18. Natives carrying a mummified ancestor in November. Source: Guamán Poma de Ayala 1613/1936: 256.

alive during the celebrations. He characterized these rituals as a communion between the living and the dead.[106]

Cosmology as Politics

Absent a system of writing in Peru, memory, history, and values were transmitted through story, song, ceremony, and structure. The practice of rituals, which often used stories and songs, reinforced the dominant Andean worldview at both the imperial and local levels and promoted unity. The investiture, for example, included a sacrificial procedure for consulting the ancestral powers to determine the right candidate for succession. At both imperial and provincial levels, a finite, elite conclave kept private the debates and jockeying for influence involved in arriving at a consensual decision. The selection was eventually announced to the realm without making any of the infighting public, because this would have undermined the confidence in the sanctity of their divine leaders. The investiture ceremony was most solemn and significant at the moment that the incoming Inca or lord sat on his tiana. The seat represented hegemony and dominion. He, then and there, imbibed or became invested with the essence of his predecessors' vital energy, the breath of life. The white-feather presentations and the salute—in which individuals raised their open hands, palm forward and up, and made kissing or smacking sounds with their lips—has been likened to the moment when divine power infused the leader's body. With it he received the acknowledged wisdom of the past. Henceforth, the delegated power of the gods radiated out from him. Back home in the provinces, commoners worshipped and gave special status to all those who had direct contact with the supreme earthly power of the Inca. This held true for the living and the dead.[107]

The obligatory progresses to visit their people also acted out behavior associated with the mythical creators and founding heroes of each social group. Gods were not stationary. They moved in the mythical narrations, and, when they did, there was a lapse in orderly life. Representations of gods were taken to battle, and they accompanied the descendants when on the move themselves. While seated and still, the authority (like a god) could order the universe, despite movement all around him. Carried in a litter as if an idol or god, upheld, yet moving and seated, he became the mobile nucleus of the Andean universe, somewhere between human and deity—on this earth, but no longer of it. The processions reiterated this fact and reminded onlookers that the divine king and curaca were above, but among them. The Inca's travels suggested the movement of the sun that each day crossed the sky, sequentially visiting and warming all. The fact that the Inca donned the dress and imitated the hairstyles of the groups he visited indicates that he was attempting to embody the founding heroes of the group's mythical history and transcendent genealogy.[108]

Both Inca and curaca were carried in elaborate litters from ceremonial complex to ceremonial complex, where they feasted with "their people," thus establishing or reinforcing the personal ties, allegiance, and loyalty upon which the system and survival depended. Like the legendary gods, rulers took the occasion to reward the meritorious with women, textiles, and drinking vessels, and punish those who had dared break the covenant. Progressions made after the death of his predecessor had several functions. For the incoming lord, they allowed him to establish bonds of reciprocity and trust on his own account. Simultaneously, he visited and mourned at the places that his predecessor had frequented. Such trips, no doubt, served propagandistic purposes: emphasizing the insurance that the lord represented to the present and reemphasizing the divine line of the predecessor; sanctifying sites of significant accomplishments of these purported man-gods; and ultimately helping to mythologize his person, his regime, and his line.[109]

A curaca, too, visited the dispersed, pre-reducción populations of his followers, magnanimously plying adherents with chicha and corn at each stop. Feeding followers established his right to ask for confederation to face the mundane tasks or the exigencies of the day. He fed them to be himself fed and remembered. Reciprocity and redistribution were not ideals or mere unfulfilled promises and expectations, divorced from state ritual and everyday life and death.

Reciprocity was again the message reiterated in the funeral, which underscored the phased continuity between life and death and the interdependence between both worlds—this and the next. Even as a corpse, the dead played a significant role in daily life. Descendants assumed that the dead influenced the quality of their existence on earth. As part of the memorializing activities of last rites, partisans retraced the steps and revisited the person's old haunts, remembering him and thus summarizing his life and times. The body was paraded at ceremonials and received food sacrifices throughout the year.

The songs that were sung in each of these instances taught the living about the past of their line. Old women sang "*aillis* and *taquies* from ancient times invoking ancient memories." Arriaga in 1621 recognized the power of songs as historical repositories. In the songs, sung in their mother tongue, provincial peoples remembered their valiant past; recalled the biographies of their adored guacas, malquis, and powers; and invoked them for assistance. In so doing, they relived history and recognized that the past determined the future. Such songs and dances, as counternarrative, posed a real and constant threat to the imperial enterprise. The potential for subversion that such sung tales represented obligated the Inca to be present among the ethnicities, attempting to co-opt with honor and prized gifts and to incorporate local lords with presents of women. For these same reasons, Spanish colonial authorities threatened songsters with whippings, shaving of the head, and worse.[110]

Songs and dances, like propaganda elsewhere, were selected, and their performance was controlled. Each king appointed three or four elders to remember and compose ballads recounting all remarkable events during his reign. These were chanted in the presence of the ruler. After his death, these songs were heard by his successor. Later, only on days of great celebration or profound sadness "was it permitted to tell the greatness of them and their origin and birth, and except for these [times] no one was permitted to deal with the subject." Thus, the successor controlled the historical information in the ballads. The sung biographies of some, judged unworthy of future memory, were expunged from the performers' repertoire. Thus could the past be manipulated or reconstructed.[111]

Participation in the rites of rule, which were themselves staged in suggestive architectural settings, was tantamount to acceptance of the cosmological bases of the religio-political legitimacy that organized society at all levels. Repeated viewings provided a context in which culture was taught and inculcated. Comprehension provided the moral and ethical guidelines that regulated and constrained participants' behavior; and it maintained social unity and political continuity in a society that did not yet include a widespread, institutionalized penal system. To sing and dance with the dead was to honor them and proclaim partisanship and dependence. Over several generations, a growing, prosperous lineage had to spread out to take advantage of the resources of the broken Andean landscape. Large numbers were good, though a centrifugal force, because they represented the labor power that could be mustered in times of need. Family and lineage reunions to celebrate the departed brought relatives back together. Such lineage or ayllu cults, as countervailing and centripetal forces, helped dispersed family members remember their beginnings, no matter where they lived or where they moved.[112]

The devotees of a cult to their grandparents were also members of a larger congregation that adored the grandparents of their grandparents. Dancing at a ceremony honoring an ancestor-hero implied his worship. But individuals had multiple loyalties that reflected the kinship and hierarchy of the empire. They might dance to propitiate the malquis at various levels of the administrative structure—that is, the malqui of their immediate lineage and the malqui of their paramount lord. The latter was also their protector, though further removed. To send dancers to the rituals of others was a sign of adherence and solidarity. The ability to attract wider groups of followers enhanced the position of the ancestor on the always-shifting hierarchy of prestige and power in this segmented, nested society. Perceived power attracted additional devotees.

But gods were fickle; and humans, fallible and imperfect. This recognition was the proverbial loophole to explain hard times. Periodic crises motivated whole groups and their leaders to redouble their efforts to please their gods: to feed in order to be fed. They adored, loved, and respected in order to be protected. Failure to please the divine ancestors, in contrast, threatened the disaccreditation of the lords and the dispersal and death of their followers. Could the periodic and prolonged climate shifts have been interpreted as the wrath of the gods? If so, individual leaders would have been delegitimized and rejected. In fact, if climate shifts were prolonged, a whole line of rulers would have been shunned and eventually condemned as powerless to atone and appease the supernatural beings—to end the drought, stop the uncommonly heavy rains, or quiet the rumblings and trembling of the earth. Eventually, confidence in the rulers would have waned, and the ideological cement would have come unglued. Former devotees would leave, looking elsewhere for protection against the uncertainties of life. Such a scenario may explain the eclipse of the mighty Tiwanaku culture, whose decline is already associated with a major and long-lasting drought.[113]

The strength of such local cults could be and was used by the disgruntled to challenge Cuzco domination. But the imperial system was flexible. Elasticity allowed local heroes to be grafted onto the dominant pantheon. This practice, the command to learn Quechua, and gifts of reproductive power, which were meant to engender a biological unity, fostered the association and incorporation of their ethnic followers into the ranks of Inca adherents and Sun worshippers.

In contrast, the more rigid colonial conversion of these people to Catholicism meant a dramatic repudiation of these beliefs and practices, a negation of their accustomed, ancestor-based sense of self. Andeans were denied self-expression. Instead, they were commanded to disassociate from their mythical past and to give up their beliefs: that they all came from a single origin—a pacarina, a person and a place—and that they were all children of the ancestor gods.[114]

Part Four

THE SOCIAL BASES OF AUTHORITY

6 *A Sense of Selves*

If that ancestor did not exist, I would not exist.
—Bernabé Cobo

What we call our data are really our own constructions of other people's constructions of what they and their compatriots are up to.
—Clifford Geertz

This book is part of a trend that revisits the spiritual and ideological dimensions of Andean life. After decades in which the investigative efforts concentrated on the material and economic, recent scholarship has gravitated toward a reconsideration of native religion as a key to values and behavior. In this vein, this effort is designed to begin to decolonize and decenter the past by explaining—to the extent possible given the extant written sources and my status as an outsider—the legitimizing cosmology of the people of the Andes just before and as they underwent the uneven process of Hispanicization in the sixteenth and seventeenth centuries. I cannot make claims concerning periods before that time because of the scarcity of written testimonials that refer back to those eras. But plentiful indirect evidence and archaeological research suggest that the belief in the everyday power of the ancestors, around which the legitimating ideology was constructed and continually being manipulated, predated Inca hegemony.

My journey began with a contradiction and incongruity in the earliest European accounts over the meaning of the phrase "el Cuzco." The first Spanish chronicles used the expression consistently to indicate a person and only indirectly to refer to a place. Heretofore, these writings have been dismissed as the imperfect understandings of European observers who themselves depended on the interpretation of young natives. But their basic translations proved to be more accurate than not. My studies show that only after Francisco Pizarro founded the Spanish villa and anointed it as the city of "el Cuzco" did the heretofore "place of the gods," or the "place of the sun," and most elaborate of the many ceremonial complexes scattered throughout the Andes become known by that name.

The fact that el Cuzco was a title taken by one Andean lord from another elucidates the conceptualization of the Andean polity as an abstract construction, based on kinship and the claim to a common sacred ancestry. The aim of the Andean rulers was to create a polity, a mega-association, united by a belief that all members were of "one birth" and lived under "one law." In this order, established by the rulers in the name of the overarching solar deity, el Cuzco was a divine ruler, the navel of the body politic (in literal and fictive terms), and the giver and enforcer of the corpus of customary laws that (theoretically) regulated everyday life. I argue, in short, that certain of the Andean peoples recognized a sacred center or nexus between themselves and the gods. The polity headed by el Cuzco was not defined as specific, fixed territorial units or delimited, contiguous regions. Rather, it was conceived of in personal, affiliative terms—in some respects like the vast system of clientelism that made up the sociopolitical tissue of the Nyoro people (in Uganda), described by Heusch and others. In other words, el Cuzco was more the king of the Andeans than king of the Andes in an abstract, geographic sense. Social construction predominated over the physical dimensions of occupation of noncontiguous space. Political authority over people equated sovereignty with a group of devotees and subjects, or a congregation, rather than a defined and demarcated topographical area. The Inca's was a jurisdictional state, where a religious and moral hegemony was probably more real than direct, day-to-day political control, with elements of or similarities to the theater states and galactic polities of Southeast Asia and the kingdoms of Africa. A peripatetic, celestial-inspired imperial court overcame the centrifugal forces of division. The ruler traveled to visit groups who worshipped him or who he expected would acknowledge him as overlord and sovereign. The multiple pilgrimage centers, denominated as "Cuzcos" by the chroniclers, were built to resemble the model in the south. They served as platforms that received the incarnation of the sun on earth and functioned as monumental stages for elaborate, authorizing ceremonials and the accompanying generous hospitality of the unifying state.[1]

This argument does not deny that individual families or ayllus possessed fields associated with their founding ancestors. But individual families sometimes moved seasonally; ayllus fissured, establishing distinct, but related entities on unoccupied lands. This process of rupture and recomposition meant that kin groups lived scattered over a wide Andean landscape interspersed with other households belonging to other ayllus. Their ethnic affiliation was their shared worship—their dancing, their singing of common histories, and their feasting. Participation in ritual activities provided the experiential adhesive that drew individuals together around a founding ancestor: the marcaioc. Their biographies, highlighted with heroic and valuable deeds, provided the history and pride of belonging to their group. These sometimes real (in that their mummies continued to exist) and sometimes mythical beings served as integrating poles of attraction to their cult and memory. Only once fixed in place by the Spanish colonial state did the natives' sense of self become associated with a given, assigned homeland. This creeping territorialization was a piecemeal process that took decades, even centuries, as the Spanish imperial government defined, alienated, and ratified, often in imperfect ways, different types and categories of tenure rights to physical space.

Chapter 3 elaborates on the idea of el Cuzco as the center of the center. Kingship was embedded in religio-political institutions. The reigning Cuzco was advertised as and acted as a guaca or god. Ideally, his dress, demeanor, and comportment fit the collective imaginings of multiple ethnicities, carefully prepared by ritualized songs and dances, myths, architecture, and iconographies to accept him as son of the Sun, chief diviner, soothsayer, and theocrat—representing guardian spirits whose power extended over a large, changing number of social groups living interspersed in an almost unimaginable range of habitats and backward into historical and inexperienced times. Like the Chinese kings of the Shang dynasty, the emperor and his advisers determined through divination the will of ancient souls. The king's ability to communicate with them proved his divinity. He was believed to be able to influence these ancients through prayer and sacrifice. Thus, he could promise bountiful harvests, health, and victories. He had the power, like the gods, to dispense life-giving food and clothing in times of emergency. He and the representations of his ancestral guacas moved together around the landscape and were even carried into battle to ensure triumph. In the latter case, any indication of impotence signaled that the favor and power of the gods had slackened or were being withdrawn. In these instances, supporters scattered and retreated, leaving the other camp to celebrate the power and invincibility of their forebears.[2]

Chapter 4 parallels the previous discussion, focusing on such ethnic authorities as the curacas and principal lords. At the lineage level, too, the ruler acted, to the extent that his resources allowed, like the ancestor-heroes of his past, the subjects of their songs and celebrations. He was carried on litters; he sat on sacred stools, his head above the rest; he was venerated as the choice of his forebears to bring order to their heirs and adherents and guarantee life and stability. The cherished ancestors passed their power to him, as the most able of the living, as a divine essence or breath (*soplo divino*). Through this wind or breath, they conferred upon their chosen representative their blessing and the wisdom to rule and protect the people.

As their representative and spokesman, he took responsibility for the ancestral cult that was the defining basis of their ethnic identity. He orchestrated the activities, organizing workforces to serve the gods. During the curaca's visitations, he sought help in maintaining sacred buildings and spaces;

in cultivating fields to produce surpluses of corn and other products offered as sacrifices; and in herding the animals killed at the ceremonials. He also originated and directed the observances, anointing the participants and those responsible; ordering the preparation of the chicha; and proportioning the clothes and other insignia of power that were displayed at such affairs.

Curacas and their followers worshipped at the graves of their ancestors, in their pueblos viejos, so vilified and feared as locations of demonic practices and worship by Spanish prelates and royal authorities. Pilgrims from scattered homesteads gathered at these otherwise empty or minimally staffed religio-political centers to celebrate periodically in song and dance the beneficial presence of the dead in their lives and their continuing affiliation and community. At these observances, drinking from the lord's chicha and eating from the carcasses of numerous sacrificial animals consecrated their communion and ethnic solidarity.

Sickness, failed crops, earthquakes, and bad weather, especially if they continued beyond a season or two, signaled the nonfeasance of ethnic authorities—to propitiate the ancestors properly or to live up to sacred expectations. In several cases, such inept leaders were scorned or shunned and eventually permanently recalled, being removed—usually summarily executed—by their own subordinates and replaced with a person whom the gods confirmed through ceremony and divination. Should a series of lords fail to ameliorate adverse conditions, such as in the case of a prolonged drought, an entire lineage or elite might be discredited. The faithful would no longer have reason to respond to invitations to celebrate their forebears. Without material support from below, the elite would be rendered powerless, and their hegemony and memory would quickly wane. This seems to have been the case of the Tiwanaku and explains, in part, the abrupt Andean capitulation to the Spanish in Cajamarca in the 1530s.[3]

What this detail demonstrates is that both at the imperial and local levels, the multiethnic populace shared the certainty that the ancestral gods participated in and determined the life of the living. In their own voices, Andean peoples related their belief in a continuing interconnectedness, indebtedness, and interdependence between this realm and the other. For these reasons, the forebears had to be propitiated. Sacrifices demonstrated the living love of the devoted, who beseeched the protection and favor of the departed. Commoners obeyed their leaders, as the anointed man-gods of the Andes, who were alive and well and capable of transmitting otherworldly favor on their devotees. A lord's mandate was divine. It was evidenced on the battlefield and in the wisdom of his quotidian decisions. Should he lose the enabling sanction of the guacas, for whatever reason, he forfeited his legitimacy—a traditional legitimacy made manifest in the remains and representations of those who preceded him. He would lose control of the labor and allegiance of his followers. He could then only watch, harangue, and evoke the spirits, as some of his subjects flocked to a rival lord's protection and aid. Eventually, without a reversal of fortune, he would be helpless in the face of supposed supernatural ire or disdain and run the risk of being deposed and disposed of by the guardians of order.[4]

Finally, I show how these legitimizing precepts were displayed, codified, transmitted, and taught. Enthronements sanctified the person of the lord. Investitures depicted the accepted transfer of divine wisdom and prowess to the next ruler. Processions provided an opportunity to symbolize the order and redistribution of goods associated with the center of sociopolitical and religious life. The lord's ability to supply goods, sumptuary items in normal times and subsistence in periods of crisis, served as a proxy measure of the authority's power and greatness. Funerals memorialized the life of the dead both in song and in observances that—even when serious and sad—carried not-so-subtle messages about hierarchy and order. The act of redistributing to the living their offerings to the ancestors underscored the responsibilities between the dead and the living, between the leader and led, and among neighbors. Such acts also reinforced the idea that life and death were a continuum, not a duality. These and other rituals socialized participants, encouraged bonding, and nurtured feelings of belonging.[5]

Architecture, going back millennia, encapsulated in the silence of stone or sun-dried adobe brick the ideographical representation of the king as sacred center. The ushnu's placement within U-shaped structures at many ceremonial centers, however small and localized, communicated the idea that the ruler represented the origin and beginning of life. He carried the sacred seed and was the navel and womb, or center, of the state—a state made up of persons and conceived of in sociopolitical and religious terms, not as a given "land." Thus, as the monument builders of the Indian subcontinent represented Shiva as an androgynous duality, so imperial architects idealized the person of el Cuzco as the potentially androgynous embodiment of an overarching, all-encompassing deity, sometimes labeled as Viracocha. As such, the Andean rulers represented life, fertility, and continuity, extending back to the beginning of history.

The Incas, it can be argued, were just the last of a long series of ethnicities whose gods had vanquished the ancestral deities of their neighbors and assumed dominance. Persons rushed to ally with the powerful because of the dangers inherent in life in the Andes, where the phenomenon of the periodic El Niños, the recurring earthquakes and tremors, and other disasters were more than occasional. Ideas about order were reinforced by symbol, enacted in ritual, propagandized in song and dance, and retold in legend. They were also disseminated through gifts of painted pottery, tightly woven textiles, and beautifully rendered insignia meant to convey promises of sociocosmic solace to an audience in need of such reminders. All this was meant to manipulate ideologies and memory to win the "battle of identities" (to use Edward Said's phrase), to reinforce fickle and quickly shifting allegiances, and to buttress the power of the center, which without human support would falter and fail. Thus, we are reminded again of the Andean definition of wealth—as people and not material possessions.[6]

Thus, cosmology as political ideology and system provided a model for succession; the legitimacy for its rulers; a justification for mastery and colonialism; a mechanism for the removal of the weak and incompetent; and an explanation for the vicissitudes of life in the Andes. To preach that the life force of a corpse continued to exist and had to be sustained and nourished by its descendants established solidarity. Andeans felt that they were children of the gods.

The supposed man-gods of the Andes, as sons of the Sun, were in the process of establishing a "sovereign" or "jurisdictional" state in which persons and their labor were of more concern than where they lived and worked. From the rather tenuous beginnings of the legendary sinchi or "big man" Manco Capac, the Inca polity became one of many chieftains, before starting its imperial phase after the defeat of the Chancas. This empire was organized along patrimonial lines. In theory, the Sun was to the Inca as he was to ethnic lords and they were to commoners. El Cuzco endeavored, through gift brides that represented prized values, to bind the favored to a religio-political administrative structure captained by himself, his relatives, and his closest retainers. These recipients, then, regarded their duties as personal service to their ruler. Recall that Pachacuti Inca Yupanqui advised his successor to name his relatives to positions of confidence. Kolata has likened such a structure to a Grecian hyper-oikos.[7]

Because of the authenticating role of the religious ideology and the related activities of the elite, such a governing apparatus can also be labeled a theocracy. In theory, the solar cult and its supporting ritual were invented and inherited traditions that served to incorporate and override distinct, even hostile or opposite self-representations and competing local histories to forge a new universalizing, Pan-Andean identity that would broaden Inca sway and make it capable of meeting new challenges. To paraphrase Lewis Wurgaft, the political use of cultural symbolism and ritual encouraged a sense of group identity on otherwise disparate ethnicities. History became, as Hobsbawm reminds us, a "legitimator of action and cement of group adhesion." In the process, it was hoped, a people of one blood would be forged.[8]

In theory, the Tawantinsuyu appeared as a tightly centralized state, thanks to the rhetoric of the Inca elites as recorded in early chronicles. El Cuzco served as a nexus between several dozen ethnicities. The links established by exchanging women or by sacrifice were personal: between local lord and divine ruler. El Cuzco established a multidimensional universe in which his person was the bond and mediator among disparate minorities—much like the Spanish Hapsburg kings united the kingdoms of their realm, at least in theory. In practice, however, the degree of Inca centralization was overstated, the wishful recollections of a surviving native elite. The strongest ties were vertical. But these were also fragile. Especially during the interregnums, when society symbolically returned to a state of behetría, local ethnicities exerted their independence. The number of revolts against the hegemony of the Cuzco indicates that the unification efforts of the navel of the universe were still incomplete. For this reason, the passing of one king was hushed (to the extent possible) until the ascension of the next. For this reason also, upon succession, the new Cuzco had to make the rounds of his subjects to rededicate himself to their protection and well-being and to receive their assurances and signs of obligation. In short, this vast network of personal relationships and political alignments that was the essence of the Tawantinsuyu had to be reconstituted at each succession.

The emperor's sagacious endeavor to forge a more homogeneous congregation of one birth, under one law, can be seen as a brilliant and farsighted effort to overcome the factiousness, tenuousness, and instability inherent in the system—as then constituted—which favored stronger vertical relationships more than horizontal, interethnic ones. It was a conservative ploy to maintain el Cuzco's hegemony that acknowledged the existence of other nested hierarchies of powers, which could potentially challenge the center's right to rule, especially if two or more subordinate groups were to fuse to fight as one against it. By defeating adversaries' gods and their adherents on the battlefield, and reducing the survivors to tributary status, el Cuzco promised, in the long run, peace and life.

The grand illusion of Incafication that the cosmological lesson tried to convey ultimately failed. The Inca conquests proceeded too quickly, trying to unite state-level societies, such as Chimor, and kin-based groups, such as those encountered near Pasto in modern Colombia. Local groups revered and trusted their ancestors, convinced that they produced local cloudbursts and safeguarded the crops against blight and frost. The Incas came along, claiming that their father, the Sun, did so for the entire universe. Worship and work for the Sun and his son would bring big benefits. But without prolonged, continuous, and intimate exposure to the message and its reiteration at close and regularly scheduled intervals, local groups continued to turn to their own leaders and the fathers of their own forefathers for protection and aid when needed. They acquiesced to demands of work from el Cuzco to escape his promised wrath. People may also have come to scheduled celebrations and rituals out of need for aid or fear, unwilling to be absent and unaccounted for and incur the ire of human and supernatural powers. There the visitors expected to be regally treated and entertained. The representatives of one guaca visited the representatives of another. Lavish hospitality was a way to demonstrate the strength and well-being of the host god and his congregation. Commoners were attracted to power, especially beneficent power. One can imagine elaborate ceremonies impressing the newcomers and arguing for incorporation and absorption. The more elaborate, the more impressed. As one imbibed the host's chicha, one drank in a feeling of community and partisanship. Statecraft was tied to stagecraft. One sees a parallel with the ostentatious "theater states" of Southeast Asia, so ably characterized by Clifford Geertz.[9]

The tragedy is that the players believed their own constructed and inherited cosmological propaganda: the strongest gods win, and their followers get served. This was the basic rule of the game, whether it was a struggle between the siblings of a previous Inca for succession, a battle between the Incas and another known adversary, or the struggle between the Andeans and the Christians. In the end, the devastating demographic decline (where less than 10 percent of the population alive at the time of the Spanish invasion still survived at the end of the sixteenth century) and their cosmology (which predicted and underpinned legitimacy) led the populace to expect a cataclysm, a pachacuti—in which the world turned upside down and in on itself—leaving the Spaniards on top to change and dominate, and to begin the negotiated and contentious process that would try to re-create the world in the European image. As the Incas appeared doomed, another chieftain proclaimed that he was the son of the Sun, and undaunted, wanted to begin the process, the struggle, anew. Thus, the Inca cosmology and ploy succeeded in establishing a measure of internal stability in the short run, but could not overcome rifts in the uniting fiction that translated to weakness in the face of such an external challenge that was the Spanish invasion.[10]

This generalized reconstruction of the Andean legitimizing cosmology, besides arguing that native religion was as important as Catholicism for explaining certain behaviors and events in the sixteenth and seventeenth centuries, invites reflections on the concept of community, the bases of identity, and the methodology that has brought me to these conclusions. Until I began this research project, when I heard the word *community*, I imagined a place. In colonial Spanish America, the word elicited visions of a settlement or town, with a central plaza, a church, a town hall, and local authorities. Traditional Andean communities were also associated with communal lands. But this visualization of an Andean community is a Spanish creation, an imposition, very unlike what existed prior to the arrival of the Europeans.

Before the 1570s, Andean peoples lived in sites scattered over an extensive landscape. Members of a lineage or broader ethnic group lived side by side and interdigitalized with members of others. The "community" of Jayanca, a well-known example, was composed of thousands of persons concentrated on the north coast. A Spanish administrative inspection in

1540 documented that this population lived in hundreds of compounds or homesteads over at least a two-league radius measured from one residence of the curaca. But the curaca revealed to the visiting Spanish officials that he had hundreds of subjects several days' walk away, living in the mountains among people subject to the lord of Túcume, a leader associated with the coast. They had migrated during the lifetime of his predecessor, probably to work lands to produce foodstuffs (such as pigweed and potatoes) that could not be grown well on the hot, irrigated coastal plain. Other curacas in the same era are also known to have had villagers scattered over a distance as great as thirty leagues inland and east from the Pacific seashore. Thus, individual but related families often worked resources far removed one from the other. Members of one family also shifted their productive activities from field to field and resource to resource (e.g., salt pan, seashore, lomas) depending on the season. Sites of production also changed from year to year, as the yields of last season's vegetable field fell to the point where a new plot of land had to be plowed and planted. Such diversity of work sites enabled inhabitants to better cover their basic necessities and lowered the risk of total subsistence failure. Add to this the pilgrimages to worship their origins and travels to serve the authorities, and I conclude that the Andean peoples were almost incessantly on the move.[11]

The conceptual glue that bound these dispersed peoples together was not where they lived, not a concrete idea of a fixed and delineated homeland, but a belief that they were all children of a common ancestor, whom they still recalled and whose mummified body or representation they still worshipped after sometimes hundreds of years. The lord, as the incarnation of the founders of their line, made the rounds to connect his people. They gathered for recurring festivals and celebrations to sing and dance their history, sometimes with their ancestral guardians or their representations strapped to their backs. While worshipping their progenitors under the direction of their lord, they imbibed quantities of chicha, ate of the sacrificial animals, and were entertained by court jesters and buffoons (*truhanes*). Rituals and state theater embodied the sacred sovereignty of their lords and the idealized system of reciprocity and redistribution. Although the celebrations took on a tone of mass festival or carnival, they were quite serious. To participate implied a personal purification, deference, and dedication to authority and the acceptance of overlapping networks of association and exchange. The totality of the experience was designed to reinforce allegiances and ties between individual persons, their families, and their lords and the transcendental hierarchies they represented to create a common identity and sense of self.

Thus, the Andean imagining of community was (ideally) an authority and his kin who participated in the cult to their ancestors in order to preserve their world. On an imperial scale, the "community" of believers encompassed the son of the Sun and all his relatives plus members of the ethnicities that were, through marriage, sacrifice, extraordinary service, or defeat, incorporated into his expanded realm. This imposed orthodoxy institutionalized the worship of the ever-shining sun and obviated the problem that the emperor would eventually die. In more general terms, it also set the limits of a lord's sovereignty, wherever he might fit into the hierarchy of relationships, to wherever he had adherents to his ancestral cult.

But members of non-Cuzco ethnicities also had other allegiances. They worshipped their own parents, grandparents, and great-grandparents as lineage leaders. In this segmented and nested society, they likewise participated in the adoration of the illustrious antecedents of authorities above their own, regardless of where they resided. The worship of one deity did not mitigate the worship of others. Such bases of identification explain why people who owed allegiance to one authority lived among the adherents of another, a settlement pattern best described as "scattered occupation" (*ocupación salpicada*).[12]

Andeans did not see themselves as clusters of people whose religio-political affiliations could be delineated as bounded wholes by closed lines on a Western map. Guamán Poma de Ayala's map of the Tawantinsuyu (reproduced in Figure 2.1) represents a Europeanized understanding of the native empire, having been drawn approximately eighty years after the collapse of Inca domination. Other of his drawings (see Figures 4.4, 4.5, 5.10, 5.14, 5.15, 5.16, and 6.1, for instance) and that of Murúa (Figure 2.3, drawn after 1600) harken back to and reveal original indigenous understandings, where the four suyus were four native peoples, each depicted in characteristic dress. According to ancient conceptualizations, Andeans thought of themselves as part of a lineage within a larger population ranked by religio-political criteria. To think or say, as one Quechua-speaking informant did in the 1970s, that he "belonged" to don Diego, in response to my question of where he was from, was to situate himself in a common imagining within a particular group on a living, constantly shifting hierarchy of nested power and prestige. Only outsiders, such as myself, would be puzzled at such a response, and not know either where the informant fit in the local and regional socioreligious scheme of life of the group to which he identified or the strength and number of the vertical connections in that hierarchy. Such worldviews and self-representations reinforce my belief that the Andeans—like the Maori, discussed by Sahlins, and the Africans, described by Thornton—did not recognize the distinction between sovereignty and landed property rights. As long as a chief and his people maintained residence on the land they used and were willing to defend the crops they planted thereon, no other ruler and his people could use it (without a fight or permission). That is the distinction between jurisdiction and occupation of and "title to"

1057

FIGURE 6.1. The city of Potosí, showing el Cuzco surrounded by the natives of the four suyus. Source: Guamán Poma de Ayala 1613/1936: 1057.

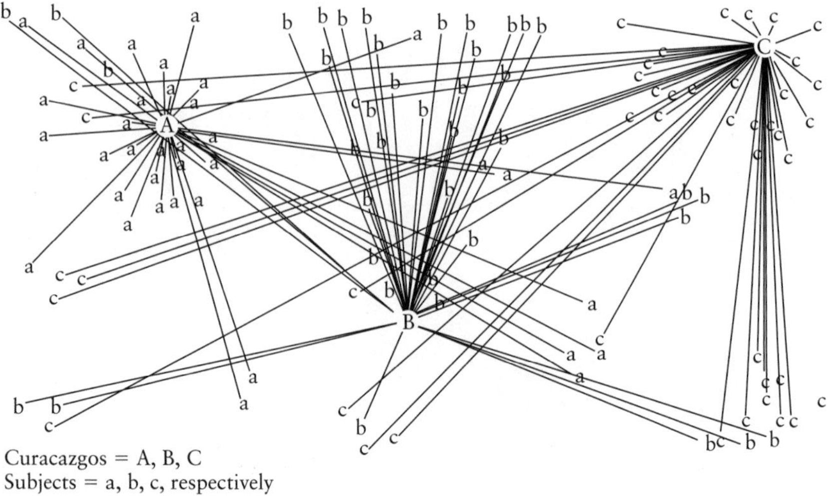

FIGURE 6.2A. Settlement pattern of three curacazgos, before the reducciones.

land. Absolute, fee-simple ownership was not pertinent to the Maori, the Africans, or the Andeans.[13]

Any Western attempt to plot the comings and goings of the members of such a group would result in an amoeba-like outline of their activities, which would be constantly changing over the course of the year and from year to year and often overlap the outline of other internally affiliated, self-representing groups (Figures 6.2a, b, and c). Thus, "community" (like empire) was, in a sense, an intangible, borderless, variable entity defined by a cult and history with social frontiers that were only fixated in place by the Spanish colonial state.[14]

Because of the multiple loyalties of any one individual and the polytheism of this society as a whole, the power of an Andean authority, had he the allegiance of hundreds or millions, was fluid and flexible. The fortunes of the gods rose and fell in keeping with the accuracy of their oracular predictions and their perceived aid to the living. Some were known to help in some circumstances but not in others. People's devotions shifted in keeping with the effectiveness of their prayers and invocations to the god of the moment, be he the progenitor of the extended family, the lineage, the ethnic group, or the empire. In this sense, gods, like rulers, competed against each other for adherents. The various ancestor-gods—be they local hero or imperial Sun—attracted as if they were multiple magnetic poles, radiating concentric circles of power through the ranks of the populace. Some nodes of attraction exerted more pull than others. They represented overlapping spheres of alternative forces that reinforced allegiances at times and interfered with

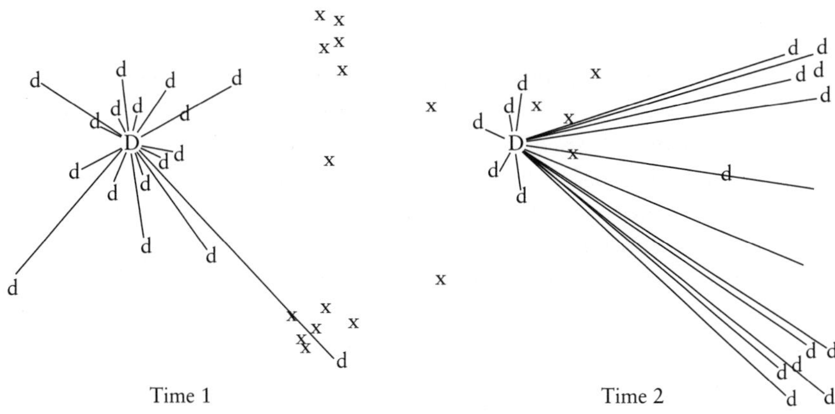

D = Curaca
d = Subjects
x = Uninhabited houses at that time

FIGURE 6.2B. Seasonal changes in residence.

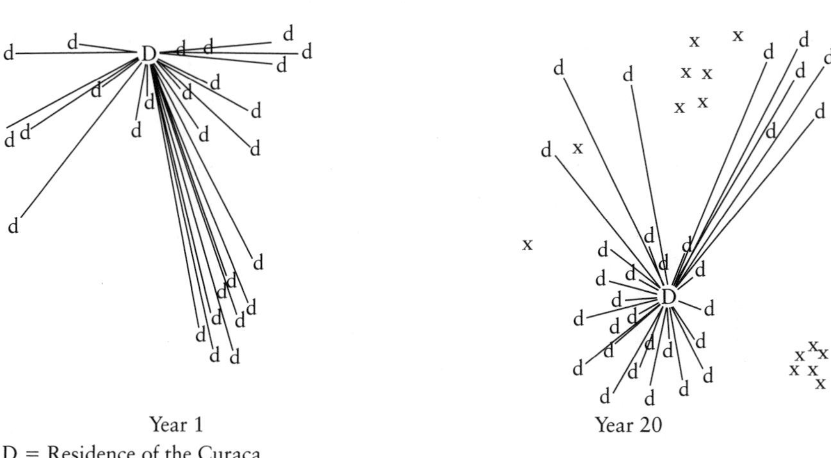

D = Residence of the Curaca
d = Residence of subjects
x = Unoccupied residence

FIGURE 6.2C. Change in residence of the population of a curacazgo over twenty years.

them at others. Therefore, devotions could be unstable and fickle, shifting up and down the pantheon from local, more specific ancestral gods, to the empire-encompassing Sun. Myriad fonts of supernatural aid could be a mechanism for righting instances of ineffectiveness or abuse. Devotion to nested supernatural forces provided choice and gave rise to a corresponding multitude of overlapping identities, depending on the circumstances and the contrasting "other."[15]

People who were naturally attracted to a winner gravitated to demonstrated power that could defeat enemies and ensure their survival through periodic times of scarcity and need. Familial identifications could coalesce into a feeling of belonging to a larger whole if reinforced by perceived, mutually beneficial interactions. One person could be simultaneously the subject of a chief, the member of his cult, and devoted to the ancestors of his own lineage. Thus, we have documentary evidence that describes how one guaca with five idols attracted in pilgrimage "Caracaras Yanparaes and Chichas and Zuras and Bisisas and Asanaques and Carangas and Chuyes," who Saignes identifies as "nations" of the Charcas confederation. These peoples did not necessarily live concentrated in one area but were united by ties of reverence to a common cult and mutual obligations. On pilgrimage, they temporarily abandoned parochial concerns to become part of a larger fellowship of devout tourists. They formed a congregation of devotees, which is, of course, the essence of the meaning of ayllu, writ large. But this confederation was, at times, and in theory, incorporated into ever-larger and more comprehensive congregations of believers, to fit grand imperial aspirations. Given this scenario, the phrase *ethnic group* and the word *ayllu* lose precision and remain flexible concepts. And the overall picture of the empire appears more disarticulated and fluid than strongly centralized and unified.[16]

The Inca process of state building was abruptly interrupted by the Spanish invasion. Christian evangelization, which began at first contact, asked more from the Andeans than did native efforts. Catholic dogmatizers made Andeans pledge to honor one, all-encompassing god and a host of saints that replaced their devotions to their guacas. This was different from just grafting another deity onto their already existing pantheon of immortals, as required under el Cuzco's domination. Acceptance of Christian demands promised prosperity, but this alien orthodoxy meant the repudiation of their senses of self. Unlike Inca demands—to accept the Sun as the primary god—which allowed persons to continue to worship ethnic deities and retain lineage affiliations, the Spanish demanded the total abnegation of these. This implied a repudiation of their guacas, heroic history, and common rituals. It implied behavior and thought modification. Natives were asked to stop singing their songs; they could no longer dance in devotion to their gods. They were commanded to devalue and forget their ancestors, who had given them life; who had built the terraces, the irrigation canals, and the roads; and who had defended and favored them over the generations. They were asked to substitute for their own an irreconcilable Christian history of which they were not a part and could not identify.

Some natives, ultimately, accepted baptism and attended catechism. They learned the basic vocabulary and conceptualization of the imported religion. But many, too, feigned ignorance and used it as a weapon to defend their past. Imposition of Christianity may have even fortified their cultural identity. They realized that the Christian god brought benefits, even riches, to the Europeans, but hardship and deprivation to most of them. So they risked apostasy and continued to practice their traditional cults, but not openly. To expose them was to destroy their hopes, histories, and identities. To accept the Europeans' religion was to turn their world upside down. To accept a foreign social structure and economic system, and their dependent political status, ran contrary to the values they held dear. Such considerations explain the surreptitious resistance to European dogmatizers and the underground survivals of pre-Hispanic religious practices in the central Andes and elsewhere.

The settlement pattern of native society was changed dramatically and fixed in place by the Spanish policy of reducción in the 1560s and 1570s. This concentration of native populations was at least thirty years (between 1570 and 1600), or one lifetime, before the drawings in the unpublished Galvin or Dublin manuscript (attributed to Murúa) and those of Guamán Poma de Ayala were completed. Implementation aimed at moving scattered cult members far from their shrines and pueblos viejos, where their ancestors were interred and were believed to visit. Removal concentrated the native population into towns, similar in construction to Spanish villas, to facilitate conversion and indoctrination, tribute collection, labor distribution, and generalized Spanish control. Forced migrants often received different lands to work, in one or more locations. These were surveyed and marked in a process that took centuries to complete. Even then, boundary markers were often impermanent and ambiguous. In sorting out followers of one lord from another and moving each group as a whole far from its cult centers, this policy helped destroy the traditional bases of legitimacy of native leaders. This policy and forced conversion, though successfully resisted for decades and even longer by some groups, also very gradually fostered an identity associated with place. A new imagining tied to a geographically conceived world replaced one based on multiple, overlapping allegiances to common ancestral heroes. People, over time, lost their sense of being children of the guacas—the catchall word that defined with imprecision a loaded, sacred category—which originally were humans and then became associated with stones and peaks. Little by little, the people began to identify with a place, a place created to facilitate European state control and represented as little black dots or lines on a Western map.[17]

The discussion of community and identity underscores the ethnocentrism and shortsightedness of many outsiders' visions of the Andean past. Chroniclers and more modern observers alike could not and cannot easily escape their times. Eyewitnesses, scribes, and royal officials described what they saw and experienced in terms of their own culture. The descriptors employed in certain instances skewed modern understanding. Like the Portuguese and other European observers in Africa, they used the word for land *(tierra)* to mean people. *Tribute* originally meant service, but was often later interpreted as goods. Many wrote in terms of ownership when they meant possession. The dispute between Pizarro and Almagro and their partisans made them confuse commemorative monuments for boundary markers (*mojones*) and speak of imperial frontiers when only loose and personally defined jurisdictions over groups of widely scattered peoples existed. The Spanish substituted Western concepts of a territorially defined and clearly bordered community or town for the ayllu and lineage. They replaced the lord as a divinely endorsed creature with the chief, who was an administrator and community leader, charged with the duties of managing labor and resources for the colonial state. The Incas, which one chronicler names and numbers at about a hundred, were more usually condensed into a European-style dynasty of about a dozen legitimate emperors. The tentacles of a state bureaucracy were said to reach to the smallest provincial centers, leading to an image of a strong and highly articulated state in which almost every aspect of life was supervised and controlled. Western ideas of father-to-son hereditary succession displaced legitimacy based on lineage and election for the perceived ability and wisdom (imparted to the lord by the ancestors) to guarantee the continuity of the group. Inheritance was assumed to be patrilineal. European distinctions between the living and the dead sought to replace the notion of the power of past generations to condition the everyday life of their descendants. A native society without money, merchants, or markets, in which gold and silver had political and ritual ends, was quickly transformed, starting with the payout of Atahualpa's ransom.[18]

Yet in certain respects the Spanish view of phenomena was closer to the Andean than our own. Sixteenth-century Spaniards were subjects of a monarchy that did not have one fixed, recognized capital until the 1560s. The monarchy united the peoples of the various, sometimes not contiguous, kingdoms. Administration was not uniform or highly centralized. People served two sovereigns: the king, who administered justice on earth, and the god he represented. Service and loyalty were personal and rewarded. To be grateful (*agradecer*) was a royal obligation (*deber*) and had a political dimension. Asymmetrical reciprocities were personal and took the form of the benefice (*beneficio*), the concession (*gracia*), the gift (*don*), and the grant (*merced*). Authority was constructed with symbols in public rituals and ceremony. Common folk learned the etiquette of service and court decorum by observing spectacles and participating in provincial and imperial rites.

What cultural filters still blind modern students to native understandings of their realities? My answer returns our attention to historiography and the problems of translating native cultures into terms that will be intelligible to Westerners. The completion of this study has taught me to go beyond being alert and sensitive to the biases and exaggerations in the sources. It showed me the value of inconsistencies, of seeking clues in the interstices of contradictions. What is inconceivable to a modern reader, à la Darnton and Demarest, can become an avenue into the thinking of "the other." Students must open up to the other, without dismissing such perplexities and incongruities as past generations of historians have too facilely done, as mistakes or irrationalities, or worse, as the work of the devil or as barbarisms.

Future investigators should consider philology as an important key. Period manuscripts cannot be taken literally. Context is as important as content and authority. Concomitantly, scholars should not neglect the study of native languages, because "history" is shaped by the words and phrases used. The vernacular employed to describe cultural phenomena conditions interpretation. Whorf, for example, argues that European languages have an inherent bias for object classes rather than qualities or processes (e.g., a body of water versus waters). Moreover, the translations of words are imprecise, and the definitions of words, such as *guaca*, *ayllu*, or *community*, change over time. In writing this book, I have grappled with the basic, often multiple and conflicting definitions of terms in native Andean languages, such as Quechua, as well as Spanish and English. A few of the most critical examples are such nouns as *guaca*, which at one point may have been synonymous with tomb and house, but over time became a generic signifier for a sacred thing or a place and, as shown previously, must also be extended to include holy essences. Another problematic word that I often hesitated to use was *Inca*. Should, given my findings, the individual Inca be called el Cuzco as used in the initial Spanish sources? I often substituted such generic words as *emperor*, *king*, or *ruler*. But these words, to my mind, have overt and strong secular connotations. I, therefore, occasionally wrote *theocrat* to convey the sacred element that king and emperor lack now. The word *empire*, too, I found deficient for my purposes. Many students know there are many shapes and forms of empires. But I admit to having usually thought of them in terms of bounded spaces, certainly the legacy of courses in Western civilization. My thesaurus helped, giving synonyms, such as *country*, *government*, and *sovereignty*. Among these equivalents only *polity*, *realm*, and *dominion* approximated the meanings that fit this study. Nevertheless, I found myself using less precise words such as *nation*, *state*, *kingdom*, and *province* in the text for variety and flow. I usually rejected words such as *land(s)*, *republic*, and *territory* for obvious reasons. In doing this, I felt that I was making the same type of translating decisions as the first interpreters and chroniclers must have made in writing their texts.[19]

Furthermore, the close reading of multiple sixteenth- and seventeenth-century texts made me realize, as never before, that Spanish observers often used their words according to their own, sometimes gendered, understandings. For example, a Spanish witness identified Pachacamac as a fortress in 1571. This source and others, as well as discussions with archaeologists, suggest, however, that Pachacamac more likely was a huge complex that served as a temple and tomb and simultaneously could offer sanctuary as needed. I also realized that a king did not always have just one capital and that cities might not be places of permanent residence with primarily socioeconomic purposes. In the Andes, they could be and often were temporarily occupied sites for religious commemorations and celebrations with political ends. Consider, for instance, the previous pre-Hispanic understanding of the city founded by Pizarro in 1534. It was, in theory and practice, the pueblo viejo of the Inca ayllu, not solely the political center indicated by the term "capital."[20]

Likewise, my own native language and culture dictated the categories of my sometimes unconscious thought. Instead of considering Andean classifications such as hot/cold, up/down, left/right, and raw/cooked, I thought in terms of religious, social, economic, and political divisions. Andeans, in contrast, did not separate the economic from the religious, the religious from the political or the social, and the less sacred and animated from the more sacred and animated. Thus, I came to appreciate that one of the challenges in writing the anthropological history of the other is thinking outside one's own cultural parameters to bridge the gap between other understandings and my own. Scholars must seek out native voices—even those recorded in recognized imperfect translation—and tease out meanings from between the lines. Historians doing anthropology or anthropologists and archaeologists doing history must learn to read words such as *king* and *empire* within the context of their times. Often they are not literally translatable. Then we must think backward to try to find the Quechua, Aymara, or Mochica equivalents for the Spanish term chosen to express their thought. Comparing what natives said with what they did also helps. Students endeavoring to understand symbols must be particularly careful to document when they were drawn or made, by whom, and for what purpose. To dismiss what does not coincide with Western views, cultural preconceptions, and stereotypes is to impose through selection an alien worldview on those studied. In so doing, researchers would deny the subjects of their inquiry self-expression and forever condemn our studies to the invention of interpretations in our own cultural image, echoes of our own collective voices.[21]

Why has this basic outline of another reality (or should I say "construction") taken me so long to achieve? One answer is that for many years the European and outsider visions and interpretations of the Andeans and their culture coincided, in part, with my own Western filters and imagination. Therefore, I did not question them. This is no longer true.[22]

REFERENCE MATTER

Notes

ABBREVIATIONS

Archivo Arzobispal del Cuzco (AAC)
  Quejas
Archivo Arzobispal de Lima (AAL)
  Hechicerías
Archivo Arzobispal de Trujillo (AAT)
Archivo de Comunidades Indígenas (Lambayeque) (ACI)
  Monsefú
  Paquete (P)
Archivo Departamental del Cuzco (ADC)
  Corregimiento, Ordinario (CoO)
Archivo del Fuero Agrario (AFA)
Archivo Histórico de La Paz (Bolivia) (ALP)
  Expediente Colonial (EC)
Archivo General de las Indias (AGI)
  Audiencia de Lima (AL)
  Audiencia de Charcas (ACharcas)
  Audiencia de Quito (AQ)
  Escribanía
  Estado
  Justicia (J)
  Patronato (P)
Archivo de Límites (Lima) (ALL)
Archivo Nacional de Bolivia (ANB)
  Expediente Colonial (EC)
Archivo Nacional del Perú (ANP) (now, Archivo General de la Nación)
  Derecho Indígena (DI)
  Notarial
  Real Audiencia (RA)
  Residencia (R)
  Tierras y Haciendas
  Títulos
Archivo Notarial de Carlos Rivadeneira (Lambayeque) (ANCR)
  Collús
Archivo Regional de Piura (ARP)
  Corregimiento (Co)
Archivo Regional de Trujillo (ART)
  Corregimiento, Asuntos de Gobierno (CoAG)

Corregimiento, Compulsa (CoCompa)
Corregimiento, Juez de Comisión (CoJuez de Comisión)
Corregimiento, Juez de Residencia (CoR)
Corregimiento, Ordinario (CoO)
Corregimiento, Pedimento (CoP)
Escrituras Notariales
Intendencia Compulsa (IntCompa)
Martínez de Escobar
Mata
Pedro de los Rios

Biblioteca Nacional de España (BNE)
Biblioteca Nacional del Perú (Lima) (BNP)
A—sixteenth century
B—seventeenth century

Biblioteca de la Real Academia de Historia (Madrid) (BAH)
Mata Linares

British Museum (BM)
Colección Vargas Ugarte (Lima) (CVU)

KEY TO SPANISH ABBREVIATIONS

año, year
c. (cuaderno), individual case, file, or folder
caja, box
cajon, drawer
cap. (capítulo), chapter
chap., chapter
Dec. (década), decade
est. (estante), shelf
exp. or E. (expediente), individual case or file
fol. (folio), manuscript page
l. or leg. (legajo), bundle or box of papers
ley, law
lib. (libro), book
Ms. (manuscrito), manuscript
P (paquete), package
r. (ramo), subheading
s.f. (sin folio), without folio
t. (tomo), volume
tit. (título), title
Notation is sometimes unique to an archive or library and cannot be standardized.

Note references internal to a paragraph explain or document the text on a specific point. Note references at the end of the paragraph explain and document the text of the entire paragraph. Multiple references to the same phenomena or institution(s) are meant to indicate the extent of its appearance in the historical record. In some of the notes I give references to various editions of the same (usually primary) sources to facilitate finding the citation for those without access to complete libraries.

CHAPTER 1

1. Guamán Poma de Ayala 1613/1980: 185 [187]; Vaca de Castro; Rostworowski 1981b. The page numbers in this 1980 edition of Guamán Poma de Ayala appear as folio number as written by Guamán Poma de Ayala, followed by the actual or corrected folio number (in brackets) as supplied by the editors. After folio 155, pagination errors by the author result in discrepancies between given and actual folio numbers.

2. Prescott; Cunow; Wittfogel; Patterson 1992; Mariategui; Kagan.

3. Rowe 1946, 1948, 1957; Murra 1967a; Zuidema 1964; Espinoza Soriano 1969a, 1969b, 1975, 1977, and many other subsequent publications; Rostworowski 1963, 1970, 1981–82; Pease 1977; Cook 1975.

4. Millones 1990, 1992; Cock Carrasco 1983; Cock Carrasco and Doyle; Doyle 1988; Huertas 1978, 1981; Regalado de Hurtado 1992, 1996a; Demarest 1981, 1992b; Conrad and Demarest 1984; Gose 1995, 1996; Mills 1997; Álvarez 1588/1998.

5. Urton 1990b; Powers 1998; Rowe 1946; Warren; Ivan Ghezzi, personal communication, September 3, 2001; Rostworowski 1999b: 84. See also Adorno 1982, 1986; and Paz Soldan 1877: especially ix–xiii.

6. Hiltunen 1999: 212; MacCormack 1997a: 280, citing Estete.

7. Distortion still occurs. On the "stereotyped construct" of the Iquichanos, see Méndez 2001: especially 131. Méndez also discusses lack of evidence as "not-finding as a finding" and the "absence of clues" as the clue (134, 137). On filters, see Saignes 1991: 95; Tantaleán Arbulú 1997: 50; Rostworowski 1978b: 90.

8. See Chapter 2, for example.

9. Guillén Guillén 1974; Rowe 1960: 417–18 (who argues that Viracocha also referred to a class of supernatural forces); Demarest 1981. I am aware that the "fact" that central Mexican populations thought that the Spanish were gods is now being debated in scholarly circles. I find the Spaniards being equated with gods in so many instances in the local Andean sources of the sixteenth and seventeenth centuries that I presently have no doubts that this was the case in the minds of Andean peasants. I revisit this topic again later. See Chapter 3, note 131, and Townsend, with whom I respectfully disagree.

10. Werner and Campbell; Ramírez 1996: chap. 3.

11. Porras Barrenechea 1986; Pease 1995; Means 1928, 1973; Adorno 1982, 1986. Ramos (2001: especially chaps. 1–2) does a superb job at analyzing chroniclers, unmasking their depictions and the motivations behind them.

12. Pease 1990b: 193; Porras Barrenechea 1967: 74, note 25.

13. Cosmology is the corpus of ideas common to a culture that expresses the basic order of the universe, that is, the general geometry of space and time, the moving force of the natural and social events, and the interconnecting principles among them, as well as the classification of these phenomena in a coherent model. In brief, it is the framework that permits the ordering of the natural and social forces of the

universe, which facilitates its manipulation by the people of society, according to Earls and Silverblatt 1978: 300; Sherbondy 1993: 343.

14. MacCormack 1991.

15. Rostworowski 1997; Hiltunen; Betanzos, 1551–57/1987; Conrad and Demarest 1984; Ramírez 1985, 1987, 1996: chap. 3; Verdesio 2001: 85.

16. See Chapter 2; Warren; Julien 1991; Keith 1971; Lockhart; Rowe 1946. On the intercultural approach to world history, see Von Laue 1987: xvii.

CHAPTER 2

1. Special thanks are due to the following people (in alphabetical order) for bibliographical input and/or helpful suggestions on the chapter: Margot Beyersdorff; Christopher Boehm; David Noble Cook; Gary Dickson; Karen Graubert; Catherine Julien; Richard Kagan; Susan Kellogg; Jeffrey Klaiber, S.J. [Society of Jesus, Jesuit Order]; Enrique Mayer; Sabine MacCormack; Luis Millones; Amy Remensnyder; Teofilo F. Ruiz; Frank Salomon; and Helaine Silverman.

2. Means 1928/1973; Porras Barrenechea 1967, 1986; Pease 1989b; Murra 1967b (note his assumption of territoriality, for example, on p. 339); Adorno 1982, 1986.

3. Darnton 1985.

4. The word *Inca* refers to the emperor, the Cuzco elite, and to the empire and its people as a whole, depending on context. See Franklin Pease's review (1990b: especially 193–95) of the construction of and usage of the word *Inca*. The word was first used as a proper name in the "Ordenanzas para los vecinos del Cuzco" (March 26, 1534) and in several royal decrees issued during the following months. The word is not used commonly to refer to the Andean kings and ethnicity until almost thirty years later. See Pease's discussion of these (1995: especially 16–19, 53). See also Wilson 1995: 2 (on Spanish ethnocentrism).

5. Hyslop 1984; Von Hagen; Lanning; Zuidema 1964; Cieza l985: 21; Sancho de la Hoz 1938: 178; Farrington 1998; Agustinos ca.1550/1992: 32 (on the Temple of the Sun as its home).

6. Pease 1990b. Toponyms and personal names have been standardized, except in direct quotes.

7. Levillier 1921: 2:12–13, 19–20; Cortés 1986. The news was later confirmed, proving that the interpreters were indeed conveying basic information in this regard accurately (Mena 1534/1967: 100). Note that Pease (1995: 18) questions the possibility that Mena is the author of this account.

8. Oviedo 1535–45/1959: 84, 85, 87–88.

9. The "dried images" are Spanish references to mummies or mummy bundles of ancestors.

10. For Mena's biography, see Porras Barrenechea 1986: 85, 87–88. See Pedro Sancho's testimony of the distribution of Atahualpa's treasure (Sancho 1533/1917: Appendix B, especially 217), where it is recorded that Mena received 366 marks of silver and 8,380 pesos of gold. Mena 1534/1967: 79–80, 83, 86, 89, 92–93, 95–100.

11. For Xerez's biography, see Porras Barrenechea 1986: 95. Pease (1995: 18) questions whether or not Xerez's account is a response to *La conquista del*

Perú, attributed to Mena. Xerez 1534/1917: 30, 35, 37, 41–43, 65–69, 72, 74–75. See also Molina, el cuzqueño 1574/1943: 43 (who equates Cuzco with people).

12. Sancho de la Hoz 1534/1938: 117, 136–37, 167, 174, 176–77; Romero 1917.

13. Oviedo 1535–45/1959: 91.

14. Pease 1992b: 66.

15. Porras Barrenechea 1967: 74, note 25. Pease (1990b: especially 193) also distrusts the interpreters' work.

16. Seed 1991: 23; MacCormack 1989: 153. See Valera 1945: 140–41; Betanzos 1551–57/1987: 7; Pease 1989a: 181–82; 1992b: 73 (on the quality of the translation).

17. There is no consensus about when babies were named. Cabello Valboa reports after birth (1586/1951: 294). Cieza writes at fifteen to twenty days old (1864/1964: 190, 230). Betanzos notes that babies were named at one year of age (1987: 191). Garcilaso de la Vega says they were named at age two, citing Cieza 1864/1964: 230–31. Silverblatt writes that girls were renamed at age four to five (1987: 78). Again during puberty rights, both males and females received new names (MacCormack 1991: 116–17; Classen 1993: 62). For an overview of naming practices, see Medinaceli 1995.

18. Betanzos 1551–57/1987: 83, 113, 207; 1557/1996: 189; Rostworowski 1970: 154, 162; BNE/Ms. 2010, 1576 [?], 40.

19. Garcilaso de la Vega 1602/1960–63: 2:37; and Lastres 1947: 8 (on not pronouncing the Inca's name); Cieza 1987: 146 (on Huáscar's name). On Tupac Inca Yupanqui, see Guamán Poma de Ayala 1613/1980: 262 [264]; see also Valera 1596/1945: 113. These leaders could also be addressed in other ways. *Huachacuyac* (Betanzos 1551–57/1996: 60) or "lover and do-gooder of the poor"; *capac* or "richly magnanimous"; *intip churin* or "sons of the Sun" (Garcilaso de la Vega 1602/1960–63: 390); *ticci capac*, which meant "richest of monarchs" (*sumo* or *monarca rico*) (Sarmiento de Gamboa 1572/1965: 219) were titles applied to various Incas at various times; (Quipucamayocs 1542–44/1920: 27; Martínez 1981: 70).

20. Xerez 1534/1917: 42. This interpretation is also strongly supported by Santacruz Pachacuti Yamqui. The text reads: "And later [Manco Capac] saw a rock that the natives of that place who are the Allcay Uicças and the Cullin Chimas and the Cayao Cachis called Kkuzko casa (or rumi). And since then it was called Cuzco pamppa or Cuzco llacta, and the yngas later called themselves Cuzco capac or Cuzco ynca" (1613/1993: 8). Margot Beyersdorff (whom I thank for this citation) thinks that *khuska qaqa* (rocky outcrop in the middle) is the promontory between the Watanay and Tullumayo rivers, where a people predating the arrival of Manco Capac, the Allca Wisas, lived. This landform still exists in Cuzco; one can walk up the steps to the top of the promontory, which faces on its west side the Avenida Sol and at the southern end the Post Office bordering the street Mat'u chaka. The last sentence of the quotation clearly substantiates the use of Cuzco as a title (personal communication, August 5, 1998). Also see Ramírez 1990 (on local chiefdoms); Montesinos 1644/1930 (for the long list of kings); Valera 1596/1879: 173, 178 (on Pachacuti Inca Yupanqui); Cunnison 1951; 1956: 29, 38 (on perpetual kinship in Africa); Ramírez

2004 (on "positional inheritance" and "perpetual kinship" in the Andes); Gama 1540/1975: 270 (for Jayanca).

21. Santo Tomás 1560/1951; Gonçales Holguin 1608/1952: 142; Garcilaso de la Vega 1602/1960–63: 2:30; Cerrón-Palomino 1997: 168; 1998: 443; Sarmiento de Gamboa 1572/1965: 217; 1572/1967: 55. Garcilaso de la Vega wrote that the Incas spoke a private, sacred language "to speak one with the other" that by the time he wrote his history had "been totally lost" (1602/1960–63: 2:37). On the translation of the term "Cuzco," see Espinoza Soriano 1977: 110, 120, 140. A twentieth-century observer, Anibal S. Villar Cordova (1929: 48), notes that children in the sixteenth century were taught that the word *Coscco* meant navel. It was associated with valor. For Acamama, see Rostworowski 1993a: 220. Note a curious use of the term that appears in titles of lands near Cuzco. One of the sides of a piece of land being described abutted "with lands of the Indians Paullo-Cusco." Paullo was named Inca by Diego Almagro when Manco Inca fled to Vilcabamba in rebellion. He became a puppet ruler of the Spanish (Varón Gabai 1997: 177). Might this phrase refer to lands worked by subjects of Paullo Inca? Another plot and field extended to the "mountain named Cuxco-Orco" (after Inca Urcon?) (Sarmiento de Gamboa 1572/1965: 290; 1572/1967: 55). See also Rostworowski 1962: 160, 163; 1999a: 8 (on the origin of the name "Cuzco"); Farrington 1998: 53.

22. Cabello Valboa 1586/1951: 365; Xerez 1534/1917: 65; Betanzos 1551–57/1987: 261; 1551–57/1996: 233, 291; Guamán Poma de Ayala 1613/1980: 185 [187], 407 [409]; Cieza 1553/1959: 342–43, cited by Hyslop 1985: 8–12; Cobo 1653/1956: 2:94–95 (on a new Cuzco in Quito); Saignes 1991: 99 (on other "new Cuzcos"); Lazaro Llantoy 1996: 20 (on Vilcabamba as a new Cuzco). Craig Morris (1993: 37) notes the need for "administrative cities" for ceremonial exchange and gift giving. See also Morris and Thompson. Farrington (1998: 54) observes that Inca toponyms like those found around Cuzco, e.g., at Hanacaure and Kenko, have been located in the areas surrounding Huánuco Pampa, Tomebamba, and Incahuas. This suggests that the Inca was re-creating the original, historical scenario of their origins for state theater—as a way of inculcating their worldview on new recruits, converts, and devotees. These other Cuzcos had ushnus (*uznos*), plazas, and sun temples as well. Cobo (1653/1956: 2:140) writes that el Cuzco had houses and royal palaces wherever he went. On ceques in the provinces, see Polo 1990: 47–88; Abercrombie 1998: 186–87. On Vilcabamba, see Regalado de Hurtado 1992: 45. She translates the word as land of the sun, or the sacred, or the ancestors. She also states that Vilcabamba became sacred "only after the presence of Manco Inca [a sacred person]." Lazaro Llantoy (1996: 57) writes that Vilcabamba was also designed as a replica of the original. Zuidema (1989a: 250) suggests that such Inca sites were populated only when the ruler was there. See also his discussion of another "Cuzco" built in the Valley of Lunahuana (1968: 45), "or in other words a city built following the model of the Cuzco." Note also Murúa's version, where a "Cusco Guanca" (stone Cuzco) conquered the city, "and he made it the head of all the provinces and pueblos of this kingdom of Piru, and no one mentions the history of the Incas since Cusco-Guanca, because he died after conquering the great city of the Cusco, before being sworn in as King" (1590/1946a: 183).

23. Geertz 1983: 125, 128, 132, 136–37; Trimborn 1979: especially 69; Silva Santisteban 1982: 298–99; ANCR, 1586–1611; Ramírez 1995a; Ibarra Rojas 1985–86: 95. See Rex González's mostly futile attempts (1982) to identify local capitals or "centers" of Inca "provinces" in Tucumán; Hyslop's problems (1976) doing the same among the Lupaca; and Silva Santisteban's thought (1982: 298–99) on the same in Cajamarca. An ayllu was an extended family or lineage believed to have a common ancestor.

24. Helaine Silverman wonders whether references to multiple Cuzcos refer to the successive construction of ancestral temple palaces in honor of the Sun, the mythical and legitimizing father of the reigning Inca emperor, as sites for provincial religious observations. She points out, however, that archaeologists accept the present site of the city of Cuzco as the Inca capital on the basis of its size and architectural elaboration. No other Inca site rivals it (personal communication, June 1998). I found Clifford Geertz's article (1985) on centers, kings, and charisma very suggestive on the idea of multiple centers.

25. Geertz 1985: 14, 19; Zuidema 1989a: 251; 1973b: 21, 25; Pease 1991: 65, 68, 70–71. See also Garcilaso de la Vega 1602/1963: 73; Regalado de Hurtado 1993: 42; Rivière 1986: 13; 1995: 120 for a statement on Bolivian authorities as "center" (*taypi*) in the 1970s and 1980s.

26. See Mignolo on just such a process of "colonial semiosis" (1989: 94).

27. Xerez 1534/1917: 65; Cabello Valboa 1586/1951: 257–58, 260, 274 (on Sinchi Ruca). See Garcilaso de la Vega 1602/1960–63: 2:37 (on the adoration of dead rulers); Bandera 1557/1920 [1921]: 62 (on the number of subjects). The phrases "one birth" and "one law" are taken from the Huarochirí myths that are transcribed, translated, and published by Salomon and Urioste 1991: 71. For a native statement on the idea of order and chaos and confusion (*vehetría* or *behetría*) and the importance of people (as opposed to land), see ANB/EC 1686, exp. 34, fol. 2. On the multiple definitions of behetría, see Covarrubias 1611/1943: 203–4. On the surplus, see Cobo 1653/1956: 2:140. The demographic motivation for expansion supports the common saying that "all the universe is *ayni* [collective, reciprocal labor]" and contradicts the argument that the state expanded to control land (Conrad and Demarest 1984: chap. 3). On the divinity of the Inca, see Sarmiento de Gamboa 1572/1942: chap. 31 (p. 108), chap. 44 (p. 132); Julien 2000: 263–64.

28. See Betanzos 1551–57/1996: 273–74 (on the demographic aspects of conquest); Bachmann 1905 (for a traditional geographic analysis); Ramírez 1987 (on the *dueño de indios*); 2002 (where I show that the phrase is a translation of *marcayoc*, *llactayoc*, and *pacarina*, referring to origins and the act of creation); Hyslop 1976: 101–3, 138 (on the Lupaca). See also Regalado de Hurtado 1993: 64, 86; Netherly 1993: 13.

29. Betanzos 1551–57/1996: 87–89, 226–27, 252; 90 (on the gallery); MacCormack 1997b: 13. Compare this description to the Spanish ceremony of taking possession of lands. Rostworowski publishes a 1590 document, which describes how several natives from the town of San Gerónimo took possession of lands near Cuzco:

> The orders . . . for the possession by me the said scribe read. . . . he took by the hands the said don chistoual [*sic*] cosirimache and luis yucay and gonsalo suno

> and don diego tancar to whom he gave the said possession of the said lands guaynacarisno and machocarismo who as a sign of the said possession entered the said lands and paced and walked and threw dirt from one part to another and uprooted grasses and did other acts of possession quietly and peacefully. (1962: 156)

In contrast, in the ceremony conferring possession of an encomienda, people were ordered to do different tasks (ANP/DI, 39, exp. 806, 1673, fol. 30). Santacruz Pachacuti Yamqui 1613/1968: 285; Zuidema 1989a: 257; Cerrón-Palomino 1998: 424, 433 (for the quote), 438–39, 441 (on sayas as women's dress). On this point, see also Las Casas 1555/1948: 127.

30. Garcilaso de la Vega 1602/1960–63: 2:30; Bandera 1557/1920[1921]: 59. See Quipucamayocs 1542–44/1920: 60 (on the suyus); Murúa 1590/1946b: 3:28, 231; Santillán 1927: 15; Stenberg and Carvajal 1988: especially 182, for example; Rostworowski 1999a: 142, 178 (on the late use of the term "Tawantinsuyu," specifically); Zuidema 1964, 1982. Regalado de Hurtado questions the conventional definition of Tawantinsuyu, but still considers the Tawantinsuyu in geographic terms as "a cosmic and ceremonial space" and "a space or world experienced and ordered ceremonially" (1996a: 89–90).

31. Guamán Poma de Ayala 1613/1980: 982 [1000]; Espinoza Soriano 1577/1977: 113–14, 120; Titu Cusi 1570/1916: 33; Santacruz Pachacuti Yamqui 1613/1993: 33v; Escobar Zapata 1992 (for a comprehensive overview of definitions of *suyu*); Garcilaso de la Vega 1609/1957: 89–90, as cited by Hinojosa Cuba 1999: 33; Molina's sixteenth-century definition of *suyu* as "*partida*" (Molina, el cuzqueño, 1574/1943: 77) and as cited by Lastres 1947: 10. See Zuidema and Poole's assessment (1982) of Espinoza Soriano's analysis of the "Memorial." On don Diego Saire Tupac Mancocapac, see Wachtel 1977: 245, note 130; Garcilaso de la Vega 1609/1941: 1:141; 1602/1960–63: 14. In the dictionary of Cuzco Quechua prepared by Gonçalez Holguin, one of the definitions of *suyu* is "a task assigned to a province or person." It derives from the verb *suyuni*, which means "to divide fields or tasks in order to give out work assignments" (1608/1952: 333). Note the suggestive parallels to the definition of *chapas* and my discussion of the Inca Guayna Capac's activities in the Valley of Cochabamba later in the text. Murra, citing Polo, reports that the task of each family was also called a "suyu" (1967b: 342). Rostworowski's research (1988a: 140) in the south reveals three additional, nonofficial "suyus": Omasuyu, Orcosuyu, and Colesuyu. See also Las Casas 1555/1948: 109; Castro and Ortega Morejón 1558/1974: 94. Similarly, Szemiñski (1996: 8–9) writes on the meaning of the Aymara word *marka*, which can be the union of two Aymara *parcialidades* (parts, lineages, halves): today a parcialidad can have from four to twenty communities, or towns, cities, or nations, etc. Additionally, he concludes that the game of chance played by the Inca was a way to redistribute the holdings of the Sun. These holdings were native peoples, not lands: "of labor and not of land ownership" (1996: 16). Note, too, that Murúa writes of the four versions of Viracocha among the four peoples of the empire (in Gisbert 1991: 348). Luis Valcarcel, writing in 1949, also refers to the Inca's four "virreyes, the chiefs [*jefes*] of suyus" (37).

32. Some describe the four suyus as composed of provinces (Santillán 1927: 16; Murua 1590/1946a: 99–101). *Province*, however, was a political code word that was nowhere consistently defined. Chroniclers and modern scholars alike used it

haphazardly and indiscriminately as a synonym for ethnic group, town, lineage, and chiefdom (curacazgo). Others write equally vaguely of "nations" (*naciones*), referring to peoples who had a common and recognizable identity, such as those called the Huancabilcas, Cayambes, and Pastos. But given the sacred nature of the Inca and his indispensable role in the management of the empire, "nations," the last descriptive, best fits the Inca's conception of his domain. See also Bandera 1557/1920 [1921]: 60. On local lords, see Guamán Poma de Ayala 1613/1980: 65. On local lords as rulers of people, see Rostworowski 1999a: 140, who cites Gonçáles Holguin (1608/1952) and Bertonio for the definition of *mallco* or *mayco*; Szemiñski 1996: 13–14. On Chincha, see Castro and Ortega Morejón 1558/1968: 479; and Crespo 1558–1974. Las Casas (1559/1909) and Heinrich Cunow, cited by Wedin (1965: 10, 20–21), stated that the decimal system may have existed before Inca rule. Juan Polo de Ondegardo said it was established by the Inca (1571/1917a: 51).

33. Bandera 1557/1920[1921]: 62; Guamán Poma de Ayala 1613/1980: 189 [191], 456 [458]. See also Regalado de Hurtado 1993: 67; Espinoza Soriano 1969b: 132 (note the use of the term "señorío" to denote control of subjects and vassals). Zuidema (1989a: 250) writes that rank of a group is also expressed in terms of the genealogical distance from the Inca. On this point, see also Lorandi 1995: 86.

34. Julien 1982; Varón Gabai 1993: 726, especially note 15 (for Guaylas); Regalado de Hurtado 1984b; Murra 1984: 13, 81; Wedin 1965: 10.

35. Rowe 1946: 255 (on the ayllu as a territorial unit). Ana Raquel Marques da Cunha Martins Portugal (1996) analyzed the changing meaning of the word *ayllu* in six Spanish chronicles. She shows how the word's meaning evolved over time from one that designates family, lineage, or social group to one that had an implied or explicit territorial dimension. Saignes also makes this point when he writes that "legal actions about lands and waters tended to become a major forum for *ayllu* mobilization [that] may have bent the social form toward a more territorial definition than Andean tradition required" (1999: 104). In Harald O. Skar's article on Andean pilgrimage, he notes that "ayllu units . . . may involve a town, a village, a province or a total country" (1985: 100). This statement underscores the flexible nature of the concept and approximates, in its maximal extension, the grand lineage that the Incas were trying to forge as a basis for their cult and rule. This metamorphosis is undoubtedly the origin of past confusion. Population pressure was not the only reason for fragmentation of polities. Others include conflict and disagreements. (Zuidema 1989b: 125).

36. Pedro Pizarro 1844: 244; Julien 1997; Sancho de la Hoz 1534/1938: 125; Betanzos 1551–57/1987: 290; 1551–57/1996: 278; Garcilaso de la Vega 1602/1960–63: 77 (on painting and making models of geography). The 1996 translation of Betanzos incorrectly gives *repartimiento* a territorial dimension that it did not have at the time (p. 312). See also p. 308 for a better gloss. Also on this point, see Regalado de Hurtado 1993: 97; Martínez Cereceda 1995b: 259, 261; 1995c: 298.

37. Quipucamayocs 1542–44/1920: 35, 37–41. For more specific information on continuing Spanish demands for gold and silver, see Rostworowski 1970: 158, 185, 212, 225. For another example of the use of the word *tierra* to mean "people," see Las Casas 1555/1948: 83.

38. Betanzos 1551–57/1996: 154 (in describing the chosen women of Tupac Inca Yupanqui), 160 (on the prevention of rebellion); 1551–57/1987: 57, 77, 167, 175, 179 (on gifts of women to local lords); Espinoza Soriano 1969a: 18, 55; 1976: 259, 263; 1980a: 180 (on Chuptongo and his hundred wives); Urbano 1990: 282 (on women as memory); Molinié Fioravanti 1986–87: 278–79; Caillavet 2000: 165–66, 444 (on polygamy in Ecuador); Bandera 1557/1920[1921]: 84. Sometimes sources state that the Inca rewarded his henchmen—faithful servants—with people (*aldeas*) (Espinoza Soriano 1978: 3–4). See also Espinoza Soriano 1969a: 24 (for the Guanca); Río 1990: 86 (for Tapacarí). For a sampling of the numbers of wives that provincial lords of Guaylas still kept in 1558, see the visita published by Aibar Ozejo (1968–69). Note that in early colonial times, some provincial lords, perhaps in imitation of the Incas, married their sisters or women identified as such (Millones 1990: 290 [for 1584]).

39. BM/Add.13992: 412v; Betanzos 1551–57/1987: 99–100, 137; 1551–57/1996: 105–6; Sarmiento de Gamboa 1572/1942: 90; Pease 1990a: 8–10; 1992a: 116–18; Espinoza Soriano 1976: 247, 264; 1977: 112. Compare these figures to others provided by Guamán Poma de Ayala, who says that routinely provincial caciques and principals had fifty women "for his service and the increase of his people" (1613/1980: 189 [191]); a lord of myriad households (huno [huño] curaca) had thirty women; a captain (*guamanin apo*) had twenty; a lord of a thousand households (guaranga curaca) had fifteen; and a lord of a hundred households (*pachaca camachicoc*) had eight.

40. On Guaylas, see AGI/AL 1, no. 146, cited by Varón Gabai 1993: 730–31. Atahualpa even tried this with Pizarro, presenting him with a woman who became known as doña Angelina so as to establish a kinship link (Varón Gabai 1997: 194). Espinoza Soriano 1976: 249, 254; Varón Gabai 1997: 177–78, 183–84, 186. Compare this to Pachacuti's gift to his principal wife of "certain small towns" and a hundred cloistered women dedicated to the service of the Inca gods or elite (*mamaconas*) for her service. She received fifty more mamaconas from a steward of the Temple of the Sun. Lords gave her another two hundred yanacona servants, besides gifts of gold and silver (Betanzos 1551–57/1996: 78). See also Pease 1990a: 10. For another example of lords taking multiple wives for the purpose of forming and perpetuating alliances, see Río 1990: 86 (for the Tapacarí).

41. Anónimo 1571/1995: 142; AGI/J461, 850–67, 1480–81, 1482v, 1484–89, 1579v; AL 128, 2-June-1587, 12v–13; Ramírez 2001a; Salomon and Schwartz 1999: 479. The male relatives of the wives of curacas also became obligated to support him. See, for example, Garavaglia 1999: 4, 7 (on the Guaraní of the La Plata basin); Saeger 1999: 267 (on the Guaraní of the Chaco and Paraguay).

42. Pease 1990a: 20. On negotiation of rights and responsibilities between el Cuzco and local peoples, see Sternfeld 2000. See Morris (1993: 46) on Huánuco Pampa, where the public architecture appears to have been devoted to ritual and feasting. He found "no positive evidence of a marketplace, little to indicate systematic exchange with areas outside the center itself." Local leaders also told the Spanish that they made periodic rounds for the same types of purposes, saying that "we have Indians to command and visit" (AGI/J458, 1802).

43. Cobo 1653/1956: 2:145 (for the quote); Silverblatt 1988a: 91.

44. Anónimo 1571/1995: 142. See also Eric Van Young (1996: 73) on a Mexican analogue to guaca hostage in colonial times.

45. Salomon and Urioste 1991: 71.

46. Silverblatt 1988a: 85. Idolatry records show that the Sun did not long remain an important deity in local eyes; on this point see also Chapter 4 herein. See also Duviols 1986; MacCormack 1991; Ellefsen 1982: 12; Laurencich-Minelli 1991 (on labor as a state cult).

47. The fragility of the Inca empire is explored further in Chapter 3. For a contrary characterization, see Farrington 1992: 370.

48. This is one way to account for what María Rostworowski (1988b: 227–33) and others have called diarchy.

49. Salomon and Urioste 1991: 71; Cabello Valboa 1586/1951: 371–79 (on the rebellion against Guayna Capac); Pease 1990b: 198 (on the failure of Manco Capac's siege).

50. Sallnow 1987: 36. See also Chapter 3 herein.

51. Ramírez 1985, 2001b; Pease 1990b: 194; Regalado de Hurtado 1996b: 210 (on *control vivo* [living control]); Molinié Fioravanti 1986–87: 255–56.

52. Sahlins 1989: especially 28, 55, chap. 7.

53. Hampe Martínez 1988: 60. Rostworowski has wrestled with this problem, concluding about Inca "provinces" that "their descriptions are confused and they only refer to vague geographic areas, without specifying their territories, their borders, or their jurisdictions" (1993b: 202). Pease describes the Spanish conceptualization of provinces in the sixteenth century as "territorial jurisdictions" (1998: 234). Note that Río (1990: 85) reports that the Aymara word *mamani* means *cóndor, halcón*, province, or district, and "lord of many vassals" (based on L. Bertonio's dictionary 1612/1984: 213). We might hypothesize that originally *mamani* identified an ayllu's leader and only under the Spanish came to connote/denote province or district. See Taylor (1987: 30–31), who translates the term "llacta" as guacas and their devotees, on how quickly the term lost its original meaning; and Cerrón-Palomino's discussion (1998: especially 427–28). Salomon and Schwartz recognize the problem when they note that "early European observers often used European-style classifiers such as 'nation' (inappropriately implying territoriality and linguistic affiliation) when other kinds of social organizations—phratries, clans, lineages, alliances—were being described" (1999: 448). See also my article on decentering (Ramírez 2002).

54. Regalado de Hurtado 1996a: 89; Salomon and Urioste; Hyslop 1984: 2; Schaedel 1978: 292–93; Dillehay 1988: 3, especially 6–8; Netherly 1988: especially 105; Galdos Rodríguez 1985–86; Murra 1980: chap. 2, especially 32; Stenberg and Carvajal 1988: 181–260; Dillehay and Netherly 1988: 273–75. Craig Morris (1988) takes a more nuanced approach to the boundary debate.

55. I want to restrict myself here to early manuscripts because the Spanish overlay of institutions, language, and culture made it increasingly difficult to see the shadows of the pre-Columbian legacy as time went on.

56. Cabello Valboa 1586/1951: 336 (on Chile), 384 (on the Valley of Atres); Bibar 1966: 165 (on Chile); Sarmiento de Gamboa 1572/1942: 144–45 (on penetrating the jungles to the east); Rex González 1982: 337 (on Tucumán); González

Suárez 1968: especially 129–30; Julien 2000: 142–43, 153, 161. John Hyslop (1988: especially 37–40) discusses the tendency to include within the Inca empire areas that the Incas never controlled, where their presence was only occasional and unlasting through special emissaries or war parties. On the supposed frontiers in northwestern Argentina, see Garcia 1998.

57. Rostworowski 1993a: 227; 1993b: 207; Guamán Poma de Ayala 1613/1980: 852 [866]. On task-defined limits, see Cieza 1967: 83, 215; Polo de Ondegardo 1571/1917a: 56, 79; Melo et al. 1582/1925: 272; Guamán Poma de Ayala 1613/1980: 1074 [1084]; and later in this chapter. See also Álvarez (1588/1998: 77–78) on *apachetas*, piles of rocks and stones, amassed at certain locations along the routes between uplands and lowlands, that may have been mislabeled by the Spanish as boundary markers. Are such human-made piles of rocks what Rowe (1946: 211) refers to as *saywas*, which marked the boundaries of all fields?

58. It is often unclear whether or not the word *pueblo* refers to an urban settlement or the abstract notion of a "people" who lived dispersed over the countryside (Gama 1540/1975, and later in this chapter). See also Las Casas 1555/1948: 108. Note that he states that a *province* is ten thousand "vecinos" or households, but this is not how other authors use the word.

59. Betanzos 1551–57/1996: 169, 175; Guamán Poma de Ayala 1613/1980: [58], [111], 353 [355]; Melo et al. 1582/1925: 272, 275, 285; Murúa 1590/1946b: 231. For other clear examples of the use of the word *province* to refer to people, see Las Casas 1555/1948: 85; Szemiñski 1996: 3, 16.

60. AGI/AL 137, as mentioned by Hart 1983: 233 (on Jayanca and Motupe). See also Rostworowski 1993b: 202; Rodríguez Suy Suy 1997: 20 (who also doubts that Andeans recognized fixed territorial limits). He concludes that "the borders of Andean space were moveable and very sensitive: alive" (22).

61. Rostworowski 1962: 141, 144, and other subsequent pages; 1963: 234; 1999b: 70, 75, 78, 83, 86–88, 90, 95, 99, 118, 163–64 (on the establishment of fences in Pachacamac in the 1560s and 1570s).

62. AGI/AL 123, cited by Rostworowski 1993a: 219–20.

63. Julien 1991: 1–2, 4, 43, 48, 85, 88, 105–6, 109, 129; Gibson 1987: 269.

64. AGI/J457, 1144v–45; see also CVU, 1-1, 1-July-1550. Another list showing how north coast polities were divided between multiple Spanish masters is published by Loredo 1958: especially 250–58. See also Rostworowski 1990: 6–7; 1999b: 11 (who quotes Fray Domingo de Santo Tomás on how the Spanish divided polities of two or three thousand households and the confusion that resulted); Huertas 1998: 16–17.

65. Julien 1991: 5, 11, 34. Central to Julien's efforts (1991: 42, 85, 107) is mapmaking of the Inca provinces. A major problem of that effort is that many prereducción settlements cannot be found on maps and that there is no sure way to tell that those located had been in the same place between Inca times and the date the map was drawn. Complicating map locations is the fact that a toponym may appear more than once (1991: 107; Polia Meconi 1999: 563). See Morales 1977; Wachtel 1982: 200, 222–23, 232; Gama 1540/1974: 225; Murra 1967a (on subjects of various curacas who lived in close proximity).

66. When Julien's data do not correspond to discrete areas, she states that "the structure of the parish is complex, and additional documentation will be necessary to interpret the lists we have" (1991: 11).

67. Rex González 1982: 327, 329–30, 332, 335–46, 354, 369.

68. Hyslop 1976: 2, 179\80, 185–86, 189–90. For don Martín Cari, see Diez 1567: 14; Hyslop 1976: 165–66. Note that Hyslop constructs a tentative map of the probable territorial extent of the land pertaining to each Lupaca province based on a fragment of a 1574 visita to the area. Unfortunately, he erroneously equated ayllu with lands and did not take into consideration the fact that the 1574 visita probably reflected the result of the crown's resettlement policy. Ayllus, which he defined as family and geographic units (1976: 180), were not conceived of as land areas, and as Gabriel Martínez (1981) discovered some years later, ayllu members did not live in one location. Also, there may be little or no correspondence between the settlement pattern of pre-reducción ayllus and their later configuration. As noted later, it is at the time of the reducciones that natives were given specific bounded lands on which to work (Hyslop 1976: 165). On the changing meaning of the word *ayllu*, see Marques da Cunha Martins Portugal 1996.

69. Martínez 1981: 263–65, 268–71; Hyslop 1976: 184; Murra 1967a.

70. Martínez 1981: 271–72.

71. On the lack of stable geographic zones, see Silva Santisteban 1982: 294 (on the Guzmango); Caillavet 2000: especially 105 (for Ecuador). On dispersed settlement, see Rostworowski 1978b: 91; 1990: 15; 1993a: 223, 226, citing Jiménez de la Espada 1881–97, vol. 2; 1993b: 10 (on the Lima Valley); BAH/Mata Linares, t. 2, año 1787); 1981–82: 146, 150 (for the quote); 1999b: 19; 1988a: 142; Julien 1991: 43, 85, 88, 105–6, 109. See also Julien for the same phenomena among the Quolla (1983: 82–83); Martínez 1981: 264–65; Hyslop 1976: 165–66, 183–84, 208–12; Pease 1982; Huertas 1998: 11–13, 17; Remy 1986; Rostworowski and Remy 1992 (on Cajamarca); Castro 1993: especially 362; Espinoza Soriano 1969b: 122, 124, 131, 140 (for the Quillacas and Soras); Río and Presta 1995; Rivera and Platt 1978: 101, 105; Saignes 1991: 98, 100 (footnote 9), 106; Benavides 1988: 51 (on the Colca Valley); Regalado de Hurtado 1996b: 210 (on Acarí, Arequipa); Arze O. 1996: 179; Cañedo-Argüelles 1998: 5; Adrián 1997: 248; Caillavet 2000: 118, 140–41, 214–15, 220, 231–32, 442 (for Ecuador); Cook 1976–77 (on Conchucos): especially 28, 38–40, 43.

72. According to Hart's analysis of the Jayanca visita (Gama 1540/1975), settlements were of four to sixty structures with a median size of eight. There were one to twenty-nine tribute payers per settlement. Gama 1540/1974: 225 (on Guambos); AGI/J458, 1749, 1829–30v, 1835v, 1838; J460, 377v, 385–85v; J462, 1860v; Rostworowski 1985; 1990: 14; 1993b: 210; Loredo 1958: 251, 269–71; Rostworowski and Remy 1992 (on Cajamarca); Carrera 1644/1939: 7–9; Silva Santisteban 1982: 294 (based on Reichlen 1970: 480); Remy 1986: especially 49–50; 1992: 62; Rubiños y Andrade 1782/1936: 303; Aibar Ozejo 1968–69: 6, 18 (on Huaraz).

73. Ramírez 1996: chap. 3 (on the absence of private property); Rostworowski 1962 (for a contrasting view); 1981c: chap. 2; Hernández Príncipe 1621–22/1923:

27 (on the Recuay); Salomon and Urioste 1991: 49 (for the Huarochirí); Masuda 1985 (on natural resources). Salomon (1986: 90) also reports that individuals could lay claim to newly broken virgin land (based on Anónimo 1573/1965: 228).

74. Ramírez 1995b; Garcilaso de la Vega 1602/1942: 2:2, 85.

75. Farrington 1992: 378, 381 (on Quispeguanca); Betanzos 1551–57/1996: 170, 190. Most workers were probably yanaconas, because this situation is different from that at Abancay and Cochabamba where mitimaes returned home after 1532 (Wachtel 1982: 218–21). Wachtel also publishes native testimonies from the valley that say that mitimaes ("that means Indians who have just arrived") served him as yanaconas (1977: 74, 110). Varón Gabai (1980: 88) further glosses the term, stating that strangers or outsiders were so judged not because of where they were born, but because they had a different ancestral origin than others. Polo de Ondegardo (1917a: 70–71) noted that different groups of outsiders sowed lands for the Inca and the Sun. On "private estates," see Betanzos 1551–57/1996: 170; Wachtel 1982: 219–20; Farrington 1992: 378. Betanzos relates another example (1551–57/1996: 51). On lands created by order of Huáscar (or Topa [Tupac] Cusi Guallpa Inga), see Rostworowski 1962: especially 135, 142. Wachtel (1982: 215) mentions property in the Cochabamba Valley that "had been given by Huayna Capac to one of his sons." This, then, was property of the "private type" (218). Since I have not seen the source from the Archivo Histórico de Cochabamba on which this statement is based, I cannot comment on it at this time.

76. Betanzos (1551–57/1996: 170) related that Guayna Capac sent yanaconas to cultivate some land assigned to the lords of Cuzco, both living and dead. Such was the case of the lands created by order of Huáscar (Rostworowski 1962: 135). Such lands could also have supported the office of the Inca and not a particular ruler (see Farrington 1992: 379 on lands associated with Tupac Inca Yupanqui in the Valley of Yucay). He also mentions royal estates in the Limatambo and Chinchaypukio valleys and at Zurite on the Pampa de Anta, which were claimed by the sons and grandsons of Guayna Capac or "are associated with his panaqa," based on work by K. J. Heffernan (1989). I cannot comment on these because I have not had access to Heffernan's work (Farrington 1992: 378–79).

77. ANP/RA, Civiles, l. 4, c. 26, 1559, fol. 6.

78. AGI/Escribanía 501A, especially fols. 17, 21, 62, 101.

79. Rowe 1987, cited by Farrington 1992: 378–81; Rostworowski 1970: 159, 181, 253. The court case over doña Beatriz Coya's claims to peasants and lands in the Yucay Valley also confirmed my belief that what the Spanish identified as "private estates" belonging to the Inca were originally lands worked to support royal panacas. See also Murra on estates (1987: especially 340–41.)

80. Cieza 1985: 21; Sancho de la Hoz 1534/1938: 158; Ramírez, forthcoming; Wachtel 1982: 234 (for the quote); Rostworowski 1993b: 207 (on Mala). Calero reports for southern Colombia that native peasants who sold land did not understand its implications—permanent alienation of the resource. After the sale, the natives sought to return to their land (1997: 107). They may have conceived of it as a modernized, updated version of traditional "resource sharing," in which after the harvest they could regain possession of the land that they had originally used. See also Rostworowski 1990: 22 (for a similar example of natives who did not understand

the concept of "to sell"); Assadourian 1987: 70; Salomon 1986: 90, 200; Golte 1970: 474–75. For evidence of pre-Hispanic resource sharing in the Upper Saña Valley, see Dillehay and Netherly 1983. Resource sharing included "sharing" worked land with outsiders, who were given part of the harvest in return for their labor, and situations in which outsiders colonized and used an unexploited part of an ecological niche to take advantage of a given resource.

81. Morales (1977: especially 28) indicates the Cochabamba was first conquered by Tupac Inca Yupanqui. On private estates there, see Rostworowski 1966: 31; Wachtel 1982: 205–6, 214; Morales 1977: 5–10, 14, 20–21, 24, 30; Farrington 1992: 378; Schramm 1995: 165. See also Espinoza Soriano 1993: 50 (on the abandonment of Cochabamba after the Spanish arrived).

82. Hernández Príncipe 1621–22/1923: 34. Curacas competed for the allegiance of subjects. A test of the loyalty of new adherents or subjects was for them to propitiate the community's ancestors; this was also a way of honoring the curaca and his subjects. In this way, outsiders, in time, might become accepted members of a group. On "corporate ownership" of the means of production, see Sherbondy 1996: 179.

83. Sherbondy 1996: 177–78, 183, 188, 195.

84. Quipucamayocs 1542–44/1920: 6; Guamán Poma de Ayala 1594/1991. "Behetría" was a term that the Spanish applied "to any culture escaping the direct control of the Inka state, wherever its habitat" (Taylor 1999: 197) and thus was part of the propaganda that the Inca civilized and established order out of chaos. See also note 27 in this chapter.

85. Betanzos 1551–57/1996: 10–11, 15; Cabello Valboa 1586/1951: 261–63. See Polo de Ondegardo 1906 (on the columns): 213; Polia Meconi 1999: 266 (on the Jesuit report); BNE/Ms. 2010, 1576, fol. 35v (on four pillars around the city of Cuzco to guide planting according to the sun); Agustinos ca. 1550/1918: 32. The structures identified as fortresses to guard against the Chiriganaes may also suggest a boundary. If, in fact, they were fortresses, they served to protect certain Inca subjects. But had the Chiriganaes come in peace to work a resource, would such structures have been built or would the newcomers have been welcomed or tolerated as other workers among other ethnicities of the empire were? See Espinoza Soriano 1987–89: 257–58 (about the erection of pillars in the 1580s to delineate the provinces of Chiquicache and Huancané).

86. Salomon and Urioste 1991: 48, 52, 59, 62–63, 66, 77, 93; Hernández Príncipe 1621–22/1923: 37, 55; Doyle 1988: 11, 87; Polia Meconi 1996: 222 (on animals). As will be developed later in the chapter, pacarinas might also have denominated a person as well as the place the person originally appeared, a position favored by Doyle (1988) and Ramírez (2002). See Polia Meconi 1999: 226 (for the Chinchaycochas in 1613). See also the ambiguity of the definition cited by Negro 1996: 132, note 6.

87. On songs, see Harrison 1989; Métraux 1969: 41; Ramírez 1986: especially 592–608. On "sacred or ritual geography," see Farrington 1992; Regalado de Hurtado (1996a: 89); Niles 1999: especially 53–54. On the cliff, see Farrington 1992: 377. Farrington considers the cliff and other places as boundary markers. I am unconvinced that his heartland boundary was one designated by the Incas. For the quote, see Anónimo 1571/1995: 168. See Landázuri 1993: 285, who cites another

example of the Incas imposing new meanings on a given landscape. On quipus, see Urton 1990a; 1997; Quilter and Urton 2002.

88. Regalado de Hurtado 1996a: 89. On how names and geographical features in a small place amount to a local history, see Scott, Tehranian, and Mathias 2002: especially 5.

89. Castro and Ortega Morejón 1558/1968: 481; Ramírez 1995a; Neale 1969; Bandera 1557/1968: 509; Duviols 1986: 471 (for 1621). Direct control of people was the essence of political dominance that gave native authorities a theoretical and potential basis for claiming territory under the Spanish. The "land is to rule" principle was also embodied in the Treaty of Madrid of 1750, where the "as you possess" (*uti posedetis*) principle was used to establish the international frontiers between Portuguese and Spanish America in the eighteenth century (Whitehead 1999: 425).

90. Harley 1990: 61. This particular map is named because it was the earliest extant map of America. Many early maps were more concerned with coastlines and wind directions needed for navigation than on the possessions of the Spanish empire.

91. The capitulación giving Pizarro the governance of the lands and provinces of Peru, signed in Toledo on July 26, 1529, is published in Levillier (1921: 2:1–5) and in Sancho (1533/1917: 203–13, especially 204). See the letter from Francisco Pizarro, dated June 8, 1533, in Levillier 1921: 1:1–2, 6 (dated January 10, 1535). See also Pease (1980: 6), who cites a June 1541 letter from Francisco Pizarro, published by Porras Barrenechea (1959: 400–402), regarding "the disputes about the delineation of the southern boundary of his jurisdiction" ["pleitos por la delimitación del ámbito sur de su gobernación"]. See also Hampe Martínez 1988: 62–63; Cuzco 1926: 18; Levillier 1921: 1:76–77. Molina Argüello states that "after the initial settlement in the territory or because with the years the area becomes familiar to the citizens, Spanish American legislation frequently specifies the jurisdiction in territorial terms, usually to avoid encounters between captains" (1972: 448–49).

92. Sancho de la Hoz 1534/1938: 167; Cuzco 1926: 10–11, 13–27, 34–37; MacCormack 1997b: 21; Espinoza Soriano 1977: 113; Bromley 1935: chap. 3. Compare these vague limits of Cuzco with the much more exact limits of the city of Cuenca in Ecuador, which was founded more than twenty years later (see Chacón Zhapán 1990: 99). See also Cobo 1935: 1:19–20 (on Lima); Porras Barrenechea 1978: 458–59 (on Trujillo).

93. Mena 1534/1967: 89, 92–100; Hernando Pizarro, in Oviedo 1535–45/1959: 86, 88–90; Sancho de la Hoz 1534/1938: 117, 176–77; and 1917; Diego Molina 1533, in Oviedo 1534–45/1959: 91, 98; Obispo de Tierra Firme Don Tomás de Berlanga to S.M., February 3, 1536, in Levillier 1921: 2:39, 41; Quipucamayocs 1542–44/1920: 27; Pease 1990b: 194–95; Betanzos 1551–57/1987: pt. 1; Bromley 1935: 114.

94. Hampe Martínez 1988: 67–68.

95. Vargas Ugarte 1949: 141–43, 157–58; Valcarcel l982: 16 (gives the date as 1559). For further information on the permutations of the Audiencia of Charcas, see Maurtua 1906: vols. 2–3; Levillier 1921–22: 458 (for 1566).

96. Rowe 1957: 161–63; Maurtua 1906: 76–77; Keith 1969, 1971; Lohmann Villena l957: 187–89. See Molina Argüello (1972: especially 446–47, 452–53) on the same phenomena in Guatemala.

97. Lisson y Chaves 1943: 1:4, 127–32, quoting AGI/P 185, r. 39 (on Vaca de Castro's establishment of bishoprics [*obispados*]), r. 59; Rostworowski 1982a: 227. In 1616, the jurisdictions of various bishoprics were further refined by Viceroy Marqués de Montesclaros. See ALL/LB-169, leg. 248, s. 18, 1616 (the original is from AGI/AL, est. 70, cajon 1, leg. 36.)

98. Armas Medina 1952: 122 (for the quote); Adrián 1997: 242–43 (on the demographic definition of parishes). See also Sherbondy 1996: 177; Mörner 1973: 6. Duviols (1972: 315–20, 328, 414) states that the first parishes were sort of a continuation of the ayllus (Jeffrey Klaiber, S.J., personal communication, January 28, 1998). Rowe (1946: 229) gives parishes boundaries that he says were established in the middle of the sixteenth century.

99. For the quote, Romero 1924: 159–70, as cited by Julien 1991: 99, 131. Gibson 1987: 369; Lisson y Chaves (1944: 2:5, 43–55), who publishes a sixteenth-century list of the Bishoprics of Cuzco, La Plata, Guamanga, and Arequipa and the amount of income generated by the population of each. See also Adrián 1997: 241–42.

100. On cities, see Angulo 1920: especially the map following p. 299 (for Saña); 1921: 38–41, 47–66 (on Cañete); Cobo 1935: 1:20–22 (on Lima); Vargas Ugarte 1949: 128–29; Ayacucho 1966: 45, 47–48, 51 (for Guamanga); Rostworowski 1962: 141 (on Cuzco, including a document from 1555); Ramírez 1995b (on Chicama); on land disputes and Spanish orders to establish boundary markers, see Rostworowski 1999b: 70, 75, 78, 83, 86–88, 90, 95, 99, 118, 163–64; and BNP/A16, 1560, especially 147, 148, 171. On gardens, see, for example, Vargas Ugarte 1949: 128–30.

101. AGI/J418, 1573, 219–219v. On the equivalence between reducción and doctrina, see Mörner 1973: 65.

102. Viceroy Toledo was not the first to concentrate population, as claimed by Murra (1970: 9). See Ramírez 1996: chap. 2; and Hart 1983: 298 (on Dr. Gregorio González de Cuenca's efforts in the 1560s); see also Varón Gabai 1980: 51 (on Viceroy Lope Garcia de Castro's effort); Mörner 1973: 6 (on reducción). On the four hundred households, see Toledo 1924: 174; Garcilaso de la Vega (1602/1960–63: 2:33) says five to eight ayllus were reduced in one reducción. My research shows that these numbers do not hold everywhere. Toledo wanted natives moved far from their "idolatries and the tombs of their ancestors" (AGI/AL 29, document dated La Plata 7-November-1573). See also Toledo 1924: 165; AGI/P, l. 189, r. 11, 1566 (on Jayanca); AGI/J460, fol. 365v (on Chicama); Rostworowski 1993b: 205 (on Yauyos); Huertas 1998: 17, 19 (on Huamanga); AGI/AL 123, cited by Rostworowski 1993a: 220 (on Colesuyu); Cook 1976–77: 25 (on Conchucos).

103. Mörner 1973: 66; AGI/AL 132, fol. 4; Toledo 1924: 165, 67–68; 1986: 43 (translation of this and all Spanish quotations is mine; translation is more literal than literary); Duviols 1986: 61; Saignes 1991: 112; ART/CoJuez de Comisión, l. 272, exp. 3369, 26-July-1557, s.f. (on mobility).

104. Ramírez 1978; Espinoza Soriano 1981: 125.

105. On Mocupe, see AFA/l. 2, c. 2, 1712, fols. 7–9; ART/CoCompa, 21-January-1712; on Monsefú, see ACI/Monsefú, P. 110-5345; and ANCR/Collús,

1807; on llacta, see Gonçalez Holguin 1608/1952: 207, 608; and note 53 in this chapter.

106. Many of these reducciones were eventually abandoned (Espinoza Soriano 1981: 125) due to their poor location, which in some cases caused the natives to sicken and die (AGI/J458, fols. 942v; Ramírez 1978; *Recopilación de las Leyes de las Indias*, ley 14, tit. 3, lib. 6, 2:199v). Other natives fled to the dubious protection of Spanish employers and landholders (ART/CoO, l. 154, exp. 222, 22-November-1585, fol. 1v [for Chuquisongo]; CoO, l. 157, c. 301, 14-December-1595, fols. 6, 24–30; Glave 1986: 4, 9; Ramírez 1986: 72). Or, once the visitador left, natives moved back to be near their former fields and guacas (Espinoza Soriano 1981: 122; Murra 1970: 9; Flores and Gutierrez 1992: 203; Andrien 1991: 135; Saignes 1987: 145; Hart 1983: 48; Doyle 1988: 265). On boundaries, see ART/Pedro de los Rios, 1579; ART/Martínez de Escobar, 1609; Anónimo 1571. On first grants, see Ramírez 1986: appendix 3.

107. ANP/Títulos, l. 23, c. 611, 1783, fol. 6. According to Enrique Mayer (personal communication, September 1998), this picture holds even today in some places. On permanent boundaries, see ANP/Tierras y Haciendas, l. 26, c. 236, 1805, fol. 47. See the court cases in ANP/RA, l. 283, c. 2511, 1789, fol. 22v; and ANP/Tierras y Haciendas, l. 21, c. 131, 1805, fols. 76–76v.

108. ART/CoCompa, 15-January-1781, fol. 23 (on Sialupe); ART/IntCompa, 11-December-1787 (on Éten and Reque). See also ANP/RA, l. 283, c. 2511, 1789, fol. 8; Comisión 1947. On eighteenth-century mapping, see Lafuente and Mazuecos 1978; Comisión 1947.

109. The distinction between sovereignty and territoriality also exists in Eastern thought from at least the time of the Shang state. As David N. Keightley has shown, "It is unlikely that the full Shang state, except at its center, can be associated with a defined and bounded territory. . . . There is, in fact, no evidence in the [oracle-bone] inscriptions that the Shang thought in terms of specific territorial units or delimited boundaries. The polity seems to have been conceived in terms of personal power (*who* was in control) and kinship association (*what* relationship he had to the center) rather than land area (*where* he was in control)" (1979–80: 26).

110. Gottman 1973: 22, 28, 32, 34.

111. Gottman 1973: 36, 41–43, 46, 48–49; Sahlins 1989: 7, 28.

112. Schramm; Farrington 1992. Another possible example of Western observers and scholars imposing their ideas on Inca institutions is the idea that the Inca ritual center ordinarily referred to as the city of Cuzco was laid out in the form of a puma or lion. See Barnes and Slive 1993; Zuidema 1983b.

113. Barth 1970; Regalado de Hurtado 1996b: 210. In Africa (and, more specifically, in what is now Liberia), according to Murphy and Bledsoe (1986: 123), kinship and territory had "many overlapping meanings and could be used interchangeably." See also Pease 1979: 98.

114. Sarmiento de Gamboa 1572/1967: 88; Cobo 1653/1956: 2:10; Guillén Guillén 1991: 76; Zuidema 1979. Zuidema (1968: 45) points out that around Quito are four hills with the same names as the four hills near Cuzco that played important roles in religious life. See Pease 1965: 130–31 (on the model of a ceremonial center). On Huánuco Pampa, see D'Altroy 1987: 87, citing Morris 1982; Zuidema

1968: 49; Hagar 1905: 217; see also Bromley 1935: 114. Cobo (1653/1956: 2:291) states that the name "Los Reyes" originated from the day chosen to officially found the city. This does not necessarily negate my suggestion that "Los Reyes" may also have been chosen as an analogue to the city of "el Cuzco." Huertas (1998: 13) also describes sixteenth-century Vilcasguamán as a royal inn (*tambo real*) with sun and moon temples, royal residences, house of the chosen women (acllahuasi, acllawasi), ushnu, storehouses, etc. On Lima as "Los Reyes," see the paragraph in the text preceding note reference 93.

115. Polo de Ondegardo 1571/1916: 55; 1990: 44–45; Sarmiento de Gamboa 1572/1965: 231; 1572/1967: 89; Cobo 1653/1956: 2:107; Barnes and Slive 1993; Pease 1998: 236.

CHAPTER 3

1. Pease 1990b; Bauer 1992: 39. I agree with Pease (1989b: 13–14) that the Inca state was not as closely centralized as some chroniclers would have readers believe.

2. Gibson 1969: 99.

3. As mentioned in passing previously, this term "province" is used inconsistently and is nowhere precisely defined in the literature of the times. "Province," depending on the context, might have referred to suyu or any large administrative jurisdiction, an ethnic group, or even dispersed people who through dress, language, political, or religious affiliation demonstrated that they acted, at times, as a unit. In most cases, the word should be defined and interpreted in terms of population and jurisdictions and sovereignty over people, not territory.

Sabine MacCormack suggests that the solar cult was most likely universalized only after the Inca conquest (1991); whereas Cabello Valboa states that the sun was the preeminence (*superioridad*) of all other sacred things and the "universal creator of all things and provider of all the created" (1586/1951: 258). This view most likely reflects the relatively late Inca imposition, the fact that the author was recording the information decades after the Christians had arrived, and his own parochial education that favored one overarching, omnipotent religious focus.

The statement on "lords" applies to their "*caçiques y señores*" who were worshipped if they were tractable, generous, and affable (*mansos*, *liberales*, *y afables*) (Cabello Valboa 1586/1951: 258).

4. Garcilaso de la Vega 1602/1963: 19. The same sentiment was expressed later, when it was said that "the God of the Christians only serves them" ("el Dios de los cristianos sólo sirve para ellos") (Cock Carrasco 1983: 144). See also Rostworowski 1983: 11; Szemiñski and Ansion 1982: especially 190–91; Chapter 4 herein.

5. Sallnow 1987: 32.

6. Schaedel (1978: 289) writes that in the mid-thirteenth century the Incas were one tribal group among others. In the fourteenth century, the Incas established their chiefdomship within the Cuzco basin. He believes they achieved statehood in the fifteenth century.

7. Pease 1991: 20–21.

8. Sallnow 1987: 49; Schaedel 1978: 290; Sarmiento de Gamboa 1572/1965: 260. Pease's analysis and that of his students and colleagues, such as Liliana Regalado de Hurtado (1993), imply that the elite consisted of two distinct groups: the

sinchis, or military leaders, and the amautas, or priests and intellectuals. My reading of the historical record of the late pre-Hispanic and early colonial periods suggests that this is a false dichotomy. The Inca was simultaneously god or guaca, religious leader, and military commander. Guayna Capac specifically dismissed a person identified as the high priest of the Sun and took the position himself. Later in the era of the encounter, the person of the high priest became the most forceful advocate of military resistance in the immediate postinvasion years, perhaps realizing that the Christians were a much greater threat than their small numbers made them appear. Both personages had multiple and overlapping roles. The biographies of several Incas, after Pachacuti Inca Yupanqui, suggest that they focused on their military roles at one point in their lifetime and ritual roles in another, that is, they had sequential roles. The confusion may, in part, be due to the fact that the Spanish secularized the Inca, because they used European categories to describe what they saw and heard. In deemphasizing or neglecting the religious aspects of the myriad parts of native life, including the governing system, they missed the fact that the political, military, economic, and social systems were intimately related to and aspects of the religious. Ziólkowski's observations support this interpretation (1997: 36, 87, 121, 152–53, 239, 266, 335, 372, 383).

9. Guamán Poma de Ayala 1613/1980: 84 [84], 101 [101].

10. On Pachacuti Inca Yupanqui, see Rostworowski 1997. Pease (1991: 22) has advanced the hypothesis that Pachacuti Inca Yupanqui may not have been an individual; instead, the name may represent or symbolize a period or a "Cuzqueño solar archetype" (*arquetipo cuzqueño solar*). See my effort to elaborate on this hypothesis further (2004).

Schaedel (1978: 290) dates the defeat of the Chancas archaeologically to the early fifteenth century. He states that the victory marked the turning point in converting the Inca chiefdomship into a predatory superchiefdom and, under Pachacuti Inca Yupanqui, to a state (ca. 1425–50).

11. Urton 1981: 113 (for other possible identifications of the stars), 130–31 (on the Southern Cross); Cieza 1550/1985: 21 (on the "çercado de oro"); Cabello Valboa 1586/1951: 306 (for the quote on the seat of the empire), 333; Molina, el almagrista, n.d./1968: 75; Mena 1534/1938: 320; Pizarro 1571/1978: 59 (on the House of the Sun). On assignment of servants, see Cabello Valboa 1586/1951: 310–11; Bandera 1557/1968: 494, 500; and Guamán Poma de Ayala 1613/1980: 109 [109]. Both the sun and thunder gods were represented in several ways, each with its own name. For example, the Sun could be Inti or Punchao and be depicted with its rays as a heavenly body or could be depicted as a human. Thunder had three manifestations (MacCormack 1991: 340–41; Rostworowski 1983: 39–42). The multiple aspects of these gods added to the confusion of the Spanish and accounts for some of the contradictions on this issue in their writings. See also Ziólkowski 1997: especially chap. 1. Landázuri (1993: 277) believes that the Sun replaced Viracocha as the dominant god in the time of Pachacuti.

12. Polo de Ondegardo (1906: 214) relates that the Incas had three statues of the Sun. Molina n.d./1968: 76; Betanzos 1551–57/1987: 51–52 (on the bulto); 1551–57/1996: 92 (on divine descendance); Calancha 1638/1974–81: 1:223; Cabello Valboa 1586/1951: 333; Sarmiento de Gamboa 1572/1967: 97 (on the image of the

Sun being the size of a man), 100–101 (on the two additional statues); Pizarro 1571/1978: 59 (on the throne); Silverblatt 1988a: 90 (on ceremonies); Urteaga 1928: especially 36 (on "divine consanguinity"). Before 1555, one-fiftieth of a gold mark = one peso de oro de minas = eight tomines = one castellano.

13. Sarmiento de Gamboa 1572/1967: 100–101; BNP/A635, 1557–62, fol. 10; Hinojosa Cuba 1999: 30–31.

14. Cabello Valboa 1586/1951: 260, 311; Molina, el almagrista, n.d./1968: 75; Sarmiento de Gamboa 1572/1967: 114; Pease 1965: 129. Pachacuti Inca Yupanqui was said to have burned many guacas, "throwing salt on the place where they were, [but] despite that they did not disappear or stop multiplying in number" (Santacruz Pachacuti Yamqui 1613/1993: 25). Cabello Valboa relates how the Inca realized that the Sun was "not powerful for everything" and how he determined that there was "only one powerful and universal creator of all the creations," an omnipotent god, which he called Ticci Viracocha Pachacamac (Cabello Valboa 1586/1951: 309–10). Was this view due to Cabello Valboa's instruction and beliefs as a Catholic priest?

15. Cieza 1864/1964: 242, note 2; Molina, el almagrista, n.d./1968: 75; Agustinos ca. 1550/1918: 27–32 (where it is said that many guacas had people assigned to them).

16. Sarmiento de Gamboa 1572/1967: 106–8; 127. Francisco Pizarro heard of one such incident when he encountered the curaca of the Pavor in the north. The lord said that "he was a great lord and he ruled many people some time ago, and he was at present destroyed, because he said that the lord of the Cuzco, father of Atabaliba [Guayna Capac], had burned and leveled twenty towns, and he had killed the people of them because he had not welcomed him peacefully" (Oviedo 1535–45/1959/1992: 121:39).

17. Rowe 1948: 40; Pizarro 1571/1978: 80–81; Pease 1965: 129; Landázuri 1993: 296.

18. AGI/P 188, r. 22, 1561, fol. 13. See also Cobo 1653/1956: 2:167 (on guaca hostage). Polo de Ondegardo adds that the institution of guaca hostage guaranteed "holding that people wholly subdued, and so that they would not rebel against him, as well as because they could contribute things and persons for the sacrifices and guard of the guacas and for other things" (1906: 229–30).

19. Santillán 1927: 32; Cobo 1653/1956: 2:110; Silverblatt 1988a: 91; Pease 1965: 129. See also Valcarcel 1961.

20. Silverblatt 1988a: 93, 97.

21. Valera 1596/1879: 149.

22. Sallnow 1987: 40; Molina, el cuzqueño, 1574/1916: especially 56; Sarmiento de Gamboa 1907/1972/1999: 91. On lineage houses, see Chapter 4.

23. Santillán 1927: 33 (on guacas speaking); Molina, el almagrista, n.d./1968: 76; Bandera 1557/1968: 494, 500; Polo de Ondegardo 1559/1916: 3; Agustinos ca. 1550/1865/1964: 36 (on guacas causing sickness or death); Zuidema 1989b: 275; Ziólkowski 1997: 29–34; Gose 1996: 14.

24. *Illa Tecce* translates as "eternal light" (Valera 1596/1879: 137).

25. Valera 1596/1879: 137–38; Calancha 1638/1974–81: 1:210; Cieza 1550/1985: 8 (for the quote). See also Titu Cusi 1570/1916: 8; Demarest 1981: 9 (on Viracocha).

26. Betanzos 1551–57/1987: 14 (for the quote); Calancha 1638/1974–81: 1:210.

27. Valera 1596/1879: 138; Cieza 1550/1985: 8–10; Calancha 1638/1974–81: 207, 216; Pease 1968: 194; Isbell 1997: 96. At this point I leave unanswered and unresolved the very controversial questions of the identities of and relationships between Viracocha, the Sun, Thunder, Pachacamac, and Guanacaure. Viracocha was associated with Pachacamac in Inca tradition (Sallnow 1987: 37). Calancha reports that Manco Capac ordered that Pachacamac, which means "he who creates and gives life to the universe," be worshipped, suggesting that he equated Viracocha with Pachacamac. According to Pease (1991: 20, 22, 27), Viracocha was "solarized" during the time of Pachacuti Inca Yupanqui. Arthur Demarest, in a tantalizing short book, writes that Viracocha overlaps and merges with the sun god Inti; the thunder god Illapa or Thunupa (in Aymara); the coastal creator god Pachacamac; regional mythical ancestors; and even many of the important geographic guacas, such as Pariacaca, the sky god or creator god of the Guancas of Jauja, and Catiquilla, a thunder and rain god of the Huamachucos and Conchucos. He further points out that Viracocha did not have one ceremony dedicated to him and he lacked an endowment to support his worship (1981: 2–3, 19–21, 36, 50, 52). Such evidence suggests that direct worship of Viracocha was minimal. For two more short treatments of the subject of Viracocha and his multiple identities, see Pease 1968; Rowe 1960. See also Szemiñski 1985.

Not all Andean peoples would have agreed with such an interpretation. For example, in 1573 several informants, including Martín Tocari, a cacique principal of the town of Cocan Uta and parcialidad of the Atun Yauyos, reported seeing a separate sun temple at the shrine of the idol Pachacamac on the central coast in 1532–33 (Guillén Guillén 1974: 59, 72, 94.) Garcilaso de la Vega notes that Viracocha was "a modern god that they worshiped," making me wonder whether this god was not a guaca invented or resurrected to explain the European invasion. On this point, see also Duviols 1977a. That would account for the paucity of early references to his being and the relative absence of temples dedicated to his cult (Garcilaso de la Vega 1602/1963: 2:80). Ziólkowski (1997: chap. 1) devotes an entire chapter to the topic of deity identity and representation.

28. Cabello Valboa 1586/1951: 258; Pizarro 1571/1978: 73. Note that Cobo (1990: 26–27) and Gonçalez Holguin (1608/1952: 123) replace inti-guauqui with *churi inti* or child sun (Demarest 1981: 14, 23). See also Arriaga 1621/1968: 22. Mena describes the throne, or "golden seat" where they sacrificed, as weighing nineteen thousand pesos and large enough so that two men "could recline . . . on it" (1534/1967: 93). A secondary account states that it weighed eighteen thousand pesos, or eight *arrobas*, and could be converted to a litter. Its value is variously estimated at eighteen thousand to seventy thousand pesos (Lothrop 1938: 28, 49, 52).

29. Mena 1534/1938: 320–21; Molina, el almagrista, n.d./1968: 75.

30. Sallnow 1987: 37; Betanzos 1551–57/1996: 95; Calancha 1638/1974–81: 1:232; Estete 1534–45/1938: 202, 213; Guillén Guillén 1974: 94. For a more complete list of the sun temples, see Cieza 1550/1985: 56. Tupac Inca Yupanqui established the cult of the Sun in Copacabana on the shore of Lake Titicaca. According to Ziólkowski (1997: 299–300), the Inca did this to divide the priesthood and

escape the limitations of entrenched elites. Note that although most scholars accept Estete's publication date as circa 1535, Pease (1990b: 194) believes that it was written in the decade of the 1540s, hence my notation of 1534–45. Other mentioned, though minor, celestial bodies important to the Inca belief system included the planet Jupiter, which for guarding the provinces and empire was assigned the first fruits of the harvest, which were delivered to its shrines; and the planet Mars, which was in charge of war and soldiers. Mercury directed travelers (Valera 1596/1879: 138–39).

31. Cobo 1653/1956: 2:156–58, 160–61; Demarest 1981: 14.

32. Silverblatt 1988: 88; 1987: 45; Calancha 1638/1974–81: 1:216; Guamán Poma de Ayala 1613/1980: 185 [187], 912 [926]; Rowe 1946: 295. One aspect of Silverblatt's analysis that unsettles me is the fact that in the primary sources, pachamama is considered female, not male, as indicated in her interpretation. Duviols publishes the testimony of Francisco Poma in 1657, who in the town of San Pedro de Hacas related the following:

> The said ministers of idols taught every Indian to adore the sun because it is the father and who created humans and the moon as creator and mother of the women and the Venus of the morning that they call chachaguara as father and creator of the curacas and two little stars that are near each other that they call chuchuicollor as creators of twins and the seven cabrillas that they call vncuicollar so that their planted fields do not freeze and so that there will be no disease. (1986: 189–90)

33. Garcilaso de la Vega 1602/1963: 38; Anello Oliva 1998: 167; Grebe 1995–96: especially 141–43.

34. Aporimac or Apurimac means "the lord who speaks." Pizarro 1571/1978: 81–82.

35. Pizarro 1571/1978: 83; Estete 1542?/1987: 301, 303; Calancha 1638/1974–81: 1:209, 216; Guillén Guillén 1974: 20; Garcilaso de la Vega 1602/1963: 2:80; Hernando Pizarro 1533, in Oviedo 1535–45/1959/1992: 121:71; Patterson 1992: 9; MacCormack 1993: 109; Rostworowski 1983: 42–49; Santillán 1927: 29–31; Ziólkowski 1997: 28; Lastres 1947: 8. Other important oracles functioned at Chincha and Quito (Rostworowski 1999a: 157). On the role of oracles in the Inca governing system, see Gose 1996.

36. Mena 1534/1938: 318–19; Hernando Pizarro (1533), in Oviedo 1535–45/1959/1992: 121:89 (for the quotes). See also Santillán's account of Pachacamac speaking to Tupac Inca Yupanqui (1927: 29–31).

37. Estete, in Oviedo 1535–45/1959/1992: 121:72; Santillán 1927: 29–31. Population figures are cited by Guillén Guillén 1974: 20–21.

38. Rostworowski 1978a: 214; 1983: 70; Santillán 1927: 29–31; Santacruz Pachacuti Yamqui 1613/1968: 309; Albornoz 1967: 33–35; Dávila Brizeño 1965: 163; Ávila 1598/1966: 113–19; Netherly 1977: 321; Ramírez 1996: chap. 5, especially 127 (on Yamayoguán); Santillán 1563–72/1968: 111.

39. Bandera 1557/1968: 493; Urton 1981; Cieza 1550/1985: 16–17, 20–21; Betanzos 1551–57/1987: 19; Rowe 1946: 283 (on the Huarachicoy); Guamán Poma de Ayala 1613/1980: 299 [301]; Ziólkowski 1997: 135, 174.

40. Polia Meconi 1996: 220; Cieza 1550/1985: 6; Cabello Valboa 1586/1951: 258; Sallnow 1987: 32; Doyle 1988: ix. According to Doyle (1988: 87), pacarina is a dual notion, being the place of origin of a *malqui* (or *mallqui*), or founding ancestor, and the malqui itself.

41. Molina, el cuzqueño, 1574/1916: 7; Bandera 1557/1968: 493; Urton 1981.

42. Cabello Valboa 1586/1951: 258; Guamán Poma de Ayala 1613/1980: 337 [339]; Gonçalez Holguin 1608/1952: 165.

43. Cabello Valboa 1586/1951: 258; Molina, el cuzqueño, 1574/1943: 58 (on chipanas [tinpanas?]).

44. Molina, el almagrista, n.d./1968: 76.

45. Arriaga 1621/1968: 196 (for the quote); see also Baines and Yoffee 2000: 14.

46. Farrington 1992: 370; Pizarro 1571/1978: 52, 63; Aguirre Palma 1986: 27; Santacruz Pachacuti Yamqui 1613/1993: 29v; Arriaga 1621/1920: 14; 1621/1968a: 19, 27, 222; Rostworowski 1983: 67; Calancha 1638/1974–81: 1:236; Anónimo 1571/1995: 145–46, 148–49; Cobo 1653/1956: 2:163–65; Polo de Ondegardo 1559/1916: 7–10; Guamán Poma de Ayala 1613/1980: 257 [259]; Acosta 1590/1979: 309; Rostworowski 1983: 67. See also Molina, el almagrista, n.d./1968: 76; Las Casas 1555/1948: 71–72; Zuidema 1989a: 261; Valera 1596/1879: 153; MacCormack 1991: 85, 87, 89.

47. Santacruz Pachacuti Yamqui 1613/1993: 36v; Betanzos 1551–57/1996: 163, 166, 167; Sarmiento de Gamboa 1572/1967: 154, 172; Rostworowski 1997: 26, 28; 1999a: 32; Calancha 1638/1974–81: 1:219; Polo de Ondegardo1561/1940: 154; 1559/1916: 7–10; Acosta (1590/1979: 309), who states, "The elders confirm that this Guaynacapa was adored by his followers as a god, in life"; Varón Gabai 1997: 182 (on the postconquest veneration of the statue of Paullu Inca). See also Zuidema 1989a: 265, citing Acosta 1590/2002 lib. VI, chap. 22; Sancho de la Hoz 1534/1938: 183; Hinojosa Cuba 1999: 37.

48. Sancho de la Hoz 1534/1938: 167, 185; Estete 1542?/1987: 317; Pizarro 1571/1978: 52–53, 89–90; Cabello Valboa 1586/1951: 260; BNP/A635, 1557–62, fol. 10.

49. Classen 1993: 85–86; Levillier 1935: 266; Niles 1999: 1, 21.

50. Gama 1540/1974: 225; Cabello Valboa 1586/1951: 267; Pease 1990b: 195; Molina, el almagrista, n.d./1968: 74; Garcilaso de la Vega 1602/1963: 37 (for the quote); Bauer 1996: 337; Taylor 1999: xxiv. See also the word's use in Polia Meconi 1999: 345 (for Guamanga in 1614).

51. Julien 1997: 3; 1999: 1 (for the quote), 4, 7. This paper was subsequently published in Julien 2000: chap. 2; Betanzos 1551–57/1987: 132 (for the quote). On the Inca as a sacred being, see also Pease 1976, 1978, 1991: 65; Tantaleán 1981; Garcilaso de la Vega 1602/1963: 2:38; Guillén Guillén 1984: 76. Rowe uses the term "demi-god" (1946: 202).

52. Garcilaso de la Vega 1603/1963: 2:37; Molina, el almagrista, n.d./1968: 74.

53. Pizarro 1571/1978: 33; Mena 1534/1967: 83; Hernando Pizarro 1533, in Oviedo 1535–45/1959/1992: 121:86; Dammert Bellido 1997: 125.

54. Estete 1542?/1987: 292 (for the quote); Hernando Pizarro 1533, in Oviedo 1535–45/1959/1992: 86; Mena 1534/1967: 84.

55. Estete 1534–45/1938: 222; 1542?/1987: 294–95; Cieza 1550/1985: 29; Pease 1990b: 196–97; 1994: 10; Cabello Valboa 1586/1951: 291.

56. Cabello Valboa 1586/1951: 257; Cieza 1550/1985: 34, 36; Betanzos 1551–57/1987: 111; 1557/1996: 177; Pizarro 1571/1978: 33–37.

57. Betanzos 1551–57/1996: 193.

58. Betanzos 1551–57/1996: 227; Sherbondy 1992: 56.

59. Cabello Valboa 1586/1951: 458; Pizarro 1571/1978: 37. The display's symbolism was important. Cobo suggests that through its brilliance, the Sun communicated with humans: "The Indians said that with its light the Sun sent its virtue" (1653/1956: 2:157).

60. MacCormack 1988: especially 967–68, 982; Melo et al. 1582/1925: 281, 285; Betanzos 1551–57/1987: 185–86; 1551–57/1996: 168–69; Molina, el cuzqueño, 1574/1916: 6; Salomon and Urioste 1991: 65, 75, 81, 116, 121; Earls and Silverblatt 1978: 20.

61. Betanzos 1551–57/1987: 185–86, 220; 1551–57/1996: 154, 205; Sarmiento de Gamboa 1572/1965: 219–20 (for Manco Capac), 220 (for Sinchi Roca), 221 (for Lloqui Yupanqui), 222 (for Mayta Capac), 223 (for Capac Yupanqui), 230 (for Viracocha Inca), 253 (for Pachacuti Inca Yupanqui), 258–59 (for Tupac Inca Yupanqui), 265 for (Guayna Capac). Gose (1996) thinks that statues of the Incas became an integral part of a delegated system of power, where social distance prevented mere mortal subjects from interacting with their divine kings.

62. Pease 1990b: 195; 1991: 35; Wachtel 1977: 40; Zuidema 1989a, 261. *Ucu* (*hurin*, *urin*, or *uku*) *Pacha* was the underworld (*mundo del subsuelo*) where the fertility gods and the dead lived (Pease 1991: 64; Regalado de Hurtado 1993: 21). According to Monica Barnes this tripartite division reflects sixteenth-century Christian beliefs (discussed by Dover 1992: 10).

63. Zuidema 1992: 18, 28, 33, 35; Cabello Valboa 1586/1951: 266; Guamán Poma de Ayala 1613/1980: 113 [113]; Betanzos 1551–57/1987: 185–86. See also Anónimo 1571/1995: 153.

64. Cabello Valboa 1586/1951: 257, 266; Pease 1991: 75–75; Pizarro 1571/1978: 51; Hart 1983: 320. Note that Betanzos, who interviewed "all the oldest nobles and gentlemen of Cuzco, the majority of whom had been with Atahualpa and his father, Guayna Capac, during their time in Quito," says that Atahualpa was never a prisoner of anyone (1551–57/1996: 212). The fact that stories to this effect circulated and were believed and repeated shows that history was already turning into myth. On the sacred language, see Garcilaso de la Vega 1609/1943: vol. 7, 1:88, quoted by Cerrón-Palomino 1998: 417; or Garcilaso de la Vega 1609/1987: 403; 1609/1942: vol. 2, book 7, chap. 1, 240. See also Cobo 1653/1956: 2:64.

65. Betanzos 1551–57/1987: 169–73; Cabello Valboa 1586/1951: 309; Cieza 1550/1985: 35. During Pachacuti Inca Yupanqui's reign, the Andes suffered seven years of famine during which time many people died. His brother, Amaro Tupac Inca, fed the starving people from his harvests and the surplus stored in the granaries (Santacruz Pachacuti Yamqui 1613/1993: 24v). See also Valcarcel 1961: 6 (on surplus). Polia Meconi and Chávez Hualpa (1994: 11) discuss the Inca as a curer.

66. Pease 1990b: 195–96; 1991: 68; Bauer 1996: 331; Garcilaso de la Vega 1609/1941–45: 2:141; Wachtel 1977: 40; Espinoza Soriano 1976: 250, 264.

67. Estete 1542?/1987: 313, 315.

68. Salomon 1987b: 208.

69. Salles-Reese 1997: 46; Patterson 1992: 181–89.

70. Garcilaso de la Vega 1602/1963: 26; 1987: 42 (for the quote); Betanzos 1551–57/1987: 85–86; 1551–57/1996: 54–55.

71. Viracocha rather than the Sun was the creator, according to Sarmiento de Gamboa (1572/1967: 44).

72. Silverblatt 1987: 47; Sarmiento de Gamboa 1572/1967: 43–44, 51; 1572/1965: 216; Cabello Valboa 1586/1951: 260–63; Garcilaso de la Vega 1602/1963: 20, 26–27, 30; 1609/1941–45: 1:54–58; Cieza 1550/1985: 13, 21; Pizarro 1571/1978: 45; Molina, el almagrista, n.d./1968: 73; Santacruz Pachacuti Yamqui 1613/1993: 6v; Urton 1981. Garcilaso de la Vega, in reporting one brother-sister pair, may have tried to sanitize Inca history to make it acceptable to his Christian readers. Most chroniclers commonly state that there were three or four pairs (Santacruz Pachacuti Yamqui 1613/1993: 6; Cieza 1550/1985: 13; Sarmiento de Gamboa 1572/1967: 45; Guamán Poma de Ayala 1613/1980: 84 [84]). Sarmiento de Gamboa contradicts the story of the peaceful invasion of the valley, saying that the Incas took water from the Alcabizas by force. As a result, the locals were forced to forfeit the space that the Incas coveted and serve them as masters (*señores*) (Sarmiento de Gamboa 1572/1965: 219). This emphasis may have been part of his effort to label the Incas as tyrants.

73. Cieza 1550/1985: 14–15; Sarmiento de Gamboa 1572/1967: 44; Cabello Valboa 1586/1951: 265–67, 363.

74. Garcilaso de la Vega 1602/1963: 39.

75. Garcilaso de la Vega 1602/1963: 26–28.

76. Cieza 1550/1985: 27–28; Abercrombie 1998: 195–96. See also Rostworowski 1984. These songs continued to be sung after 1532. A Franciscan missionary in Pantaguas listened to a cacique's "sad song in which he named the Ingas of Perú and the death that the Spanish gave to the king Atahualpa Inga" (Córdova Salinas 1651/1957: 222, as cited by MacCormack 1985b: 458). In Huarochirí, songs with very good "epithets" were sung to the Sun and the Inca (Ares Queija 1984: 462). Others conveyed the accepted origin myth (Abercrombie 1998: 14).

77. Abercrombie 1998: 215; Molina, el almagrista, n.d./1968: 74; Schwartz 1982 (on how collective memory is constructed to place part of the past in the service of conceptions and needs of the present).

78. Santillán 1563–72/1968: 104 (for the quote); Garcilaso de la Vega 1602/1963: 74, 84–85. On the rainbow as a good omen, see Sarmiento de Gamboa 1572/1965: 216; MacCormack 1991: 340–41. A solar eclipse was feared. The priests explained that the Sun's face was "disturbed" because it was mad about a real or imagined offense committed against it. They predicted "that a grave punishment would befall them."

Equally cataclysmic was a lunar eclipse. Such a celestial event was explained by saying that the Moon was sick. If it got totally dark, the Moon might die and fall from the sky, crushing to death all those on earth, and the world would end. So people played trumpets, horns, conch shells (*caracoles*), kettle drums (*atabales*), drums, and other instruments to make noise. They made dogs howl to get the attention of the Moon, which "fancied dogs, for a certain service that they had done her, and that hearing them cry, she would have had pity on them and would have reminded her of the dream that the illness caused." When the Moon began to reappear, they said that the Moon was recovering because "Pachacamac, that was the sustainer of the Universe, had given her health and ordered her not to die to save the world." When the Moon recovered, they thanked it for not falling (Garcilaso de la Vega 1602/1963: 74).

79. Garcilaso de la Vega 1602/1963: 31; Cieza 1864/1964: 233; 1984: 201; 1550/1985: 78; Calancha 1638/1974–81: 1:246; Santacruz Pachacuti Yamqui 1613/1993: 32v, 35–36; Regalado de Hurtado 1992: 44. On comets that appeared in the skies of the Andes in 1531–32, see Villareal 1894–95: especially 274–79; Ziólkowski 1997: 367–68, 387. See also Hiltunen (1999: 271–72, 327), who gives the dates of major solar eclipses and comets. I am aware that some of these omens resemble those that announced the eclipse of the central Mexican Mexica empire and some stories imported from Europe.

80. Sarmiento de Gamboa 1572/1942: 138; Betanzos 1551–57/1987: 81; Cabello Valboa 1586/1951: 307.

81. Sarmiento de Gamboa 1572/1967: 135–36; Rostworowski 1970: 168, 199–200 (for the long quote); Lazaro Llantoy 1996: 72.

82. Garcilaso de la Vega 1602/1963: 75; Cabello Valboa 1586/1951: 287–89; Betanzos 1551–57/1987: 81; Guamán Poma de Ayala 1613/1980: 81 [81]; Rostworowski 1999a: 158. In this regard, chroniclers often also refer to the high priest of the Sun, and sometime military leader against the Spanish (Guillén Guillén 1974: 171), who was second only in power to the Inca or el Cuzco (when the Inca did not hold the position himself, e.g., Guayna Capac) (Titu Cusi 1570/1916: 47; Agustinos ca. 1550/1865/1964: 33). Some Andean specialists (Molina, el almagrista, n.d./1968: 75–76; Valera 1596/1945: 34; Pizarro 1571/1978: 91, 94) think that the high priest (Villac Umu or Vil[l]aoma), a name or title that Garcilaso de la Vega translated as *villac* (to say or he who speaks) and *oma* or *umu* (one who divines or the one who communicates with the divine) (1609/1941–45: 285–87; Betanzos 1551–57/1996: 313; Cieza 1550/1985: chap. 17], was elected by the amautas (Cock Carrasco 1983: 136), probably from the relatives of the Inca (Lothrop 1938: 21). This may be true, because Sarmiento de Gamboa (1572/1967: 104) records that Pachacuti's brother, Inca Roca, was a great necromancer, and most authors refer to him as the Villaoma. Molina describes such a person as Vilaoma, *Indivianan*, or "servant or slave of the Sun." As such, he talked to the image and "gave his replies," serving in general as the sun statue's caretaker or *camayoc* (Guillén Guillén 1991: 77). He lived in the temple; supervised, perhaps indirectly, the four thousand servants that Molina described as Coricancha's assets (Molina, el almagrista, n.d./1968: 75); and with the help of other religious specialists performed sacrifices and directed worship (Guillén Guillén 1974: 171). He also announced messages from the gods (guacas) (Guamán Poma de Ayala 1613/1980: 278 [280]). Guillén Guillén believes that Vilaoma was the son or brother of Guayna Capac and that Vilaoma was a personal name of the individual who was priest of the Sun and not the name of the position. Other known priests of the Sun were named Colla Topa (or Kolla Thupa) and Apu Chalco Yupangui

(or Auqui Challco Yupanqui) (Guillén Guillén 1974: 30; 1991: 77). His title was *intip apun* (or *Indip yanan* or *Inti phuillac*) (Molina, el almagrista, n.d./1968: 76), which translates as "high priest of the Sun" or "servant or slave of the Sun" (Guillén Guillén 1991: 75–76). On the person of the chief priest of the Sun, see Ziólkowski 1997: 157–59, who argues that usually (during the reigns of the last five Incas) the older brother of the ruler became the high priest of the Sun. On priests and shamans in general, see Cock Carrasco 1983: especially 141. See also Conrad and Demarest 1984: 102; Ziólkowski 1991b.

83. Sarmiento de Gamboa 1572/1967: 89, 158; Garcilaso de la Vega 1602/1963: 19; Ziólkowski 1997: 247. Sometimes the calpa was interpreted wrongly (Sarmiento de Gamboa 1572/1965: 232). See Gonçalez Holguin 1608/1952: 44–45 (on calpa); see also Santo Tomás 1560/1951: 245 (on *callparicuni*, to tell the future by looking at the entrails or lungs of animals or birds). See also Molina, el cuzqueño 1574/1943: 22 (on *Calparicuqui*, which means "they who answer questions about the fortune and success of things," who for this reason kill birds, lambs, and sheep and blow into a vein of the lungs to find in them certain signs through which they predict the future). See also Cobo 1653/1964: 2:229–31 (on Inca and Andean divination); Guamán Poma de Ayala 1613/1980: 880–82; Rostworowski 1988b: 206–7; Guillén Guillén 1991: 71; MacCormack 1998: 339.

84. Guamán Poma de Ayala 1613/1980: 113 [113], 262 [264]; Bandera 1557/1968: 503–4; Cobo 1653/1964: 2:78; Montesinos 1644/1930: 94; Pease 1991: 80–81; Sarmiento de Gamboa 1572/1967: 90; 1965: 222, 229, 232; 1907/1999: 81 (Atun Tupac Inca was Inca Viracocha's adolescent name); Molina, el cuzqueño, 1574/1916: 18; Rostworowski 1997: 20; Cabello Valboa 1586/1951: 283, 310–11; Ziólkowski 1991b: 60; Santacruz Pachacuti Yamqui 1613/1993: 34; Santillán 1879: 34. Some say that Inca Viracocha took the title after his puberty rites, during which the god Viracocha was named as his godfather and sponsor. See also Álvarez 1588/1998: 74.

85. Santacruz Pachacuti Yamqui 1613/1993: 12–12v; Betanzos 1551–57/1987: 131–32, 137; Regalado de Hurtado 1992: 44.

86. This was not so far-fetched; the news may have been spread at the same time as the European disease that eventually claimed Guayna Capac's life. Manuel Ballesteros Gaibrois believes that the news traveled along trading links between the Ecuadorian coast and Central America (Guillén Guillén 1974: 137). See Garcilaso de la Vega 1602/1963: 11 (on the date 1515).

87. Garcilaso de la Vega 1602/1943: 3:149. MacCormack (1985a: 430) questions the veracity and telling of this story.

88. Pizarro 1571/1978: 241; Garcilaso de la Vega 1609/1943: 3:148–52; Herrera y Tordesillas 1728 and 1601–15: Dec. 5, lib. 5, cap. 1, 105, as cited by Calancha 1638/1974–81: 1:234.

89. Calancha 1638/1974–81: 1:234.

90. MacCormack 1991: 306.

91. Sarmiento de Gamboa 1572/1965: 214, 220; 1967: 60, 101; Gose 1996: 3; Ruiz de Arze 1543/1933: 372; Alonso Sagaseta de Ilurdoz.

92. Guamán Poma de Ayala 1613/1980: 113 [113]; Molina, el almagrista, n.d./1968: 78; Betanzos 1551–57/1987: 249–50; Agustinos ca. 1550/1865/

1964: 22–26. See also Sarmiento de Gamboa 1572/1967: 176; Dammert Bellido 1997: 52; Rostworowski 1983: 49.

93. Pizarro 1571/1978: 49, 57; Guillén Guillén 1974: 21; Cieza 1550/1985: 89; Santacruz Pachacuti Yamqui 1613/1993: 39; Gose 1996: 6; Álvarez 1588/1998: 74. See also Zuidema 1989b: 139.

94. Pease 1991: 14, 17, 114; Titu Cusi 1570/1916: 60; Rostworowski 1960: 421; 1983: 154–73; 1997: 73; Sherbondy 1993: 72; Regalado de Hurtado 1993: 47, 73; Sarmiento de Gamboa 1572/1965: 220; 1967: 70, 140; Schaedel 1978: 302; Cieza 1550/1985: 19–20; Garcilaso de la Vega 1602/1963: 38.

95. Rostworowski 1960: 417. Pease (1991: 102–3) believes, based on the chronicles, that persons who were not a king's son (*pretendientes irregulares*), but perhaps members of the same age-grade (generation), could try to assume power. This implies that they could gain control even without right (*derecho*) if they had strength (*fuerza*) and prestige enough to support them. See also Sarmiento de Gamboa 1572/1965: 259–60; Murua 1946b: 175.

96. Guamán Poma de Ayala 1613/1980: 118 [118]; Rostworowski 1953: 213–15; 1960: 419; 1981–82: 109; 1997: 66; Quipucamayocs 1542–44/1920: 12, 26; Pizarro 1571/1978: 47; Betanzos 1551–57/1996: 27, 72–73; Varón Gabai 1997: 181–82; Salles-Reese 1997: 103; Sarmiento de Gamboa 1572/1967: 54, 64, 69, 123; 1965: 221; Ziólkowski 1997: 151–54.

97. Garcilaso de la Vega said that the successor was "the son best loved by his vassals," which emphasizes election and not inheritance (as cited by Rostworowski 1960: 419).

98. We do not know if they kept track of birth order (See Zuidema 1977: 276).

99. Cabello Valboa 1586/1951: 294; Sarmiento de Gamboa 1572/1965: 220, 223; 1572/1967: 63, 69–70, 81, 85, 88, 123, 163; Sancho de la Hoz 1534/1938: 122; Salles-Reese 1997: 103; Betanzos 1551–57/1996: 72–73; Gibson 1969: 18; Rostworowski 1981–82: 108; 1997: 66; Garcilaso de la Vega 1609/1942: 2:144; Santacruz Pachacuti Yamqui 1613/1993: 10; 1613/1879: 300; Molina, el cuzqueño, 1574/1916: 56; Ziólkowski 1991b: 67; Abercrombie 1998: 86l; Guillén Guillén 1974: xvi; Pease 1991: 20; Schaedel 1978: 302. Ziólkowski (1997: 141) adds also his ability to overpower his enemies (i.e., prowess in battle); his ability to control rain and water, in general; and his fecundity.

100. Santo Tomás 1951: 139, 245. Note that *callpachini* (?) means "to endow someone with force" and *callpaicuni* means "to divine by looking at the entrails or lungs of a mammal or bird." See also note 83 in this chapter. On the use of such divination, see Sarmiento de Gamboa 1572/1965: 112–13 (on the crisis caused by the uprising of the Collas), 140 (regarding Guayna Capac's conquest of the Chachapoyas), 147–48 (on choosing the successor to Guayna Capac). See also MacCormack 1998: 339.

101. The ceremony was performed by Colla Topa, according to Pease 1991: 105. Note that Sarmiento de Gamboa (1572/1942: 158) says that Ninan Cuyoche was an adolescent before Guayna Capac died.

102. Pease 1991: 106; Sarmiento de Gamboa 1572/1967: 168–69. For a different version, see also Guamán Poma de Ayala 1613/1980: 118 [118]; Betanzos 1551–57/1996: 183–84; Quipucamayocs 1542–44/1920: 21–23, 26–27.

103. Atahualpa is the exception. He was anointed by Cuxi (Tupac?)Yupanqui in Tumibamba, perhaps because of the extraordinary arrival and interventions of the Spanish (Cieza 1550/1985: 212; Regalado de Hurtado 1993: 100).

104. See the statement of repudiation of sun worship and the acknowledgment that oracular pronouncements were staged, given by Inca Tupac Amaro in "De virreyes" 1867: 280.

105. Patterson 1992: 69; Sarmiento de Gamboa 1572/1965: 196, 215, 235; 1572/1907/1999: 97; 1572/1967: 96–97 (where the sun statue is described as a man); Molina, el almagrista, n.d./1968: 74; Cabello Valboa 1586/1951: 290; Guamán Poma de Ayala 1613/1980: 118 [118]; 1613/1936: 118; Betanzos 1551–57/1996: 93; Cobo 1990: 105; Kubler 1944: 253; Santacruz Pachacuti Yamqui 1613/1993: 36; MacCormack 1990: 18; Pease 1991: 81.

106. Cabello Balboa 1586/1951: 290, 333–34, 357–58, 460; Sherbondy 1993: 346; Sarmiento de Gamboa 1572/1965: 248–49; 1572/1967: 49, 96–97, 126–29, 138, 140, 153–55; Pease 1991: 33–34; Rostworowski 1997: 69; Pizarro 1571/1978: 241–42; Sancho de la Hoz 1534/1938: 123–24, 159, 183; Cieza 1550/1985: 29; Betanzos 1551–57/1996: 131, 160; Guamán Poma de Ayala 1613/1980: 113 [113]. Specifically on the succession of Tupac Inca Yupanqui, see Pease 1991: 33–34; Rostworowski 1997: 69; Ziólkowski 1997: 245; Cabello Valboa 1586/1951: 290, 333–34, 460; Sarmiento de Gamboa 1572/1967: 49, 126–29, 138, 140; Pizarro 1571/1978: 241–42; Sancho de la Hoz 1534/1938: 123–24, 159, 183; Cieza 1550/1985: 29; Betanzos 1551–57/1996: 131. On the succession of Guayna Capac, see Guamán Poma de Ayala 1613/1980: 113 [113]; Guillén Guillén 1974: xvi; Cabello Valboa 1586/1951: 357–58; Sarmiento de Gamboa 1572/1967: 153–55; Cobo 1653/1959: 2:138–39; Betanzos 1551–57/1996: 160.

107. Classen 1993: 86.

108. Arriaga 1621/1968: 22–24, 50; Garcilaso de la Vega 1602/1963: 38.

109. Sarmiento de Gamboa 1572/1943: 163; 1572/1965: 263; Arriaga 1621/1968: 26; Albornoz 1967: 31 (on Catequil(a) [or (Apo)catiquil(lay)]); Rostworowski 1983: 56; 1997: 16–17; Santacruz Pachacuti Yamqui 1613/1993: 26v, 32v; Cabello Valboa 1586/1951: 383–84; Cobo 1653/1956: 2:273–75; Pizarro 1571/1978: 53; Ávila 1598/1966: 113–19; Murúa 2001: 142–45. On permission to marry, see Santacruz Pachacuti Yamqui 1613/1993: 32v; Pizarro 1571/1978: 53–54; Cobo 1653/1956: 2:250. See also Alonso Sagaseta de Ilurdoz 1990: 96; Lazaro Llantoy 1996: 17, 38 (on movable guacas); Hinojosa Cuba 1999: 35 (on the same). For an example of people moving to a new location and taking their guacas with them, see Cook and Cook, forthcoming: chap. 4

110. Santacruz Pachacuti Yamqui states that they were to take the image of Guanacaure with them (1613/1993: 35v). See Ziólkowski's exhaustive treatment (1997: especially 66–68, 234–35, 247, 254–55, 269, 392) on the confusion between the Sun and Guanacaure. María Rostworowski (1999a: 93) mentions both the statues of Manco Capac and Guanacaure.

111. Cabello Valboa 1586/1951: 371–76; Pizarro 1571/1978: 53–54.

112. Cieza 1550/1985: 30; Cabello Valboa 1586/1951: 306.

113. Molina, el almagrista, n.d./1968: 75; Pizarro 1571/1978: 53, 90–91; Estete 1542?/1987: 309–10; Mena 1534/1967: 96 (for the quote); Betanzos 1551–57/1996: 166–67.

114. On tectonic and climatic changes as causes of major shifts in socioeconomic and political organization in Peruvian history, see Zuidema 1989b: 46; Browman 1996: 230; Huertas 1992; Ortloff and Kolata 1993: 195, 204, 214.

115. Mena 1534/1967: 93; Estete 1542?/1987: 302.

116. As cited by Pease 1991: 77, 117; 1989: 15; 1965: 133–34, citing Anello Oliva 1598/1998: 65.

117. Pease 1968: especially 183–84; 1989b: 16; Castro-Klarén 1993: 167; Santacruz Pachacuti Yamqui 1613/1993: 8v, 38v–39; Spalding 1984: 63–65. On war, see Espinoza Soriano 1980a.

118. Titu Cusi 1570/1916: 86–88 (on Manco Inca); Kubler 1944: 269; Santacruz Pachacuti Yamqui 1613/1993: 15, 22v–23, 26v–27; Cobo 1653/1956: 2:256. On the symbolism of the conflict between the eagle and the snake, see Zuidema 1989b: 278. According to Ávila, the struggle between Tupac Inca Yupanqui and the Colla was won with the help of the god Pariacaca's son (1598/1966: 130–35; see also Patterson 1992: 117–18), that is, the Incas needed the help of the guacas to put down rebellions. Recall that Guayna Capac sent guacas from the Cajamarca, Guamachuco, and Chachapoyas people and their followers south during the Chiriguanos threat. Such contests continued after 1532. Several lifetimes after Pachacuti Inca Yupanqui's death, Manco Inca, while marching through Jauja, sought revenge on the Guancas for allying with the Spanish in 1533 to free themselves from their servitude under the Incas. Once Manco Inca had defeated them, he destroyed their sacred guaca, Huarivilca, and killed all its retainers and servants "so that they would understand that he [Manco Inca] was the lord." I might also speculate that the Inca institution of "guaca hostage," to the extent that it actually deprived local peoples of their god and sacred image, might be a calculated means to discourage rebellions, especially if the subject people were accustomed to take their guaca into battle as an amulet necessary for support and victory. See Polo de Ondegardo 1906: 210 (on the practice of taking guacas to war).

119. Betanzos 1551–57/1987: 32, 49–50 (on the confusion between the Sun and Viracocha); Sarmiento de Gamboa 1572/1965: especially 232–33; 1907/1972/1999: 97. The latter sometimes mentions the Sun and Viracocha or both. Inca Yupanqui acquired the title "Pachacuti" after he became the king. Because so many rulers had Yupanqui in their name and to prevent confusion, he is usually identified with the name Pachacuti Inca Yupanqui.

120. Pachacuti Inca Yupanqui also heard of a lord named Ruquiçapana of Hatun Colla who claimed to be the "son of the Sun." The Inca met and defeated Ruquiçapana in battle to prove that he still held the favor of his gods. See Betanzos 1551–57/1996: 93–95; 1551–57/1987: chap. 17; Albornoz 1967: 28; Sarmiento de Gamboa 1572/1965: chap. 26; Cabello Valboa 1586/1951: 299–300.

121. Although the report adds that "[those who survive and surrender] look for one hundred ways to kill him and flee, and for this the Inga had so little confidence in them" (Anónimo 1571/1995: 149). See also Ziólkowski 1991: 63–64; Titu Cusi

1570/1916: 128; Estete 1534–45/1938: 250 (on "well, you beat me, [so now] I will serve you").

122. Betanzos 1551–57/1987: 49–50; 1551–57/1996: 76; Sarmiento de Gamboa 1907/1972/1999: 91.

123. Viceroy Francisco de Toledo captured the guaca Punchao during an expedition to Vilcabamba. He recognized it as the last legitimizing guaca of the rulers of the Tawantinsuyu (Ziólkowski 1997: 375).

124. Sánchez Concha 1996: 289–91, discussing Santillán 1563–72/1968: 2, 104 (for the quote); Betanzos 1551–57/1987: 22–28, 49–50; 1996: 93; Sarmiento de Gamboa 1572/1965: 44–45, 228–34; Ziólkowski 1997: 159, 160, 162, 215–21, 265, 357, 375; Gose 1996: 23; Millones 1987: 88; Querejazu 1995: 44; Niles 1999: 72. Note that Betanzos portrays Uscovilca as a living person, whereas Sarmiento de Gamboa states emphatically that Uscovilca had been one of the founders of the Chancas and that by the time of this war he was dead and embalmed. Because he had been so ruthless and courageous in his lifetime, his followers carried his statue "with them in the wars and plundering. For that reason, although they took with them other warriors, always they attributed the deeds to the image of Uscouilca" (Sarmiento de Gamboa 1572/1965: 231). Therefore, Sarmiento portrays the struggle as between the forces of the ancestor-god of the Chancas, Uscovilca, and the Inca. See Abercrombie (1998: 269) for another example of a guaca giving victory over an enemy. See also Pease (1989b: 16–17), where he shows that whether in battle or in a certain wagering game, the Inca always won. On the same point, see MacCormack 1997a: 281.

125. Pease 1991: 82, 97; MacCormack 1990: 18–20. Indications that Huáscar was already losing his mandate appeared even before the troops were amassed.

126. Betanzos 1551–57/1996: 189, 207; Pizarro 1986: 54. This is similar to the ritual wars in the African Sudan mentioned by Pease (1991: 143–44).

127. Cabello Valboa 1586/1951: 446, 453–56, 458–59; Santacruz Pachacuti Yamqui 1613/1993: 39, 42; Sarmiento de Gamboa 1572/1967: 177, 180–82. Huáscar may have initially turned to Guanacaure, because it was a guaca associated with the *Hurin* (lower moiety) half of the elite and the founding Incas. Huáscar had repudiated his *Hanan* (upper moiety or half) birth and joined the ranks of the Hurin, by declaration. It is interesting to note that Pachacuti Inca Yupanqui had changed moieties, from Hurin to Hanan. It suggests to me that Huáscar's desired switch portended the pachacuti that he planned. On Pachacuti Inca Yupanqui's switch, see Rostworowski 1999a: 19.

128. Cieza 1550/1985: 213; Cabello Valboa 1586/1951: 459–61, 465; Sarmiento de Gamboa 1572/1965: 270; Santacruz Pachacuti Yamqui 1613/1993: especially 42; Pease 1965: 136; Rowe 1946: 209.

129. BNE/Ms. 2010, 1576.

130. Guamán Poma de Ayala (1613/1980: 370 [372]) says Santa rather than Túmbez.

131. Titu Cusi 1570/1916: 8, 13–14, 37, 77; Betanzos 1551–57/1987: 235, 255, 262, 264; 1996, 269; Cieza 1550/1985: 11; 1987: 146; Santacruz Pachacuti Yamqui 1613/1993: 43; Guamán Poma de Ayala 1613/1980: 381 [383], 378 [380]; Cabello

Valboa 1586/1951: 296–97; Sarmiento de Gamboa 1572/1967: 172; Guillén Guillén 1974: 142; Torero 1993: 229; MacCormack 1988: 981; Calancha 1638/1974–81: 1:232 (for the quote); Moreno Yáñez 1991: especially 532–37 (on Viracocha in Ecuador). The Spanish were still called viracochas by some rural groups in the seventeenth century (Duviols 1986: 21, 452; Polia Meconi 1999: 480), but the Inca elite fast realized that the bearded white men from the sea were mere mortals. See the text for further elaboration, and Kicza 1994: 395, 397 (on analogous reactions in North America and Mexico). Wilson (1995: 1) reminds readers that "Harris questions the legitimacy of such mythologies of 'white gods' and indicates that they are perhaps more likely to have been strategies of conquest promoted by the Spanish." Townsend also debunks the "white gods" stories for Mexico. I believe that the Inca elite did at first explain Pizarro and his company's arrival as the return of Viracocha. They quickly learned otherwise. Commoners, however, continued to equate the Spanish with powerful, godlike creatures and to call them Viracochas into the seventeenth century.

132. Or were these boys destined to be human sacrifices (*capac cochas*)? (Pizarro 1571/1978: 5–6). Note that Capac (*qhapaq*) cocha literally translates as "opulent presentation." It refers to a royal (capa[c]) sacrifice of goods and humans from all parts of the empire that were reassigned bureaucratically and dispatched. Humans (especially unstained and unblemished children and young women) were sacrificed by drowning or by being buried alive. Santacruz Pachacuti (1613/1993: 14v) writes that Capac Yupanqui invented this type of sacrifice. (See Salomon and Guevara-Gil 1994: 4; Besom 2000: chap. 1).

133. Guillén Guillén 1974: 7, 20, 62–63, 139; Cabello Valboa 1586/1951: 297, 466, 477–78; Cieza 1550/1985: chap. 5; Molina, el almagrista, n.d./1968: 73; 1943: 32; Betanzos 1551–57/1996: 269; Guamán Poma de Ayala 1613/1980: 380 [382]; Estete 1534–45/1938: 202; 1542?/1987: 303–4; Calancha 1638/1974–81: 1:248, 252; Pizarro 1571/1978: 32.

134. Guillén Guillén 1974: 78–80.

135. This is a simple enough message that the interpreters probably had no trouble with it.

136. Pease 1989a: 189; Titu Cusi 1570/1916: 11, 13, 30, 41; Guillén Guillén 1974: 80–82; Molina, el almagrista, n.d./1968: 65; Sancho de la Hoz 1534/1938: 157. Pizarro also began to confirm heirs to curacazgos. See the claims of don Simon Curi paucar in 1577 in ANP/DI, l. 39, c. 805, 1673, fol. 171v.

137. Cabello Valboa 1586/1951: 466, 469; Sarmiento de Gamboa 1572/1967: 187; Guamán Poma de Ayala 1613/1980: 370 [372]; Calancha 1638/1974–81: 1:247; Betanzos 1551–57/1987: 261–62, 264; 1551–57/1996: 260; Titu Cusi 1570/1916: 26; Guillén Guillén 1974: 141–42. Reports about these godlike visitors were soon contradicted (Betanzos 1551–57/1987: 264). Atahualpa's generals were only briefly fooled (Betanzos 1551–57/1996: 270; 1551–57/1987: 282). Guillén Guillén also reports that the impression that the Spaniards were gods changed quickly. After he was imprisoned, Atahualpa called the Spanish *zuncazapas*, or the bearded ones (*barbudos*) (1974: 141). See also Titu Cusi 1570/1916: 30–32, 45; Cieza 1987: 3:148.

138. I say "briefly" because documents exist suggesting that Atahualpa realized that the Spanish were not divine by the time he encountered them in Cajamarca (Guillén Guillén 1994: 271).

139. Calancha 1638/1974–81: 1:247–48; Mena 1534/1938: 318; Cieza 1550/1985: 11; Polo de Ondegardo 1561/1940: 154; Acosta 1590/1979: 309–10; Cobo 1653/1956: 2:256; Abercrombie 1998: 192; Guillén Guillén 1974: 20; Salomon and Urioste 1991: 41–42. To some degree, the idea of the Christians' supernatural favor persisted for years, as evidenced by Manco Inca, who already in revolt, sent word to Almagro that "he would come peacefully and he would worship him" (Molina, el almagrista, n.d./1968: 90). On Huáscar's consultations of oracles during the fratricidal war of succession against Atahualpa, see Gose 1996: especially 6. See also Polo de Ondegardo 1906: 226–27.

140. See also the same idea related to the Taqui Onqoy movement as a struggle between the Andean and the Christian gods. Ares Queija 1984: 461; Castro-Klarén 1993: 161, 163; Guillén Guillén 1984: 74, 79. See also Dammert Bellido 1997: 49.

141. Ziólkowski 1991b: 67; Santacruz Pachacuti Yamqui 1613/1993: 27v; Betanzos 1551–57/1996: 212–13; Titu Cusi 1570/1916: 72, 77; Urbano 1981: 84–85; Cook 1981; 1998.

142. Molina, el cuzqueño, 1574/1916: 98; MacCormack 1985a: 423, 434. Cock and Doyle remind readers that Pease wrote, in this regard, that "the sun of the Cuzco was defeated then in Cajamarca" (1979: 57; discussing Pease 1973: 27). See also Castelli 1998: 84.

143. Pease 1968: 183–84, 187; Castro-Klarén 1993: 159; Pizarro 1571/1978: 140; Titu Cusi 1570/1916: 67; Guillén Guillén 1974: 141–42. Betanzos's account states that native witnesses said that the fire on the straw roof of the church was put out by "a Spanish lady dressed all in white" (1551–57/1996: 290). In contrast, Titu Cusi reports that blacks extinguished the fire (1570/1916: 67). Zuidema 1989a: 250; Anónimo 1571/1995: 142, as cited by Regalado de Hurtado 1984a: 186; MacCormack 1985a: 423; Álvarez 1588/1998: 75. On population decline, see also McAlister 1987: especially 120–21.

144. Betanzos 1551–57/1996: 50, 95. Gisbert (1991: 358) also writes about the legendary conflict between the god Cons and Pachacama.

145. Cabello Valboa 1586/1951: 365, 378; Betanzos 1551–57/1996: 291; Álvarez 1588/1998: 75. Standard reasons for his defeat include (1) Manco's hesitation in pressing his initial advantage; (2) a ritual warfare calendar that dictated ceremonies every twenty days and launched attacks at full moon; (3) his untrained popular militia, levied largely from the ranks of the peasants; (4) the large numbers of soldiers regularly demobilized and dispatched to search for food or to cultivate; (5) weak armaments and strategy; and (6) Manco's lack of control over native allies of the Spanish who served as spies, domestic providers, and nurses (Kubler 1944: 262–64; Pizarro 1571/1978: 141). For other analyses of the military prowess of both Andeans and Spanish, see Guilmartin; Wachtel 1977: especially 25. On atisca, see Duviols 1984: 173, 217; Albornoz 1967: 37; Cabello Valboa 1586/1951, 378; Espinoza Soriano 1981: 116; Guillén Guillén 1984: 79. See also Taylor 1987: 16, 25–27 (on calpa).

146. Pizarro 1571/1978: 148; Betanzos 1551–57/1996: 207; Rostworowski 1997: 22; Estete 1542?/1987: 297; 1534–45/1938: 225; Mena 1534/1967: 91; 1534/1938: 317, 319; Guamán Poma de Ayala 1613/1980: 388 [390]. See also Sahlins 1983: 520 (on the same phenomenon among the Fiji). Analogously, Chan Chan was largely abandoned after the Inca conquest of the Chimu, with just squatter settlements in various parts during the Late Horizon. Thus, the end of urban life at Chan Chan predates the Spanish conquest (Daniel Sandweiss, personal communication, December 4, 2001).

147. Pizarro 1571/1978: especially 186–88; Cieza 1991: especially chap. 89, 380–83; Herrera y Tordesillas 1728 and 1601–15: Dec. 6, lib. 6, cap. 8, 138; Kubler 1944: 269. Ziólkowski (1997: 175, note 97) shows that victory in war confirmed the Sun's choice and favor even after 1532, citing the case of Manco Inca. Titu Cusi (1570/1916: 72) thought the Spanish might have succeeded in breaking Manco Inca's siege of Cuzco with the help of "Viracocha." These ideas persisted into the second half of the sixteenth century. See Rodriguez de Figueroa's (Pietschmann 1910: 110) account of his encounter with the renegade Inca Titu Cusi Yupanqui, who declared that he wanted to demonstrate his right to the natives' obedience "by force of arms and not by reasoning."

148. Ramos 1993: 151–52, 153 (on the "war of the guaca"). See also Castro-Klarén 1993: 161, 163, 167; Hinojosa Cuba 1999: 39; Millones 1998: 35.

149. Generosity was one of the hallmark virtues of a good god-king. Once Tupac Inca Yupanqui was accused of being stingy (*escasso*) during the celebration of Capac Rayme. So disturbed was he by this characterization that for the next year he ordered huge drinking beakers (*queros grandíssimos*) made. "And thus, for the next year, he gave drink three times a day, with fearfully big beakers, without allowing them to go to urinate etc." (Santacruz Pachacuti Yamqui 1613/1993: 29).

150. Pease 1989a: 180; MacCormack 1991: 301, 308; Gose 1996: especially 7.

151. Garcilaso de la Vega 1942: 2:141.

152. Garcilaso de la Vega 1942: 2:145 (for the long quote); Valera 1596/1879: 172–73; Varón Gabai 1980: 40; Bandera 1557/1968: 494 (for the last quote). See also Abercrombie (1998: 217) on the relation of don Pedro Ochatoma, cacique of the town of Puna Quiguar, who believed that as a result of the Spanish colonization he was "of" (belonged to) the Christian god.

153. Quipucamayocs 1542–44/1920: 19; Betanzos 1551–57/1996: 121, 128, 131; Rostworowski 1997: 73–74; Sarmiento de Gamboa 1572/1967: 82.

154. Quipucamayocs 1542–44/1920: 20; Sarmiento de Gamboa 1572/1965: 228–29; Cabello Valboa 1586/1951: 339. For a catalog of revolts, see Cabello Valboa 1586/1951: 290, 300, 301, 314, 331, 335, 338, 365.

155. Anderson 1992: 6, 19.

156. For examples of the multiple devotions that multiple gods implied, see Polia Meconi 1999: 209 (for 1592–94 Cuzco and Vilcas), 233 (for 1599 Huamanga), 242 (for 1601 Cuzco), 275 (for 1609 Lima), 285 (for 1609 Chuquiabo), 292, 305 (for 1611 Lima), 328–29 (for 1613 Guancavelica), 369 (for 1614 central Andes), 405 (for 1617 Guaylas), 418, 422 (for 1618 Cajatambo), 444 (for 1620 Tambo, Acobamba, and Huayllay), 479 (for 1639–40 Cuzco), 488 (for 1654 Huarochirí), 514 (for 1664–66 Guamanga).

157. Patterson 1992: 104. An example of such propaganda is related by Cieza, who writes that the Incas did "good works . . . not consenting that they be harassed or that they be charged excessive tribute or that other outrages be done to them" (1550/1985: 35). "El Niño" refers to the cold current of ocean water that rises in the south and travels along the western coast of South America about Christmastime, hence it is named for the Christ child. It can bring unusual rains or drought to sections of the desert coast, and snow or drought to the highlands.

158. On the failure to achieve complete integration of all subject peoples, see Rostworowski 1993b: 214; Caillavet 2000: 168–69, 172 (on Ecuador).

159. MacCormack 1991; Gibson 1969: 99; Millones 1992: 210; Romero 1916: xxv. Patterson (1991: 123) states that the hegemony that existed at the end of Guayna Capac's reign collapsed within ten years.

160. Guayna Capac built the sacred center of Tumibamba to resemble Cuzco. He built palaces, one for his mother in the place where he was born. Inside he placed chaquira and a statue. He also built temples to the Sun, Ticiviracocha Pachacamac, and Thunder. The plaza had a judgment seat (ushnu or uzno) where chicha was offered to the Sun (Cabello Valboa 1586/1951: 364–65). See also Morris 1973: especially 130–35 (on Huánuco Pampa); Hyslop 1985 (on Incahuasi). Ziólkowski (1997: 164, 300–301) suggests that regional sacred centers such as Tomebamba and the others mentioned in Chapter 2 served as additional places for the Inca to communicate with the gods and places of escape from the meddling, prying, and limiting activities of other factions of the Cuzco elite.

161. Cabello Valboa 1586/1951: 374, 394; Pease 1989b: 14; Santacruz Pachacuti Yamqui 1613/1993: 14 (on Mayta Capac), 33; Regalado de Hurtado 1993: 46.

162. Duviols 1974–76: 278, 284; Polia Meconi 1999: 224, 277, 390, 468, 516.

163. MacCormack 1990: 6; Demarest 1992a: 8. Scattered references suggest that a ruler's power was also reflected in his age, health, and vigor. Cobo, for example, states that "as a principal and respected man that one had been while his vigor and virility lasted, upon being old, they paid little heed to him for the rest of his life" (1653/1956: 2:163). Age and health may also have been part of the determination of whether or not a candidate for office was apt (Betanzos 1551–57/1996: 73). Such considerations tie into the idea that the king must be destroyed when he becomes an imperfect link between humans and the gods. Therefore, a ruler cannot be allowed to become ill or senile, lest his diminished vigor be reflected in society.

164. Conrad and Demarest 1984: especially 91, 120, 122, 125. See also Ramírez 1996: especially chap. 3.

CHAPTER 4

1. Wachtel 1977.

2. Anónimo 1571/1995: 125. Some of the local sources used for this chapter are relatively late (mid-seventeenth century). Therefore, it is not always possible to identify the paramount (*hatun*) curaca from subordinates who over time assumed and acquired the title and role. My generalizations apply most precisely to the paramount lord and to a lesser extent to other native officials lower on the religio-political hierarchical ladder.

3. On individuals, see Rostworowski 1981–82; 1982b; Cuneo-Vidal 1977: 1: 332–36; 1919; Salomon 1990; Glave 1989a, 1989b; Alva Mariñas; Rivera; Ramírez 2001b. On curacas in one region, see Millones 1984; Varón Gabai 1980; Zevallos Quiñones 1989, 1992; Diez Hurtado 1988; Espinoza Soriano 1980b; Fernández Villegas; Assadourin 1983; Rostworowski 1978c; Ravines 1972; Rossell Castro 1963. On succession, see Rostworowski 1961; Ramírez 1998; Powers 1998. On insignia, see Martínez Cereceda 1988, 1995. On wealth, see Cock 1986; Pease 1988; Powers 1991; Ramírez 1998. On power, see Wachtel 1977: 80; Ramírez 1987, 2001b; Castro and Ortega Morejón 1558/1968: 473; Gonçalez Holguin 1608/1952: 55 (regarding the *hatun rimak curaca*, literally, he who has the voice for others [*el que tiene la voz de todos*]). See also Spalding 1981, 1991. See also Assadourian 1983.

4. The last of the traditional or old-style curacas were dying off by the 1560s and 1570s on the Peruvian north coast (Ramírez 1987).

5. As representative of his people, see Álvarez 1588/1998: 77; on allocation of labor and resources, see Cock 1986; Pease 1988: especially 92–104; Spalding 1981: especially 12, 19; Diez Hurtado 1988: especially 14–15, 25, 29; Murra 1968: especially 130–134; Netherly 1977: 126, 183, 208; Powers 1995. On redistribution and ties to the state, see Varón Gabai 1980: 28, 93. On insufficiency to rule, see Diez Hurtado 1988: 27; Pease 1990a: 17; Ramírez 1996; Rostworowski 1961. On "good government," see Betanzos 1551–57/1987: 74, 150; Ramírez 1987. On hospitality, see Rostworowski 1978b: 97.

6. Cult traditions were labeled "idolatry" by the Spanish. By the seventeenth century, many distinguished "idolatry" from "witchcraft" (*hechicería*). See Flores Espinoza 1991 (for an example of such a distinction).

7. Powers 1997; Guamán Poma de Ayala 1613/1980.

8. Spalding 1981: 8; Rostworowski 1998; Sánchez 1991a: ii, 7–8, 15; Álvarez 1588/1998: 6–7.

9. Guibovich Perez 1993: 182; 1990: especially 23–35; Urbano 1993: 23, 27; Acosta 1987: especially 183; Sánchez 1991b. On the biases and problems inherent in the use of hechicería records, see Gareis 1989: especially 64–65; 1993.

10. AAC/Quejas 29.17, LXVIII, 2, 26 (for 1742); García Cabrera 1994: 12–13; MacCormack 1985a: 441; Millones 1984: 135–36.

11. Álvarez 1588/1998: 30, 36, 42–43, 83, 86, 109–10. On the difficulty of investigative reporting for the peoples of the far north, see Landázuri 1993: 299 (who cites Bishop Peña y Montenegro in 1663 [1668/1985: 173]). See also Polia Meconi 1999: especially 279, 319, 330, 423, 446; Agustinos ca. 1550/1865/1964: 12–13.

12. See, for example, the index of Duviols 1986.

13. Anello Oliva 1598/1998: especially 162–70. For Atacama, see Castro 1993: 347–66. For a summary of traditional religious practices in Charcas (that I do not cover fully here) from 1560–1620, see Barnadas 1993.

14. Pizarro 1571/1978: 19. In pre-Hispanic times, the worship of the latter was extensive. Cieza (1550/1985: 56, 198) lists provincial Temples of the Sun at Carangue, Tomebamba, Quito, Manta, Vilcas, Jauja, Bonbón, Cajamarca, Guancabamba, Latacunga, Hatuncolla, Ayaviri, Chucuito, Paria, Riobamba, Hatun

Cañar, and Túmbez. See also Landázuri 1993: 294–95, citing Juan de Velasco 1789/1978: 143. Huertas (1998) also notes a sun temple at Guamanga.

15. The 1573 manuscript on Pachacamac, published by Rostworowski (1573/1999: 52, 54, 105, 192–93, 211, 213–15, 219, 229–30), also indicates that the people of the coast near Lima were not catechized systematically until after 1550–51. This suggests that more isolated native peoples were not baptized as Christians until much later; they thus were able to practice their ancestral religion much longer than those in core and high-contact areas. For coastal peoples, see Cabero 1906: 183; Calancha 1638/1974–81: 1242–43; Hart 1983: 190; Rubiños y Andrade 1782/1936: 300. See also Lizarraga 1604/1907: 290–91. On ancestor worship in Manta (Ecuador), see Landázuri 1993: 289–91.

16. Ruiz de Arze 1543/1933: 357; Álvarez 1588/1998: 17–18. See also Rubiños y Andrade 1782/1936: 292–93.

17. Agustinos ca. 1550/1865/1964: 15–17, 22. Some scholars have equated Ataguju, Sagad zabra, and Vaungrabrad to the Christian trinity. I suspect that the original story explained the existence of the nobles and the commoners. On the interpretation of Andean religion in Christian terms, see Landázuri 1993: 276, 282, 301; Griffiths 1996: chap. 1. Landázuri writes that the Andeans had no abstract conception of a god, especially a creator god. There was, instead, a multilayered hierarchy of gods: major, minor, and personal. See also Rostworowski 1983: 9.

18. Agustinos ca. 1550/1865/1964: 19, 21, 23–27.

19. Agustinos ca. 1550/1865/1964: 13, 27–30, 32, 49.

20. Álvarez 1588/1998: 8, 12, 14, 21, 24, 27.

21. Álvarez 1588/1998: 74–75, 77–85, 103. See also Anello Oliva 1598/1998: 162–70. Duviols (1986: 61) gives another example of people taking their idols with them when they moved. On the thunder god and its transformation, see Silverblatt 1988b.

22. Romero 1918: 181–82, 189, 192.

23. Romero 1918: 183–85.

24. Romero 1918: 184–85, 188; Saito 1997: 58 (on mummies as guacas). Ancestor worship is ubiquitous in the Andes. See, for example, Polia Meconi 1999: 305, 321, 323, 329, 332, 369, 377, 385–88, 409, 418, 440–42, 471, 504, 506, 508–9, 519, 539–40.

25. On Fray Francisco, see Anello Oliva 1598/1998: 167.

26. Hernández Príncipe 1621–22/1923: 25, 52–53.

27. The three manifestations are suspiciously analogous to Christian creed.

28. Hernández Príncipe 1621–22/1923: 26, 29–30; Huertas 1978: 3; Pizarro 1571/1978: 73.

29. See also Polia Meconi 1999: 324 (for the Chincha[y]cocha in 1613, where it refers to a place). The term "pacarina" is used as the place where the founder emerges or originates. Crisóbal de Albornoz, the author of the "Instruccion para descubrir todas las guacas del Piru," which Duviols dates as late sixteenth century, defines *pacariscas* as "creating ancestor" or "criadores de donde descienden" (Albornoz 1967: 37). The Jesuits use the term "pacarina" in 1601 to refer to a place in Cuzco (Polia Meconi 1999: 245). Some years later (in 1613) they report that the

bodies of the ancestors among the Chincha[y]cocha were called pacarinas (Polia Meconi 1999: 324). In two later letters, the term refers to both person and place (Polia Meconi 1999: 345, for the Chincha[y]cocha in 1614) or is used ambiguously for a people who lived near Huánuco between 1632 and 1634 (Polia Meconi 1999: 463). If it refers to the ancestral founder and the place where he originated, the lakes mentioned earlier could logically represent the place of emergence, and most probably an ancestor, both of which might have shared a common name. Doyle (1988) also believes that the term refers to the founding ancestor and the place of emergence. Salomon equates pacarina or *paqarisqa* with "dawning place" (1987b: 224). On the pacarina of northern groups, see Landázuri 1993: 284. See also Ramírez 2002.

30. On the word *camachico*, see Doyle 1988: 119; Gonçalez Holguin 1608/1952: 46.

31. Duviols 1986: 466–67.

32. The religious specialists mentioned included some who spoke to the malquis and others who interpreted dreams, divined, or made chicha. On types of religious specialists in the central Andes, see Polia Meconi 1999: 425–26 (for 1618).

33. Hernández Príncipe 1621–22/1923: 51, 54, 57; Duviols 1986: 151, 464–65, 470–71; Abercrombie 1998; Saignes 1999: 122; ALP/1691, c. 35, exp. 16, fol. 46. See AGI/AQ, 23, nos. 5–5a, 1579–83, fol. 24 (on Puento); Polia Meconi 1996: 237 (on Barranca); Espinoza Soriano 1969a: 57 (on Jauja in 1585), based on ANP/DI, l. 13, c. 622 (1598). On separate origins, see Duviols's 1983 study of myths recorded by the Jesuits; Calancha 1638/1974–81: especially 388–89; Zuidema (1973b: 17). Hamilton (1978: 34) believes that a hierarchical division existed among parcialidades, based upon the tracing of ancestors. The oldest, associated with the region's settlers and conquerors, were the most prestigious and central. I believe size was also a criterion for ranking and genealogical subordination. It is easy then to generalize that the hierarchy of native authorities is correlated at each level with the prestige and power rankings of their founding gods (Sánchez Farfán 1981: 151). Note that curacas and hechiceros came from the same line, which suggests their original convergence. For other examples of a line of indigenous priests, see Polia Meconi 1999: 285, 305. See also D'Altroy (1987: 92), who writes that his reconstruction of Guanca succession indicates that Inca-appointed and recognized offices were inherited lineally during the sixteenth century. Karen Spalding (1991: 403) writes that before the Inca, the most "valient" (*valiente*) succeeded each other as chief. Under the Incas, chieftainships became hereditary.

34. Hernández Príncipe 1621–22/1923: 51–53. See also Flores and Gutierrez 1992: 204, citing a Jesuit letter from 1621. For similar descriptions, see Polia Meconi 1999: 262 (of a guaca sitting on his stool [tiana] in the province of Parinacocha in 1606), 419 (of the mummies of curacas in the provinces of Ocros and Lampas [Corregimiento de Cajatambo] in 1618).

35. Hernández Príncipe 1621–22/1923: 26–27, 61–63; Hinojosa Cuba 1999: 33.

36. Hernández Príncipe 1621–22/1923: 28, 34, 36–37, 39, 41, 65. The fact that each ayllu had its own guaca, ceremonies, and customs is also evident in the Jesuit reports. See, for example, Polia Meconi 1999: 223 (for the Aimaraes of 1599),

271 (for the natives of Chorrillo [distrito de Çiçicaya] in 1609), 405 (for the Guaylas of 1617), 473 (for the Yanaguares of 1639 Cuzco), 507 (for the 1664–66 Cajatambos), 516 (for the population of Cuzco in 1664–66), 539 (for the Pueblo of San Miguel de Aquia in 1675). On the multi-ayllu worship of an idol or god, see also the previous discussion of the worship of Llaiguen.

37. Duviols 1986: 504–7. See also Viceroy Esquilache's 1619 summary report, where he, too, quantifies the extirpators' activities, listing how many malicious witches (*brujos malefiros*), idols, and mummified bodies they encountered and suppressed or punished (Pease 1968–69; Duviols 1967a: 87–100).

38. Earlier examples exist. The first comes from Atacama. Because I have not seen the primary source itself, only an article based on it, it will not be used here. See Castro 1993. The second, references to which appear in the notes, is not presented because Europeans reported their observations.

39. Sánchez 1991a: 14, 55, 58, 68, 84–85 (for the year 1662), 133, 134 (for the year 1665), 136 (from AAT/l. 1, exp. 7, 1665; AAL/Hechicerías, l. 2, exp. 7, 1647, 6–7 [for 1647]).

40. Trimborn 1979: 10; Sánchez 1991a: 136; García Cabrera 1994: 199 (for 1640s), 205. See also the previous note.

41. There are also a few extant cases from the second decade of the seventeenth century in Duviols (1986). See also the documents published by Polia Meconi (1999) on the Cajatambo.

42. Duviols 1986: 224. *Dueño* is best translated as "creator or maker" in this context, not the literal "owner." See Ramírez 2002.

43. Duviols 1986: 79, 89, 97, 172, 224, 280, 301, 346, 359. Lubiac's name suggests that it represented the thunder god. Griffiths (1996: 13) highlights the fact that guacas responded to Christianity's threat by changing their form and altering their behavior.

44. Duviols 1986: 52, 224. See also García Cabrera 1994: 199; Polia Meconi 1999: 306 (for a report of an eight-hundred-year-old mummy), 419 (for a report of one that was two or three centuries old). Acosta (1590/1979, lib. 5, cap. 6, 226) mentions that mummies of kings and lords were conserved for more than two hundred years.

45. Duviols 1986: 327, 329, 333–46, 349–50, 352, 380. For other examples, see Duviols 1986: 155, 301, 382–84, 396–97, 414 (for the middle of the seventeenth century), 444, 448 (for 1617). See also Polia Meconi 1999: 294 (for a guaca that was the descendant of indigenous leaders in the Lima area in 1610).

46. Duviols 1986: 333–34 (for the quote), 380. See also Polia Meconi 1999: 511.

47. Duviols 1986: 169–70 (for the quote), 248, 472. For more on local human sacrifice, see Doyle 1988: 128, note 12; Cock Carrasco 1980: 158; Duviols 1976a; Zuidema 1977: 231–33; 1979: 339–42; Santacruz Pachacuti Yamqui 1613/1993: 10, 14v.

48. Duviols 1986: 72, 77–78, 80, 89, 97, 99, 121, 151, 159–60, 189, 201, 212, 220, 226, 238, 241, 243, 245, 265–66, 269, 274, 466, 480. Note that the celestials are not a presence in the cases published by García Cabrera in 1994 either. Millones (1998: 36) writes that neither the Sun, Viracocha, nor Illapa is mentioned in the records of the Taqui Onqoy movement as part of the revitalized confederation of

ethnic group guacas that promised to defeat the Christian god. See also Castro and Ortega Morejón (1558/1968: 478, 488) for 1558 Chincha, where they report that these coastal peoples did not worship the Sun. In a later case from Chancay, the local lord had only vague notions of god: "and asking him who was god he responded that the sky and the earth" (AAL/Hechicerías, l. 7, no. 13, 1676, fol. 2 of the second series of numbers). The people in the mountain hinterland of Lima in 1571 (Polia Meconi 1999: 198–99) and the Chupas in 1614 (Duviols 1966: 501, 504) also mention the celestials, in addition to their ancestors, in their confessions.

49. AAL/Hechicerías, l. 3, exp. 9, 1656, fols. 3–3v; l. 7, exp. 14, 1677, fols. 1v-2, 10v–12v, 34–34v, 38, 40v–41, 44v; Polia Meconi 1999: 252; Duviols 1986: 89, 99, 151, 159, 189, 212, 220, 226, 238, 241, 243, 245. Landázuri (1993: 288–89, 296) states that the Sun was an Inca imposition onto the pantheon of the peoples of what is today Ecuador. See also Cock Carrasco and Doyle 1979: especially 55, 58–63. Other exceptions are reported in the Jesuit annual letters published by Polia Meconi 1999: 227, 233–34, 238, 247, 266, 283, 355, 376, 405, 520, 541.

50. García Cabrera 1994: 131 (for 1623), 135, 503, 505, 508, 516, 521, 526–27, 536.

51. Hernández Príncipe 1621–22/1923: 29–30, 39, 58, 66; Duviols 1986: 169 (for the quote). On the worship of the Sun by provincial people, see Cock Carrasco and Doyle 1979: especially 55–56. See also Negro 1996: 132; Huertas 1981: 60. This principle also holds for ranking of a person or group on the social structure: the closer to the Inca/god, the higher the status.

52. For example, Romero 1918; Agustinos ca. 1550/1865/1964.

53. Mills (1997: 46) describes this process as lohomorphosis.

54. Duviols 1972: 382, 387–88; 1974–76: 278, 288–89 (for the 1614 Chinchaycocha); 1986: 56–60 (for the quote), 89, 112–14, 128, 169, 210–11 (for the quote) (I say "his or her" because it is not clear whether the mentioned gods were a brother-sister pair or two men who both had children once settled down), 218, 227, 247 (for masks that represent persons and malquis), 271, 279, 313; Doyle 1988: 64, 66; Villagómez 1649/1919: 144–45. See also Cock Carrasco and Doyle 1979: especially 60–61, 70; Saignes 1999: 82, 112. Zuidema observes that Hernández Príncipe used the term "guaca" for the ancestors of the local native elite, "guaca malqui" for those of an intermediate class, and "malqui" for the forebears of commoners. He also observes that "huaca refers to all sacred stones or religious places constructed of stone, and mallqui means [ancestor] mummies." He speculates, in explanation, that only the elite could enumerate ancestors so far back (*tan lejanos*), that they had had time to turn to stone. But, he continues, commoners could worship stone guacas "without these being considered their direct ancestors" (1989b: 120–21). Polia Meconi (1999: 252) relates a case where natives worshipped at a tomb of a principal on a high mountain peak in 1604 near Cuzco. See Polia Meconi 1996: 214 (on the god Xamuna); Molina, el cuzqueño, 1574/1916: vi (for the date it was written), 6 (Molina says, "And they say that the first who was born in that place became stones").

55. Hernández Príncipe 1621–22/1923: 66; Duviols 1972: 382, 387; 1986: 59, 197 (for the quote); Huertas 1978: 3; AAL/Hechicerías, l. 7, exp. 14, 1677, fol. 42; Gose 1995: 205–7. See also Polia Meconi 1999: 306 (for the central Andes in 1611).

Bodies and their representations were also moved to high mountain peaks for ease of visibility for sacrifice and recall, difficulty of access, and dryness of climate that would preserve the remains. This move shifted the association from mummified body or its representation to place. In 1662 a fiscal of the archbishopric reported that native women sang as they danced, "extolling the men for their descendants or mountains or heights . . . saying that they were born of said mountains or heights" (García Cabrera 1994: 459, citing AAL/Hechicerías, l. 4, exp. 9, 1662). Hastorf (1993: 50–51) reports that ancestors return to reside with the local mountain deity (*wamani*) and to act as mediators between the living and their spiritual hosts. This is confirmed in a 1677 court case in which guancas are identified as once having been soldiers and malquis who helped descendants communicate with the mountains (AAL/Hechicerías, l. 7, exp. 14, 1677, fols. 35v, 36v, 41). Santacruz Pachacuti Yupanqui (1613/1993: 15–15v) relates how Ttonapa Uihinquira exiled all the guacas and idols to the snow-capped mountains. See also Duviols 1977b: 373. On mountaintop worship among the people of Atacama in the seventeenth century, see Castro 1993: especially 355. On the same in the eighteenth century, see Cook and Cook, forthcoming: chap. 10.

56. Duviols 1986: lxiv (citing a criminal case against Pedro de la Cruz, alias Quiñones, in the AAL), 52–53; Arriaga 1621: 6; Abercrombie; Bauer 1992: 101 (for Paururo, south of Cuzco); personal interviews, Racthie, Cuzco 1997. Salles-Reese (1997: 12) reports that Aymara speakers, following long-standing custom, refer to snowy peaks as grandparents (*achachilas*), believing that they are vigilant deities who protect their homes. See Zuidema 1989a: 261 (on how ancestors became identified with a locality through the people who lived there and worshipped them).

57. Mills (1997: 210) agrees.

58. Hernández Príncipe 1621–22/1923: 26–27, 51 (for the quote); Duviols 1986: 149, 464 (for 1621), 499; Doyle 1988: 66; AAL/Hechicerías, l. 7, exp. 14, 1677, fol. 41; Arriaga 1621/1968: 204–5; Huertas 1978: 6; Ferrero and Iwasaki Cauti 1984: 79. On "suffering god [*dios penante*]," also see Landázuri 1993: 291.

59. ANB/EC 1605, E. 2, fol. 62; Guamán Poma de Ayala 1613/1980: 65 [65]–66 [66]; Sarmiento de Gamboa 1572/1967: 146, 149; D'Altroy 1987: 95; Anónimo 1571/1995: 126; Rostworowski 1981–82: 108–9; Cieza 1985: 7; Cabello Valboa 1586/1951: 356; ANP/DI, l. 1, c. 7, 1566, fols. 10–10v, 12; Ramírez 1995a: 249, 253; 1998. Valient curacas in Chicama are given *camarico* or labor (*yndios de servicio*) (Guamán Poma de Ayala 1613/1980: 870 [884]).

60. Polia Meconi 1996: 234, 236; 1999: 198–99, 235, 339, 357; Calancha 1638/1972: 231–32, cited by Polia Meconi and Chavéz Hualpa 1994: 37–38; Pease 1968–69: 90; AAL/Hechicerías, l. 2, exp. 4, 1646, fol. 171; l. 2, exp. 7, 1647, fol. 4; l. 3, exp. 9, 1656, fols. 14, 15v; Polo de Ondegardo 1559/1916: 31–34; 1906: 198, 210–11, 219, 221–22; Duviols 1974–76: 278, 281–82 (for descriptions of such a ceremony among the Chinchaycochas [Junin] in 1614), 288; 1986: 55, 62–63, 66; Martínez Cereceda 1995: 48, 50; Cobo 1653/1956–64: 2:225 (for the quote); Doyle 1988: 137–38, 142–43, 201, 255–57; Zuidema 1973b: 17 (for a description of such a ceremony among the 1622 Recuay); Álvarez 1588/1998: 92. For other instances of divination in a variety of forms, for a number of reasons, see Polia Meconi 1999: 311–12 (for the Juli in 1611), 367, 369 (for the Checras in 1614),

388, 390 (for the people of Barranca and Cajatambo in 1617), 417 (for the Guaylas in 1618), 431 (for the Conchucos in 1618), 521 (for those of Juli between 1664 and 1666); Romero 1918: 194; Martínez Cereceda 1995: 48, 50. On elections of local lords, see Taylor 1987: 131–35; Sternfeld 2000: 10; Rostworowski 1961: 99; Hart 1983: 143–44; Valcarcel 1949; BNP/A379, 1596, fol. 47v. This last manuscript also contains a hint that old ceremonies continued into the 1580s and 1590s. See folio 33v. For evidence that the Huarochirí also practiced divination, see, for example, Taylor 1987: 91; Sternfeld 2000: 23 (on "divinely wise men" [*amawtakuna adivinos*] that "practice sorcery" [*hacen sortiligios*].

61. The stool of office could be a chair, if a tiana was not available. ALL/Pra-120, 1792–98, fol. 2 (for 1792 Asangáro); Espinoza Soriano 1969a: 17.

62. Loaiza 1998; Martínez Cereceda 1995: 120–31; Duviols 1986: 67, 174, 180, 189, 196, 219–20, 237, 239, 242, 272, 280, 352, 380, 387. The souls of the ancestors were sometimes referred to as "shadows." Rostworowski 1998: 155, citing Taylor 1987: 21, 24–25; Sternfeld 2000: 23, citing Taylor 1987: 244–45 (on the word *kamasqakuna*: "those animated by those who give vital force"). For continuities in late twentieth-century Bolivia, see Rivière 1995: 118, 120, 122.

63. AAL/Hechicerías, l. 7, no. 13, 1676, fol. 7v; Lumbreras 1985: 20; Torero 1990: especially 250–51; Duviols 1978: 133–34; 1986: 143, 361. See Romero (1918: 188) regarding the relationship between being seated on a tiana and then being worshipped, in this case referring to twins. For recent examples of the same phenomenon, see Rivière 1995: 122.

64. Saignes 1987: 155, 157; 1995: 191 (on the curaca as a divine ruler); 1999: 62; Martínez Cereceda 1982: 145–46; 1988: 62; 1995: 37, 180; MacCormack 1993: 112; Hernández Astete 1998; BNP/A379, 14-July-1596; B1087, 4-March-1629, fol. 29. See also Rivière 1995: 121.

65. Anónimo 1571/1995: 126–27; Pease 1990a: 19; Lumbreras 1985: 30 (on the Chimu Capac as god); Millones 1987: 81, 83 (on the divine character of local rulers); Krapovickas 1978: 77 (quoting a letter from the Audiencia de Charcas, dated June 10, 1566, in Levillier 1921–22: 2:437–56. I, however, upon reading this letter could not find this exact quote). See also BNE/Ms. 19569, n.d., fol. 28, which Murra thinks may have been written by Polo de Ondegardo; Río 1990: 85 (for the quote); Pease 1992a: 21; Las Casas 1555/1948: 29, 31, 73, 51, 72–73; Martínez Cereceda 1982: especially 230–36; BNP/B1945, 1602, fols. 27–27v (among the Chonos of the "province" of Daule of Guayaquil); A371, 1594, fols. 11–11v, 34v (for Soras in pre-Hispanic times); ANP/DI 3, c. 19, 1574, fol. 40 (for the time of Tupac Inca Yupanqui); ART/CoP, l. 280, exp. 3583, 9-August-1568 (for Jequetepeque); García Cabrera 1994: 502; Trimborn 1979: 35, citing Cieza 1553/1984: 205 (on 1547 Jayanca); AGI/AL 128, fol. 6v (for a description of the retinue of the wife of a high lord of Cajamarca); Ramírez 1987; 2002 (on "old-style" curacas as heirs of creator ancestors); Cieza 1864/1964: 239, 242; Polia Meconi 1999: 224 (on the curaca as wife-giver in 1599); AGI/AL 128, 2-June-1587, fol. 13v; ANB/EC 1605, exp. 2, fol. 93. See Sahlins for the Fijian belief that chiefs were gods (1983: 520). The ethnographer Gilles Rivière (1997) reports that the authorities of communities in the south of Oruro become possessed by the energy of their ancestral founders, giving them shamanistic powers, including the ability to speak to the gods. The continuities

between Oruro in the late twentieth century and the Andes in general in the sixteenth and seventeenth centuries are obvious.

66. ANB/EC 1605, exp. 2, fol. 23 (for 1602); EC 1662, exp. 11, fol. 5 (for 1662 Chayanta [Charcas]); EC 1673, exp. 26, fol. 33 (for 1667); EC 1686, exp. 34, fol. 9v (for 1658 Larecaja); ALL/Pra-36, caja 449, 1715, fol. 13; ALL/LB-581, caja 269, fol. 4v (for 1747 Huancane [Paucarcolla]), 17v (for 1790), 30; BNP/A379, 1596, fols. 30v (for 1586 for the people of Coto in the province of the Omasuyus), 59; B1087, 1629, fol. 29v; ADCuzco/CoO, l. 17, no. 348, c. 7, 1664, fol. 35; ANP/DI 3, c. 19, 1574, fol. 40v (for the Recuay); DI 31, c. 622, 1597, fol. 83 (for the pre-Hispanic Hurin Guaylas); Cieza 1864/1964: 239; Salomon 1990: 57 (for Catocollao, Ecuador, in 1606); Rivera and Platt 1978: 120 (for the Pacajes in 1592); Cobo 1653/1956–64: 2:138, 204; Arriaga 1621/1968: 212, 214; Saignes 1999: 81. A variation on this form of mochar is found in Polia Meconi (1999) among the population of Aimaraes in 1599. He describes the gesture of worship: "They who adored the huaca, in the ancient way, put their left hand on their head and with the right in front of their face and toward the place where the huaca was, making a certain sound with their lips and offering whatever they carried; others pulled out their eyebrows and prostrated themselves on the floor" (223). See also pp. 227, 247, 259, 283, and 358.

67. Martínez Cereceda (1982: 138–40) suggests that the expulsion of air and the subsequent smacking sound made by the lips in the traditional act of worship may represent the exchange of life force or vital energy. See Sternfeld 2000: 20; Taylor 1987: 87, 341; Molina, el almagrista, n.d./1968: 76; Sancho de la Hoz 1534/1938: 158; Cieza 1864/1964: 239; AGI/AL 120, 1572, fols. 67, 68v, 69v–70 (quoted in Ruiz de Pardo 2000: appendix, 20–27); AL 128, 1587, fols. 32–32v, 33v, 34v (for the quote); Dammert Bellido 1997: 124 (for the quote); Espinoza Soriano 1976: 253, 280. See also BNP/A635, 1557, fols. 14, 15v, 16v, 18v, 20v, 22; Martínez Cereceda 1988: 70; Hernández Astete 1998: 103, 109 (on the coya as a Huaca). Note that the characterization of the curaca in this chapter and Chapter 5 also applied to local chiefs in the Amazon region (Wright and Carneiro da Cunha 1999: 345).

68. Sánchez 1991a: 20; Spalding 1981: 14–15; Sánchez Farfán 1981: 151. See also Huertas 1981: 20, 24, 28; Polia Meconi 1996: 252, especially note 77; Duviols 1986: xxviii; 1972: 364.

69. AAL/Hechicerías, l. 2, exp. 4, 1646, fol. 35v; Duviols 1972: 364, 380 (on the local lord as cult leader); 1977b: 247–48; 1986: 325, 348; Saignes 1987: 154–55; García Cabrera 1994: 387–91, 510; Romero 1918: 194; Sánchez 1991a: 135–42; Espinoza Soriano 1981: 116, 118; Spaulding 1981; Mills 1997: 31; Gose 1995: 217; Vargas Ugarte 1951–54: 21–22, 254, 340; Pease 1968–69: 83 (for 1619); Polia Meconi 1999: 224 (for the 1599 Aimaraes and quote), 327 (for the 1613 Guancavelicas); Calancha 1638/1974–81: 1367. The malquis gave permission to participate in Christian celebrations. See also Polia Meconi 1996: 223–24 (for the Chinchaycochas in 1611–13).

70. AAL/II-12b, fols. 3v–4, as cited by Doyle 1988: 179; Duviols 1986: 56, 97, 108, 138, 145 (for the quote), 155, 164, 176, 180, 189, 194, 196, 200, 205, 212, 219, 230, 235, 237, 240, 244, 248, 267–68 (for the quote), 273, 277, 281, 294, 297, 299, 325 (for the quote), 334; Vargas Ugarte 1951–54: 252 (no. 95 for 1567–68).

See also Polia Meconi 1996: 223–24 (for the Chinchaycocha in 1611–13); 1999: 279 (for 1609 Lima), 319 (for the 1613 Chinchacochas), 330 (for Guancavelicas), 423 (for 1618 Cajatambos), 446 (for 1620 Julis).

71. Duviols 1986: 32, 44, 325, 334. See also Duviols 1972: 371; 1986: 329–31, 333–34, 349, 352; Las Casas 1555/1948: 55 (on clothing as an indicator of status); Osorio 1990: 165–66; Medinaceli and Arze 1996: 305.

72. On promoting festivities, see Duviols 1986: 5, 12, 27 (for the quote), 28–29, 33–35, 95, 97, 101, 142, 147, 221, 243, 277, 290; Martínez Cereceda 1982: 173. On setting the date, see Duviols 1972: 364. There are a few examples of lords who rejected and worked against the ancient religion of their forebears. See, for example, ANP/DI, l. 39, c. 805, 1673, fol. 273; Polia Meconi 1999: 429 (for the 1618 Conchucos); Rostworowski 1981–82: 172. For an example of curacas serving as priests, see Polia Meconi 1999: 291–92 (for Lima in 1610), 311, 451, 516–17. See also Polia Meconi 1999: 221 (for the example of a curaca of Cuzco's efforts to congregate his people for the ancient rites in 1599).

73. They could also inherit the position or volunteer to serve (Villagómez 1649/1919: 154). Such holy men or priests were considered "retainers and servants of idols and ancestors" (*yanaconas y criados de idolos y mallquis*) (Huertas 1981: 24–25). Saignes suggests that curacas and religious specialists shared the power that in precolonial times belonged to the "sorcerer king" (1999: 83).

74. Duviols 1986: 56, 140, 165, 325 (for the quote), 326–27, 331, 335, 341, 444; 1967: 117; Cobo 1653/1956–64: 2:225; Cock and Doyle 1979: 68–69; Pease 1968–69: 83 (for 1619); Polia Meconi 1999: 327 (for 1613 Guancavelicas); Martínez Cereceda 1995: 40; Polo de Ondegardo 1906: 221.

75. Duviols 1986: 337, 368–69 (for the quote).

76. Duviols 1986: 341. See also Cobo 1653/1956–64: 2:225; Villagómez 1649/1919: 154; Guibovich 1993: 191, citing AGI/AL 332 Carta de F. Avendaño al Rey, 1653.

77. Cock Carrasco 1983; Duviols 1986: 10, 12, 36, 44, 147, 168, 174–75, 179, 199, 216, 221, 225, 232, 234, 253, 267, 272, 327, 334, 372, 403, 408; Martínez Cereceda 1982: 124 (mentions that Caxa Atoc used a religious specialist to carry out a ceremony when he was not yet a lord, usually in the *pueblos viejos*); AAL/Hechicerías, l. 2a, no. 7, 1659, fol. 7; BNP/B1701, 1671, fols. 3v, 5 (for the Condesuyus of Arequipa); Cervantes 1996: 9–10; Hernández Príncipe 1621–22/1923: 58, 66 (for the Recuay); Polia Meconi 1996: 223 (for the Chinchaycochas, whose communal burial place is described as an "old house"). One reason that the reducciones failed was the desire and need to be near these sites for observance of the rituals of ancestor cults. See also Viceroy Francisco de Toledo's (1924: 190) instructions to his deputies and other royal officials, where he recognizes the reluctance of the natives to leave the tombs of the adored and venerated grandparents in or near the pueblos viejos. In one case, published by García Cabrera (1994: 501–2), Sevastian Mendoza, an elder of Palpas, showed the Spanish a form (an idol) that spoke to them. It was identified as Apu Casapaico, an ancient malqui whose "entire body" was in a cave in a place called Cotomarca ("town of heathens" or pueblo viejo). On feeding the ancestors as a traditional practice today, see "La Pachamama tiene hambre en agosto y espera las ofrendas," *La razon*, La Paz, Bolivia, July 31, 2002, A15.

78. Duviols 1986: 8, 38, 189 (for the last quote), 334–37 (335 for the first quote), 340–41, 343–46, 353 (for one quote), 363, 368, 372; Varón Gabai 1980: 22, 57; ART/CoR, 30-June-1576; CoO, l. 154, exp. 208, 11-August-1582; Polo de Ondegardo 1917: 57. On houses of communities, see Polia Meconi 1999: 537 (for 1675 Ocros). On llamas, see Río 1990: 107–8.

79. Feather headdresses were worn by a lord as a symbol of high rank (Cieza 1553/1984: chap. 62, 195, as quoted by Cock Carrasco 1986: 176).

80. Polia Meconi 1999: 198–99 (for 1561–71 Huarochirís), 201 (for 1576 Lima), 203 (for 1578 Julis), 204 (for 1582 Julis); Ramírez 1978: 119; 1998; Duviols 1974–76: 278, 284, 291; 1986: 65–66, 71, 140; Pease 1968–69: 83; Rostworowski 1961: 16–17; 1982b: 519; Cock Carrasco 1984: 147–51; ART/Mata, l. 11, 23-January-1570, fol. 6; CoR, l. 274, exp. 3426, 30-June-1576, especially fols. 112–13v; CoO, 11-August-1582; AGI/J404, fols. 167v, 186, 227, 373, 653; BAH/9-4664, no. 20, f. 4; Silva Santisteban 1982: 300; Álvarez 1588/1998: 94–108; Polia Meconi 1999: 235, 242, 299; Guamán Poma de Ayala 1613/1980: 297 [299]. The fact that curacas were also buried with servants underscores that, like the Incas, they were believed to go on "living" after death. See also a 1598 will of a curaca of Machachi (Quito) published by Caillavet (1983) and the will of don Diego Caqui (1588) published by Cuneo-Vidal (1977: 1:332–36). Burials often contain sacrificial llama bones (Ubbelohde-Doering: 1967: 25, 27). See also Polia Meconi (1996; especially 228) for various ethnicities in the Andes in 1611–13.

81. AGI/J404, fols. 26v, 53v–54, 106, 133, 159, 252–252v, 272, 277v–78 (for the quote), 830. See Polia Meconi 1999: 223, 227, 233, 242, 555; 1996: 230, 233, 247 (for 1611–13).

82. He is also described as a "wizard with whom they consulted to find lost mules and other things" (Duviols 1986: 139). In the pueblo of Hacas, he was considered "highly educated and wise" (Duviols 1986: 142). See also Millones 1984: especially 138.

83. Sánchez Farfán 1981; Duviols 1986: 32, 88, 139–40, 142; Polia Meconi 1999: 291–92; Szemiñski 1987; Salomon 1987a: 160; Castro 1993: 349. Martínez Cereceda (1982: 30–31, 33–34; 1995: 33) thinks that "the priesthood and the curacaship . . . are nothing more than facets, moments of one and the same institution." See also similar statements in Duviols 1986: 30; in Osorio 1990: 176; and in AAL/Hechicerías, l. 6, no. 1, 1668, f. 7v (for San Juan de los Sondores, Junin). On Cárdenas, see Saignes 1987: 155. See also Polo de Ondegardo 1571/1917b: 105; Arriaga 1621/1968: 222. On the persistence of idolatrous beliefs, see AGI/Estado 75, no. 109 (1), chap. 5. For African counterparts, see Heusch 1997: 229.

84. Duviols 1972: 367, 369, 374, 387–88; 1986: 69, 90, 94, 98, 100, 128, 142, 148, 159, 175, 181, 186, 204, 224–25, 232, 243–44, 250, 271, 273, 279, 287–88, 301, 325, 329, 333, 335, 337, 341, 344–45, 352, 355, 372, 381–83, 396–97, 414, 469, 486; Las Casas 1555/1948: 64; Polia Meconi 1999: 207 (for Cuzco in 1594); Doyle 1988: 16, 61, citing AAL/V-3, fols. 18v–19, 66; Mills 1997: 60. McDowell (1992: 100), who studied the Sibundoy of Colombia, states that the ancestors left lands in perpetuity to their descendants. Salomon (1987a: 161) reports that in eighteenth-century Andagua (Arequipa) the ancestors were seen as the true owners

of the land. I would not translate "owners" literally. Their role is more akin to creator or maker. The head of the lineage had a say about the resource thereafter, but did not own it in the Western sense. Sherbondy (1973: 72–73) states that ancestors emerged from water sources and are linked with water sites (see also Sherbondy 1993: 344, 346). Spalding (1981: 14–15) writes that ancestors were believed to be proprietors of the irrigation canal of the ayllu. Again, "proprietor" is taking the word literally, which I think leads to misunderstanding the situation. Doyle (1988: 57–58, 68) writes that malquis are revered so that irrigation ditches would be protected from damage.

85. Duviols 1986: 288, 333, 341, 355; see also 380; Polia Meconi 1999: 369–70, 419 (for the quote), 441, 536 (for the central Andes in 1675); Huertas 1978: 2; Saito 1997: 56.

86. Doyle 1988: 72; Duviols 1986: 344 (for the long quote).

87. For other examples, see Duviols 1972: 386; 1986: 206, 232, 244, 363 (for the quote), 364, 372; Polia Meconi 1999: 208–9 (for the Vilcas in 1594), 222–23 (for the Aimaraes in 1599); AAL/Hechicerías, l. 3, exp. 9, 1656, especially fol. 9v (for the Huamantangas in the 1650s); Gose 1995: 213. See also Polia Meconi 1999: 260 (for 1606 Condesuyus), 264 (for 1606 Cuzco), 277 (for 1609 Lima), 320–21 (for the 1613 Chinchaycochas), 458 (for 1630–31 Cuzco), 473 (for 1639 Cuzco). On health, see Lastres 1947: 3, 6, 10; Hinojosa Cuba 1999: 33.

88. Las Casas 1555/1948: 51; Polia Meconi 1999: 243, 252, 277, 332, 337, 340, 365, 371–72, 381, 421, 433, 498, 554; 1996: 233; Duviols 1986: 337, 340, 365, 381; AAL/Hechicerías, l. 2, exp. 7, 1647, fol. 3v; Saito 1997: 55–56.

89. Pinillos 1977: 13; Villagómez 1649/1919: 146; Duviols 1986: 7–8, 11, 64, 171, 183, 198, 211, 311–12, 407, 447, 471, 473, 502, 505 (for 1614), 519–20; García Cabrera 1994: 502, 504; Millones 1984; Romero 1918: 187; Las Casas 1555/1948: 73 (for the quote), 74–75; Earls and Silverblatt 1978: 310; Jones 1999: 153 (for the Mapuche of Chile); Polia Meconi 1996: 222 (for the Chinchaycochas in 1611–13), 229, 231 (for the Guancavelicas in the same years), 237 (for the La Barranca and the Cajatambos), 255 (for the Guaylas); Saignes 1987: 155 (on Charcas); Hinojosa Cuba 1999: 30. See Polia Meconi 1999: especially 214 (on celebrating the ancestors with food and drink). Martínez (1983: 88, 91) writes that Andeans still believed in the 1980s that the dead ancestors were alive and, therefore, it was incumbent on the Andeans to feed them.

90. This contrasts with Salomon's observation (1987b: 226) that a dead person was considered to be present and active as long as he or she has physical existence. He says that when Cañari dead were taken from their tombs, exposed, and broken, they ceased to be honored and potent ancestors. See also Eric Van Young's musings (1996: 73) in answer to the question of "where" the locus of divinity lies.

91. Polia Meconi 1999: 216; Las Casas 1555/1948: 51, 57, 60, 72, 88; Gareis 1991: 248, 249; Duviols 1986: 7, 68, 97, 113, 156, 185, 203 (for the quote), 280; see also Duviols 1986: 112–13, 128–29, 145, 147, 169, 206, 219, 242, 271, 313, 382, 397, 451, 458 (for the second decade in the seventeenth century); Polia Meconi 1999: 247, 319, 421, 508, 537.

92. Duviols 1986: 20, 55, 103, 142–44 (for the quote of Hacaspoma), 146–47, 154–55, 158, 175–76, 187, 198, 219, 235, 343, 345, 465–66; Pizarro 1571/1978: 206; Garcilaso de la Vega 1941: 1:112; Santillán 1927: 29–31, 33; BNP/B1701, 1671, fol. 6; AAL/Hechicerías, l. 2, exp. 4, 1646, fols. 17, 19v, 25v, 35; l. 3, exp. 9, 1656, fol. 8; l. 7, exp. 14, 1677, fol. 43. See also Polia Meconi 1999: 217 (for the Julis in 1598), 220 (for Cuzco in 1599), 241, 243, 258, 261–62, 224–25, 272, 286, 290, 312, 331, 342, 386, 405, 420, 443, 448, 456, 473–74, 481–82, 488, 493, 504, 510, 512–13, 515, 523, 535, 538–539, 548; Villagómez 1649/1919: 155, 163; AAL/2–6, 7, 8, as quoted by Doyle 1988: 103.

93. Duviols 1986: 61, 142 (for the quote), 150, 154–55, 187, 235, 453, 466, 472. For other examples, see 61, 150, 154–55, 187, 235. See also Aguirre Palma 1986: 32 (for Otavalo); Saito 1997: 55; Barnadas 1993: 98–100; Polia Meconi 1996: 217, 230, 238–39, notes 53–54 (on modern practice).

94. Martínez Cereceda 1995: 49; Duviols 1986: 187 (for the quote), 232, 243–44 (for the quote); for another example, see Sánchez 1991a: 135–36.

95. Duviols 1986: 186, 232, 244; AAL/Hechicerías, l. 2a, no. 7, 1659, fol. 1; l. 4, no. 5, 1617, fols. 1–2. See also AAL/Hechicerías, l. 3, exp. 9, 1656, fols. 3–4 (for an example of the ex-governor of the repartimiento of Huamantanga who sacrificed repeatedly to the sun and the sea so that he would win a court case to recoup his office).

96. The right to sentence their subjects to death was true at least into the late 1560s.

97. Cabello Valboa 1586/1951: 235; Saignes 1999: 116; Abercrombie 1998: 312 (for a twentieth-century manifestation of luring away the sympathies and affiliation of a neighboring ayllu); Rivière 1995: especially 120 (for a late twentieth-century example of the importance of proper ritual to ensure good communal outcome).

98. Álvarez 1588/1998: 76, 103; Duviols 1986: 12, 76, 90, 112 (curse), 141, 167, 170, 173, 184, 191, 196, 198, 200, 211, 217, 219, 223, 243 (for the quote), 284, 361; Mills 1997: 233, 282; Guamán Poma de Ayala 1613/1936: 267; Romero 1918: 187. See also Doyle 1988: 208; Huertas 1998: 9 (on the profanization of Pachacamac as a cause for illness in times of Pachacutec), 15–16 (for Guamanga); Spalding 1981: 13; Cock Carrasco and Doyle 1979: 53; Polia Meconi 1999: 223, 227, 242, 510, 555; Ramírez 1987: 597; AGI/J404, fols. 277v–78; Martínez 1983: 88. See also similar statements in Duviols 1986: 58, 63, 87, 89, 173, 198, 200; Sánchez 1991a: 68, 134–35; MacCormack 1991: 306.

99. García Cabrera 1994: 186, 198 (for 1641–45 Cajatambo); Duviols 1986: 54 (on sin), 198, 217; Martínez Cereceda 1986: 109 ("and to avoid said labors many of my Indians and natives have left their birth place and their homes and wives and children"). See also Polia Meconi 1996: 230, 233, 247 (for 1611–13).

100. See also Huertas (1987) for an account of a natural disaster and its consequences. Sins included engaging in prohibited types of sexual relations, breaking a prescribed fast, and concealing wrongdoing (Doyle 1988: 153, 160). Doyle (1988: 152–53) reports that in general, an "affront" to the ancestors resulted in sickness, misfortune, and death. See also Polia Meconi and Chávez Hualpa 1994: 13.

101. Villagómez 1649/1919: 159; Saignes 1987: 147; Rostworowski 1981–82: 125 (for Lima); Duviols 1986: 230, 234; ART/CoP, l. 280, exp. 3611, 31-July-1583; Rubiños y Andrade 1782/1936: 291–92 (for a pre-Spanish example of flight), 300 (for an example of 1548); ANB/EC 1605, exp. 2, fol. 93. On the discrediting effect of the El Niño phenomenon on the pre-Hispanic Moche society, see Uceda and Canziani 1993; Shimada et al. 1991; Erickson 1999. For the same phenomenon among the Mayans, see Ness 2003. For continuities with highland Bolivia in the 1970s and 1980s, see Rivière 1995: especially 117–18; 1986: 22.

102. ART/CoP, l. 280, exp. 3611, 31-July-1583, fol. 1; BNP/A538, 1580 (this manuscript was published in Huertas 1987); Rivera and Platt 1978: 110–111, 114; ARP/Co, l. 17, exp. 320, 1693, fol. 1v; Zuidema 1973b: 29; Diez Hurtado 1997: 163. For an analogous situation in Christianity, see Poole 1991b: 670.

103. Rostworowski 1961: 15, 45, 47, 51; Valcarcel 1949: 37. Resistance to an inept leader is also a theme of the myths of Huarochirí; see Taylor 1987: 471–72; Cabello Valboa 1586/1951: 328–29, 468 (on the murder of the cacique of Lambayeque by his subjects ca. 1532–33); Río and Presta 1995: 196; Trimborn 1979: 22; Regalado de Hurtado and Castelli 1982: 164; Hamilton; Zevallos Quiñones 1989: 59, 64, 114; Hart 1983: 199–200.

104. Polia Meconi 1996: 228; 1999: 327 (for 1613); Spalding 1981: especially 16–18; 1984: 264; Martínez Cereceda 1995: 110; Rivera and Platt 1978: 105, 112; Trimborn 1979: 23; ART/CoO, l. 148, exp. 46, 13-July-1565 (for Malabrigo); Agustinos ca. 1550/1865/1964: 46. The Inca was subject to the same sanctions when inept; see Guamán Poma de Ayala 1613/1980: 107 [107].

105. A prayer suggests that malquis could also help alleviate the suffering caused by the Spanish: "And you lord ancestors and lady guacas give us life [and] health, that there be no illnesses in the town [or among the people], [that there be] fertility, good harvests, belongings, that there not be freezes nor worms in the planted fields and that the Spanish do not aggrieve them" (AAL/2–6, 7, 9, as cited by Doyle 1988: 135). See also Varón Gabai 1980: 28.

106. Powers 1991: 238; Anónimo 1571/1970: 127–28; Polo de Ondegardo 1916: 194; Duviols 1974–76: 290; Polia Meconi 1996: 222; García Cabrera 1994: 492 (for 1725). See also AAL/Hechicerías, l. 3, exp. 9, 1656, fol. 6v; Sánchez 1991a: 105; Polo de Ondegardo 1906: 193–97; 200, 202–3, 205–6, 209, 212; Querejazu Lewis 1995: 48. For other examples taken from Jesuit letters, see Polia Meconi 1999: 260, 272, 329, 334, 336, 368, 419, 431, 434, 445, 473, 504, 509, 519, 530; Negro 1996: 128; Las Casas 1555/1943: 147.

107. During celebrations, natives "sang songs in their language according to ancient custom referring to the histories and ancient ways of their ancestors and guacas" (Duviols 1986: 145).

108. Duviols 1986: 473; Martínez Cereceda 1988: 64; 1986: 108–9; Pease 1994: 10; Salomon 1995. Cobo reminds us that lords were remembered longer than commoners, whose memory usually did not extend past the lifetimes of their children and grandchildren. Is this the basis for Zuidema's belief that a lord's memory had to last four or more generations to belong to the ranks of the honored "grandparents"? (Cobo 1653/1956–64: 2:165; Zuidema 1989b: especially 137–38; 1990).

For a description of these stools or thrones and the correlation between height and elaboration with authority, see Guamán Poma de Ayala 1613/1980: 453 [455]–456 [458]; Martínez Cereceda 1982: 83; 1988: 70; Dammert Bellido 1997: 125. Note that Christian missionaries portrayed the Christian god as seated on a chair to denote sacredness.

In the "Catechism Questions on the Nature of the Eucharist," one of the question-and-answer exchanges is illustrated as follows:

Q: Son, where is Jesus Christ?
A: He is in heaven and in the Holy Sacrament of the altar.

In the "Catechism Questions on the Existence and Nature of God," another exchange is illustrated as follows:

Q: Where is God?
A: In heaven, earth, and all places.

Heaven is depicted as a seated god raised above the line.

Source: Jaye and Mitchell 1999: 35, 41, 61.

109. Duviols 1986: 61, 97, 100, 145, 156. See also Mills 1997: 238; Polia Meconi 1999: 209 (for Vilcas in the 1590s); Negro 1996: 133.

110. Duviols 1986: 465; Polia Meconi 1999: 371; Millones 1990: 12; Varón Gabai 1990: 339, quoting Molina, el cuzqueño, 1959: 100. The belief that a bad

death would be forthcoming if ancient traditions were neglected is also found in Mills (1992).

111. Romero 1918: 189–90; Duviols 1986: 191, 296, 407. See also MacCormack 1988: 993.

112. García Cabrera 1994: 510; Ramírez 1996; 1998; Cock Carrasco 1984, 1986.

113. See Polia Meconi 1999: 516–17 (for an example of a two-faced curaca); Zevallos Quiñones 1989: 59 (on the rejection and murder [by hanging] of the lord of Jequetepeque, whom the people believed was illegitimate).

114. Sánchez Farfán (1981: 186) comes to the same conclusion; see also Saito 1997: 57.

CHAPTER 5

1. Pizarro 1571/1978: 59, 91–92; Molina, el almagrista, n.d./1968: 94.

2. Zuidema 1991; Pizarro 1571/1978: 66–67.

3. Martínez Cereceda 1995: 27–28.

4. Querejazu Lewis 1995: 43.

5. Cieza 1967: 32; 1553/1984: 191–92; Martínez Cereceda 1986: 106; Rostworowski 1961: 16; Cobo 1653/1956: 2:135.

6. Quilter; Cock Carrasco 1996: 88; Martínez Cereceda 1986: 114–20; Isbell and Cook 1987: especially 31–32; Kauffman Doig 1978: especially 301, 304; Silverman 1984.

7. Cabello Valboa 1586/1951: 327; Rostworowski 1961: 16.

8. Pease 1991: 32.

9. Doyle 1988: 149; Varón Gabai 1990: 366, 368–69, 379; "Relación anónima" 1583/1925: 292; Isbell 1978: 270; Salomon and Urioste 1991: 71.

10. Martínez Cereceda 1982; 1995; Ares Queija 1984: 448, 451. See also Dean 1999.

11. Molina, el almagrista, n.d./1968: 74.

12. Molina, el almagrista, n.d./1968: 74; Gibson (1948/1969) (on the process).

13. Pease 1991: 33–34; Rostworowski 1997: 69. Note that Pease writes of the elite as military men and priests. As noted previously, I do not totally accept this interpretation.

14. See note 132 in Chapter 3 regarding capac cocha. See also Cabello Valboa 1586/1951: 290; 333–34, 460; Sarmiento de Gamboa 1572/1967: 49, 126–27; Betanzos 1551–57/1996: 122; Cobo 1653/1956: 2:138–39: 238; Murúa 1962: 54.

15. Cieza 1550/1985: 29; Sancho de la Hoz 1534/1938: 123–24.

16. Pizarro 1571/1978: 241–42; Sancho de la Hoz 1534/1938: 123–24. See also Cobo 1653/1956: 2:138. Note that Sancho de la Hoz and Xerez both use the word *Cuzcos* as a synonym for *Incas*.

17. Cabello Valboa 1586/1951: 333–34; Sarmiento de Gamboa 1572/1967: 49, 126–29; Cieza 1550/1985: 29; MacCormack 1990: 13. There are other examples of successors ruling for an old, disabled lord. See, for example, Rostworowski regarding the chiefs of the Valley of Lima in the 1530s: "Because he was old he [Taulichusco] did not govern the natives of this valley of Lima. Instead Guachinamo who they said was his son [did]" (1981–82: 117, 142).

18. Betanzos 1551–57/1996: 131; Sancho de la Hoz 1534/1938: 159, 183; Sarmiento de Gamboa 1572/1967: 138, 140.

19. Guamán Poma de Ayala 1613/1980: 113 [113]. Guayna Capac also immediately ordered that siblings who were potential rivals be killed. This practice was commonplace. See Titu Cusi 1570/1916: 89; Kubler 1944: 256 (on Manco Inca); Calancha 1638/1974–81: 1:237 (who reports that Atahualpa had Huáscar, all of his sons, and forty-three of his brothers, the sons of Guayna Capac, killed). That may have been part of the reason that Mena (1534/1938: 326) reports that the half brothers of Atahualpa were afraid of him.

20. Guillén Guillén 1974: xvi; Cabello Valboa 1586/1951: 357–58; Sarmiento de Gamboa 1572/1967: 153–55; Betanzos 1551–57/1996: 160 (who gives another version).

21. Larrea 1953: 104–6, 109, 112, 114; 1960. See also Cobo 1653/1956: 2:139, 237. Murua (2001: 441) places the number of children as five hundred. Cobo more conservatively estimates the number as two hundred.

22. Larrea 1953: 109–10, 116–21, 126–28; Río 1990: 93–94. Elena Phipps (2002) writes that the color red implied royal and sacred.

23. Larrea 1953: 114–15; Zuidema 1989a: 260–61. See also Molina, el almagrista, n.d./1968: 74.

24. The emperor did not always sit on the same seat. Pedro Pizarro (1571/1978: 67) notes that when Atahualpa ate, he sat on a beautifully painted wooden stool just over a "palm" (of a human hand) high, covered by a very finely and tightly woven mantle. See Pizarro 1571/1978: 66–68; Zuidema 1989a: 261; 1991; Rodriguez de Figueroa [Pietschmann] 1910: 98; Kauffman Doig 1978: 300–1; Río 1990: 94; Estete 1542?/1987: 317; 1534–45/1938: 249. In late twentieth-century Bolivia, an important insignia of power was the poncho. See Rivière 1995: 118.

25. Martínez Cereceda 1995: 70, 137–45.

26. Julien 1999.

27. Isbell 1978: especially 275, citing Gonçalez Holguin (1608/1952); Torero 1990: 254–56; Guamán Poma de Ayala 1613/1936: 329. On Cuyusmango, see Zuidema 1966: 47–48.

28. Isbell 1978: 286; Zuidema 1966: 48; 1979 (on the ushnu).

29. Isbell 1978: 277–78; see also Silverblatt 1987 (on gender).

30. Isbell 1978: 278, 295; Morris 1993: 41; Hyslop 1984; Burger and Salazar-Burger 1993: 101; Kolata 1997: 247. Isbell (1978: 2:288–89) shows that the form is repeated at the earlier ceremonial centers of Garagay and Chavín de Huantar. See also Rostworowski 1979; Caillavet 2000: 171; Niles 1999.

31. Such investitures also hold for curacas, segundas personas, and principales—at least to the rank of pachaca. Martínez Cereceda 1995: 33–36, 44–47; ANP/DI, l. 3, c. 19, 1574, fol. 48v; ADC/CoO, l. 17, no. 348, c. 7, 1664, fol. 4; AGI/AL 128, 2-June-1587, fols. 6, 8–10, 13, 14v; Las Casas 1555/1948: 65–66, 142; Hart 1983: 183. There was a third method to achieve power: usurp power through a successful revolt. A lord who succeeded attracted followers who gave him tribute service. See Ramírez 1995b: 302; Kolata 1997: 248–49.

32. ANP/DI, l. 1, c. 7, 1566, fol. 6; l. 3, c. 19, 1574, fols. 15v–16; l. 6, c. 75, 1623, fols. 22, 33; l. 39, c. 805, 1673, fols. 162, 164, 171, 226–27, 233v–34, 235v,

237; Pease 1989b; Anónimo 1571/1995: 127, 141; Dunbar Temple 1942: 149; BNP/B454, 1621; ANB/EC 1605, exp. 2, 54v; EC 1662, exp. 11, fol. 5; EC 1686, exp. 34, fol. 2. On Inca-presented stools, see BNP/A371, 1594, fol. 8.

33. ART/CoAG l. 266, exp. 3068, 12-November-1604, fol. 2; ANP/DI, l. 31, c. 622, 1597, fol. 71v; ALL/Pra-36, caja 449, 1715, fols. 17–17v; Pra 212, l. 456, siglo 18, 1794, fol. 1; ARP/Co, l. 17, exp. 320, 1693, fol. 94v; l. 22, exp. 432, 1711, fol. 22; ANB/EC 1673, exp. 26, fol. 33 (for 1667); Cobo 1653/1956: 2:138; Pizarro 1571/1978: 241–42; Río 1990: 84; Espinoza Soriano 1969a: 19, 36 (for the Huancas). According to Cummins, "The object, by its physical presence and use, becomes a transitional sign between the ancient authority invested by the Inka in a kuraka and the colonial authority conferred on a kuraka by the Spaniards" (1998: 108–9). On don Diego Canqui, see Rivera and Platt 1978: 116.

34. ART/CoP, l. 280, exp. 3583, 9-August-1568, fol. 4v.

35. ART/CoP, l. 280, exp. 3583, 9-August-1568, fols. 5–6v.

36. Rivera and Platt 1978: 114, 120 (for another such order for the year 1590).

37. ALL/Pra-188, caja 455, 1793, fols. 6v–7v, 15v, 21; Dammert Bellido 1997: 125, based on Guamán Poma de Ayala 1613/1936; Martínez Cereceda 1995: 75. See also García Cabrera 1994: 185 (for an inventory of the goods of the cacique principal of Ocros, who still had his "wooden stool of ancient custom" in 1644).

38. BNP/A371, 1594, fol. 29v; ANP/DI, l. 3, c. 19, 1574, fols. 40v, 42v, 44v, 48v; ART/CoAG, l. 266, exp. 3068, 12-June-1604, fol. 1v; Dunbar Temple 1942: 149; Arriaga 1621/1968: 202; Martínez Cereceda 1988: 66–67; 1995: 85, 97, 117, 120–31, 148; Duviols 1986: 113 (regarding disorder without authority). See also ANP/Notarial, Protocolo 731 de Francisco Huaman Minollulli, 27-September-1775, especially fol. 777v (for 1690 Pueblo of San Juan de Labaytambo, Huarochirí, and the investiture of doña Isabela Pomaticlla as segunda persona of the guaranga of Chaucarima). In the 1790s, natives of the altiplano believed their lord, who claimed descent from the Incas, to be an oracle (ALL/Pra-188, caja 455, 1793, fol. 18). In Bolivia in the late twentieth century, being "seated" at inauguration was considered the time when the authority required the energy or spirit of his predecessors (Rivière 1995: 120).

39. ADCuzco/CoO, l. 17, no. 348, c. 7, 1664, 4, 5v, 35; ALL/LB-581, caja 169, 17v; ANB/EC 1605, exp. 2, fols. 27, 109; EC 1662, exp. 11, fol. 5; EC 1673, exp. 26, fol. 34; ART/CoO, l. 154, exp. 223, 15-March-1585, fol. 13; Rubiños y Andrade 1782/1936: 293; Gisbert 1991: 350, 356; Martínez Cereceda 1995: 120–31.

40. Bandera 1557/1968: 506; AGI/AL 128, 2-June-1587, fol. 44; ART/Escrituras Notariales, l. 41, 7-July-1594, fols. 259–61 (for don Pedro Amco Guamán, cacique principal del Pueblo of Moche, who left in his will "a beaker of silver"); Duviols 1966: 502–3, 505; AGI/AL 128, 2-June-1587, fol. 44.

41. ANP/DI, l. 39, c. 805, 1673, 221–22; Cummins 1998: 103; Murra 1998: 56. For the letter, see Polia Meconi 1999: 537.

42. Albornoz 1967: 35; Pizarro 1571/1978: 37; Oviedo 1535–45/1992: vol. 5, libro 46, cap. 6, 55.

43. Murua 1962: 175; Guillén Guillén 1974: 97, 106–7.

44. Cobo 1653/1956: 2:140; Guamán Poma de Ayala 1613/1936: 334. Gonçalez Holguin defines the word *rampa* as "the litter in which the Inca is

carried on the shoulders of men," or as the litter of a woman (1608/1952/1989: 311–12).

45. Martínez Cereceda 1995: especially 106–7; Betanzos 1551–57/1987: 85, 149–50; Calancha 1638/1974–81: 1:249.

46. Rodriguez de Figueroa [Pietschmann] 1910: 98–103; Quipucamayocs 1542–44/1920: 44–45. See also Regalado de Hurtado 1992: especially 53–55.

47. Martínez Cereceda 1986: 108–11.

48. Rodriguez de Figueroa [Pietschmann] 1910: 99.

49. Rodriguez de Figueroa [Pietschmann] 1910: 99; Pizarro 1571/1978: 39.

50. Martínez Cereceda 1995: 93, 156; Cieza 1967: 195; Melo et al. 1582/1925: 281; Pizarro 1571/1978: 37.

51. ANB/EC 1605, exp. 2, fols. 54v, 107v; Larco Herrera 1917: February 1, 1556; Hart 1983: 184; AGI/J456, fols. 97v–98v; J458, fol. 1778; Espinoza Soriano 1969b: 148 (in the 1580s). See also Ruiz de Arze 1543/1933: 354; Martínez Cereceda 1982: 103, 107.

52. ANB/EC 1605, exp. 2, fol. 54v; AGI/J458, fols. 1778, 1835v, 1838; Gama 1540/1974: 225; ART/CoJuez de Comisión, l. 272, exp. 3369, 26-July-1557.

53. AGI/AL 128, 1587, fols. 6v–7; AL 204, 1572, fols. 69–72.

54. BNP/A371, 1594, fols. 8, 34v; ANP/DI, l. 3, c. 19, 1574, fols. 40, 43, 44v; Dammert Bellido 1997: 125–26.

55. Pizarro 1571/1978: 17; Rostworowski 1981–82: 139. See also Martínez Cereceda 1986: 112; 1995: 95, 97, 155. In the south, centuries later, a pretender to a lordship continued to be accompanied by fifteen, twenty, or even fifty people (ALL/Pra-188, Caja 455, 1793, fol.1v).

56. ANP/R, l. 3, c. 7, 1582, fols. 93, 164, 205, 457, 475v, 571v.

57. AGI/AL 128, 1587, fol. 7; J458, fol. 1836; see also Martínez Cereceda 1995: 55; and Rivière 1986: 17; 1995: 118, 121 (on the visits that communal authorities still made to their peoples in the 1970s and 1980s in Bolivia).

58. AGI/J458, fol. 1802.

59. ANP/DI, l. 39, c. 806, 1673, fol. 44v; AGI/J458, fols. 1778v–79, 1829v, 1830v–31, 1835v; J461, fol. 866v.

60. AGI/AL 128, 2-June-1587, fols. 6, 14v; Ramírez 1998: especially 242–45; BNP/A371, 1594, fol. 8 (which suggests that a lord might have such residences in all settlements under his mandate and at the sites of some chacras as well); Saignes 1999: 61, 89 (who points out that both caciques and peasants might keep more than one home). Niles (1999: especially 52) documents the enshrined "houses" of Pachacuti Inca Yupanqui: Cusicancha, his birthplace; Tambo Machay, a house "where he lodged when he went hunting"; Condorcancha, "a house in which he lived"; Coracora, "a building in which he slept"; and Patallacta, "the house in which he died." His golden idol that served as his guauqui also had a "house" in Totocache.

61. First quote cited by Río 1990: 81; Duviols 1986: 334–35, 337, 341, 451–52; Molina, el almagrista, n.d./1968: 73; Huertas 1998: 8. On kullqa, see Guamán Poma de Ayala 1613/1980: 1095. The use of the word *house* (*huasi*, *wasi*) recalls the Chimú people's description and legal defense of the site named Yamayoguán. See Ramírez 1996: chap. 5.

62. Duviols 1986: 343–44 (for the quote), 386, 346; see also 340–41, 345, 351, 354, 359–65, 370, 380, 383, 386, 396, 404–6, 414–15, 435, 468, 470. Could these houses be provincial analogues for the so-called Inca estates? Caillavet (2000: 142–43) describes what appear to be similar structures in Ecuador. Saignes (1991: 108) describes how inhabitants of the Andes built houses in the state-mandated reducciones but kept others near their fields, a phenomenon he labels double domicile (*doble domicilio*). See also Adrián 1997: 249 (on this last concept in Chayanta); Cook 1976–77 (on the same concept among the Conchucos in 1543).

63. Duviols 1986: 354–55, 359, 361, 383.

64. Duviols 1986: 128, 248, 279, 380 (for the quote), 386, 396, 405; Ramírez 2002 (on marcayoc and llactayoc as first founders and "back translations" [here, a technical term for translations from Spanish to Quechua or Aymara] for "dueño de indios").

65. Duviols 1986: 406.

66. Duviols 1986: 414–15.

67. Duviols 1986: 19, 415, 451–53; Cieza 1553/1984: 275; Eckert 1945: 91–92; Caillavet 2000: 369. Note the parallels with the Mayans in Freidel and Schele 1992: 123.

68. Dammert Bellido 1997: 126; Rostworowski 1961: 16; Polo de Ondegardo 1906: 214, 216; AGI/AL 128, 1587, fols. 7, 12. See also Arriaga 1621/1968: 212–14.

69. Betanzos 1551–57/1987: 85.

70. Santacruz Pachacuti Yamqui 1613/1993: 22–22v.

71. Mena 1534/1938: 326; Estete 1542?/1987: 302, 306; Pizarro 1571/1978: 69–70.

72. Dammert Bellido 1997: 18; Cabello Valboa 1586/1951: 360–61; Murúa 1962: 76; MacCormack 1990: 15.

73. Betanzos 1551–57/1987: 85.

74. Betanzos 1551–57/1987: 86, 176.

75. Betanzos 1551–57/1987: 86.

76. Santacruz Pachacuti Yamqui 1613/1993: 26; Pease 1991: 99; Betanzos 1551–57/1987: 149–50; 1557/1996: 162, 171–72, 190, 192.

77. Valera 1596/1879: 151; Santacruz Pachacuti Yamqui 1613/1993: 26; Calero 1997: 43; Cabello Valboa 1586/1951: 198; Cieza 1864/1964: 221–23.

78. Cabello Valboa 1586/1951: 263, 337 (on the death ritual of Tupac Inca Yupanqui), 360–61, 394–96, 399; Santacruz Pachacuti Yamqui 1613/1879: 290 (for Tupac Inca Yupanqui); Garcilaso de la Vega 1602/1963: 38; Mena 1534/1938: 323; Cieza 1550/1985: 201; Valera 1596/1879: 152; Betanzos 1551–57/1987: 141–42; Calancha 1638/1974–81: 1:236.

79. Cieza 1550/1985: 31; Betanzos 1551–57/1987: 142 (for the quote); Las Casas 1555/1948: 209.

80. Cieza 1550/1985: 92; Betanzos 1551–57/1996: 134; 1987: 145. See also Cieza 1967: 205 (for the end-of-the-year or first-anniversary celebration [*cabo de año*] for Paulo Inca [Paullo Topa (Tupac) Inca]). Kaulicke (2000: 94), citing Cieza,

states that the ceremony was held for those who had been "good" during their lifetimes.

81. Betanzos 1551–57/1996: 134–36; 1557/1987: 146–47; Pease 1991: 199–200. Bolas (*aillos*) are hunting weapons thrown to entangle the legs of prey. They consist of three cords (sometimes made from the nerves of animals) that are tied together, each of which has a heavy ball affixed to its end (Zuidema 1989a: 257; 1967: 41–51.) The following illustration shows a child hunting birds with a bola.

Source: Guaman Poma de Ayala 1613/1936: 256.

82. Pease 1991: 30–32; 1994: 11; Gibson 1969: 57. The message of such a fiesta, had one been held after Atahualpa's death, almost certainly would have been that the ancestor-gods had ordained his defeat and death. If the supernatural had already determined his fate, there was nothing he or his followers could have done to change it. Therefore, they could not be blamed.

83. Betanzos 1551–57/1996: 136–37, 154, 162.

84. Cabello Valboa 1586/1951: 198–99 (for the first quote); Cieza 1553/1984: 197–98 (for the second quote), 275–76. See also Martínez Cereceda 1995: 87 (for a discussion of the burial goods of the deceased).

85. Cieza 1553/1984: 193–94, 275–76; Duviols 1977b: 96; 119–20; 1986, xxviii.

86. Cieza 1553/1984: 275–76; Negro 1996: 126, 136. As far north as Anserma in the Colombian Andes, the procedure was the same. See Eckert 1945: especially 81–82. For a short description of a funeral in Guaylas, see Polia Meconi 1999: 407 (for 1617); Negro 1996: 136 (for the people of Hacas in the central Andes in the middle of the seventeenth century).

87. Duviols 1986: 98–99, 171; Huertas 1981: 61–62; Cabero 1906: 184; Negro 1996: 135, 137; Polia Meconi 1996: 253–54; Villagómez 1919: 170–71. The

manuscript in Duviols (1986: 452) is dated 1619. Therefore, the Spanish at this time were finding bodies of ancestors who lived, according to this estimate, in the early fourteenth or fifteenth century. The Jesuits reported finding an eight-hundred-year-old mummy named Tutayquiri, who was believed to be the son of Pariacaca, had fought the people of the lowlands, named the ayllus, and established the religious practices of each. Such a ruler, if the dating is correct, represented a local lord, who in early 1611, antedated the Incas and might have lived in the ninth century (see Polia Meconi 1996: 214).

88. Negro 1996: 125; Doyle 1988: 208; Duviols 1986: 9, 15, 63–64, 92–93, 150, 171; Cabero 1906: 184; Guamán Poma de Ayala 1613/1980: 1086. Kaulicke (1997: 14) includes a drawing of a mummified body in this position.

89. Duviols 1986: 9, 15, 63–64, 149, 183, 205, 212, 238, 273.

90. Duviols 1986: 157, 212; Hernández Príncipe 1621–22/1923: 42.

91. Duviols 1986: 157, 170, 183, 273, 276.

92. Duviols 1986: 149–50. For help with the translation of the phrase *magsas echiceros*, I am indebted to Alfredo Alberdi. He translates the phrase, writing that "they are the wizards who were born twins, from *macsa*, the old Quechua word for 'two from one womb.'" The phrase could also refer to wizards who poison using copper oxide, from the word *maxa* (personal communication, February 18, 2004).

93. A parpa (*sancu*) is a cornmeal cake used as an offering to the gods (Arriaga 1621/1968: 211; Duviols 1986: 99, 472).

See Duviols 1986: 63 (for the quote), 64. Alfredo Alberdi translates the word *arguay* as special ears of corn that are placed in an important location in the storage bins as an amulet protecting the grain. These sometimes have multicolored kernels and, at other times, are two ears that have grown together (personal communication, February 18, 2004).

94. Ares Queija 1984: 456; Duviols 1986: 13, 26, 30, 93, 150, 170, 184, 221, 276; Negro 1996: 125, 136. Note that singing and dancing were ways of worshipping among the Aimaraes in 1599. To sing and dance was "to make the huaca happy" (Polia Meconi 1999: 224; see also 277, 390, 468, 516.) This procession sounds like the *vecosina*, which took place, according to Huertas, during important festivals in honor of their malquis. In the vecosina, the ayllus and parcialidades followed their leaders through the streets, accompanied by old women who played little drums and sang songs in their own language in the old style, recounting the histories of their malquis and guacas (Huertas 1978: 1, who cites AAL/l. 4, exp. 19, 1656–57, fol. 10). It helped relay their worldview to the younger members of society and kept their past alive. Both served as bases for an encompassing fellowship. On the vecosina or vecochina, see also Duviols 1986: 93, 142, 145, 160, 167, 181, 189, 197. See Poole (1991b: 659–60), who shows that Andean Catholic dancers continue to participate as a "profoundly personal gesture performed as part of a heartfelt religious vow [*voto*] to a powerful saint, virgin, or Christ figure. . . . It also encompasses a serious commitment to his community or *aylly* [ayllu?], since the future well-being . . . is considered subject to the whims of the religious image which dance is meant to please."

95. Duviols 1986: 9–12, 15–16, 19, 26, 63–64, 150, 157, 198, 212, 238, 240, 274, 276, 278, 285, 382; AAL/Hechicerías IIa: fols. 6–7; Doyle 1988: 168; Negro 1996: 137; Heyerdahl, Sandweiss, and Narvaez 1995: 154–55.

96. AAL/Hechicerías, l. 1, exp. 14, 1604, fols. 2–3v, 5; Doyle 1988: 241–42. Duviols (1972: 355–56) publishes a manuscript from 1614 in which natives of San Francisco de Musca identify the mummies of their relatives by name and kinship relation. The documents he publishes in the appendix also show clearly that each lineage buried its members apart from members of other ayllus and parcialidades, following their own customs and idiosyncrasies (1972: 368, 370–72, 381).

97. Duviols 1986: 92–93, 281, 296; García Cabrera 1994: 493; Guamán Poma de Ayala 1613/1980: 1083.

98. Duviols 1986: 63–64, 92–93 (for the quote); Negro 1996: 137. Doyle's research (1988: 156) indicates that to spit or expectorate was a way to expel sins and sickness from the body.

99. Duviols 1986: 12, 138, 150–51, 158, 171, 200, 222, 268; Negro 1996: 127, 137; Doyle 1988: 205. See also Duviols 1986: 171 (on the funeral of a curaca), 222 (of a principal).

100. Cieza 1553/1984: 196–97, 275; 1864/1964: 229; Pizarro 1571/1978: 237; Zuidema 1977–78. Reed beds were used on the north coast (Izumi Shimada, personal communication, May 8, 2000). See also note 96 in this chapter. Isbell (1997) and Kaulicke (1997: 12) discuss several types of burials and mortuary monuments. Kaulicke also includes drawings on pp. 12, 22–23.

101. Duviols 1986: 10, 13, 16, 26, 55, 72, 452; Doyle 1988: 230.

102. Duviols 1986: 64 (for the quote); Negro 1996: 137; Rostworowski 1981a. A fanega is a unit of dry measure equal to 130 pounds (of flour in sixteenth-century Peru) or 6 checos (of corn) or 12 almudes (of corn) (Ramírez 1986: 279).

103. Duviols 1986: 150, 157, 200, 218; Doyle 1988: 231–35; Hernández Príncipe 1621–22/1923: 41 (for the Recuays).

104. Duviols 1986: 150. For variations on the name of the bridge, see also Duviols 1986: 171, 184, 268; Negro 1996: 138.

105. Duviols 1986: 200, 227, 268, 276, 281, 285; Negro 1996: 138–39.

106. Polo de Ondegardo 1559/1916: 18–24; Aguirre Palma 1986: 11, 34; Baines and Yoffee 2000: 14–15.

107. Duviols 1986: 271, 288, 467, 473; Martínez Cereceda 1995: 117–18, 120–31, 205; Las Casas 1555/1948: 144. For capacochas, see Duviols 1986: 169, 246, 248, 472, 489, 491, 499.

108. Zuidema 1989a: 251; Martínez Cereceda 1995: 205; Guillén Guillén 1979: 85; Pease 1979: 98.

109. Duviols 1986: 204, 218, 337.

110. Duviols 1986: 145, 148, 517–18; Doyle 1988: 102.

111. Cieza 1550/1985: 27–28, 30–31; Varón Gabai 1990: 368; Pease 1994: 10; Garcilaso de la Vega 1609/1942: 2:120–22; 1602/1963: 2:79; Estete 1542?/1987: 318; Betanzos 1551–57/1996: 56, 79, 87–89, 121, 138–39, 153, 167; Cobo 1653/1956: 2:148.

112. Duviols 1986: 12–13, 15, 26, 28, 30–31, 33–34, 52, 54, 56, 60–61, 63, 65, 93, 142, 155.

113. Cabello Valboa 1586/1951: 198–99; Ares Queija 1984: 462, citing Santillán; Cieza 1553/1984: 277; Uceda and Canziani Amico; Shimada et al.; Erickson.

114. Rostworowski 1993b: 212. For statements on being children of gods, see

Duviols 1986: 147, 204, 206, 210, 249, 279, 335–36, 343, 397, 405–6, 408, 412, 414–15, 464, 470, 479–80.

CHAPTER 6

1. Hagar 1906: 593; Heusch 1997: 216–17; Geertz 1973: chap. 12; Thornton 1992: especially chap. 3; Timbiah 1976; Verdesio 2001: 106. A theater state implied a political edifice that was "not so much a bureaucratized centralized imperial monarchy as a kind of galaxy-type structure with lesser political replicas revolving around the central entity and in perpetual motion of fission and incorporation." I considered it as a model and ultimately rejected it as not a strictly coincident analogue for the Inca state ideal. In Southeast Asia, the king depended on lesser kings who, in turn, depended on still lesser rulers to maintain control over many culturally and linguistically diversified groups (Timbiah 1976: 70, 102–31).

2. Keightley 1979–80: 28–29 (on the Shang).

3. Binford et al.; Shimada et al.; Erickson. See Heusch 1997: 217–19, 226 (on this phenomenon in Africa); Ness 2003 (among the Mayans).

4. Sallnow 1981.

5. This recalls small-town Japanese tradition today, where "the dead remain an integral part of life and offer constant solace to the living" (Kristof 1996: 1, 8). See also Salomon 1988: 330; Noejovich. On the importance of ideology, see Conrad and Demarest 1992.

6. Said 1995; 1999. Recall that lords were competing for and fighting over people rather than land as late as 1558 (ART/CoJuez de Comisión, l. 272, exp. 3370, 29-March-1558).

7. Kolata 1996: 70, 75; 1997: 252–53; Baines and Yoffee 2000: 14; Schaedel 1988. On the oikos, see Weber 1978: 381, 1013.

8. Wurgaft 1995; Hobsbawm 1983: 12; Kolata 1997: 251. On patrimonial ruler, see Weber 1978: 1006; Wheatley 1971: 52.

9. Geertz 1980; Saignes 1987: especially 158.

10. I base the figure of 10 percent on population figures of the Valley of Saña: there were 3,000 tribute payers in the year 1532; 300 in 1563; and 219 in the early 1590s (Ramírez 1996: 26–18).

11. Río and Presta 1995: 214; Méndez 2001: 144; Saignes 1999: 91 (on cyclical mobility).

12. Regalado de Hurtado 1984a: 182; 1981: 41–42; Duviols 1972: 369, 388 (for 1656).

13. Sahlins 1983: 532–33; Thornton 1992: chap. 3, especially 74–91. He discusses, in particular, Benin, Kongo, Ndongo, and Sierra Leone. Murúa's unpublished manuscript, known as the Galvin or Dublin manuscript, is dated by Juan Ossio as after 1600, despite the addition of a later title page dated 1590.

14. Ramírez 1986; Maldi 1997: 186, 192; Adrián 1997: 248–49; Schaedel 1998.

15. Zuidema 1983a: 49; Geertz 1973: chap. 12, especially 336 (for Balinese parallels to this analysis of the Andean state).

16. Cabello Valboa 1586/1951: 356; Saignes 1987: 157, citing AGI/ACharcas 79; 1995: 182; Ramírez 1986; Méndez 2001: 142; Poole 1991a.

17. Pease 1977: especially 179; Ramírez 1986; Méndez 2001: 144–45; Duviols 1972: 368–69; Said 1995. For Africa, see Murphy and Bledsoe.

18. Ramírez 1996: chap. 3; Thornton 1992: chap. 3, especially 76–79; Verdesio 2001: 93; Saito 1997: 57–58; Millones 1998: 33, 44; Boehm 1980: especially 2; Martínez Cereceda 1996: 249; MacCormack 1997a: 282–83, 303 (on European models of empire); Guillén Guillén 1984: 79; Zuidema 1973a.

19. James Hess on Whorf, personal communications, November 18, 2000, and May 1, 2001; Carroll; Whorf. See also Restrepo Arcila 1995: especially 119 (on guaca). See Pease 1998: especially 234–35 (where he discusses the problematic meaning of some words, such as *province*), 237 (where he reminds us that words such as *aclla*, the Quechua word for "chosen woman of the Inca and Sun," have described a woman living in a harem with eunuch guards [reflecting a Moorish legacy on Spain] and later, a woman compared to a Roman vestal virgin). See also Caillavet 2000: 163 (on the imprecise use of the word *mitimaes*); Restall 2003; Powers 2002 (on women).

20. Rostworowski 1573/1999b: 84; Ivan Ghezzi, personal communication, September 3, 2001; Kolata 1997; H. Silverman; Diez Hurtado 1997: 154; Ramírez 1996: chap. 3. See also Lazaro Llantoy 1996: 29 (for another example of a sacred city and fortress).

21. Sahlins 1983; Ramírez 2002.

22. Geertz 1973: 9.

References

Abercrombie, Thomas A. 1998. *Pathways of Memory and Power: Ethnography and History Among an Andean People*. Madison: University of Wisconsin Press.

Acosta, Antonio. 1987. "La extirpación de las idolatrías en el Peru: Origen y desarrollo de las campañas." *Revista Andina* 5, no. 1 (July): 171–95.

Acosta, Joseph de. 1590/1979. *Historia natural y moral de las Indias*. México: Fondo de la Cultura Económica.

———. 1590/2002. *Natural and Moral History of the Indies*. Ed. Jane E. Mangan. Durham, NC: Duke University Press.

Adorno, Rolena. 1982. *From Oral to Written Expression: Native Andean Chronicles of the Early Colonial Period*. Syracuse, NY: Maxwell School of Citizenship and Public Affairs, Syracuse University.

———. 1986. *Guamán Poma: Writing and Resistance in Colonial Peru*. Austin: University of Texas Press.

Adrián, Monica. 1997. "El espacio sagrado y el ejercicio del poder: Las doctrinas de Chayanta durante la segunda mitad del siglo 18." *Anuario del Archivo y Biblioteca Nacionales de Bolivia (Sucre)*: 239–55.

Aguirre Palma, Borris. 1986. *Cosmovisión Andina: Una aproximación a la religiosidad indígena*. Quito: Ediciones Abya-Yala.

Agustinos. ca. 1550/1918. "Informaciones acerca de la religion y gobierno de los Incas." In Horacio H. Urteaga, ed., Colección de libros y documentos referentes a la historia del Perú, 11:3–56. Lima: Imprenta y Librería Sanmartí y Ca.

———. ca. 1550/1865/1964. "Relacion de la religion y ritos del Peru, hecha por los primeros agustinos que alli pasaron para la conversion de los naturales." In Luis Torres de Mendoza, ed., *Colección de documentos inéditos relativos al descubrimiento, conquista y colonización de las poseciones españoles en América y Oceanía*. 5–58. Madrid: Imprenta de Manuel B. de Quiroz. Reprint, Vaduz: Kraus.

———. ca. 1550/1992. *Relación de los Agustinos de Huamachuco*. Lima: Pontificia Universidad Católica del Perú.

Aibar Ozejo, Elena. 1968–69. "La visita de Guaraz en 1558." *Cuadernos del Seminario de Historia (Lima)* 9 (January 1968–December 1969): 5–21.

Albornoz, Cristóbal de. 1967. "Instrucción para descubrir todas las guacas del Piru y sus camayoc y haciendas." *Journal de la Société des Americanistes* 56 (1): 7–39.

Alonso Sagaseta de Ilurdoz, Alicia. 1990. "Los guauquis incaicos." *Revista Española de Antropología Americana* 20: 93–104.

Alva Mariñas, José Pedro. 1999. "Don Juan de Collique." *La Industria (Chiclayo)*. Sunday Magazine, October 11, 5–6.

Álvarez, Bartolomé. 1588/1998. *De las costumbres y conversión de los indios del Perú: Memorial a Felipe II (1588)*. Ed. María del Carmen Martín Rubio, Juan J. R. Villarías Robles, and Fermín del Pino Díaz. Madrid: Ediciones Polifemo.

Anderson, Benedict. 1992. *Imagined Communities: Reflections on the Origin and Spread of Nationalism*. New York: Verso.

Andrien, Kenneth J. 1991. "Spaniards, Andeans, and the Early Colonial State in Peru." In Kenneth J. Andrien and Rolena Adorno, *Transatlantic Encounters: Europeans and Andeans in the Sixteenth Century*. 121–48. Berkeley: University of California Press.

Anello Oliva, Giovanni. 1598/1998. *Historia del reyno y provincias del Perú y vidas de los varones insignes de la Compañía de Jesus*. Lima: Pontificia Universidad Católica del Perú.

Angulo, Domingo. 1920. "Fundación y población de la Villa de Zaña." *Revista del Archivo Nacional del Perú* 1 (2): 280–99.

———. 1921. "Don Andres Hurtado de Mendoza y la fundación de la Villa de Cañete." *Revista histórica* 5:21–89.

"Anónimo de Yucay [1571]: Dominio de los yngas en el Peru y del que Su Magestad tiene en dichos reynos." 1571/1970. *Historia y cultura* 4: 97–152.

Anónimo. 1571/1995. *El anónimo de Yucay frente a Bartolomé de las Casas (edición crítica del parecer de Yucay [1571])*. Ed. Isacio Pérez Fernández, O. P. [Ordo Praedicatorum]. Cuzco: Centro de Estudios Regionales Andinos "Bartolomé de las Casas." Original in the BNE/Ms. 19569, titled "Dominio de los Ingas."

———. 1573/1965. "La cibdad de Sant Francisco del Quito." In Marcos Jiménez de la Espada, ed., *Relaciones geográficas de Indias*. Biblioteca de autores Españoles, 184: 205–32. Madrid: Ediciones Atlas.

Ares Queija, Berta. 1984. "Las danzas de los indios: Un camino para la evangelización del virreinato del Perú." *Revista de Indias* 44 (174): 445–63.

Armas Medina, Fernando de. 1952. "Evolución histórica de las doctrinas de indios." *Anuario de Estudios Americanos* 9: 101–29.

Arriaga, Pablo Joseph de. 1621. *La extirpación de la idolatría en el Perú (1621)*. Lima: Geronymo de Contreras.

———. 1621/1920. *La extirpación de la idolatría en el Perú*. In Horacio H. Urteaga, ed., Colección de libros y documentos referentes a la historia del Perú, 2nd ser., vol. 1. Lima: Imprenta y Librería Sanmartí y Ca.

———. 1621/1968. "La extirpación de la idolatría en el Perú." In Francisco Esteve Barba, ed., *Crónicas Peruanas de interés indígena*. Biblioteca de autores Españoles, 209: 191–278. Madrid: Ediciones Atlas.

Arze O., Silvia. 1996. "Fragmentación e integración: Estrategias de los ayllus del norte de Potosí en situación colonial." In Xavier Albó, ed., *La integración surandina: Cinco siglos después*. 175–87. Antofagasta, Chile: Universidad Católica del Norte de Antofagasta.

Assadourian, Carlos Sempat. 1983. "Dominio colonial y señores étnicos en el espacio Andino." *HISLA* 1: 7–20.

———. 1987. "Los señores étnicos y los corregidores de indios en la conformación del estado colonial." *Anuario de Estudios Americanos* 44:325–426.

Ávila, Francisco de. 1598/1966. *Dioses y hombres de Huarochirí (1598?)*. Lima: Museo de Historia and Instituto de Estudios Peruanos.

Ayacucho, Perú, Cabildo. 1966. *Libro del Cabildo de la Ciudad de San Juan de la Frontera de Huamanga, 1539–1547*. Lima: Ediciones de la Casa de Cultura del Perú.

Bachmann, Carlos J. 1905. *Historia de la demarcación política del Perú*. Lima: Imprenta G. Clauss y Ca.

Baines, John, and Norman Yoffee. 2000. "Order, Legitimacy, and Wealth: Setting the Terms." In Janet Richards and Mary Van Buren, eds., *Order, Legitimacy, and Wealth in Ancient States*, 13–17. Cambridge: Cambridge University Press.

Bandera, Damían de la. 1557/1920 [1921]. *Informaciones sobre el antiguo Perú*. In Horacio H. Urteaga, ed., Colección de libros y documentos referentes a la historia del Perú, 2nd ser., vol. 3. Lima: Sanmartí y Ca.

———. 1557/1968. *Relación del origen é gobierno que los Ingas tuvieron y del que había antes . . . (1557)*. Biblioteca Peruana: El Perú a través de los siglos, 1st ser., vol. 3, 491–510. Lima: Editores Técnicos Asociados, S.A.

Barnadas, Josep M. 1993. "Idolatrías en Charcas (1560–1620): Datos sobre su existencia como paso previo para la valoración del tema de su extirpación." In Gabriela Ramos and Henrique Urbano, comps., *Catolicismo y extirpación de idolatrías, siglos XVI–XVIII*. 89–103. Cuzco: Centro de Estudios Regionales Andinos "Bartolomé de las Casas."

Barnes, Monica, and Daniel J. Slive. 1993. "El puma de Cuzco: Plano de la ciudad Ynga o noción europea?" *Revista Andina* 11, no. 1 (July): 79–102.

Barth, Frederick, ed. 1970. *Ethnic Groups and Boundaries: The Social Organization of Culture Difference*. Oslo: Universitets Forlegat.

Bauer, Brian S. 1992. *The Development of the Inca State*. Austin: University of Texas Press.

———. 1996. "Legitimization of the State in Inca Myth and Ritual." *American Anthropologist* 98 (2): 327–37.

Benavides, María A. 1988. "La división social y geográfica hanansaya/urinsaya en el valle del Colca y la provincia de Caylloma (Arequipa)." *Boletín de Lima* 60:49–53.

Bertonio, Ludovico. 1612/1984. "Vocabulario de la lengua Aymara." Cochabamba, Bolivia: Centro de Estudios de la Realidad Económica y Social.

Besom, John Thomas. 2000. "Mummies, Mountains, and Immolations: Strategies for Unifying the Inka Empire's Southern Quarters." Ph.D. diss., State University of New York–Binghamton.

Betanzos, Juan de. 1551–57/1987. *Suma y narración de los Incas*. Madrid: Ediciones Atlas.

———. 1551–57/1996. *Narrative of the Incas*. Austin: University of Texas Press.

Bibar [Vivar], Gerónimo [Jerónimo] de. 1558/1966. *Crónica y relación copiosa y verdadera de los Reynos de Chile*. Santiago: Fondo Histórico "J. T. Medina."

Binford, Michael W., Alan L. Kolata, Mark Brenner, John W. Janusek, Matthew T. Seddon, Mark Abbot, and Jason H. Curtis. 1997. "Climate Variation and the Rise and Fall of an Andean Civilization." *Quaternary Research* 47 (2): 235–48.

Boehm, Christopher. 1980. "Exposing the Moral Self in Montenegro: The Use of Natural Definitions to Keep Ethnography Descriptive." *American Ethnologist* 7 (1): 1–26.

Bromley, Juan. 1935. *La fundación de la Ciudad de Los Reyes.* Lima: n.p.

Browman, David L. 1996. "Evolving Archaeological Interpretations of Inka Institutions: Perspectives." *Latin American Research Review* 31 (1): 227–43.

Burger, Richard, and Lucy Salazar-Burger. 1993. "The Place of Dual Organization in Early Andean Ceremonialism: A Comparative Review." In Luis Millones and Yoshio Onuki, eds. *El mundo ceremonial Andino.* 97–116. Osaka, Japan: National Museum of Ethnology.

Cabello Valboa, Miguel. 1586/1951. *Miscelánea antártica.* Lima: Universidad Nacional Mayor de San Marcos.

Cabero, Marco A. 1906. "El corregimiento de Saña y el problema histórico de la fundación de Trujillo." *Revista histórica* 1, no. 2 (1906): 151–91; no 3: 336–73; no. 4: 485–514.

Caillavet, Chantal. 1983. "Ethno-histoire équatorienne: Un testament indien inédit du XVIe siecle." *Cahiers de monde hispanique et luso-bresilien (Toulouse)* 41:5–23.

———. 2000. *Etnias del norte: Etnohistoria e historia de Ecuador.* Quito: Ediciones Abya Yala.

Calancha, Antonio de la. 1638/1974–81. *Crónica moralizada (del orden de San Agustín en el Perú [1638]).* 6 vols. Lima: Edición de Ignacio Prado Pastor.

Calero, Luis F. 1997. *Chiefdoms Under Siege: Spain's Rule and Native Adaptation in the Southern Colombian Andes 1535–1700.* Albuquerque: University of New Mexico Press.

Cañedo-Argüelles, Teresa. 1998. "Supervivencia de la comunidad andina y claves para su identidad." *Histórica* 22 (1): 1–23.

Carrera, Padre Fernando de la. 1644/1939. *Arte de la lengua Yunga de los Valles del Obispado de Truxillo . . . [1644].* Tucuman: Instituto de Antropología.

Carroll, John B., ed. 1956/1962. *Language, Thought, and Reality: Selected Writings of Benjamin Lee Whorf.* Cambridge, Mass.: MIT Press.

Castelli, Amalia. 1998. "Una aproximación al estudio de los Incas desde un documento editado en 1547." *Histórica* 22 (1): 81–91.

Castro, Fray Chr[is]toual de, and Diego de Ortega Morejón. 1558/1968. "Relación de Chincha (1558)." *Biblioteca Peruana: El Perú a través de los siglos,* 1st ser., 3 vols., 465–89. Lima: Editores Técnicos Asociados.

Castro, Victoria. 1993. "Un proceso de extirpación de idolatrías en Atacama, siglo 17." In Gabriela Ramos and Henrique Urbano, comps., *Catolicismo y extirpación de idolatrías, siglos XVI–XVIII,* 347–66. Cuzco: Centro de Estudios Regionales Andinos "Bartolomé de las Casas."

Castro-Klarén, Sara. 1993. "Dancing and the Sacred in the Andes: From the Taqui Onqoy to Resu-ñati." In Stephen Greenblatt, ed., *New World Encounters,* 159–76. Berkeley: University of California Press.

Cerrón-Palomino, Rodolfo. 1997. "Cuzco y no cusco ni menos Qosqo." *Histórica* 21, no. 2 (December): 165–70.

———. 1998. "El cantar de Inca Yupanqui y la lengua secreta de los incas." *Revista Andina* 32:417–52.

Cervantes, Fernando. 1996. "Conversión o sincretismo? Una reinterpretación de la conquista espiritual en la América española (1521–1767)." Paper presented at the workshop "Making Sense of the World: Perceptions of Change in Mesoamerica and the Andes," Amsterdam, June 6–7.

Chacón Zhapán, Juan. 1990. *Historia del Corregimiento de Cuenca (1557–1777)*. Quito: Banco Central del Ecuador.

Cieza de León, Pedro de. 1864/1964. *Travels of Pedro de Cieza de Leon*. London: Hakluyt Society.

———. 1967. *El señorio de los Incas*. Lima: Instituto de Estudios Peruanos.

———. 1553/1984. *La crónica del Perú: Primera Parte (1553)*. Vol. 1. Lima: Pontificia Universidad Católica del Perú, Academia Nacional de la Historia.

———. 1550/1985. *La crónica del Perú: Segunda Parte*. Vol. 2. Lima: Pontificia Universidad Católica del Perú, Academia Nacional de la Historia.

———. 1987. *La crónica del Perú: Tercera Parte*. Vol. 3. Lima: Pontificia Universidad Católica del Perú, Academia Nacional de la Historia.

———. 1991. *La crónica del Perú: Quarta Parte (Guerra de Las Salinas)*. Vol. 1. Lima: Pontificia Universidad Católica del Perú.

Classen, Constance. 1993. *Inca Cosmology and the Human Body*. Salt Lake City: University of Utah Press.

Cobo, Bernabé. 1935. *Monografías históricas sobre la ciudad de Lima*. Lima: Consejo Provincial.

———. 1653/1956–64. *Historia del Nuevo Mundo*. Biblioteca de autores Españoles, vols. 91–92. Madrid: Ediciones Atlas.

———. 1990. *Inca Religion and Customs*. Austin: University of Texas Press.

Cock Carrasco, Guillermo A. 1980. "El sacerdote Andino y los bienes de las divinidades en los siglos XVII y XVIII." Bachelor's thesis, Pontificia Universidad Católica del Perú, Lima.

———. 1983. "Sacerdotes o chamanes en el mundo Andino." *Historia y cultura* 16:135–46.

———. 1984. "Poder y riqueza de un Hatun Curaca del Valle del Jequetepeque en el siglo XVI." *Historia y cultura* (Lima) 17:133–55.

———. 1986. "Power and Wealth in the Jequetepeque Valley During the Sixteenth Century." In C. B. Donnan and Guillermo A. Cock Carrasco, eds., *The Pacatnamu Papers*, 1:171–80. Los Angeles: Museum of Cultural History, University of California.

Cock Carrasco, Guillermo A., and Mary Doyle. 1979. "Del culto solar a la clandestinidad de Inti y Punchao." *Historia y cultura* 12:51–73.

Comisión del Estatuto y Redemarcación Territorial. Ley 10553. 1947. *La demarcación territorial y política del Departamento de Lambayeque: Informe de la Acesoría Técnica*. Lima: n.p.

Conrad, Geoffrey W., and Arthur A. Demarest. 1984. *Religion and Empire: The Dynamics of Aztec and Inca Expansionism*. Cambridge: Cambridge University Press.

———. 1992. *Ideology and Pre-Columbian Civilizations*. Santa Fe, NM: School for American Research.

Cook, Noble David. 1975. *Tasa de la visita general de Francisco de Toledo*. Lima: Universidad Nacional Mayor de San Marcos.

———. 1976–77. "La visita de los Conchucos por Cristobal Ponce de Leon, 1543." *Historia y cultura* 10:23–45.

———. 1981. *Demographic Collapse: Indian Peru, 1520–1620*. Cambridge: Cambridge University Press.

———. 1998. *Born to Die: Disease and New World Conquest, 1492–1650*. Cambridge: Cambridge University Press.

Cook, Noble David, with Alexandra Parma Cook. Forthcoming. *People of the Volcano: Andean Counterpoint in the Colca Valley of Peru*. Durham, NC: Duke University Press.

Córdoba [Cordova] Salinas, Diego de. 1651/1957. *Crónica Franciscana de las Provincias del Perú*. Washington, DC: Academy of American Franciscan History.

Cortés, Hernán. 1986. *Hernán Cortés: Letters from Mexico*. Trans. Anthony Pagden. New Haven, CT.: Yale University Press.

Covarrubias, Sebastián de. 1611/1943. *Tesoro de la lengua Castellana o Española*. Ed. Martin de Riques. Barcelona: S.A. Horta, I.E.

Crespo, Juan Carlos, 1558/1974. "Relación de Chincha (1558)." *Historia y cultura (Lima)* 8:91–104.

Cummins, Tom. 1998. "Let Me See! Reading Is for Them: Colonial Andean Images and Objects 'como es costumbre tener los caciques Señores.'" In Elizabeth Hill Boone and Tom Cummins, eds., *Native Traditions in the Postcolonial World*, 91–148. Washington, DC: Dumbarton Oaks Research Library and Collection.

Cuneo-Vidal, Rómulo. 1919. "El cacicazgo de Tacna." *Revista histórica* 6 (4): 309–24.

———. 1977. *Obras completas*. 7 vols. Lima: Editora.

Cunnison, Ian. 1951. "History on the Luapula." *The Rhodes-Livingstone Papers*, no. 21. London: Oxford University Press.

———. 1956. "Perpetual Kinship: A Political Institution." *Rhodes-Livingstone Journal* 20:21–48.

Cunow, Heinrich. 1933. *La organización social del Imperio de los Incas*. Lima: Librería y Editorial Peruana de D. Miranda.

Cuzco, Perú, Cabildo. 1926. *Fundación española del Cuzco y ordenanzas para su gobierno*. Lima: Talleres Gráficos Sanmarti y Cia.

D'Altroy, Terence N. 1987. "Transitions in Power: Centralization of Wanka Political Organization Under Inka Rule." *Ethnohistory* 34, no. 1 (Winter): 78–101.

Dammert Bellido, José. 1997. *Cajamarca en el siglo XVI*. Lima: Pontificia Universidad Católica del Perú.

Darnton, Robert. 1985. *The Great Cat Massacre and Other Episodes in French Cultural History*. New York: Vintage Books.

Dávila Brizeño, Diego. 1965. "Descripción y relación de la provincia de los Yauyos toda, Anan Yauyos y Lorin Yauyos, hecha por Diego Davila Brizeño, corregidor de Huarochiri." In M. Jiménez de la Espada, ed., *Relaciones geográficas de Indias—Perú*. Biblioteca de autores Españoles, 183:155–65. Madrid: Ediciones Atlas.

Dean, Carolyn. 1999. *Inka Bodies and the Body of Christ: Corpus Christi in Colonial Cuzco, Peru*. Durham, NC: Duke University Press.

Demarest, Arthur A. 1981. *Viracocha, The Nature and Antiquity of the Andean High God*. Monographs of the Peabody Museum, no. 6. Cambridge, MA.: Peabody Museum Press.

———. 1992a. "Archaeology, Ideology, and Pre-Columbian Cultural Evolution." In Geoffrey W. Conrad and Arthur A. Demarest, *Ideology and Pre-Columbian Civilizations*, 1–13. Santa Fe, NM: School of American Research.

———. 1992b. "Ideology in Ancient Maya Cultural Evolution: The Dynamics of Galactic Polities." In Geoffrey W. Conrad and Arthur A. Demarest, *Ideology and Pre-Columbian Civilizations*, 135–58. Santa Fe, NM: School of American Research.

"De virreyes y gobernadores del Pirú." 1867. *Colección de documentos inéditos relativos al descubrimiento . . . de América*. Comp. D. Luis Torres de Mendoza, VIII. Madrid: Imprenta de Frias y Compañia.

Diez de San Miguel, Garci. 1567/1964. *Visita hecha a la Provincia de Chuquito*. Lima: Casa de la Cultura del Perú.

Diez Hurtado, Alejandro. 1988. *Pueblos y caciques de Piura, siglos XVI y XVII*. Piura, Perú: Centro de Investigación y Promoción del Campesino.

———. 1997. "Caciques, cofradías, memoria y parcialidades: Un ensayo sobre el origen de la identidad cataquense." *Antropológica* (Lima) 15:151–72.

Dillehay, Tom D. 1988. "Introduction." In Tom D. Dillehay and Patricia J. Netherly, eds., *La frontera del estado Inca*. 3–33. Oxford: BAR International.

Dillehay, Tom D., and Patricia J. Netherly. 1983. "Exploring the Upper Zaña Valley in Peru: A Unique Tropical Forest Setting Offers Insights into the Andean Past." *Archaeology* 36 (July/August): 22–30.

———. 1988. "Epilogo." In Tom D. Dillehay and Patricia J. Netherly, eds., *La frontera del estado Inca*, 273–75. Oxford: BAR International.

Dover, Robert V. H. 1992. "Introduction." In Robert V. H. Dover, Katerarine E. Seibold, and John H. McDowell, eds., *Andean Cosmologies Through Time*, 1–16. Bloomington: Indiana University Press.

Doyle, Mary Eileen. 1988. "The Ancestor Cult and Burial Ritual in Seventeenth and Eighteenth Century Peru." Ph.D. diss., University of California at Los Angeles.

Dunbar Temple, Ella. 1942. "Los caciques Apoalaya." *Revista del Museo Nacional* 11 (2): 147–78.

Duviols, Pierre. 1966. "La visite des idolatries de Concepción de Chupas (Pérou, 1614)." *Journal de la Société des Américanistes* 56 (2): 497–510.

———. 1967a. "La idolatría en cifras, una relación peruana de 1619." *Colloque d'études péruviennes* (Aix-en-Provence) 61:87–100.

———. 1972. *La lutte contre les religions autochtones dans le Pérou colonial*. Paris: Institut Français d'Etudes Andines.

———. 1974–76. "Une petite chronique retrouvée: Errores, ritos, supersticiones y ceremonias de los yndios de la provincia de Chinchaycocha y otros del Piru." *Journal de la Société des Americanistes* (Paris) 63:275–97.

———. 1976a. "Un symbolisme andin du double: la lithomorphose de d'ancestre." In *XLII International Congress of Americanists* (Paris, 1976). 4:359–64. Paris: Actes.

———. 1977a. "Los nombres quechua de Viracocha, supuesto 'Dios creador' de los evangelizadores." *Allpanchis (Cusco)* 10 (10): 53–63.

———. 1977b. *La destrucción de las religiones andinas.* México: Universidad Nacional Autónoma de México.

———. 1978. "Camaquen, Upani: Un concept animiste des anciens peruviens." In Roswith Hartmann and Udo Oberem, eds., *Amerikanistische Studien/Estudios Americanistas: Festschrift für Hermann Trimborn*, 132–44. St. Augustin, Germany: Haus Völker und Kulturen, Anthropos-Institut.

———. 1983. "La *Contra Idolatrum* de Luis de Teruel y una versión primeriza del mito de Pachacámac-Vichama." *Revista Andina* 2, no. 2 (December): 385–92.

———. 1984. "Albornoz y el espacio ritual andino prehispánico." *Revista Andina* 2, no. 2 (July): 169–222.

———. 1986. *Cultura Andina y represión: Procesos y visitas de idolatrías y hechicería. Cajatambo, siglo XVII.* Cuzco: Centro de Estudios Rurales Andinos "Bartolomé de las Casas."

Earls, John, and Irene Silverblatt. 1978. "La realidad física y social en la cosmología Andina." *Actes du XLIIe Congrès International des Américanistes (1976)* 4:299–325. Paris: Société des américanistes.

Eckert, Georg. 1945. "El culto a los muertos." *Revista de Indias* 19:73–122.

Ellefson, Bernardo. 1982. "Las concubinas de los Sapa Incas difuntos." *Bulletin de l'Institut Français de Etudes Andines* 11 (1–2): 11–18.

Erickson, Clark L. 1999. "Neo-environmental Determinism and Agrarian 'Collapse' in Andean Prehistory." *Antiquity* 73: 281 (September): 634–42.

Escobar Zapata, Emerita. 1992. "Suyu y longitud en el espacio Andino." *Boletín de Lima* 83:12–14.

Espinoza Soriano, Waldemar. 1969a. *Lurinhuaila de Huacjra: Un ayllu y un curacazgo Huanca.* Huancayo, Perú: Casa de la Cultura.

———. 1969b. "El Memorial de Charcas: Crónica inédita de 1582." *Cantuta* 4:117–52.

———. 1975. "El Valle de Jayanca y el reino de los Mochica, siglos XV y XVI." *Bulletin de l'Institut Français de Etudes Andines* 4 (3–4): 243–74.

———. 1976. "Las mugeres secundarias de Huayna Capac: Dos casos de señorialismo feudal en el imperio Inca." *Revista del Museo Nacional* (Lima) 42:247–98.

———. 1577/1977. "Los cuatro suyos del Cuzco, siglos XV y XVI." *Bulletin de l'Institut Français de Etudes Andines* 6 (3–4): 109–22.

———. 1978. "La vida pública de un príncipe Inca residente en Quito, siglo XV y XVI." *Bulletin de l'Institut Français de Etudes Andines* 7 (3–4): 1–31.

———. 1980a. "Acerca de la historia militar inca." *Allpanchis* 16:171–86.

———. 1980b. "El curaca de los Cayambes y su sometimiento al imperio español, siglos XV y XVI." *Bulletin de l'Institut Français de Etudes Andines* 9 (12): 89–110.

———. 1981. "Un testimonio sobre los idolos huacas y dioses de Lampa y Cajatambo, siglos XV–XVII, Supervivencias en Cajamarca." *Scientia et praxis* (Lima, Peru) 15:115–30.

———. 1987–89. "Migraciones internas en el reino Colla: Tejedores, plumereros y alfareros del estado Inca." *Revista histórica* 36:209–305.

———. 1993. "Los mitmas ajiceros-maniceros y los plateros de Ica en Cochabamba." *Historia y cultura* 22:47–74.

Estete, Miguel de. 1534–45/1938. *Noticia del Perú*. Los cronistas de la conquista, 1st ser., no. 2, 195–251. Paris: Desclée, De Brouwer.

———. 1542?/1987. "El descubrimiento y la conquista del Perú (De los papeles de la arca de Santa Cruz)." In Alberto Mario Salas, José Moure, and Miguel A. Guérin, eds., *Crónicas iniciales de la conquista del Perú*, 253–319. Buenos Aires: Editorial Plus Ultra.

———. 1533/1559/1992. "Relacion del viaje desde Caxamalca a Pachacamac (1533)." In Gonzalo Fernández de Oviedo, *Historia general y natural de las Indias (1535–45)*. Biblioteca de autores Españoles, 121:68–78. Madrid: Ediciones Atlas.

Farrington, I. S. 1992. "Ritual Geography, Settlement Patterns and the Characterization of the Provinces of the Inka Heartland." *World Archaeology* 23 (3): 368–85.

———. 1998. "The Concept of Cusco." *Tawantinsuyu* 5:53–59.

Fernández Villegas, Oswaldo. 1991. "Un curaca de la sierra central del Perú: Siglo XVII." *Boletín de Lima* 13, no. 78 (November): 49–55.

Ferrero, Onorio, and Fernando Iwasaki Cauti. 1984. "Idolatrías de los indios checras: Religión andina en los Andes Centrales." *Historia y cultura* 17:75–90.

Flores Espinoza, Javier. 1991. "Hechicería e idolatría en Lima colonial, siglo XVII." In Mirko Lauer, ed., and Henrique Urbano, comp., *Poder y violencia en los Andes*, 53–74. Cuzco: Centro de Estudios Regionales Andinos "Bartolomé de las Casas."

Flores Espinoza, Javier, and Laura Gutíerrez. 1992. "Dos documentos sobre los Jesuitas en Huarochirí." *Boletín del Instituto Riva Agüero* 19:201–16.

Freidel, David, and Linda Schele. 1992. "The Trees of Life: Ahau as Idea and Artifact in Classic Lowland Maya Civilization." In Geoffrey W. Conrad and Arthur A. Demarest, *Ideology and Pre-Columbian Civilizations*. 115–33. Santa Fe, NM: School of American Research.

Galdos Rodríguez, Guillermo. 1985–86. "Collasuyu, Collisuyu y Colesuyo en la documentación de fines del siglo XVI." *Revista histórica* 35:35–41.

Gama, Sebastián de la. 1540/1974. "Visita hecha en el Valle de Jayanca [Trujillo] (1540)." *Historia y cultura* (Lima) 8:215–28.

———. 1540/1975. "El Valle de Jayanca y el reino de los Mochica, siglos XV y XVI." *Bulletin de l'Institut Français de Etudes Andines* 4 (3–4): 243–74.

Garavaglia, Juan Carlos. 1999. "The Crises and Transformations of Invaded Societies: The La Plata Basin (1535–1650)." In Frank Salomon and Stuart B. Schwartz, eds., *The Cambridge History of the Native Peoples of the Americas*, vol. 3, pt. 2, 1–58. Cambridge: Cambridge University Press.

Garcia, Alejandro. 1998. "La ubicación de la frontera suroriental del Tawantinsuyu." *Sequilao: Revista de historia, arte y sociedad* 7 (12): 1–8.

García Cabrera, Juan Carlos. 1994. *Ofensas a Dios: Pleitos e injurias: Causas de idolatrías y hechicerías, Cajatambo, siglos XVII–XIX*. Cuzco: Centro de Estudios Regionales Andinos "Bartolomé de las Casas."

Garcilaso de la Vega, Inca. 1609/1941–45. *Los comentarios reales de los Incas*. 6 vols. Lima: Librería e Imprenta Gil, S.A.

———. 1602/1960–63. *Obras completas del Inca Garcilaso de la Vega*. In Carmela Saenz de Santa María, ed., Biblioteca de autores Españoles, vols. 132–35. Madrid: Ediciones Atlas.

———. 1609/1987. *Royal Commentaries of the Incas and General History of Peru*. Austin: University of Texas Press.

Gareis, Iris. 1989. "Extirpación de idolatrías e inquisición en el Virreinato del Perú." *Boletín del Instituto Riva-Aguero* 16:55–74.

———. 1991. "La metamorfosis de los dioses: Cambio cultural en las sociedades andinas." *Antropológica* 9 (December): 247–57.

———. 1993. "Las religiones andinas en los procesos de idolatrías: Hacia una crítica de fuentes." In Pierre Duviols, ed., *Religions des Andes et langues indigènes*, 281–95. Aix-en-Provence: Université de Provence.

Geertz, Clifford. 1973. *The Interpretation of Cultures*. New York: Basic Books.

———. 1980. *Negara: The Theatre State in Nineteenth-Century Bali*. Princeton, NJ: Princeton University Press.

———. 1983. *Local Knowledge: Further Essays in Interpretive Anthropology*. New York: Basic Books.

———. 1985. "Centers, Kings, and Charisma: Reflections on the Symbolics of Power." In Sean Wilentz, ed., *Rites of Power: Symbolism, Ritual and Politics Since the Middle Ages*, 13–38. Philadelphia: University of Pennsylvania Press.

Gibson, Charles. 1948/1969. *Inca Concept of Sovereignty and the Spanish Administration in Peru*. Austin, TX: Latin American Series.

———. 1987. "Indian Societies Under Spanish Rule." In Leslie Bethell, ed., *Colonial Spanish America*, 361–99. Cambridge: Cambridge University Press.

Gisbert, Teresa. 1991. "La cuatripartición andina y la relación Pachacamac-Viracocha." In Raquel Thiercelin, comp., *Cultures et sociétés, Andes et Méso-Amérique: Mélanges en hommage a Pierre Duviols*, 343–74. Aix-en-Provence: Université de Provence.

Glave, Luis Miguel. 1986. *El virreinato Peruano y la llamada 'Crisis general' del siglo XVII*. Lima: Universidad de Lima.

———. 1989a. "Un caracazgo [*sic*] Andino y la sociedad campesina del siglo XVII." *Allpanchis* 21 (33): 11–39.

———. 1989b. *Trajinantes: Caminos indígenas en la sociedad colonial siglos XVI/XVII*. Lima: Instituto de Apoyo Agrário.

Golte, Jurgen. 1970. "Algunas consideraciones acerca de la producción y distribución de la coca en le estado Inca." *Proceedings of the 38th International Congress of Americanists* (Stuttgart-Munchen, FRG, 1968), 2:471–78. Munich: Kommission Verlag, Klaus Renner.

Gonçales [Gonzalez] Holguin, Diego. 1608/1952/1989. *Vocabvlario de la lengva general de todo el Perv llamada qquichua o del Inca*. Lima: Universidad Mayor de San Marcos.

González de San Segundo, Miguel. 1982. "Pervivencia de la organización señorial aborigen." *Anuario de Estudios Americanos* 39:47–92.

González Suárez, Federico. 1968. *De prehistoria y de arqueología.* Cuenca, Ecuador: Universidad de Cuenca.

Gose, Peter. 1995. "Contra Pasqual Haro: Un proceso de idolatrías, Cusco, 1697." *Ciencias Sociales* 1 (1): 203–18.

———. 1996. "Oracles, Divine Kingship, and Political Representation in the Inka State." *Ethnohistory* 43, no. 1 (Winter): 1–32.

Gottman, Jean. 1973. *The Significance of Territory.* Charlottesville: University Press of Virginia.

Grebe, María Ester. 1995–96. "Continuidad y cambio en las representaciones icónicas: Significados simbólicos en el mundo sur-Andino." *Revista Chilena de Antropología* 13:137–54.

Griffiths, Nicholas. 1996. *The Cross and the Serpent: Religious Repression and Resurgence in Colonial Peru.* Norman: University of Oklahoma Press.

Guamán Poma de Ayala, Felipe. 1613/1936. *Nueva corónica y buen gobierno.* Paris: Institut d'ethnologie.

———. 1613/1980. *El primer nueva corónica y buen gobierno.* In J.V. Murra and Rolena Adorno, eds., 3 vols. México: Siglo XXI Editores, S.A.

———. 1594/1991. *Y no ay remedio.* Lima: Centro de Investigación y Promoción Amazónica.

Guibovich Pérez, Pedro. 1993. "La carrera de un visitador de idolatrías en el siglo XVII: Fernando de Avendaño (1580–1655)." In Gabriela Ramos and Henrique Urbano, eds., *Catolicismo y extirpación de idolatrías, siglos XVI–XVIII,* 169–239. Cuzco: Centro de Estudios Regionales Andinos "Bartolomé de las Casas."

Guillén Guillén, Edmundo. 1974. *Versión Inca de la conquista.* Lima: Editorial Milla Batres.

———. 1979. *Visión peruana de la conquista (La resistencia incaica a la invasión española).* Lima: Editorial Milla Batres.

———. 1984. "Las parcialidades de Hatun Rukana y Laramati en el siglo XVI." *Boletín de Lima* 32:73–96.

———. 1991. "Wila Oma: El último gran Intip Apun del Tawantinsuyo." In Mariusz Ziólkowski, ed., *El culto estatal del Imperio Inca,* 75–80. Warsaw: Universidad de Varsovia, Centro de Estudios Latinoamericanos.

———. 1994. *La guerra de reconquista Inka.* Lima: R. A. Ediciones.

Guilmartin, John F., Jr. 1991. "The Cutting Edge: An Analysis of the Spanish Invasion and Overthrow of the Inca Empire, 1532–39." In Kenneth Andrien and Rolena Adorno, eds., *Transatlantic Encounters: Europeans and Andeans in the Sixteenth Century,* 40–69. Berkeley: University of California Press.

Hagar, Stansbury. 1905. "Cuzco, the Celestial City." In *International Congress of Americanists,* 13th Session, New York, 1902, 217–25. Easton, PN: Eschenbach Printing Co.

———. 1906. "The Peruvian Asterisms and Their Relation to the Ritual." In *Internationaler Amerikanisten-Kongress* (Stuttgart, 1904), 593–602. Stuttgart: Verlag W. Kohlhammer.

Hamilton, Joe. 1978. "Plebe and Potentate: History and Society of Prehispanic North Central Coast Peru." Unpublished manuscript.

Hampe Martínez, Teodoro. 1988. "La división gubernativa, hacendistica y judicial en el Virreinato del Perú (siglos XVI–XVII)." *Revista de Indias* 48 (182–83): 59–85.

Harley, J. B. 1990. *Maps and the Columbian Encounter: An Interpretive Guide to the Travelling Exhibition: American Geographical Society Collection*. Milwaukee, WI: The Golda Meir Library.

Harrison, Regina. 1989. *Signs, Songs, and Memory in the Andes: Translating Quechua Language and Culture*. Austin: University of Texas Press.

Hart, Elizabeth Ann. 1983. "Prehistoric Political Organization on the Peruvian North Coast." Ph.D. diss., University of Michigan, Ann Arbor.

Hastorf, Christine A. 1993. *Agriculture and the Onset of Political Inequality Before the Inka*. Cambridge: Cambridge University Press.

Hernández Astete, Francisco. 1998. "Roles sexulaes en la organización incaica." *Histórica* (Lima) 22:1, 93–134.

Hernández Príncipe, Licenciado Rodrigo. 1621–22/1923. "Mitología Andina (1621–22)." *Inca: Revista trimestral de estudios antropológicos* (Lima) 1:25–78.

Herrera y Tordesillas, Antonio de. 1601–15. *Historia general de los hechos de los castellanos en las islas i tierra firme del mar oceano*. Madrid: La Emprenta Real.

———. 1728. *Historia general de las Inkas Ocidentales*. 4 vols. Amberes: J. B. Verdussen.

Heusch, Luc de. 1997. "The Symbolic Mechanisms of Sacred Kingship: Rediscovering Frazer." *Journal of the Royal Anthropological Institute* 3 (2): 213–32.

Heyerdahl, Thor, Daniel H. Sandweiss, and A. Narvaez. 1995. *The Pyramids of Tucume*. New York: Thames and Hudson.

Hiltunen, Juha J. 1999. *Ancient Kings of Peru: The Reliability of the Chronicle of Fernando de Montesinos*. Helsinki: Suomen Historiallinen Seura.

Hinojosa Cuba, Carlos. 1999. "Las momias de los Incas: El corazón de una tradición." *Boletín de Lima* 21:116, 30–41.

Hobsbawm, Eric. 1983. "Introduction: Inventing Traditions." In Eric Hobsbawm and Terrence Ranger, eds., *The Invention of Tradition*, 1–14. New York: Cambridge University Press.

Huertas Vallejos, Lorenzo. 1978. *Dioses mayores de Cajatambo*. Ayacucho, Perú: Universidad Nacional de San Cristóbal de Huamanga.

———. 1981. *La religión en una sociedad rural Andina, siglo XVII*. Ayacucho, Perú: Universidad Nacional de San Cristóbal de Huamanga.

———. 1987. *Ecologia y historia: Probanzas de indios y españoles referentes a las catastróficas lluvias de 1578, en los corregimientos de Trujillo y Saña*. Chiclayo, Perú: CES Solidaridad.

———. 1992. "Diluvios, terremotos y sequías: Factores disturbadores del órden económico y social." *Rimaq* 1 (1): 99–118.

———. 1998. "Conformación del espacio social en Huamanga, siglos XV y XVI." In Luis Millones, Hiroyasu Tomoeda, and Tasuhiko Fujii, eds. *Historia, religión y ritual de los pueblos ayacuchanos*, 7–28. Osaka, Japan: National Museum of Ethnology.

Hyslop, John. 1976. "An Archaeological Investigation of the Lupaca Kingdom and Its Origins." Ph.D. diss., Faculty of Political Science, Columbia University, New York.

———. 1984. *The Inka Road System.* Orlando, FL: Academic Press.

———. 1985. *Inkawasi: The New Cuzco, Cañete, Lunahuana, Peru.* New York: Institute for Andean Research.

———. 1988. "Las fronteras estatales extremas del Tawantinsuyu." In Tom D. Dillehay and Patricia J. Netherley, eds., *La frontera del estado Inca*, 35–57. Oxford: BAR International.

Ibarra Rojas, Eugenia. 1985–86. "La desestructuración del cacicazgo en el siglo XVI." *Revista de Historia* (Heredia, Costa Rica), nos. 12–13: 85–103.

Isbell, William H. 1978. "Cosmological Order Expressed in Prehistoric Ceremonial Centers." In *Actes du XLIIe Congres International de Americanistes Congres du Centenaire*, 2–9 Sept 1976, 4:269–97. Paris: Société des Américanistes.

———. 1997. *Mummies and Mortuary Monuments: A Postprocessual Prehistory of Central Andean Social Organization.* Austin: University of Texas Press.

Isbell, William H., and Anita G. Cook. 1987. "Ideological Origins of an Andean Conquest State." *Archaeology* 40, no. 4 (July–August): 26–33.

Jaye, Barbara H., and William P. Mitchell, eds. 1999. *Picturing Faith: A Facsimile Edition of the Pictographic Quechua Catechism in the Huntington Free Library.* Bronx, NY: Huntington Free Library.

Jones, Kristine L. 1999. "Warfare, Reorganization, and Readaptation at the Margins of Spanish Rule: The Southern Margin (1573–1822)." In Frank Salomon and Stuart B. Schwartz, eds., *The Cambridge History of the Native Peoples of the Americas*, vol. 3, pt. 2, 138–87. Cambridge: Cambridge University Press.

Julien, Catherine J. 1982. "Inca Decimal Administration in the Lake Titicaca Region." In George A. Collier, Renato I. Rosaldo, and John D. Wirth, eds., *The Inca and Aztec States, 1400–1800*, 119–51. New York: Academic Press.

———. 1983. *Hatuncolla: A View of Inca Rule from the Lake Titicaca Region.* Berkeley: University of California Press.

———. 1991. *Condesuyo: The Political Division of Territory Under Inca and Spanish Rule.* Bonn: Estudios Americanistas.

———. 1997. "The Incas and the Early Encomienda." Paper presented at the American Society for Ethnohistory meeting, México, D.F., November.

———. 1999. "Who Is Capac? Redefining Dynastic Affiliation Rules in Early Spanish Cuzco." Paper presented at the American Historical Association meeting, Washington DC, January.

———. 2000. *Reading Inca History.* Iowa City: University of Iowa Press.

Kagan, Richard. 1996. "Prescott's Paradigm: American Historical Scholarship and the Decline of Spain." *American Historical Review* 101 (2): 423–46.

Kauffmann Doig, Federico. 1978. "Los retratos de la capaccuna de Guaman Poma y el problema de los tocapo." In Roswith Hartmann and Udo Oberem, eds., *Estudios Americanistas*, 1:298–308. St. Augustin, Germany: Haus Volker und Kulturen, Anthropos-Institut.

Kaulicke, Peter. 1997. "La muerte en el antiguo Perú." In *Boletín de arqueología* (Lima) 1:7–54.

———. 2000. "Muerte y memoria en el Perú antiguo." In Peru, *El Perú en los albores del siglo XXI*, 89–114. Lima: Congreso del Perú.

Keightley, David N. 1979–80. "The Shang State as Seen in the Oracle-Bone Inscriptions." *Early China* 5:25–34.

Keith, Robert Gordon. 1969. "Origins of the Hacienda System on the Central Peruvian Coast." Ph.D. diss., Harvard University, Department of History.

———. 1971. "*Encomienda, Hacienda,* and *Corregimiento* in Spanish America." *Hispanic American Historical Review* 51 (3): 431–46.

Kicza, John E. 1994. "Dealing with Foreigners: A Comparative Essay Regarding Initial Expectations and Interactions Between Native Societies and the English in North America and the Spanish in Mexico." *Colonial Latin American Historical Review* 3 (4): 382–97.

Kolata, Alan, ed. 1996. *Tiwanaku and Its Hinterland: Archaeology and Paleoecology of an Andean Civilization.* Washington, DC: Smithsonian Institution Press.

———. 1997. "Of Kings and Capitals: Principles of Authority and the Nature of Cities in the Native Andean State." In Deborah L. Nichols and Thomas H. Charlton, eds., *The Archaeology of City States: Cross-Cultural Approaches*, 245–54. Washington, DC: Smithsonian Institution Press.

Krapovickas, Pedro. 1978. "Los indios de la Puna en el siglo XVI." *Relaciones de la Sociedad de Antropología* (Buenos Aires) 12:71–93.

Kristof, Nicholas D. 1996. "For Rural Japanese, Death Doesn't Break Family Ties." *New York Times*, September 29, 1, 8.

Kubler, George. 1944. "A Peruvian Chief of State: Manco Inca (1515–1545)." *Hispanic American Historical Review* 24 (2): 253–76.

Lafuente, Antonio, and Antonio Mazuecos. 1978. *Los caballeros del punto fijo: Ciencia, política y aventura en la expedición geodísica hispanofrancesa al virreinato del Perú en el siglo XVIII.* Barcelona: Consejo Superior de Investigaciónes Científicas.

Landázuri N., Cristóbal. 1993. "Los sistemas religiosos norandinos del siglo XVI y las fuentes documentales." *Memoria del Instituto de Historia y Antropología Andinas (Quito)* 3: 275–336.

Lanning, Edward P. 1967. *Peru Before the Incas.* Englewood Cliffs, NJ: Prentice-Hall.

Larco Herrera, Alberto. 1917. *Anales de Cabildo de la Ciudad de Trujillo, 1566–71.* Lima: Sanmarti y Cia.

Larrea, Juan. 1953. "La mascapaicha." *Letras* (Lima) 49:103–34.

———. 1960. *Corona incaica.* Córdoba, Argentina: Universidad Nacional de Córdoba.

Las Casas, Bartolomé de. 1559/1909. *Apologética historia sumaria . . . de las Indias.* Nueva biblioteca de autores Españoles, vol. 13. Madrid: Ediciones Atlas.

———. 1555/1948. *De las antiguas gentes del Perú (1555) (Capítulos de la Apologética historia sumaria).* Los Pequeños Grandes Libros de Historia Americana, 1st ser., vol. 16. Lima: Librería e Imprenta D. Miranda.

Lastres, Juan B. 1947. "Dioses y templos incaicos protectores de la salud." *Revista del Museo Nacional* (Lima) 16:3–16.

Laurencich-Minelli, Laura. 1991. "El trabajo como forma de culto estatal en el imperio Inca." In Mariusz S. Ziółkowski, ed., *El culto estatal del imperio Inca*,

Memorias del 46th International Congress of Americanists (Amsterdam, 1988), 55–58. Varsovia: Centrum Studiow Latynoamerykanskich.

Lazaro Llantoy, Luis Alberto. 1996. *Vilcabamba de los Incas: El reyno del sol del amanecer*. Lima: n.p.

Levillier, Roberto. 1921–22. *Audiencia de Charcas: Correspondencia de Presidentes y Oidores*. 2 vols. Madrid: Imprenta de Juan Pueyo.

———. 1935. *Don Francisco de Toledo, Supremo Organizador del Perú*. Madrid: Espasa-Calpe, S.A.

Lisson y Chaves, Emilio. 1943–44. *La iglesia de España en el Perú*, 4 vols., 127–32. Seville: Escuela de Estudios Hispano-Americanos.

Lizarraga, Fray Reynaldo de. 1604/1907. "Descripción y población de las Indias (1604)." *Revista histórica* 2 (3): 261–93; 2 (4): 459–543.

Loaiza, Hector. 1998. *El camino de los brujos Andinos: Relato*. México: Editorial Diana.

Lockhart, James. 1992. "Three Experiences of Culture Contact: Nahua, Maya, and Quechua." *Mester* 21, no. 2 (Fall): 31–52.

Lohmann Villena, Guillermo. 1957. *El corregidor de indios en el Perú Bajo los Austrias*. Madrid: Ediciones Cultural Hispánica.

Lorandi, Ana María. 1995. "Señores del imperio perdido nobles y curacas en el Perú colonial." *Tawantinsuyu* (Guandaroo, Australia) 1:85–96.

Loredo, Rafael. 1958. *Los repartos: Bocetos para la nueva historia del Perú*. Lima: n.p.

Lothrop, Samuel K. 1938. *Inca Treasure as Depicted by Spanish Historians*. Los Angeles: Southwest Museum.

Lumbreras, Luis Guillermo. 1985. *Nueva historia general del Perú*. Lima: Mosca Azul Editores.

MacCormack, Sabine G. 1985a. "The Fall of the Incas: A Historiographical Dilemma." *History of European Ideas* 6 (4): 421–45.

———. 1985b. "The Heart Has Its Reasons: Predicaments of Missionary Christianity in Early Colonial Peru." *Hispanic American Historical Review* 65 (3): 443–66.

———. 1988. "Pachacuti: Miracles, Punishments, and Last Judgment: Visionary Past and Prophetic Future in Early Colonial Peru." *American Historical Review* 93, no. 4 (October): 960–1006.

———. 1989. "Atahualpa and the Book." *Dispositio* 14 (36–38): 141–68.

———. 1990. *Children of the Sun and Reason of State: Myths, Ceremonies and Conflicts in Inca Peru*. Working paper no. 6., University of Maryland, College Park.

———. 1991. *Religion in the Andes: Vision and Imagination in Early Colonial Peru*. Princeton, NJ: Princeton University Press.

———. 1993. "Demons, Imagination, and the Incas." In Stephen Greenblatt, ed., *New World Encounters*, 101–66. Berkeley: University of California Press.

———. 1997a. "History and Law in Sixteenth-Century Peru: The Impact of European Scholarly Traditions." In S. C. Humphreys, ed., *Cultures of Scholarship*, 277–310. Ann Arbor: University of Michigan Press.

———. 1997b. "Lords of Cuzco: From Pre-Inca Settlement to Inca and Spanish City." Draft, courtesy of the author.

———. 1998. "Time, Space, and Ritual Actions: The Inka and Christian Calendars in Early Colonial Peru." In Elizabeth Hill Boone and Tom Cummins, eds., *Native Traditions in the Postconquest World*, 295–343. Washington, DC: Dumbarton Oaks Research Library and Collection.

Maldi, Denise. 1997. "De confererados a bárbaros: A representação da territorialidade e da fronteira indígenas nos séculos XVIII e XIX." *Revista antropológica* (São Paulo, Brasil) 40 (2): 183–221.

Mariategui, José Carlos. 1977. *Siete ensayos de interpretación de la realidad Peruana: Versión popular y gráfica*. Lima: Centro de Publicaciones Educativas.

Marques da Cunha Martins Portugal, Ana Raquel. 1996. "Sintese analítica da concepçao de ayllu em cronicas do século XVI." *Estudos leopoldenses* 32, no. 148 (July–August): 87–101.

Martínez, Gabriel. 1981. "Espacio Lupaqa: Algunas hipótesis de trabajo." In Amalia Castelli and Marcia Koch de Paredes, eds., *Etnohistoria y antropología Andina*, 263–80. Lima: Museo Nacional de Historia.

———. 1983. "Los dioses de los cerros en los Andes." *Journal de la Société des Americanistes* 69:85–115.

Martínez Cereceda, José Luis. 1982. "Una aproximación al concepto andino de autoridad, aplicado a los dirigentes étnicos durante el siglo XVI y principios del XVII." Master's thesis, Pontificia Universidad Católica del Perú, Lima.

———. 1986. "El 'personaje sentado' en los keru: Hacia una identificación de los kuraka Andinos." *Boletín del Museo Chileno de Arte precolombino* 1:101–24.

———. 1988. "Kurakas, rituales e insignias: Una proposición." *Histórica* 12, no. 1 (July): 61–74.

———. 1995a. *Autoridades en los Andes, Los atributos del señor*. Lima: Pontificia Universidad Católica del Perú.

———. 1995b. "Textos y palabras: Cuatro documentos del siglo XVI." In Ana María Presta, ed., *Espacio, etnías, frontera: Atenuaciones políticas en el sur del Tawantinsuyu. Siglos XV–XVIII*. Sucre, Bolivia: Imprenta "Tupac Katari."

———. 1995c. "Papeles distantes, papeles quebradas: Las informaciones sobre Lipes en el siglo XVI." In Ana María Presta, ed., *Espacio, etnías, frontera: atenuaciones políticas en el sur del Tawantinsuyu. Siglos XV–XVIII*. Sucre, Bolivia: Imprenta "Tupac Katari."

———. 1996. "Papeles distantes, palabras quebradas: Las informaciones sobre Lipes en el sigloXVI." In Xavier Albó, ed., *La integración surandina: Cinco siglos después*, 229–59. Antofagasta, Chile: Universidad Católica del Norte de Antofagasta.

Masuda, Shozo. 1985. "Algae Collectors and *Lomas*." In Shozo Masuda, Izumi Shimada, and Craig Morris, eds., *Andean Ecology and Civilization: An Interdisciplinary Perspective on Andean Ecological Complementarity*, 233–50. Tokyo: University of Tokyo Press.

Maurtua, Victor M. 1906. *Juicio de límites entre El Perú y Bolivia*. 12 vols. Barcelona: Imprenta de Henrich y Comp.

Means, Philip Ainsworth. 1928/1973. *Biblioteca Andina*. New Haven, CT: Academy of Arts and Sciences.

Medinaceli G., Ximena. 1995. "Nombres disidentes: Mugeres Aymaras en Sacaca (siglo XVII)." In *Estudios Bolivianos* 1:321–42.

Medinaceli G., Ximena, and Silvia Arze. 1996. "Los mallkus de Charkas: Redes de poder en el norte de Potosí, siglos XVI y XVII." *Estudios Bolivianos* 2:283–319.

Melo, Garçia, Damián de la Bandera, Cristóbal de Molina, Alonso de Mesa, and Bartolomé de Porras. 1582/1925. "Información hecha en el Cuzco, por orden del Rey y encargo del Virrey Martín Enríquez acerca de las costumbres que tenían los Incas del Perú, antes de la conquista española . . ." In Roberto Levillier, ed., *Gobernantes del Perú: Cartas y papeles, siglo XVI,* 9:268–96. Madrid: Imprenta de Juan Pueyo or Sucesores de Rivadeneyra, S.A.

Mena, Cristóbal de. 1534/1938. "La conquista del Perú." In *Los cronistas de la conquista.* Biblioteca de cultura peruana, 1st ser., no. 2. Paris: Desclée.

———. 1534/1967. "La conquista de la Nueva Castilla." In Raul Porras Barrenechea, ed., *Las relaciones primitivas de la conquista del Perú,* 79–101. Lima: Instituto Raul Porras Barrenechea.

Méndez Gastelumendi, Cecilia. 2001. "The Power of Naming, or the Construction of Ethnic and National Identities in Peru: Myth, History and the Iquichanos." *Past and Present,* no. 171: 127–160.

Métraux, Alfred. 1969. *The History of the Incas.* New York: Schocken Books.

Mignolo, Walter D. 1989. "Colonial Situations, Geographical Discourses and Territorial Representations: Toward a Diatopical Understanding of Colonial Semiosis." *Dispositio* 14 (36–38): 93–140.

Millones, Luis. 1984. "Shamanismo y política en el Perú colonial: Los curacas de Ayacucho." *Histórica* 8, no. 2 (December): 131–49.

———. 1987. *Historia y poder en los Andes Centrales.* Madrid: Alianza Editorial.

———, comp. 1990. *El retorno de las huacas: Estudios y documentos del siglo XVI.* Lima: Instituto de Estudios Peruanos.

———. 1992. "The Time of the Inca: The Colonial Indians' Quest." *Antiquity* 66:204–16.

———. 1998. "Logros y azares de la cristianización colonial: El obispado de Huamanga." In Luis Millones, Hiroyasu Tomoeda, and Tasuhiko Fujii, eds. *Historia, religión y ritual de los pueblos ayacuchanos,* 29–49. Osaka, Japan: National Museum of Ethnology.

Mills, Kenneth. 1992. "Persistencia religiosa en Santiago de Carhuamayo." In Martín Leinhard, ed., *Testimonios, cartas y manifiestos indígenas,* 222–31. Caracas: Biblioteca Ayacucho.

———. 1997. *Idolatry and Its Enemies: Colonial Andean Religion and Extirpation, 1640–1750.* Princeton, NJ: Princeton University Press.

Molina, el almagrista, Cristóbal. n.d./1968. "Relacion de muchas cosas acaescidas en el Perú." In *Crónicas Peruanas de interés indígena.* Biblioteca de autores Españoles, 209:57–95. Madrid: Ediciones Atlas.

Molina, el cuzqueño, Cristóbal. 1574/1916. *Relación de las fábulas y ritos de los Incas.* In Horacio H. Urteaga, ed., Colección de libros y documentos referentes a la historia del Perú, 1:3–106. Lima: Imprenta y Librería Sanmartí y Ca.

———. 1574/1943. "Fabulas y ritos de los Incas (1574)." In *Las crónicas de los Molinas*, 3–84, Los pequeños grandes libros de historia americana, 1st ser., vol. 4, Lima: n.p.

———. 1959. *Ritos y fábulas de los incas (1575)*. Buenos Aires: Futuro.

Molina Argüello, Carlos. 1972. "Comunidades y territorialidad en las jurisdicciones." In *Memoria: Congreso Venezolano de Historia I*, 444–56. Caracas: Academia Nacional de la Historia.

Molinié Fioravanti, Antoinette. 1986–84. "El simbolismo de frontera en los Andes." *Revista del Museo Nacional* 48:251–86.

Montesinos, Fernando de. 1644/1930. *Memorias antiguas historiales y politicas del Perú (c. 1644)*. In Horacio H. Urteaga, ed., Colección de libros y documentos referentes a la historia del Perú, 2nd ser., vol. 6. Lima: Librería e Imprenta Gil, S.A.

Morales, Adolfo de. 1977. *Repartimiento de tierras por el Inca Huayna Capac*. Cochabamba, Bolivia: Universidad Boliviana Mayor de San Simon.

Moreno Yánez, Segundo E. 1991. "Los doctrineros 'Wiracochas' recreadores de nuevas formas culturales: Estudios de caso en el Quito colonial." In Segundo E. Moreno Yáñez and Frank Salomon, eds., *Reproducción y transformación de las sociedades andinas, siglos XVI–XX*, 2:529–53. Quito: Ediciones Abya-Yala.

Mörner, Magnus. 1973. "La formación de la reducción y el dualismo indiano del siglo XV." In Enrique Martínez Paz, ed., *Homenaje al Dr. Ceferino Garzon Maceda Córdoba*, 59–68. Córdoba, Argentina: Universidad Nacional de Córdoba.

Morris, Craig. 1973. "Establecimientos estatales en el Tawantinsuyu: Una estrategia de urbanismo obligado." *Revista del Museo Nacional* (Lima, Perú) 39:127–42.

———. 1988. "Más alla de las fronteras de Chincha." In Tom D. Dillehay and Patricia J. Netherly, eds., *La frontera del estado Inca*, 131–40. Oxford: BAR International.

———. 1993. "The Wealth of a Native American State: Value, Investment, and Mobilization in the Inka Economy." In John S. Henderson and Patricia J. Netherly, eds., *Configurations of Power: Holistic Anthropology in Theory and Practice*, 36–50. Ithaca, NY: Cornell University Press.

Morris, Craig, and Donald E. Thompson. 1985. *Huánuco Pampa: An Inca City and Its Hinterland*. London: Thames and Hudson.

Murphy, William P., and Caroline H. Bledsoe. 1986. "Kinship and Territory in the History of a Kpelle Chiefdom (Liberia)." In Igor Kopytoff, ed., *The African Frontier: The Reproduction of Traditional African Societies*, 123–43. Bloomington: Indiana University Press.

Murra, John V. 1967a. "El control vertical de un máximo de pisos ecológicos en la economia de las sociedades andinas." In Iñigo Ortiz de Zúñiga, *La visita de la Provincia de Leon de Huánuco en 1562*, 2:427–76. Huánuco: Universidad Nacional Hermilio Valdizán.

———. 1967b. "On Inca Political Structure." In Ronald Cohen and John Middleton, eds., *Comparative Political Systems: Studies in the Politics of Pre-Industrial Societies*, 339–53. Garden City, NY: Natural History Press.

———. 1968. "An Aymara Kingdom in 1567." *Ethnohistory* 15 (2): 115–51.

———. 1970. "Current Research and Prospects in Andean Ethnohistory." *Latin American Research Review* 5, no. 1 (Spring): 3–36.

———. 1980. *The Economic Organization of the Inka State*. Greenwich, CT: Jai Press.

———. 1984. "An Interview with John V. Murra." *Hispanic American Historical Review* (November): 1–24.

———. 1987. "Temas de estructura social y económica en la etnohistoria y el antiguo folklore andino." In Juan Manuel Perez Zenalbo and José Antonio Perez Grollan, eds., *La etnohistoria en Mesoamerica y los Andes*, 95–111. México: Instituto Nacional de Antropología e Historia.

———. 1998. "Litigation over the Rights of 'Natural Lords' in Early Colonial Courts in the Andes." In Elizabeth Hill Boone and Tom Cummins, eds., *Native Traditions in the Postconquest World*, 55–62. Washington, DC: Dumbarton Oaks Research Library and Collection.

Murúa [or Morúa], Fray Martín de. 1590/1946a. *Los orígenes de los Incas*. Los pequeños grandes libros de la historia americana, 2nd ser., vol. 11. Lima: Librería y Ed. D. Miranda.

———. 1946b. *Historia del origen y genealogía real de los Reyes Incas del Perú (1590)*. Ed. Constantine Bayle, S.J. Madrid: Consejo Superior de Investigaciones Científicas, Instituto Santo Toribio de Mogrovejo.

———.1962/2000. *Historia general del Peru, origen y descendencia de los Incas*. Madrid: n.p.

———. 2001. *Historia general del Perú*. Ed. Manuel Ballesteros Gaibrois. Madrid: Dastin.

Neale, Walter C. 1969. "Land Is to Rule." In Robert Eric Frykenberg, ed., *Land Control and Social Structure in Indian History*, 3–15. Madison: University of Wisconsin Press.

Negro, Sandra. 1996. "La persistencia de la visión Andina de la muerte en el virreinato del Perú." *Antropológica* 14:121–41.

Ness, John. 2003. "Fall of the Mayans." *Newsweek*, March 24, 38–39.

Netherly, Patricia J. 1977. "Local Level Lords on the North Coast of Peru." Ph.D. diss., Cornell University, Department of Anthropology.

———. 1988. "El reino de Chimor y el Tawantinsuyu." In Tom D. Dillehay and Patricia J. Netherly, eds., *La frontera del estado Inca*, 105–30. Oxford: BAR International.

———. 1993. "The Nature of the Andean State." In John S. Henderson and Patricia J. Netherly, eds., *Configurations of Power: Holistic Anthropology in Theory and Practice*, 11–35. Ithaca, NY: Cornell University Press.

Niles, Susan. 1999. *The Shape of Inca History*. Iowa City: University of Iowa Press.

Noejovich, Hector O. 1995. "El pensamiento dual andino y sus implicaciones socioeconómicas." *Histórica (Lima)* 19 (1): 105–18.

Ortloff, Charles R., and Alan Kolata. 1993. "Climate and Collapse: Agro-Ecological Perspectives on the Decline of the Tiwanaku State." *Journal of Archaeological Science* 20:195–221.

Osorio, Alejandra. 1990. "Una interpretación sobre la extirpación de idolatrías en el Perú, Otuco, Cajatambo, siglo XVII." *Historia y cultura* 20:161–99.

Ossio, Juan. 2002. "Guamán Poma and Martín de Murúa's Attitudes Towards Andean Oral Tradition, European Historiography and Art." Paper presented at the Newberry Library's conference "Peru in Black and White and in Color: Unique Texts and Images in the Colonial Andean Manuscripts of Martín Murúa and Guamán Poma," Chicago, April 19–20.

Oviedo, Gonzalo Fernández de. 1535–45/1559/1992. *Historia general y natural de las Indias (1535–45)*. Biblioteca de autores Españoles, vols. 117–21. Madrid: Ediciones Atlas.

Patterson, Thomas C. 1991. "Andean Cosmologies and the Inca State." In Christine W. Gailey, ed., *Dialectical Anthropology: Essays in Honor of Stanley Diamond*, 1:181–93. Civilization in Crises: Anthropological Perspectives. Gainesville: University Press of Florida.

———. 1992. *The Inca Empire: The Formation and Disintegration of a Pre-Capitalist State*. New York: Berg.

Paz Soldán, Mariano Felipe. 1877. *Diccionario geográfico estadístico del Perú*. Lima: Imprenta del Estado.

Pease, Franklin. 1965. "Causas religiosas de la guerra entre el Cusco y Quito." *Historia y cultura* 1:127–36.

———. 1968. "Cosmovisión Andina." *Humanidades* 2:171–99.

———. 1968–69. "El Principe de Esquilache y una relación sobre la extirpación de la idolatria." *Cuadernos del Seminario de Historia* (Instituto Riva-Aguero) 7, no. 9 (January 1968–December 1969): 81–118.

———. 1973. *El Dios creador andino*. Lima: Mosca Azul Editores.

———. 1976–77. "Etnohistoria andina: Un estado de la cuestión." *Historia y cultura* 10:207–28.

———, ed. 1977. *Collaguas I*. Lima: Pontificia Universidad Católica del Perú.

———. 1978. "Las visitas como testimonio Andino." In Francisco Miro Quesada, Franklin Pease, and David Sobrevilla, eds., *Historia: Problema y promesa*, 431–53. Lima: Pontificia Universidad Católica del Perú.

———. 1979. "La formación del Tawantinsuyu: Mecanismos de colonización y relación con las unidades étnicas." *Histórica* 3, no. 1 (July): 97–120.

———. 1980. "Los Incas." In *Historia del Perú*, 2:187–293. Lima: Editorial Juan Mejia Baca.

———. 1982. "The Formation of Tawantinsuyu: Mechanisms of Colonization and Relationship with Ethnic Groups." In George A. Collier, Renato I. Rosaldo, and John D. Wirth, eds., *Inca and Aztec States, 1400–1800* A.D., 173–98. New York: Academic Press.

———. 1988. "Curacas coloniales: Riqueza y actitudes." *Revista de Indias* 48 (182–83): 87–107.

———. 1989a. "La conquista española y la percepción Andina del otro." *Histórica* 8, no. 2 (December): 171–96.

———. 1989b. "Ritual y conquista incaica." *Boletín del Instituto Riva Aguero* (Lima) 16:13–20.

———. 1990a. *Inca y kuraka: Relaciones de poder y representación histórica*. College Park: University of Maryland.

———. 1990b. "Los Incas en la colonia." In Comisión Nacional Peruana del V Centenario del Descubrimiento Encuentro de Dos Américas, ed., *El mundo andino en la época del descubrimiento*, 191–206. Lima: Tall. Impresiones Benito.

———. 1991. *Los últimos Incas del Cuzco*. Madrid: Alianza Editorial.

———. 1992a. *Curacas, reciprocided y riqueza*. Lima: Pontificia Universidad Católica del Perú.

———. 1992b. "Las primeras versiones españoles sobre el Perú." *Colonial Latin American Review* 1 (1–2): 65–76.

———. 1994. "El pasado andino: Historia o escenografía?" *Cuadernos de Investigación* 2:5–21.

———. 1995. *Las crónicas y los Andes*. Lima: Pontificia Universidad Católica del Perú.

———. 1998. "Cuatro décadas de etnohistoria andina." In *Encuentro Internacional de Peruanistas: Estado de los estudios histórico-sociales sobre el Perú a fines del siglo XX*, 1:229–40. Lima: UNESCO.

Phipps, Elena. 2002. "Colors and Inka Garments: An Investigation of the Colorants in the Martín de Murúa's *Historia General del Pirv* [*sic*], in the J. Paul Getty Museum." Paper presented at the Newberry Library's conference "Peru in Black and White and in Color: Unique Texts and Images in the Colonial Andean Manuscripts of Martín Murúa and Guamán Poma," Chicago, April 19–20.

Pietschmann, Richard. 1910. "Bericht des Diego Rodriguez de Figueroa über seine Verhandlungen mit dem Inka Titu Cusi Yupanqui in den Anden von Villcapampa." *Nachrichten von der Königl. Gesellschaft der Wessenschaften zu Göttingen*, 79–122. Göttingen, Germany: Dieterich'schen Verlagsbuchh andlung.

Pinillos Rodríguez, Alberto. 1977. *Huacas de Trujillo: Derrotero para una visita turistica*. Trujillo, Perú: Ediciones Oro Chimu.

Pizarro, Francisco. 1986. *Testimonio: Documentos oficiales, cartas y escritos varios*. Madrid: Consejo Superior de Investigaciones científicas.

Pizarro, Hernando. 1533/1959/1992. "Carta de Hernando Pizarro a la Audiencia de Santo Domingo, 23 de noviembre de 1533." In Gonzalo Fernández de Oviedo, *Historia general y natural de las Indias (1535–45)*, 121:84–90. Madrid: Ediciones Atlas.

Pizarro, Pedro. 1844. "Relación del descubrimiento y conquista de los reinos del Perú . . ." In Martín Fernández de Navarrete, ed., *Colección de documentos inéditos para la historia de España*, 5:201–388. Madrid: Imprenta de la Viuda de Calero.

———. 1571/1978. "Relación del descubrimiento y conquista de los reinos del Perú . . ." Lima: Pontificia Universidad Católica del Perú.

Polia Meconi, Mario. 1996. "Siete cartas inéditas del Archivo Romano de la Compañía de Jesus, 1611–13: Huacas, mitos y ritos Andinos." *Antropológica (Lima)* 14:209–59.

———. 1999. *Cosmovisión religiosa Andina en los documentos inéditos del Archivo Romano de la Compañía de Jesus, 1581–1752*. Lima: Pontificia Universidad Católica del Perú.

Polia Meconi, Mario, and Fabiola Chávez Hualpa. 1994. "Ministros menores del culto, shamanes y curanderos en las fuentes españolas de los siglos XVI–XVII." *Antropológica* (Lima) 11 (January): 7–48.

Polo de Ondegardo, Juan. 1906. "Instrución contra las ceremonias, y ritos que vsan los indios conforme al tiempo de su infidelidad." *Revista histórica* 1 (2): 192–231.

———. 1916. "Instrución contra las ceremonias, y ritos que vsan los indios conforme al tiempo de su infidelidad." In Horacio H. Urteaga, ed. *Informaciones acerca de la religión y gobierno de los Incas*. Colección de libros y documentos referentes a la historia del Perú, 1st ser., 3:189–203. Lima: Imprenta y Librería Sanmartí y Ca.

———. 1559/1916. "Los errores y supersticiones de los indios sacadas del tratado y averiguación que hizo el Licenciado Polo (1559)." In Horacio H. Urteaga, Colección de libros y documentos referentes a la historia del Perú, 1st ser., 3:3–43. Lima: Imprenta y Librería Sanmartí y Ca.

———. 1571/1916. "Relacion de los fundamentos acerca del notable daño que resulta de no guardar a los indios sus fueros (26 de junio 1571)." In Horacio H. Urteaga, ed., *Informaciones acerca de la religión y gobierno de los Incas*. Colección de libros y documentos referentes a la historia del Perú, 1st ser., 3:45–186. Lima: Imprenta y Librería Sanmartí y Ca.

———. 1571/1917a. "Del linage de los Ingas y como conquistaron." In Horacio H. Urteaga, ed., *Informaciones acerca de la religión y gobierno de los Incas (1571), Segunda Parte*. Colección de libros y documentos referentes a la historia del Perú, 1st series, 4:45–94. Lima: Imprenta y Librería Sanmartí y Ca.

———. 1571/1917b. "Verdadero y legitimo dominio de los Reyes de España sobre el Perú." In Horacio H. Urteaga, ed., *Informaciones acerca de la religión y gobierno de los Incas (1571), Segunda Parte*. Colección de libros y documentos referentes a la historia del Perú, 1st ser., 4:95–138. Lima: Imprenta y Librería Sanmartí y Ca.

———. 1561/1940. "Informe del Licenciado Juan Polo de Ondegardo al Licenciado Briviesca de Muñatones sobre la perpetuidad de las encomiendas en el Perú." *Revista histórica* 13:125–96.

———. 1990. "Notables daños de no guardar a los indios sus fueros." In Laura González and Alicia Alonso, eds., *El mundo de los Incas*, 35–171. Madrid: Historia 16, S.A.

Poole, Deborah A. 1991a. "Miracles, Memory, and Time in an Andean Pilgrimage Story." *Journal of Latin American Lore* 17 (1–2): 131–63.

———. 1991b. "Time and Devotion in Andean Ritual Dance." In Raquel Thiercelin, comp., *Cultures et sociétés Andes et Méso-Amérique: Mélanges en hommage a Pierre Duviols*, 2:659–74. Aix-en-Provence: Université de Provence.

Porras Barrenechea, Raúl. 1959. *Cartas del Perú*. Lima: Sociedad de Bibliófilos Peruanos.

———. 1967. *Las relaciones primitivas de la conquista del Perú*. Lima: Instituto Raúl Porras Barrenechea.

———. 1978. *Pizarro*. Lima: Editorial Pizarro, S.A.

———. 1986. *Los cronistas del Perú (1528–1650) y otros ensayos*. Biblioteca Clásicos del Perú, vol. 2. Lima: Banco de Crédito del Perú.

Powers, Karen Vieira. 1991. "Resilient Lords and Indian Vagabonds: Wealth, Migration, and the Reproductive Transformation of Quito's Chiefdoms, 1500–1700," *Ethnohistory* 38 (3): 225–49.

———. 1995. *Andean Journeys: Migration, Ethnogenesis, and the State in Colonial Quito*. Albuquerque: University of New Mexico Press.

———. 1997. "Mistaken Identities: Chiefly Legitimacy and Ethnographic Performance in the Colonial North Andes." Paper presented at the annual meeting of the American Historical Association, New York.

———. 1998. "A Battle of Wills: Inventing Chiefly Legitimacy in the Colonial Andes." In Susan Kellogg and Matthew Restall, eds., *Dead Giveaways: Indigenous Testaments of Colonial Mesoamerica and the Andes*, 183–214. Salt Lake City: University of Utah Press.

———. 2002. "Conquering Discourses of 'Sexual Conquest': Of Women, Language, and Mestizaje." *Colonial Latin American Review* 11: (1): 7–32.

Prescott, William. 1957. *History of the Conquest of Peru*. New York: Heritage Press.

Querejazu Lewis, Roy. 1995. "La extirpación de idolatrias en Charcas, Bolivia." *Sequilao* (Lima) 4 (8): 43–59.

Quilter, Jeffrey. 1997. "The Narrative Approach to Moche Iconography." *Latin American Antiquity* 8, no. 2 (June): 113–33.

Quilter, Jeffrey, and Gary Urton, eds. 2002. *Narrative Threads: Accounting and Recounting in Andean Khipu*. Austin: University of Texas Press.

Quipucamayocs. 1542–44/1920. "Declaración de los quipocamayos a Vaca de Castro." In Horacio H. Urteaga, ed., *Informaciones sobre el antiguo Perú (1535–75)*. Colección de libros y documentos referentes a la historia del Perú, 2nd ser., 3:3–57. Lima: Imprenta y Librería Sanmartí y Ca.

Ramírez, Susan Elizabeth. 1978. "Chérrepe en 1572: Un análisis de la visita general del Virrey Francisco de Toledo." *Historia y cultura* 11:79–121.

———. 1985. "Social Frontiers and the Territorial Base of *Curacazgos*." In Shozo Masuda, Izumi Shimada, and Craig Morris, eds., *Andean Ecology and Civilization*, 423–42. Tokyo: University of Tokyo Press.

———. 1986. *Provincial Patriarchs: Land Tenure and the Economics of Power in Colonial Peru*. Albuquerque: University of New Mexico Press.

———. 1987. "The *Dueño de Indios:* Thoughts on the Consequences of the Shifting Bases of Power of the '*Curaca de los Viejos Antiguos*' Under the Spanish in Sixteenth Century Peru." *Hispanic American Historical Review* 67 (4): 575–610.

———. 1990. "The Inca Conquest of the North Coast: A Historian's View." In Michael E. Moseley and Alana Cordy-Collins, eds., *The Northern Dynasties: Kingship and Statecraft in Chimor*. Washington, DC: Dumbarton Oaks Research Library and Collection.

———. 1995a. "De pescadores y agricultores: Una historia local de la gente del valle de Chicama antes de 1565." *Bulletin de l'Institut Français de Etudes Andines* 24 (2): 245–79.

———. 1995b. "An Oral History of the Valley of Chicama, Circa 1524–1565." In Ari Zighelboim and Carol Barnes, eds., *Journal of the Steward Anthropological Society* 23 (1–2): 299–344.

———. 1996. *The World Upside Down: Cross Cultural Contact and Conflict in Sixteenth Century Peru.* Stanford, CA: Stanford University Press.

———. 1998. "Rich Man, Poor Man, Beggar Man or Chief: Two Views of the Concept of Wealth in Sixteenth Century Peru." In Susan Kellogg and Matthew Restall, eds., *Dead Giveaways: Indigenous Testaments of Colonial Spanish America,* 215–48. Salt Lake City: University of Utah Press.

———. 2001a. "Amores prohibidos: Del crimen y el castigo en el siglo XVI." Paper presented at the Instituto Nacional de Cultura, Sede Trujillo, Perú, August 8.

———. 2001b. "El concepto de 'comunidad' en el siglo XVI." In Hector Noejovich Chernoff, ed., *América bajo los Austrias: Economía, cultura, y sociedad,* 181–89. Lima: Pontificia Universidad Católica del Perú.

———. 2002. "From People to Places: Insights from a Definition of the Phrase 'Dueño de Indios.'" Paper presented at the conference "New World, First Nations: Native Peoples of Mesoamerica and the Andes Under Colonial Rule," University of New South Wales, Sydney, Australia, October 1.

———. 2004. "History and Memory: On the Making of Andean Genealogy." Paper presented at the conference "Empires and Archives," University of Notre Dame, April 4–5.

———. Forthcoming. "Dimensiones etnohistóricas de mineria y metalurgia del siglo XVI en el norte del Perú." *Historia y cultura (Lima).*

Ramos, Gabriela P. 1993. "Política eclesiástica y extirpación de idolatrías: Discursos y silencios en torno al Taqui Onqoy." In Gabriela Ramos and Henrique Urbano, comps., *Catolicismo y extirpacón de idolatrías, siglos XVI–XVIII,* 137–68. Cuzco: Centro de Estudios Regionales Andinos "Bartolomé de las Casas."

———. 2001. "Death, Conversion, and Identity in the Peruvian Andes: Lima and Cuzco, 1532–1670." Ph.D. diss., University of Pennsylvania, Philadelphia.

Ravines, Rogger. 1972. "Los caciques de Paucamarca: Algo más sobre las etnías de Chachapoyas." *Historia y cultura* 6:217–48.

Regalado de Hurtado, Liliana. 1981. "La relación del Inca Titu Cusi Yupanqui: Valor de un testimonio tardío." *Histórica* 5 (1): 45–61.

———. 1984a. "De Cajamarca a Vilcabamba: Una querella Andina." *Histórica* 8, no. 2 (December): 177–96.

———. 1984b. "En torno a la relación entre mitmaqkuna, poder y tecnología en los Andes." *Historia y cultura* 17:61–73.

———. 1992. *Religión y evangelización en Vilcabamba, 1572–1602.* Lima: Pontificia Universidad Católica del Perú.

———. 1993. *La sucesción incaica.* Lima: Pontificia Universidad Católica del Perú.

———. 1996a. "Espacio andino, espacio sagrado: Visión ceremonial del territorio en el período incaico." *Revista Complutence de historia de América* 22:85–96.

———. 1996b. "Padrones y retasas del partido de Acarí, Arequipa: Estratégias para el mantenimiento de antiguos modelos socio-económicos?" In Xavier Albó, ed., *La integración surandina: Cinco siglos después,* 205–27. Antofagasta, Chile: Universidad Católica del Norte de Antofagasta.

Regalado de Hurtado, Liliana, and Amalia Castelli G. 1982. "Una versión norteña del origen del Tawantinsuyu." *Historia y cultura* 15:161–83.

Reichlen, Henri. 1970. "Reconocimientos arqueológicos en los Andes de Cajamarca." *100 Años de arqueología en el Perú*. Lima: Instituto de Estudios Peruanos.

"Relación anónima sobre el modo de gobernar de los Incas (1583)." 1583/1925. In Roberto Levillier, ed., *Gobernantes del Perú: Cartas y papeles, siglo XVI*, 9:289–96. Madrid: Imprenta de Juan Pueyo.

"Relación de Piura [1571?]." 1885. In Marcos Jiménez de la Espada, ed., *Relaciones geográficas de Indias*, 2:225–42. Madrid: Tip. de M. G. Hernandez.

Remy Simatovic, María del Pilar. 1986. "Organización y cambio en el reino de Cuismanco (1540–70)." In Fernando Silva Santisteban, Waldemar Espinoza Soriano, Rogger Ravines, and Rebeca Carrión Cachot, eds., *Historia de Cajamarca*, 2:35–68. Cajamarca: Instituto Nacional de Cultura.

———. 1992. "El documento." In María Rostworowski and Pilar Remy, eds., *Las visitas a Cajamarca, 1571–72/1578*, 1:37–108. Lima: Instituto de Estudios Peruanos.

Restall, Matthew. 2003. "A History of the New Philology and the New Philology in History." *Latin American Research Review* 38 (1): 113–34.

Restrepo Arcila, Roberto A. 1995. "Instituciones sociales, políticas y económicas del Tawantinsuyu." *Revista Pumapunku (La Paz)* 4, no. 8 (January): 115–38.

Rex González, Alberto. 1982. "Las provincias Inca del antiguo Tucumán." *Revista del Museo Nacional* 46:317–80.

Río, Mercedes del. 1990. "Simbolismo y poder en Tapacarí." *Revista Andina* 8, no. 1 (July): 77–113.

Río, Mercedes del, and Ana María Presta. 1995. "Un estudio etnohistórico en los corregimientos de Tomina Yamparaes: Casos de multietnicidad." In Ana María Presta, ed., *Espacio, etnías, frontera: Atenuaciones políticas en el sur del Tawantinsuyu, siglos XV–XVIII*, 189–218. Sucre, Bolivia: Antropólogos del Surandino.

Rivera C., Silvia. 1978. "El mallku y la sociedad colonial en el siglo XVII: El caso de Jesús de Machaca." *Avances: Revista Boliviana de estudios históricos y sociales* (La Paz) 1 (February): 7–27.

Rivera C., Silvia, and Tristan Platt. 1978. "El impacto colonial sobre un pueblo Pakaxa: La crisis del cacicazgo en Caquingora (Urinsaya), durante el siglo XVI." *Avances: Revista Boliviana de estudios históricos y sociales* (La Paz) 1 (February): 101–20.

Rivière, Gilles. 1986. "Cuadripartición e ideología en las comunidades Aymaras de Carangas (Bolivia)." *Historia y cultura* (La Paz) 10:3–27.

———. 1995. "Caminos de los muertos, caminos de los vivos: Las figuras del chamanismo en las comunidades aymaras del altiplano boliviano." *Antropología* (Madrid) 1:109–32.

———. 1997. "Tiempo, poder y sociedad en las comunidades Aymaras del Altiplano (Bolivia)." In M. Goloabinoff, E. Katz, and A. Lammel, eds., *Antropología del clima en el mundo hispano-americano*, vol. 2. Quito: Ediciones Abya-Yala.

Rodriguez de Figueroa [see Pietschmann].

Rodríguez Suy Suy, Vitor Antonio. 1997. *Los pueblos Muchik en el mundo Andino de ayer y siempre*. Moche, Perú: Centro de Investigación y Promoción de los Pueblos Muchik "Josefa Suy Suy Azabache."

Romero, Carlos A. 1916. "Biografía de Tito Cusi Yupangui." In Horacio H. Urteaga, ed., *Relación de la conquista del Perú y hechos del Inca Manco II*. Colección de libros y documentos referentes a la historia del Perú, 1st ser., 2:xix–xxxiii. Lima: Imprenta y Librería Sanmartí y Ca.

———. 1917. "Francisco de Jerez y Pedro Sancho." In Horacio H. Urteaga, ed., *Las relaciones de la conquista del Perú*. Colección de libros y documentos referentes a la historia del Perú, 5:xiii–xxi. Lima: Imprenta y Librería Sanmartí y Ca.

———. 1918. "Noticias bibliográficas." In Horacio H. Urteaga, ed., *Informaciones acerca de la religión y gobierno de los Incas*. Colección de libros y documentos referentes a la historia del Perú, vol. 11. Lima: Imprenta y Librería Sanmartí y Ca.

Rossell Castro, Alberto. 1963. "Los cacicazgos de Ica." *Anales del III Congreso Nacional de Historia del Perú*, 242–47. Lima: n.p.

Rostworowski [de Diez Canseco], María. 1953. "La sucesión monárquica y el correinado entre los Incas." *Letras* 49:213–16.

———. 1960. "Succession, Cooptation to Kingship, and Royal Incest Among the Inca." *Southwestern Journal of Anthropology* 16, no. 4 (Winter): 417–27.

———. 1961. *Curacas y sucesiones, Costa Norte*. Lima: Librería Imp. Minerva Miraflores.

———. 1962. "Nuevos datos sobre tenencia de tierras reales en el Incario." *Revista del Museo Nacional* (Perú) 31:130–64.

———. 1963. "Dos manuscritos inéditos con datos sobre Manco II, tierras personales de los Incas y mitimaes." *Nueva crónica* (Lima) 1:223–39.

———. 1966. "Las tierras reales y su mano de obra en el Tahuantinsuyu." In *XXXVI Congreso Internacional de Americanistas* (1964), 2:31–34. Seville: Editorial Católica Española.

———. 1970. "El repartimiento de Doña Beatriz Coya, en el Valle de Yucay." *Historia y cultura* 4:153–267.

———. 1978a. "Estructuras políticas y económicas de la costa central del Perú precolombino." *Revista histórica* 31:203–18.

———. 1978b. "Una hipotesis sobre el surgimiento del estado Inca." *III Congreso Peruano: El hombre y la cultura andina* 1:89–100.

———. 1978c. *Señoríos indígenas de Lima y Canta*. Lima: Instituto de Estudios Peruanos.

———. 1979. "Breves notas sobre la estructura socio-económica en la costa peruana precolombina." In Roswith Hartmann and Ubo Oberem, eds., *Estudios Americanistas* 2:207–11. St. Augustin, Germany: Anthropos Institute.

———. 1981a. "Mediciones y cómputos en el antiguo Perú." In Heather Lechtman and Ana María Soldi, eds., *La tecnología en el mundo Andino*, 1:379–405. México: Instituto de Investigaciones Antropológicas, Universidad Nacional Autónoma de México.

———. 1981b. "Los pescadores del litoral Peruano en el siglo XVI: 'Yunga Guaxme.'" *Nova Americana* (Torino, Italy) 4:11–42.

———. 1981c. *Recursos naturales renovables y pesca, siglos XVI y XVII*. Lima: Instituto de Estudios Peruanos.

———. 1981–82. "Dos probanzas de Don Gonzalo, curaca de Lima (1555–59)." *Revista histórica* (Lima) 33:105–73.

———. 1982a. "Comentarios a la visita de Acari de 1593." *Histórica* 6, no. 2 (December): 227–54.

———. 1982b. "Testamento de Don Luis de Colan: Curaca en 1622." *Revista del Museo Nacional* 46:507–43.

———. 1983. *Estructuras Andinas del Poder: Ideología religiosa y política*. Lima: Instituto de Estudios Peruanos.

———. 1984. "El baile en los ritos agrários andinos (Sierra Nor-Central, siglo XVII)." *Historia y cultura* 17:51–60.

———. 1985. "Patronyms with the Consonant F in the Guarangas of Cajamarca." In Shozo Masuda, Izumi Shimada, and Craig Morris, eds., *Andean Ecology and Civilization*, 401–22. Tokyo: University of Tokyo Press.

———. 1988a. "La antigua región del Colesuyu." In Ramiro Matos Mendieta, comp., *Sociedad Andina: Pasado y presente*, 139–50. Lima: Fomciencias.

———. 1988b. *Historia del Tahuantinsuyu*. Lima: Instituto de Estudios Peruanos.

———. 1990. "Las macroetnías en el ámbito Andino." *Allpanchis* 22 (35–36): 3–28.

———. 1993a. "La antigua región del Colesuyu." In *Ensayos de historia Andina: Elites, etnías, recursos*, 219–29. Lima: Instituto de Estudios Peruanos.

———. 1993b. "Las macroetnías en el ámbito Andino." In *Ensayos de historia Andina: Elites, etnías, recursos*, 201–18. Lima: Instituto de Estudios Peruanos.

———. 1997. *Pachacutec y la leyenda de los Chancas*. Lima: Instituto de Estudios Peruanos.

———. 1998. "Un caso de hechicería en los Reyes en 1547." In *Ensayos de historia Andina II: Pampas de Nasca, género, hechicería*, 153–69. Lima: Instituto de Estudios Peruanos.

———. 1999a. *History of the Inca Realm*. Cambridge: Cambridge University Press.

———. 1573/1999b. *El señorío de Pachacamac: El informe de Rodrigo Cantos de Andrade de 1573*. Lima: Instituto de Estudios Peruanos.

Rostworowski [de Diez Canseco], María, and Pilar Remy. 1992. *Las visitas a Cajamarca, 1571–72/1578*. 2 vols. Lima: Instituto de Estudios Peruanos.

Rowe, John H. 1946. "Inca Culture at the Time of the Spanish Conquest." In Julian H. Steward, ed., *Handbook of South American Indians*, 2:183–331. Washington, DC: U.S. Government Printing Office.

———. 1948. "The Kingdom of Chimor." *Acta Americana* (México) 6 (1–2): 26–59.

———. 1957. "The Incas Under Spanish Colonial Institutions." *Hispanic American Historical Review* 37, no. 2 (May): 155–99.

———. 1960. "The Origins of Creator Worship Among the Incas." In Stanley Diamond, ed., *Culture in History: Essays in Honor of Paul Radin*, 408–29. New York: Columbia University Press.

Rubiños y Andrade, Justo Modesto. 1782/1936. "Un manuscrito interesante (1782)." *Revista histórica* 10 (3): 289–363.

Ruiz de Arze, Juan de. 1543/1933. "Relación de los servicios en Indias de don Juan Ruiz de Arce, conquistador del Perú." *Boletín de la Academia de Historia* (Madrid) 102 (2): 327–84.

Ruiz de Pardo, Carmen. 2000. "La curaca Contarhuacho: Paradigma de la reciprocidad Andina." Lima: Unpublished paper.

Saeger, James Schofield. 1999. "Warfare, Reorganization and Readaptation at the Margins of Spanish Rule—the Chaco and Paraguay (1573–1882)." In Frank Salomon and Stuart B. Schwartz, eds., *The Cambridge History of the Native Peoples of the Americas*, vol. 3, pt. 2, 257–86. Cambridge: Cambridge University Press.

Sahlins, Marshall. 1983. "Other Times, Other Customs: The Anthropology of History." *American Anthropologist* 85:517–44.

Sahlins, Peter. 1989. *Boundaries: The Making of France and Spain in the Pyrenees*. Berkeley: University of California Press.

Said, Edward. 1995. "Secular Interpretation, the Geographical Element, and the Methodology of Imperialism." In Gyan Prakash, ed., *After Colonialism: Imperial Histories and Post-colonial Displacements*. Princeton, NJ: Princeton University Press.

———. 1999. "Unresolved Geographies, Embattled Landscapes." The Annual Eqbal Ahmad Lecture, Hampshire College, Amherst, Massachusetts, September 17, 21–39. Typescript.

Saignes, Thierry. 1987. "De la borrachera al retrato: Los caciques andinos entre los legitimidades (Charcas)." *Revista Andina* 5, no. 1 (July): 139–70.

———. 1991. "Lobos y ovejas. Formación y desarrollo de los pueblos y comunidades en el sur Andino (siglos XVI–XX)." In Segundo Moreno Yáñez and Frank Salomon, comps., *Reproducción y transformación de las sociedades andinas, siglos XVI–XX*, 91–135. Quito: Ediciones Abya-Yala.

———. 1995. "Indian Migration and Social Change in Seventeenth Century Charcas." In Brooke Larson, Olivia Harris, and Enrique Tandeter, eds., *Ethnicity, Markets, and Migration in the Andes: At the Crossroads of History and Anthropology*, 167–95. Durham, NC: Duke University Press.

———. 1999. "The Colonial Condition in the Quechua-Aymara Heartland (1570–80)." In Frank Salomon and Stuart B. Schwartz, eds., *The Cambridge History of the Native Peoples of the Americas*, vol. 3, pt. 2, 59–137. Cambridge: Cambridge University Press.

Saito, Akira. 1997. "La conquista de la historia: La extirpación de la idolatría y la transformación de la conciencia histórica en los Andes." *Anuario del Archivo y Biblioteca Nacionales de Bolivia (Sucre)*: 49–71.

Salles-Reese, Veronica. 1997. *From Viracocha to the Virgin of Copacabana*. Austin: University of Texas Press.

Sallnow, Michael J. 1981. "Communitas Reconsidered: The Sociology of Andean Pilgrimage." *Man* 16:163–82.

———. 1987. *Pilgrims of the Andes: Regional Cults in Cusco*. Washington, DC: Smithsonian Institution Press.

Salomon, Frank. 1986. *Native Lords of Quito in the Age of the Incas*. Cambridge: Cambridge University Press.

———. 1987a. "Ancestor Cults and Resistance to the State in Arequipa, ca. 1748–54." In Steve J. Stern, ed., *Resistance, Rebellion, and Consciousness in the Andean Peasant World, Eighteenth Century*, 148–65. Madison: University of Wisconsin Press.

———. 1987b. "Ancestors, Grave Robbers, and the Possible Antecedents of Cañari 'Inca-ism.'" In Harald O. Skar and Frank Salomon, eds., *Natives and Neighbors in South America: Anthropological Essays*, 207–32. Göteborg, Sweden: Göteborgs Etnografisk Museum.

———. 1988. "Indian Women of Early Colonial Quito as Seen Through Their Testaments." *The Americas* 44 (3): 325–41.

———. 1990a. "Don Pedro de Zambiza un Varayuj del siglo XVI." In Manuel Mesías Carrera and Frank Salomon, eds., *Historia y cultura popular de Zambiza*, 35–72. Quito: Centro Ecuatoriano para el desarrollo de la Comunidad.

———. 1995. "'The Beautiful Grandparents': Andean Ancestor Shrines and Mortuary Ritual as Seen Through Colonial Records." In Tom D. Dillehay, ed., *Tombs for the Living: Andean Mortuary Practices*, 315–54. Washington, DC: Dumbarton Oaks Research Library and Collection.

Salomon, Frank, and Armando Guevara-Gil. 1994. "A 'Personal Visit': Colonial Political Ritual and the Making of Indians in the Andes." *Colonial Latin American Review* 3 (1–2): 3–36.

Salomon, Frank, and Stuart B. Schwartz, eds. 1999. *The Cambridge History of the Native Peoples of the Americas*. Vol. 3. Pt. 2. Cambridge: Cambridge University Press.

Salomon, Frank, and George L. Urioste. 1991. *The Huarochirí Manuscript: A Testament of Ancient and Colonial Andean Religion*. Austin: University of Texas Press.

Sánchez, Ana. 1991a. *Amancebados, hechiceros y rebeldes (Chancay, siglo XVII)*. Cuzco: Centro de Estudios Regionales Andinos "Bartolomé de las Casas."

———. 1991b. "Mentalidad popular frente a ideologia oficial: El Santo Oficio en Lima y los casos de hechicería (siglo XVII)." In Mirko Lauer, ed., and Henrique Urbano, comp., *Poder y violencia en los Andes*, 33–52. Cuzco: Centro de Estudios Regionales Andinos "Bartolomé de las Casas."

Sánchez-Concha Barrios, Rafael. 1996. "El Licenciado Hernando de Santillán y sus observaciones en torno de las formas tiránicas de los curacas." *Histórica* 20, no. 2 (December): 285–302.

Sánchez Farfán, Jorge. 1981. "Kuraqkuna, Sacerdotes Andinos?" In Amalia Castelli, Marcia Koth de Paredes, and Mariana Mould de Pease, comps., *Etnohistoria y antropología andina*, 145–59. Lima: Centro de Proyección Cristiana.

Sancho, Pedro. 1533/1917. "Testimonio del acta de repartición del rescate de Atahuallpa, otorgado por el Escribano Pedro Sancho." In Horacio H. Urteaga, ed., *Las relaciones de la conquista del Perú*. Colección de libros y documentos referentes a la historia del Perú, 5:215–24. Lima: Imprenta y Librería Sanmartí y Ca.

Sancho de la Hoz, Pedro. 1917. "Relacion de lo sucedido en la conquista del Perú." In Horacio H. Urteaga, ed., *Las relaciones de la conquista del Perú*. Colección de libros y documentos referentes a la historia del Perú, 5:124–202. Lima: Imprenta y Librería Sanmartí y Ca.

———. 1534/1938. "Relación para S.M. de lo sucedido en la conquista y pacificación de estas provincias de la Nueva Castilla (1534)." In *Los cronistas de la conquista*. Biblioteca de cultura peruana, 1st ser., 2:117–93. Paris: Descelée de Brauwer.

Santacruz Pachacuti Yamqui Salcamaygua, Juan. 1613/1879. "Relacion de antiguedades deste reyno del Perú. In Marco Jimenez de la Espada, ed., *Tres relaciones de Antiguedades Peruanas*, 231–328. Madrid: Imprente de M. Tello.

———. 1613/1968. "Relacion de antiguedades deste reyno del Piru (c. 1613)." In Francisco Esteve Barba, ed., *Crónicas peruanas de interés indígena*. Biblioteca de autores Españoles, 209:279–320. Madrid: Atlas Ediciones.

———. 1613/1993. *Relacion de antiguedades deste reyno del Piru*. Lima: Instituto Frances de Estudios Andinos.

Santillán, Licenciado Hernando (Fernando) de. 1879. "Relación del orígen, descendencia, política y gobierno de los Incas." In Marcos Jimenez de la Espada, ed., *Tres relaciones de antiguedades Peruanas*, 3–137. Madrid: Imprenta de M. Tello.

———.1927 *Relacion*. In Horacio H. Urteaga, ed., Colección de libros y documentos referentes a la historia del Perú, 2nd ser., 9:1–124. Lima: Imprenta y Librería Sanmartí y Ca.

———. 1563–72/1968. "Relación del orígen, descendencia, política y gobierno de los Incas (c. 1563–1572)." In Francisco Estete Barba, ed., *Crónicas peruanas de interés indígena*, Biblioteca de autores Españoles, 209:97–150. Madrid: Ediciones Atlas.

Santo Tomás, Fray Domingo de. 1560/1951. *Lexicon: Vocabulario de la lengua general del Perv*. Lima: Universidad Nacional Mayor de San Marcos, Instituto de Historia.

Sarmiento de Gamboa, Pedro de. 1572/1942. *Historia de los Incas*. Colección Hórreo, no. 10. Buenos Aires: Emecé Editores.

———. 1572/1965. *Histórica indica*. Biblioteca de autores Españoles, 135:195–279. Madrid: Ediciones Atlas.

———. 1572/1967. *History of the Incas*. Nendeln, Liechtenstein: Kraus Reprint Limited.

———. 1907/1972/1999. *History of the Incas*. Mineola, NY: Dover Books.

Schaedel, Richard P. 1978. "Early State of the Incas." In Henri J. M. Claessen and Peter Skalnik, eds., *The Early State*, 289–320. The Hague: Mouton Publishers.

———. 1988. "Andean World View: Hierarchy or Reciprocity, Regulation or Control." *Current Anthropology* 29 (5): 768–77.

———. 1985/1998. "Comentario: Las fronteras del estado Inca." In Tom D. Dillehay and Patricia J. Netherly, eds., *La frontera del Estado Inca*, 216–24. Quito: Ediciones Abya-Yala.

Schramm, Raimund. 1995. "Fronteras y territorialidad, repartición étnica y política colonizadora en los Charcas (Valles de Ayopaya y Mizque)." In Ana María Presta, ed., *Espacio, etnías, frontera: Atenuaciones políticas en el sur del Tawantinsuyu, siglos XV–XVIII*, 163–87. Sucre, Bolivia: Antropólogos del Surandino.

Schwartz, Barry. 1982. "The Social Context of Commemoration: A Study in Collective Memory." *Social Forces* 61 (2): 374–401.

Schwartz, Barry, and Frank Salomon. 1999. "New Peoples and New Kinds of People: Adaptation, Readjustment and Ethnogenesis in South American Indigenous Societies (Colonial Era)." In Frank Salomon and Stuart B. Schwartz, eds., *The Cambridge History of the Native Peoples of the Americas*, vol. 3, pt. 2, 443–501. Cambridge: Cambridge University Press.

Scott, James C., John Tehranian, and Jeremy Mathias. 2002. "The Production of Legal Identities Proper to States: The Case of the Permanent Family Surname." *Comparative Studies of Society and History* 44:1, 4–44.

Seed, Patricia. 1991. "'Failing to Marvel': Atahualpa's Encounter with the World." *Latin American Research Review* 26 (1): 7–32.

Sherbondy, Jeanette E. 1973. "Water and Power: The Role of Irrigation Districts in the Transition from Inca to Spanish Cuzco." In William P. Mitchell and David Guillet, eds., *Irrigation at High Altitudes: The Social Organization of Water Control Systems in the Andes*, 69–97. Arlington, VA: Society for Latin American Anthropology and the American Anthropological Association.

———. 1992. "Water Ideology in Inca Ethnogenesis." In Robert V. H. Dover, Katherine E. Seibold, and John H. McDowell, eds., *Andean Cosmologies Through Time*, 46–66. Bloomington: Indiana University Press.

———. 1993. "Irrigation and Inca Cosmology." In Ross W. Jamieson, Sylvia Abonyi, and Neil A. Mirau, eds., *Culture and Environment: A Fragile Coexistence*, 341–51. Calgary: University of Calgary Archaeological Association.

———. 1996. "Panaca Lands: Re-invented Communities." *Journal of the Steward Anthropological Society* 24 (1–2): 173–201.

Shimada, Izumi, Crystal Schaaf, Lonnie G. Thompson, Ellen Mosley Thompson, and R. Byrd. 1991. "Implicaciones culturales de una gran sequia del siglo VI d.c. en los Andes Peruanos." *Boletín de Lima* 77:33–56.

Silva Santisteban, Fernando. 1982. "El reino de Cuismanco." *Revista del Museo Nacional (Lima)* 46:293–315.

Silverblatt, Irene. 1987. *Moon, Sun, and Witches: Gender Ideologies and Class in Inca and Colonial Peru*. Princeton, NJ: Princeton University Press.

———. 1988a. "Imperial Dilemmas, the Politics of Kinship and Inca Reconstructions of History." *Comparative Studies in Society and History* 30 (1): 83–102.

———. 1988b. "Political Memories and Colonizing Symbols: Santiago and the Mountain Gods of Colonial Peru." In Jonathan D. Hill, ed., *Rethinking History and Myth: Indigenous South American Perspectives on the Past*, 174–94. Urbana: University of Illinois Press.

Silverman, Gail. 1984. *El tejido Andino: Un libro de sabiduria*. Lima: Banco Central de Reserva del Perú.

Silverman, Helaine. 1993. *Cahuachi in the Ancient Nasca World*. Iowa City: University of Iowa Press.

Skar, Harald O. 1985. "Communitas and Schismogenesis: The Andean Pilgrimage Reconsidered." *Ethnos* (Stockholm) 50 (1–2): 88–102.

Spalding, Karen. 1981. "Resistencia y adaptación: El gobierno colonial y las elites nativas." *Allpanchis* 15 (17–18): 5–21.

———. 1984. *Huarochirí*. Stanford, CA: Stanford University Press.

———. 1991. "Defendiendo el suyo: El kuraka en el sistema de producción andina." In Segundo Moreno Yañez and Frank Salomon, comps., *Reproducción y transformación de las sociedades andinas, siglos XVI–XX*, 401–14. Quito: Ediciones Abya-Yala.

Stenberg, Rubén, and Nazareno Carvajal. 1988. "Red vial incaica en los terrenos meridionales del Imperio: Tramo Valle del Limari–Valle del Maipo." In

Tom D. Dillehay and Patricia J. Netherly, eds., *La frontera del estado Inca*, 181–260. Oxford: BAR International.

Sternfeld, Gabriela. 2000. "Asambleas, negociaciones y autoridades locales en las traiciones orales de Huarochirí." Paper presented at the 50th International Congress of Americanists, University of Warsaw, July.

Szemiñski, Jan. 1985. "De la imagen de Wiraqucan segun las oraciones recogidas por Joan de Santa Cruz Pachacuti Yamqui Salcamaygua." *Histórica* 9 (4): 247–64.

———. 1987. "Why Kill the Spaniard? New Perspectives on Andean Insurrectionary Ideology in the Eighteenth Century." In Steve J. Stern, ed., *Resistance, Rebellion, and Consciousness in the Andean Peasant World, Eighteenth Century*, 166–92. Madison: University of Wisconsin Press.

———. 1996. "Las apuestas del Inqa." *Anuario del Archivo y Biblioteca Nacionales de Bolivia (Sucre)*: 3–18.

Szemiñski, Jan, and Juan Ansion. 1982. "Dioses y hombres de Huamanga." *Allpanchis* 19:187–233.

Tantaleán Arbulú, Javier. 1981. "Modo de producción asiático: Estado y sociedad Inka." *Histórica* 5, no. 1 (July): 63–103.

———. 1997. "El circuito macroeconómico incaico." *Socialismo y participación* 79:49–65.

Taylor, Anne Christine. 1999. "The Western Margins of Amazonia from the Early Sixteenth to the Early Nineteenth Century." In Frank Salomon and Stuart B. Schwartz, eds., *The Cambridge History of the Native Peoples of the Americas*, vol. 3, pt. 2, 188–256. Cambridge: Cambridge University Press.

Taylor, Gerald. 1987/1999. *Ritos y tradiciones de Huarochirí*. Lima: Instituto Frances de Estudios Andinos and Instituto de Estudios Peruanos.

Thornton, John. 1992. *Africa and Africans in the Making of the Atlantic World, 1400–1680*. Cambridge: Cambridge University Press.

Timbiah, S. J. 1976. *World Conqueror and World Renouncer*. Cambridge: Cambridge University Press.

Titu Cusi Yupangui, Don Diego de Castro. 1570/1916. "Relación de la conquista del Perú." In Horacio H. Urteaga, ed., Colección de libros y documentos referentes a la historia del Perú, 1st ser., 2:3–114. Lima: Imprenta y Librería Sanmartí y Ca.

Toledo, Francisco de. 1924. "Instrucciones elaboradas por el virrey don Francisco de Toledo para los visitadores." *Revista histórica* (Lima) 7:115–216.

———. 1986. *Francisco de Toledo: Disposiciones gubernativas para el Virreinato del Perú, 1569–1574*. Seville: Escuela de Estudios Hispano-Americanos.

Torero, Alfredo. 1990. "Procesos lingüisticos e identificación de dioses en los Andes centrales." *Revista Andina* 15:237–63.

———. 1993. "Fronteras linguísticas y difusión de culto: El caso Huari y de Contiti Viracocha." In Pierre Duviols, comp., *Religions des Andes et langues indigènes*, 219–33. Aix-en-Provence: Université de Provence.

Townsend, Camilla. 2003. "Burying the White Gods: New Perspectives on the Conquest of Mexico." *American Historical Review* 108 (3): 659–87.

Trimborn, Hermann. 1979. *El reino de Lambayeque en el antiguo Perú*. St. Augustin, Germany: Haus Völker und Kulturen Anthropos-Institut.

Ubbelohde-Doering, Heinrich. 1967. *On the Royal Highways of the Inca*. London: Thames and Hudson.

Uceda, Santiago, and José Canziani Amico. 1993. "Evidencias de grandes precipitaciones en diversos etapas constructivas de la Huaca de la Luna, Costa norte del Perú." *Bulletin de l'Institut Français de Etudes Andines* 22 (1): 313–43.

Urbano, Henrique. 1981. "Del sexo, incesto y los ancestros de Inkarré: Mito, utopía e historia en las sociedades andinos." *Allpanchis*, no. 17–18: 77–103.

———. 1990. "Huayna Capac y sus enanos: Huellas de un ciclo mítico andino prehispánico." *Historia y cultura* 20:281–93.

———. 1993. "Idolos, figuras, imágenes: La representación como discurso ideológico." In Gabriela Ramos and Henrique Urbano, comps., *Catolicismo y extirpación de idolatrías: Siglos XVI–XVII*, 7–30. Cuzco: Centro de estudios regionales andinos "Bartolomé de las Casas."

Urteaga, Horacio. 1928. "La organización judicial en el imperio de los Incas." *Revista histórica* 9:5–50.

Urton, Gary. 1981. *At the Crossroads of the Earth and Sky: An Andean Cosmology*. Austin: University of Texas Press.

———. 1990a. "From Knots to Narratives: Reconstructing the Art of Historical Record Keeping in the Andes from Spanish Transcriptions of Inka Khipus." *Ethnohistory* 45, no. 3 (Summer): 409–38.

———. 1990b. *The History of a Myth: Pacariqtambo and the Origin of the Inkas*. Austin: University of Texas Press.

———. 1997. *The Social Life of Numbers: A Quechua Ontology of Numbers and Philosophy of Arithmetic*. Austin: University of Texas Press.

Vaca de Castro, Licenciado Christobal. 1543/1908. "Ordenanzas de tambos . . . (1543)." *Revista histórica* 3:427–92.

Valcarcel, Carlos Daniel. 1982. *Historia del Perú colonial*. Lima: Editores Importadores S.A.

Valcarcel, Luis E. 1949. "El estado incaico." *Revista histórica* 18:26–44.

———. 1961. "El estado imperial de los Incas." *Revista del Museo Nacional* 30:5–18.

Valera, Blas [El Jesuita anónimo?]. 1596/1879. "De las costumbres antiguas de los naturales del Pirú." In *Tres Relaciones de antiguedades Peruanas*, 137–227. Madrid: Imprenta de M. Tello.

———. 1596/1945. "Las costumbres antiguas del Perú y la historia de los Incas (1596)." In Francisco de Loayza, ed., Los pequeños grandes libros de historia Americana, 1st ser., vol. 8. Lima: Editorial de Domingo Miranda.

Van Young, Eric. 1996. "Material Life." In Susan Migden Socolow and Luisa Schell Hoberman, eds., *The Countryside in Colonial Latin America*, 49–74. Albuquerque: University of New Mexico Press.

Vargas Ugarte, Rubén. 1949. *Historia del Perú: Virreinato (1551–1600)*. Lima: A. Bolocco y Cía, S.R. Ltda.

———. 1951–54. *Concilios Limenses (1551–1772)*. 3 vols. Lima: n.p.

Varón Gabai, Rafael. 1980. *Curacas y encomenderos: Acomodamiento nativo en Huaraz, siglos XVI–XVII*. Lima: P. L. Villanueva.

———. 1990. "El Taqui Onqoy: Las raíces andinas de un fenómeno colonial." In Luis Millones, comp., *El retorno de las huacas: Estudios y documentos sobre el Taki Onqoy, siglo XVI*, 331–406. Lima: Instituto de Estudios Peruanos.

———. 1993. "Estrategias políticas y relaciones conyugales: El comportamiento de Incas y Españoles en Huaylas en la primera mitad del siglo XVI." *Bulletin de l'Institut Français de etudes andines* 22 (3): 721–37.

———. 1997. *Francisco Pizarro and His Brothers: The Illusion of Power in Sixteenth-Century Peru*. Norman: University of Oklahoma Press.

Verdesio, Gustavo. 2001. "Forgotten Territorialities: The Materiality of Indigenous Pasts." *Nepantla: Views from the South* 2 (1): 85–114.

Villagómez, Pedro de. 1649/1919. *Exortaciones e instrucción acerca de las idolatrías de los indios del arzobispado de Lima (1649)*. Lima: Sanmarti y Cia.

Villar Cordova, Anibal Severino. 1929. *Historia de la educación peruana-educación incaica*. Huancayo, Perú: Imprenta El Heraldo.

Villareal, Federico. 1894–95. "Los cometas en tiempo de Huayna Capac." *Boletín de la Sociead Geográfica de Lima* 4:268–81.

Von Hagen, Victor Wolfgang. 1955. *Highways of the Sun*. New York: Duell, Sloan, and Pearce.

Von Laue, Theodore. 1987. *The World Revolution of Westernization: The Twentieth Century in Global Perspective*. New York: Oxford University Press.

Wachtel, Nathan. 1977. *The Vision of the Vanquished: The Spanish Conquest of Peru Through Indian Eyes, 1530–70*. New York: Barnes and Noble.

———. 1982. "The Mitimas of the Cochabamba Valley: The Colonization Policy of Huayna Capac." In George A. Collier, Renato I. Rosaldo, and John D. Wirth, eds., *The Inca and Aztec States, 1400–1800* A.D., 199–235. New York: Academic Press.

Warren, Kay B. 1992. "Transforming Memories and Histories: The Meanings of Ethnic Resurgence for Mayan Indians." In Alfred Stepan, ed., *Americas: New Interpretive Essays*. New York: Oxford University Press.

Weber, Max. 1978. In Guenther Roth and Claus Wittich, eds., *Economy and Society: An Outline of Interpretive Sociology*. 2 vols. Berkeley: University of California Press.

Wedin, Ake. 1965. *El sistema decimal en el imperio incaico*. Madrid: Instituto Ibero-Americano.

Werner, Oswald, and Donald T. Campbell. 1973. "Translating, Through Interpreters, and the Problem of Decentering." In Raoul Noroll and Ronald Cohen, eds., *Handbook of Method in Cultural Anthropology*, 398–420. New York: Columbia University Press.

Wheatley, Paul. 1971. *The Pivot of the Four Quarters*. Chicago: Aldine Publishing Co.

Whitehead, Neil L. 1999. "Native Peoples Confront Colonial Regimes in Northeast South America (c. 1500–1900)." In Frank Salomon and Stuart B. Schwartz, eds., *The Cambridge History of the Native Peoples of the Americas*, vol. 3, pt. 2, 382–442. Cambridge: Cambridge University Press.

Whorf, Benjamin Lee. 1956. *Language, Thought, and Reality*. Ed. John B. Carroll. Cambridge, MA: MIT Press.

Wilson, Richard. 1995. "Shifting Frontiers: Historical Transformations of Identities in Latin America." *Bulletin of Latin American Research* 14 (1): 1–7.

Wittfogel, Karl A. 1957. *Oriental Despotism: A Comparative Study of Total Power*. New Haven, CT: Yale University Press.

Wright, Robin M., Manuela Carneiro da Cunha, and the Núcleo de História Indígena e do Indigenismo. 1999. "Destruction, Resistance and Transformation—Southern, Coastal and Northern Brazil (1580–1890)." In Frank Salomon and Stuart B. Schwartz, eds., *The Cambridge History of the Native Peoples of the Americas*, vol. 3, pt. 2, 287–381. Cambridge: Cambridge University Press.

Wurgaft, Lewis D. 1995. "Identity in World History: A Postmodern Perspective." *History and Theory* 34, no. 2 (May): 67–85.

Xerez [Jerez], Francisco de. 1534/1917. "Verdadera relación de la conquista del Perú y provincia del Cuzco . . ." In Horacio H. Urteaga, ed., *Las relaciones de la conquista del Perú*. Colección de libros y documentos referentes a la historia del Perú, 5:1–123. Lima: Imprenta y Librería Sanmartí y Ca.

Zevallos Quiñones, Jorge. 1989. *Los cacicazgos de Lambayeque*. Trujillo, Perú: Consejo Nacional de Ciencia y Tecnologia.

———. 1992. *Los cacicazgos de Trujillo*. Trujillo, Perú: Gráfica Cuatro, S.A.

Ziólkowski, Mariusz S. 1991a. *El culto estatal del imperio Inca*. Warsaw, Poland: Universidad de Varsovia, Centro de Estudios Latinoamericanos.

———. 1991b. "El Sapan Inka y el sumo sacerdote: Acerca de la legitimización del poder en el Tawantinsuyu." In M. Ziólkowski, ed., *El culto estatal del imperio Inca*, 59–74. Warsaw, Poland: Universidad de Varsovia, Centro de Estudios Latinoamericanos.

———. 1997. *La guerra de los Wawqi: Los objectivos y los mecanismos de la rivalidad dentro de la élite inka, s. XV–XVI*. Quito: Ediciones Abya-Yala.

Zuidema, R. Tom. 1964. *The Ceque System of Cuzco: The Social Organization of the Capital of the Incas*. Leiden, The Netherlands: E. J. Brill.

———. 1967. "El juego de los ayllus y del Amaru." In *Journal de la Société del Americaniste (Paris)* 56 (1): 41–51.

———. 1968. "La relación entre el patrón de poblamiento prehispánico y los principios derivados de la estructura social incaica." *Proceedings of the 37th International Congress of Americanists* (Mar de Plata, Argentina [1966]), 1:45–55. Buenos Aires: Librart.

———. 1973a. "Una interpretación alterna de la historia incaica." In Juan M. Ossio, ed., *Ideología mesiánica del mundo Andino*, 3–33. Lima: Editorial de Ignacio Prado Pastor.

———. 1973b. "Kinship and Ancestor Cult in Three Peruvian Communities: Hernández Príncipe's Account of 1622." *Boletín del Instituto Frances de Estudios Andinos* 2 (1): 16–33.

———. 1977a. "The Inca Calendar." In Anthony F. Aveni, ed., *Native American Astronomy*. Austin: University of Texas Press.

———. 1977–78. "Shafttombs and the Inca Empire." *Journal of the Steward Anthropological Society* 10 (1–2): 113–78.

———. 1979. "The Ushnu." In I. A. Franch, ed., *Economia y sociedad en los Andes y Mesoamerica. Revista de la Universidad Complutense* (Madrid, Spain) 28 (117): 317–62.

———. 1982. "Myth and History in Ancient Peru." In Ino Rossi, ed., *The Logic of Culture: Advances in Structural Theory and Methods*, 150–75. South Hadley, MA: J. F. Bergin Publishers.

———. 1983a. "Hierarchy and Space in Incaic Social Organization." *Ethnohistory* 30 (2): 49–75.

———. 1983b. "The Lion in the City: Royal Symbols of Transition in Cuzco." *Journal of Latin American Lore* 9 (1): 39–100.

———. 1989a. "At the King's Table: Inca Concepts of Sacred Kingship in Cuzco." *History and Anthropology* 6:249–74.

———. 1989b. *Reyes y guerreros: Ensayos de cultura Andina*. Comp. Manuel Burga. Lima: Talleres Gráficos P. L. Villanueva, S.A.

———. 1990. *Inca Civilization in Cuzco*. Austin: University of Texas Press.

———. 1991. "Guamán Poma and the Art of Empire: Toward an Iconography of Inca Royal Dress." In Kenneth Andrien and Rolena Adorno, eds., *Transatlantic Encounters: Europeans and Andeans in the Sixteenth Century*, 151–202. Berkeley: University of California Press.

———. 1992. "Inca Cosmos in Andean Context." In Robert V. H. Dover, Katherine E. Seibold, and John H. McDowell, eds., *Andean Cosmologies Through Time*, 17–45. Bloomington: University of Indiana Press.

Zuidema, R. Tom, and Deborah Poole. 1982. "Los límites de los cuatro suyus incaicos en el Cuzco." *Bulletin de l'Institut Français de Etudes Andines* 11 (1–2): 83–89.

Index

Spelling variations and accentuation, especially of local toponyms, institutions, deities, and informants' words and names, are preserved, but not to the extent that could cause confusion.